Edited by Christopher

CW01621553

Human Resources at Work

Chartwell-Bratt

Studentlitteratur

British Library Cataloguing in Publication Data
Human Resources at Work
1. Personnel Management
I. Molander, Christopher
658.3

Chartwell-Bratt (Publishing and Training) Ltd
ISBN 0-86238-417-6

Printed in Sweden
Studentlitteratur, Lund
Art.nr. 6356
ISBN 91-44-00209-2

Printing/Year 1 2 3 4 5 6 7 8 9 10 | 2000 99 98 97 96

Contents

Foreword

It gives me great pleasure, both as an Industrialist and as sometime Chancellor of the University, to have this opportunity of writing a foreword to Christopher Molander's book on the management of human resources.

Firstly the book is very much in the stream of everything the University sets out to do. It is a team effort, all the contributors being members of the University's Management Centre.

It is above everything practical and pragmatic. The book explains, codifies and illuminates the processes managers and human resource practitioners follow and that alone causes one to think about, reflect upon and understand more deeply the significance and contribution of so much that we undertake.

The University is built on the twin pillars of practical applicability of the subjects taught, and the more abstruse one of 'adding value' by combining every skill we can to make the whole greater than the sum of the parts.

The second point I wish to make is a more general one. Interest in the arts and skills of different areas of business life tend to wax and wane in a cyclical fashion. Now it is the period of the accountant, now the marketing expert. From time to time the skills of the production specialist are most in fashion. I suspect for many reasons the day of the professionally equipped human resource manager may be about to dawn. So many fundamental changes are occurring in our society that industry is inevitably faced with a massive period of adjustment to external change.

The skill shortages of young people entering our ranks entail much more competition for the available talent. The development of a vicious spiral of decline in our educational system with fewer and fewer students seeking to study technical subjects again leads to more competition in recruiting, and retaining scarce skills. International and national mobility of management is intensifying. Major changes are occurring in trade union structure, behaviour and expectations. No one can fail to be aware of the different aspirations and ambitions of today's young men and women.

All this ferment of change is impacting on business organizations and is going to force major re-appraisals of the ways in which employees are managed, motivated and rewarded. In order to look at things anew and adapt to the future, one requires a profound understanding of one's craft and practice.

This is the reason why I can recommend this book, not only to human resource specialists, but also to the line managers who are, after all, the actual customers and on whom the responsibility for human resource management so clearly lies.

Sir John Harvey-Jones

Ross-on-Wye

The Editor

Christopher Molander is Senior Lecturer in Human Resource Management at the University of Bradford Management Centre. He was previously Plant Personnel Manager at the Ford Motor Company and Personal Assistant to the Director of Personnel, the Littlewoods Organization. His research and consultancy interests in Britain Europe and South East Asia are the introduction of management development systems in large scale public and private sector organizations. He is author *of Management Development – Key Concepts for Managers and Trainers, co-author with Jonathan Winterton of Managing Human Resources and Editor of Human Resource Management.*

The Contributors

All the contributors are members of the academic staff at the University of Bradford Management Centre.

John Lawler is Management Teaching Fellow. His research focus is public sector management, especially areas of public service such as health and welfare organizations. His teaching and consultancy activities cross a range of organizational behaviour and human resource management issues. He is involved with management development programmes in a wide range of contexts.

Alistair Ostell is Senior Lecturer in Occupational Psychology. His research and consultancy activities are in the areas of the development of managerial skills, the analysis and management of employee performance problems and psychological health. His main publications are in the field of stress and coping.

Andrew Pendleton is Lecturer in Industrial Relations. He has also taught at the Universities of Bath, Kent and Shanghai. His major research interest is the management of human resources in the public sector.

Gerry Randell is Professor of Organizational Behaviour. Previously he was Lecturer in Occupational Psychology at Birkbeck College in the University of London. He is joint author of *Staff Appraisal – A First Step to Effective Leadership.*

David S Taylor is Senior Lecturer in Applied Psychology. He has teaching research and consultancy experience in several areas of applied psychology. He is author of *Performance Reviews: A Handbook for Tutors and co-author of Improving Leadership Performance and Developing Interpersonal Skills through Tutored Practice.*

David Weir is Director and Professor of Management. He is Chair of the Association of Business Schools, a founder member of the British Institute of Management and is a Fellow of the British Institute of Management. He has been consultant for several large organizations including the World Bank, the Portugese Government and UNESCO.

Jonathan Winterton is Senior Lecturer in Industrial Relations and a consultant to the International Labour Office, the Organization for Economic Cooperation and Development, the European Commission and the Department for Education and Employment. His major research interests are industrial restructuring, work organization and vocational training.

Peter L Wright is Lecturer in Occupational Psychology. He is author of *Managerial Leadership and co-author of Improving Leadership Performance and Developing Interpersonal Skills through Tutored Practice.* He has conducted interpersonal skills training for a wide variety of British and European companies.

Introduction

Students of personnel management will hardly fail to be aware of the current debate about the need for change in the commonly accepted notion of the role. Whilst as yet only a limited number of firms have seriously confronted this need, some organizations, notably the larger multinationals, have re-appraised the personnel function. This re-appraisal has often been signalled by the re-titling of personnel management as human resource management.

In these cases there is hopefully more than simply a change in name. Many personnel departments are seen not to be offering the kind of service which line managers require – where and when they want it. In particular some line managers complain that personnel policies are not closely enough linked to strategic planning – both in its development and in its day to day application. Others have argued that the relationship of personnel specialist and line manager is not close enough, leading to the development of policies 'out of gear' with the operating needs of managers. Yet others have pointed to the changing environment in which personnel management operates and have suggested for example that whilst traditional industrial relations issues remain, more innovative attempts should be made to win the cooperation of the labour force – at all levels. The combative and procedural approach to IR should not, it is argued, blind personnel people to the need for additional methods of winning the hearts and minds of employees.

Rarely has such attention been paid to human resource management and never have the opportunities for development been greater. Work organizations have responded by and large to the need to adopt the most appropriate technology and accept the wisdom of tight fiscal control. The competitive edge is going to be won in the next decade by those firms which conquer the last frontier – the more effective use of people. Even a cursory reading of the quality Sunday press will reveal the increasing number of vacancies for human resource specialists at the highest levels.

The contributors to this book are members of the University of Bradford Management Centre. The University is widely recognised as a centre of excellence for the development of managers at the undergraduate, graduate and post-experience level. Human resource management is taught at all these levels and a major purpose in the production of this book is the felt need to provide one coherent text which covers the syllabus of a number of different courses. Inevitably therefore, the choice of topic covered reflects individual teaching purposes. The contributors however have experience not only of teaching in an academic context, but also of consultancy – working alongside managers and supporting them as they attempt to resolve 'real life' problems.

The choice of topics covered in this book necessarily involves the making of choices and it might be argued that there are omissions in the range of topics covered. The final product does however represent a sustained attempt to address the changes taking place in the profession of human resource management. To the contents of the third edition of this book have been added chapters on managing diversity at work, managing stress and managing change. In addition a final chapter has been added on empowerment. Naturally the content of the other chapters has been brought up to date, with a greater emphasis on strategic human resource management.

In addition to targetted suggestions for further reading, chapters are followed by a case study. Readers are recommended to use the stated objectives, presented in the form of 'bullet points' at the beginning of each chapter, as a means of evaluating their understanding. They may also wish to use the typical examination questions at the end of each chapter for the same purpose.

It is expected that this book will be useful to students of HRM, professionals already in the field who wish to keep abreast of modern developments and line managers who are anxious to get to grips with the most effective methods of managing people at work.

Christopher Molander

University of Bradford Autum, 1996

Part One

Employee Resourcing

Chapter 1

Strategic Human Resource Management: Analysis and prospects

Christopher Molander

Objectives

- To define the nature of strategic Human Resource Management
- To explore the varying managerial responsibilities for HRM
- To describe the activities involved in the management of human resources
- To emphasise the significance of HRM for organizational survival and development

Introduction

Human Resource Management is concerned with developing conditions in the workplace which are conducive to promoting commitment, flexibility, high performance and high quality output. It is a strategic approach to the acquisition, development and motivation of people at work so that they contribute effectively to the survival and growth of the organization.

HRM is a particular view of personnel management which encapsulates the approaches used by strategically-minded managers who see the need to integrate business and human resource strategies as part of an overall approach to the managing of people at work. HRM specialists are partners with other managers, capable of making an equal contribution to the achievement of organizational goals.

Essential therefore to an understanding of HRM are its strategic and integrative elements, which distinguish it from earlier forms of personnel management which tended to flourish independently of any coherent organization strategy. Generally, until the 1980's, few personnel managers were involved in the development of such strategies and felt, not surprisingly, little commitment to them. Correspondingly, managers elsewhere in the organization often had difficulty in understanding the role of personnel managers and were inclined either to leave personnel issues to them or to view such issues as tiresome interruptions to the working day. Drucker[1] went so far as to describe the traditional personnel department as the 'corporate trashcan' into which were thrown the trivial or irrelevant. (A more detailed history of the development of personnel management in Britain may be found in Human Resource Management. (Molander)[2]

The urge to take a tougher more integrated view of personnel management than that which had prevailed since the end of the second world war may be said to be the result of changes external and internal to the workplace.

We shall begin then by outlining the nature of these changes. Inevitably they have had a major impact on organization culture. The process of redefining the personnel role into one which is powered by the overall organization strategy and is decentralised and 'owned' by line managers at every level is the consequence. We shall therefore turn our attention to these issues. The practical day to day consequences of these developments will then be explored.

The reader is advised to bear in mind throughout that organization culture change is at the root of these developments in HRM. Without this basic perspective, current HRM developments will appear to the reader as little more than the random neurological spasms of a profession in its death throes. Re-engineering in its widest sense is as much about cultural shift as it is about process change. It depends on the building of workforce commitment to rapid and continuous change. Managing change is the toughest of all re-engineering challenges. Oram and Wellins[3] point out that it requires new approaches to selection, training, rewards, performance management and the core organizational values affecting day-to-day decisions.

The Changing External Environment of Work Organizations

Anyone reading a daily newspaper cannot fail to be aware of the deteriorating economic environment with which work organizations are faced. There have been clear indications of increasing difficulty for firms in maintaining economic stability, largely in consequence of increasingly global competition, fragmentation of mass markets and a general decline in consumer demand. These difficulties are currently experienced world-wide, not excluding Japan. The economic turmoil which is likely to follow political events in Eastern Europe is already aggravating economic and political instability.

Even those countries which by any standard of excellence have performed well economically – the young dragons of South East Asia such as Singapore – are keenly aware that economic growth will be maintained at present rates only if greater value added activity is generated. This implies the successful emergence of a new generation of technologically complex and desirable products together, with a trained, motivated and efficient labour force to produce them.

One of the obvious effects of this turbulence is clearly visible in the increased level of competition which firms are experiencing in every market. The push for increasing efficiency – particularly with regard to the use of labour at all levels – is widely seen as one of the few remaining means whereby organizations can hold on to or regain the competitive edge. Sadler[4] observes that the consequences of under-investment in technology are well understood; the consequences of inefficient use of the human resource has begun to be realised with an increased sense of urgency.

We have argued that external economic pressures are a strong force for internal change. There are others. Although something like fifty percent of all wage settlements are currently conducted on the basis of collective bargaining, few would deny the changing role of unions in the United Kingdom. Historically the traditional power of the unions has waxed and waned with turns of the economic cycle. During the 1980's in particular, management felt able to take a stronger position in relation to the unions, supported by the implied and actual threat of increased levels of redundancy.

It is likely that this decline in the traditional power of the unions will be replaced by a more strategic multinational approach to relations with management, following the development of the single European market. Most UK companies recognize that they will have to adapt in particular to the principles expressed in the Social Charter. In the meantime, economic conditions provide a managerial opportunity to replace the adversarial model of union relationships with an alternative more within its control.

The public sector is not immune to these pressures for change as any teacher, health worker or local government administrator will testify. Both in the private and public sector the constant search for new markets and products has become a normal feature of work experience. Private sector firms are driven to look for ever wider markets – usually abroad. The internationalization of the productive process raises new problems of control and motivation across economic and cultural boundaries, the managerial implications of which are not always properly understood.

The final external change to be mentioned at this point relates to the quality of the work force. It does not always follow that in a free economy high unemployment levels will lead to low levels of job vacancies. We have argued already that the competitive edge will be won and secured through the most effective use of people. Therefore it is more important than ever then for firms to ensure that the selection, appraisal, training and reward systems are the best possible, so that they are able to attract and retain a high quality labour force. Companies need to sell themselves to potential employees just as much as aspiring recruits must sell themselves to the organization, point out Torrington and Hall.[5]

We are talking of a change in culture. The change is concerned with customer satisfaction – that is the competitive edge; the means by which it is attained is the efficient use of the labour resource.

Such a change has to be understood, planned for and managed. It is far more than the introduction of management techniques such as Quality Circles. HRM professionals alongside line managers have a crucial role to play in the process of culture change. They have in the past frequently failed to think at the necessary strategic level.

It is easy to sympathize with managers who have memories of a less stressful economic period, who claim that 'nowadays it is one damn thing after another'. But there is no promise of a return to stability in the future. Organizations which are likely to survive in the '90's will be those which develop a view of change not as temporary turbulence but as the norm; and then go on to develop the structures and processes which will accommodate and exploit it.

The Changing Internal Environment

All organizations, if they are to survive, make an adjustment to the pressures on them from the external environment. (Molander)[6] That they do survive implies that the adjustment is to some extent satisfactory. Many work organizations perish however, and they do so because they are unable to adjust to the demands of the external environment.

In this section we shall attempt to define the elements of a satisfactory adjustment. They can be summed up in the word 'culture'.

The culture or climate of an organization is made up of traditions, habits, ways of organising and patterns of relationships at work. Anyone who has spent time in a number of work organizations will have noticed how the 'climate' differs, the ways in which things are done, levels of energy and individual freedom, and of course different kinds of people. Organizations have different sets of values, rules and beliefs and these are reflected in different formal and informal relationships and systems of working. Culture is reflected in organization structure, power distribution, reward systems, development processes and motivational levels. In short, culture is the growing medium in which the personnel of an organization operate.

Some growing mediums are hostile and arid, producing personnel who are suspicious and unresponsive. Others offer a supportive climate, encouraging employees to develop and flourish.

Organization culture materialises in the systems and processes which have emerged over time and which are responsible for the output. ‘Culture’, an American once said ‘is the way we do things round here’.

It is possible to define some of the elements of an effective work culture, given the external environment reviewed earlier in this chapter:

Flexible. The rate of technological change and the change in economic conditions, brought about by global trading, has meant that companies must be able to adjust speedily to market forces. Traditional bureaucratic systems of planning and implementation are likely to result in responses which are too slow, are inappropriate and which do not carry the commitment of trained and motivated employees.

Instead we must look for new ways of ‘lining up to get work done’ (organization structure) which is alert to market needs and can adjust output accordingly. It is likely that flat, decentralised structures will be appropriate in many instances. Increasingly what is required is a more flexible workforce, capable of handling change more effectively. Managers will need to become leaders rather than controllers, and will need to constantly update their skills to achieve this change. (Dolan)[7]

Integrated. Along with flexibility must go a greater degree of integration which the classical bureaucratic structure has always avoided. The various parts of the organization must work together, in a coherent way, to avoid the duplication and squandering of effort which is prevalent in companies which thrive on the promotion of narrow sectional interests (empire building) and internal politics. Corporate planning and the development of strategy are therefore prerequisites for survival.

The organization structure most suitable for such integration is not the common functional division of labour, with its built in barriers to cooperation, but product and project – based structures, both of which produce flexible as well as integrated activity.

Decentralised. The maintenance of a competitive edge depends upon not only satisfying customers but delighting them. (Tiernan)[8] Organizations which push the point of decision-making as far down as possible are likely to find that they are more responsive to customer need – simply because decisions are more likely to be made by those who are in closest contact with the consumer. Decentralised structures are 'flat' rather than 'vertical' or hierarchical.

Performance Oriented. Having obtained a strategy and clearly defined goals, the HRM culture is concerned with achievement of objectives. These are quantified and expressed in 'bottom line' terms. The danger of short termism is consequently a real one. One might expect to find in such organizations a concern with performance related appraisal systems and other methods of close monitoring. There will be those who lack the enthusiasm for such a 'shape up or ship out' culture and 'exiting' procedures will be in place.

There is then a strong element of individual responsibility, best understood on the basis of a contract. The organization undertakes to provide the resources and the training for the individual to achieve objectives. Where these are persistently achieved, employees will find themselves rewarded. Consistent under-achievement may lead to re-deployment or 'separation'.

Quality Conscious. Many of the functional activities to be mentioned in a later section of this chapter stem from this much espoused element in the emerging HRM culture. For example, moves to introduce flatter organization structures, perhaps based on product rather than functional lines, are designed to allow employees to respond more quickly to the needs of the customer. Recent interest in empowerment also has this as its objective, by pushing down the organizational point at which decisions affecting the satisfaction level of the customer are made.

In the search for quality, Total Quality Management (TQM) has become modish, with the consequent interest in such techniques as Quality Circles and other employee – involving devices.

Cooperative. In order for the cultural elements mentioned above to be achieved, the next factor in the changing culture relates directly to the management of people. The history of industrial relations in the United Kingdom has been characterised by pluralism. (Fox)[9] It has long been accepted that any large group of people consists of varying and irreconcilable interests. The function of management is therefore to manage the conflict so that the underlying common interest of keeping the organization running is achieved.

Central to the HRM culture however, is a return to an earlier managerial view that the organization is a unitary institution, the members of which share common interests. Since conflict is unnecessary and dysfunctional, the task of management is not the pluralist one of managing the conflict, but the unitary one of conflict avoidance. Accordingly the search is on for non-adversarial and non-collective systems of employee representation, through which the hearts and minds of employees can be won. Those whose bodily parts are not negotiable are free to work elsewhere. (Guest)[10]

Two consequences follow from this change in managerial philosophy. Firstly, and most importantly, it has effects on negotiation procedures. One of the arguments against incremental payment systems is that employees have been known to demand an extra increment if they were to take on extra responsibility.

This has led to managerial interest in *individually* negotiated wage and salary packages, as opposed to collectively negotiated incremental payment systems. Such packages are also related to appraisal or merit rating systems. Management expect that such payment systems will lead to greater scope to target rewards and also provide a greater degree of flexibility. Broad band payment systems, together with some form of group – based incentive system, are likely to be of increasing interest to managers.

Secondly, with regard to relationships at work generally, managers will look to replace the former collective systems with more direct relationships. The forging of such direct relationships between managers and individual employees is more relevant to the integrated HRM approach in which operating managers will re-assume the responsibility for those individuals who report to them. In sum, it is increasingly being seen as part of every manager's job and an important element in the new more cooperative and individualistic culture.

This view will appear to some as a resurrection of an earlier management position which reflects a more 'macho' industrial relations policy, much encouraged by the British Conservative government of the 1980's.

Segmented. The desirability or otherwise of harmonization is increasingly a matter of concern for managers. It is not only a matter of the rights and wrongs of equalising conditions of service between the various grades of employee on moral grounds.

There are more substantial issues relating to the overall managerial attitude to various grades and types of employee. Increasingly, organizations are distinguishing between core and peripheral workers. The former group are those who are identified as being particularly important to the organization and who need to be retained by providing the necessary rewards. The rest, often the most easily replaceable, are kept, as Torrington[11] asserts, 'at arms length' and encouraged to move on by the conspicuous lack of reward and development opportunities. (White)[12]

The possibility of such a new style division of labour is inherent in the human resource management culture, which Torrington[13] describes as 'demand driven'.

Empowered. Central to the points listed above is the concept of empowerment: giving authority to those who lack it to make decisions, which lead to greater customer satisfaction and, through this, to an increase in the level of personal motivation.

It is important not to be swept away by a facile view of what empowerment entails. If it is not to be seen by a cynical work force as yet another way of getting more work done without increasing payment, it must be integrated into the culture and must be the end product of a lengthy organization – wide development programme. Molander[14] argues that appraisal, training and reward systems must be supportively in tune with the philosophy of empowerment.

The major elements of HRM strategy and functions can be related to organization culture in the form of a flow chart (see Figure 1). It is questionable whether there are many organizations which actually manage to achieve an integrated corporate and human resource plan (Monks),[15] or whether HRM activities are as smoothly achieved as such models suggest but, nonetheless, they indicate the philosophy of HRM in a tidy fashion.

Strategic and Functional Aspects of Human Resource Management

Before embarking on a description of the broad areas in which professional HR staff might be expected to be involved, it is important to review the position of HR staff in the modern large scale organization. Hopefully this will avoid confusion later on.

Typically, in Britain before the 1980's, the personnel department was heavily weighted numerically towards the centre. It was primarily seen as a 'staff' function which existed to advise managers as to the best way of handling people at work: expert advisers without operating responsibility.

This alone encouraged the development of a rather aloof attitude to operating managers and a mutually felt lack of sympathy between the two managerial types. Empire building was common. Some larger organizations seemed unable to control either the growth in size of the personnel department, or the gulf between what personnel considered their role and what operating managers saw

Corporate mission and strategic plan
(giving birth to the culture)

|

Human resource plan
(defining the culture)

|

Recruitment and selection
(locating the bearers of the culture)

|

Training and development
(instilling the culture)

|

Target setting and appraisal
(enabling the culture)

|

Reward management
(reinforcing the culture)

|

Succession planning and exiting
(maintaining the culture)

Figure 1. The development of organization culture.

them actually achieving. The result was a mutual lack of respect and the widespread failure of the personnel staff to influence events to any noticeable degree. Some large-scale firms however, saw the personnel department as inevitable and a cost which had to be largely written off. Few firms saw the possibility of developing the personnel department as a cost centre or of describing its performance in the language of operating managers: profit and loss accounting.

During the 1980's there was a reappraisal of the role of the personnel department, amongst others, fuelled by adverse economic conditions and the resulting need for managerial value for money. A consequence was the decentralizing of the department and the integration of its activities with corporate goals.

The core central human resource management group was vastly reduced in size, and those HRM staff reporting to and working for operating managers were increased. By this means it was expected that the activities of the HRM professional would be more closely tied to the needs of operating managers, who were now responsible for employing and paying their HRM staff.

Whilst the majority of HRM staff now found themselves working to the agenda of operating managers, the reduced central group were also encouraged to integrate their activities with those of other top managers. They were represented on the top team and began to have a role as equally powerful as that of any other director in the development of corporate policy.

The reader will have noticed a change in title which is now common. The abandonment of the term 'personnel management' in favour of 'human resource management' was designed to emphasis a new harder-headed look at the handling of people at work. Employees were just as much a resource as any other asset and needed to be carefully acquired, used and maintained.

Care needs to be taken however to avoid the view that this change is universal and coherent. As Guest[16] has pointed out, the change is uneven and there are, no doubt, firms which have simply changed the description on the door plate of the department, whilst within much continues as before.

From here onwards, the term 'human resource management' will be used in place of personnel management. Strategic HRM staff should be taken to mean those central specialists engaged in the development of HRM policy and working as part of the top management team, whilst HRM officers are those professionals working for, and responsible to, operating managers.

This latter term refers to those managers who have an overall responsibility for and authority over others and who are not specialists – in the area of human resource management for example.

This distinction between the strategic and the functional role of the HRM specialist is important if the reader is to fully understand the changing role of the human resource specialist.

Human Resource Management Issues

In this section we shall take a more detailed look at the various activities in which HRM professionals and line managers equally may be expected to get involved and which stem from the cultural elements discussed above. Human resource management is not something which can be left to the professionals. We have already explored the importance of integration. The activities of both line manager and professional HR manager must also be integrated.

Corporate planning

It is essential that the HRM function carries directorial status and is represented at the top of the organization. It is here that corporate planning will take place and the HR director has a vital role to play in this process.

It is difficult to see how decisions affecting the activities of the organization can be properly made without a human resource input. Is the organization to move into new product areas? Is it to open a new plant in a different country and is it to decentralise? What are the implications of these possibilities for employees and are there sufficient of them to satisfy potential staffing requirements? What are the possible implications for recruitment, training, organization design and development?

This sample of questions should help to illustrate the need to have a technical HRM *input* into strategic decision making. HRM professionals also need to obtain information necessary for the development of human resource policy – to get an *output* from the strategic plan.

Human resource management policy

One should reasonably expect the top levels of HR management to concern themselves with the development of an HRM policy for use throughout the company. Its application arguably should be left to line managers. HRM specialists should concern themselves with the validation of the policy. Is it relevant to the needs of the organization? Does it promote a performance oriented culture? This is not to imply that HRM staff lay down the operating details of the policy; it might well be that the central policy allows for the operating divisions to develop their own procedures within wide margins.

There will always be personnel related issues which need central review and which require responses understood and wholly supported by board – level managers.

Human resource planning

This is an area in which centrally located HR staff might be expected to play an important role. Whatever the contents of the strategic plan, there will be human resource implications. In order for it to be developed adequately, top line managers will expect adequate information about the supply of labour now and in the future, and also about the characteristics of the labour supply.

In its turn, the HR department will expect to glean sufficient relevant information about the possible growth and decline in company assets, and outlines of any plans to change the technology or develop the product. With the data obtained, personnel staff should encourage the production of a five year rolling plan which will allow line managers, together with their operating HR staff, to develop recruitment, training and retention budgets.

Recruitment and selection

It is commonplace but true that if the wrong people are selected, then no amount of development through good management will make them effective. The whole of HRM specialist and operating manager activity hinges on this point. It is therefore important that the best selection methods are used.

Operating managers will doubtless want to make the final selection decision, since they will be responsible for new recruits and will need to find their wage or salary from their budget. No self-respecting manager would allow this selection function to fall into the hands of others and, equally, no self-respecting HRM officer would presume to make the decision on behalf of those responsible for the new employee. There is a good political reason for this. As long as operating managers can blame others for bad selection decisions, they will. It was common in the past, when personnel staff often made employment decisions, for the operating managers to give up trying to develop individual members of their teams, claiming that they should never have been selected and that 'those personnel people have messed things up again'.

There is good reason why the functional HRM officer should take an active part in the proceedings; ensuring that there is a job description, that the short list is adequate and does not, for example, offend against employment legislation and advising upon and administering selection tests. Even though the interviews for the short-listed candidates also might be usefully attended by the HR specialist, the final decision must still be made by the operating manager, whose commitment to making a good decision is the stronger for having been responsible for it.

Strategic HRM staff will, no doubt, want to develop operating procedures and encourage top management to follow their recommendations as to the use of various selection techniques. These professionals are likely to want to monitor the selection process to ensure that the head count remains in line with corporate planning.

Reward management

Generally, the policy and mechanics of payment should be a responsibility of the operating manager, rather than HR staff. Nonetheless, questions such as the type of job evaluation scheme, if any, which is to be used, if there is a policy regarding harmonization of terms and conditions of service, whether there is to be a general system of appraisal and any consequent performance-related payments, will be a matter for top management concern. This group will, of course, include the most senior HRM managers. The latter will be expected to have the available data regarding national and international trends in reward management and have relevant statistics relating to payment trends.

Both the implementation of wage and salary systems, and the policy decisions relating to the development of reward systems generally, will always involve line managers. We should expect that the latter policy decisions will involve an input by specialist HRM staff. Even so, the responsibility for final policy decisions also rests with line management.

It is worth emphasizing that there are many strategic elements in the development of reward systems. White[18] for example draws attention to the need to have a clear idea as to what the pay system is designed to achieve. Systems can encourage certain types of staff to remain loyal to the organization and at the same time discourage others from staying beyond a certain age or wage level.

Performance management and the issue of performance related pay is obviously an area with strong strategic overtones, (Fowler).[19]

Such fiscal engineering requires strategic thinking and monitoring at the highest level and is an example of an area where top-level HRM professionals will be involved.

Training and management development

It will be clear by now that almost all HRM issues involve operating managers. This is true of training. Operating managers must take responsibility for identifying the training needs of their staff – through some form of appraisal. In many instances, there is no-one better to carry out the training. 'On the job' training is frequently the least expensive and the most effective form of development. It therefore makes sense to leave it to operating managers to decide, in conjunction with the trainee, what training is appropriate and when.

It is also important that the cost of training is borne by managers and not provided for by a central fund in the control of HRM staff. A cost centre approach will help ensure that money is not wasted on training and that some thinking takes place before expense is incurred. The wider use of zero-based accounting disciplines, which oblige departments to assume no annual budget until justified, would doubtless concentrate the mind further.

By now the reader will be wondering just what responsibilities HRM staff have. We shall pursue this point in detail shortly. In the meantime, it may be said that the professional trainers, if any, are likely to be located in the operating divisions of the company and under the control of line managers. In the largest companies there may be some who will be located centrally and will sell their services on the market principle: managers will buy them as they would any material needed for production. In either case the responsibility for implementing training must rest with line managers. It is likely however that the strategic decisions as to training priorities; funding policies and provider contracting, will be handled centrally by HRM professionals and much of the training itself will involve HRM officers who work in the operating divisions.

A particular contribution which HRM staff can generally make is to help managers think through training policy. There is a tendency for managers to rely heavily on training for the resolution of employee problems, the cause of which lies elsewhere – in departmental structure and responsibilities, roles and job descriptions, motivation and rewards. In the past training has earned itself a poor reputation because it passed from the control of those who should have retained an interest; also partly because too much has been asked of it. In particular, sending people on courses might be alright as part of the reward system, but it has been the cause of much waste of money and consequent cynicism.

This last point, relating to the over use of training as the cure for problems at work, is perhaps even more valid with regard to management development. A major skill of managers is the capacity to analyse and define problems and to delay the process of looking for solutions. Whilst training is of course important, there are many factors which affect the performance of managers other than technical competence. Accordingly, training ought not to be embarked upon without caution. There are many other ways in which managers can be developed, particularly changing the circumstances in which managers are expected to produce: the internal environment of the organization or department. Much of managerial behaviour is a reflection of the prevailing culture.

Managers ought to be able to rely on up-to-date information on management development techniques from HR staff. Central staff will, as the reader might by now expect, be engaged in the production of policy as regards the development of managers. What ought to be the priorities? What methods of development does the organization favour? Who are to be the providers? The administration of training is something which HRM officers in the operating departments will be able to provide for managers.

Managers will be expected to improve their performance without necessarily increasing training costs. Desk training, external attachments and secondments, fellowships, bursaries, job rotation, shadowing, mentoring and coaching ought to be commonplace in what is often referred to as the 'learning organization'. The re-engineering of work processes alone will not ensure workforce commitment and the tunnel-visioned pursuit of leanness may involve the loss of expertise to cope with certain recurring problems. (Burgoyne)[19]

Industrial relations

Industrial relations continue to be an area of importance, despite the shift in power from unions to managers, which reflects changes in the economic environment. Many wage claims are still settled on a collective basis. Quite apart from the settlement of wage and salary issues, there is much to be done regarding the devising and setting up of systems of communication and consultation.

Line managers will require support with regard to the handling of day-to-day conflict from their own personnel staff, for the whole arena is legally complex.

There are also policy issues which will require attention by top managers,including central HRM staff. The handling of pay negotiations are strategic issues, as is policy regarding union recognition and the search for alternative forms of employee reward and also representation.

Organization design and development

As technology and the product or service change, or indeed as markets change, there will be a need to review the structure of the organization to ensure that it is best suited to the changing environment. Since the late 1980's there has been talk of flatter decentralised structures which are said to be more responsive to customer need and in any event may be necessary in the emerging multinational firm.

Changing structures is only one method of achieving organizational change and there are those who would argue that it is over-used and badly handled, being seen as the answer to all managerial problems. Certainly the process of structural change will in itself not win the hearts and minds of the employees. Without a degree of employee commitment even the most judicious of planned structural change will have little chance of succeeding in its objectives. Structural change requires the planning involvement of those who will be affected, argue Oram and Wellins.[20]

As markets, technology and processes change, so the organization will need to change or develop. Organization development is an area requiring knowledge of the social sciences and the managerial skills to plan and implement the change process. Increasingly, the change found to be the most significant is in organization culture. Frequently the objective of the change process is the development of a more customer-aware culture, with all that this implies for the development of the reward system, employee empowerment and so on.

The change effort might be directed instead at reducing the degree of bureaucracy – freeing up decision-making processes which enable decisions to be taken by those most competent to take them – an operating state which many practising managers would say is seldom present. Such changes rest on the commitment of top management and the presence of knowledge-based and skilled specialists who operate as part of the top team. As much as any of the other areas explored in this section, analysis and design constitutes an area in which the human resource professional will be expected to contribute to the efficiency of the organization.

Support services

It is hoped that the reader will have gathered that human resource management is a cooperative, strategic and hard-headed activity staffed by managers committed to the financial success of the organization. The role of honest broker, adopted in the past by personnel managers anxious to see themselves as poised between management and worker, acting as a go-between, has long gone.

So also has the image of the personnel officer as the good fairy, protecting the interests of the non-managerial employee.

There are residual issues which do not fit neatly into any of the areas described above, but are nonetheless important. Health and safety is an issue which few firms can ignore. Quite rightly there is a mounting level of legislation to protect the employee which the organization ignores at its peril. In addition, all companies ought to have a developed policy with regard to health and safety, which goes beyond the legal minimum requirements, and which will doubtless vary from country to country for multinational organizations.

Issues such as company policy regarding the provision of social amenities, health services and health promotion require thought and a coherent strategy. Much may depend on the area in which the firm operates, and there are good arguments for and against, for example, the provision of sports facilities. These need to be made and decisions taken as policy matters. Human resource professionals should see that this process takes place, but they should encourage others to participate in it.

This last point stretches to other issues, such as the provision of canteens and general administrative activities of this kind. There is no reason to think that the modern HR professional is likely to be any better than any other manager in handling these issues. The danger of HRM people falling into the corporate trashcan still remains.

Conclusion – The New Pragmatism

The following chapters in this book will alert the reader to the strategic and functional roles of the human resource specialist as they apply to the major areas of people management.

There are two myths which are difficult to dispel and which are a consequence of the history of the function and the early pioneering, but social-work oriented, activities of the 'social secretaries' in the late nineteenth century.

The first myth is concerned with the view that there is some middle ground for the human resource specialist to inhabit comfortably. The specialist is no longer required to interpret the needs of managers to the unions and of the unions to managers, much in the manner of an honest broker. HR professionals are paid by managers to represent managers in the most cost effective manner. Their interests are clearly managerial. The liberalism of the 1950's and 1960's has been replaced by a new profit – oriented pragmatism which will lead the organization to adopt those HR policies and behaviours which contribute most to profitability.

Much, if not all, of what HR staff do can be costed reasonably accurately. There is no basic difficulty in operating HR services on a cost centre basis, in which HR staff will need to sell their services to operating managers on the basis of cost and quality, and to compete with outside providers. Training services are an obvious example: it might be more cost effective to use external resources on demand rather than keep up an expensive, and often under-used, training resource.

The second myth which still prevails is that human resource specialists are blessed with a capacity to understand, like and work with people. This also is far from accurate. All management involves the motivation of others, or else it is the work of the machine or process minder. The effective management of others is not something that can be left to a limited number of HR specialists. Only alongside operating managers can they implement policies and systems which provide a more productive environment in which employees will feel sufficiently motivated to spend most of their waking hours.

The most important element of HR management is contained in the-day-to-day working relationships of manager and employee, rather than in the exercise of charm by a limited number of specialists.

Modern human resource management then is pragmatic in its concern with value for money, rather than being tied to an employee-centred philosophy. It is also strategic in its concern with the integration of human resource planning with corporate strategy.

It is appropriate now to apply this overall view of the human resource role to specific managerial issues.

References

1. Drucker, P.F. (1961) *The Practice of Management,* London, Mercury Books

2. Molander, C.F.(ed) (1989) *Human Resource Management, Bromley,* Chartwell Bratt

3. Oram,D. and Wellins, R. (1995) *Re-Engineering's Missing Ingredient,* London, IPD

4. Sadler, P. (1995) 'Turning on the Welfare Talent', *Sunday Times,* London, 5 October, 1995

5. Torrington, D. and Hall, L. (1991) *Personnel Management: A New Approach,* Hemel Hempstead, Prentice Hall (2nd Edition)

6. Molander, C.F. (1986) *Management Development: Key Concepts for Managers and Trainers,* Bromley, Chartwell Bratt

7. Dolan, S. (1995) 'A Different use of Natural Resources', *People Management,* 5 October

8. Tiernan, T. (1988) 'The Man Who Taught the Japanese about Quality Management', *Works Management,* May, 1988

9. Fox, A. (1971) *A Sociology of Industry,* London, Collier-Macmillan

10. Guest, D.E. (1987) 'Human Resource Management and Industrial Relations', *Journal of Management Studies,* 24, 5.

11. Torrington, D. (1988) 'How Does Human Resource Management Change the Personnel Function?' *Personnel Review,* 17, 6.

12. White, M. (1985) 'What's New in Pay?', *Personnel Management,* February

13. Torrington, D. (1988) *ibid*

14. Molander, C.F. (1994) 'Coming to Terms with Empowerment', *Management Development Journal of Singapore,* Vol.3 No.1, February

15. Monks, J. (1994) 'The Union Response to HRM: Fraud or Opportunity?', *Personnel Management,* September

16. Guest, D.E. (1987) *ibid*

17. White, M. (1985) *ibid*

18. Fowler, A. (1988) 'New Directions in Performance Pay', *Personnel Management,* November

19. Burgoyne, J. (1995) 'Feeding Minds to Grow the Business', *People Management,* 21 September

20. Oram, D. and Wellins, R. (1995) *ibid*

Further Reading

Guest, D.E., (1987), 'Human Resource Management and Industrial Relations', *Journal of Management Studies,* Vol. 24, No. 3, September

Sisson, K., (1994), *Personnel Management in Britain; A Comprehensive Guide to Theory and Practice,* Oxford, Blackwell

Storey, J., (1989), *New Perspectives on Human Resource Management,* London, Routledge

Storey, J., (1992), *Developments in the Management of Human Resources,* Oxford, Blackwell

Torrington, D.,(1988), 'How Does Human Resources Management Change the Personnel Function?', *Personnel Review,* Vol. 17, No. 6.

Questions

1. What, in your view, are the major factors which have led to the reappraisal of personnel management?

2. Are the developments in the personnel function, implied in the change of title to human resource management, anything more than cosmetic?

3. What are the salient elements in organizational culture which are said to have given rise to recent developments in human resource management?

CASE STUDY

D.J. ROBINSON AND COMPANY LTD.

Appointment of Human Resource Officer

At a recent Board meeting it was decided to appoint a Human Resource Officer to be responsible to the Works Manager. This decision was largely taken as a result of increasing legislation in the field of employment. The company advertised this vacancy externally and you are the successful applicant.

Your first task is to write to the Board outlining your proposals for the future of the human resource function in the company.

This report will highlight in particular:

1. The problem areas on which particular attention should be focussed.

2. Your own constructive proposals for dealing with these problems.

3. What factors you envisage might be obstacles to the implementation of these proposals.

1. Background Information

It was in 1956 that David J. Robinson, a director of a textile company in the Leeds area, decided to go into business on his own account in order to sell his own invention – an electric measuring instrument which could determine the percentage of moisture present during the drying process in the manufacture of cloth. He rented an area of 1000 square feet on the top floor of a cloth dyeing company in a poor district of Leeds, employed three men to assemble the instrument, and also a foreman, a storekeeper/clerk and a salesman. He sank all his effort and much of his capital into the venture. D.J. Robinson was born.

The success of the venture depended mainly on the ability and determination of the founder to 'sell himself and the instrument'. This Robinson achieved by tremendous personal effort. Working fourteen hours a day, he personally purchased all materials, supervised the assembly of the instrument, fixed selling prices and contacted customers.

By 1960 he had moved to larger premises on an industrial estate situated in the northern outskirts of Leeds, and had registered D.J. Robinson and Company as a private limited liability company, with himself and two former colleagues from the textile industry as directors. The latter two gentlemen merely provided capital, however, and took no part in the running of the business, which was still very much under the personal supervision of David Robinson. He now employed over fifty people and the company, which had been formed with the initial intention of closing a significant gap in the instrumentation field associated with the textile industry, had now extended its activities into the general instrumentation market as further electronic instruments (designed to measure and control such factors as temperature, pressure and level in a wide variety of industrial processes) were added to the range.

In 1965, Robinson's began an association with one of the largest textile and man-made fibre machinery manufacturers in Britain by developing heater control equipment for use on that company's machines. Due to the importance of this contract, a separate division in the Robinson organization – the Regulator Division – was formed to carry out all aspects of this work for the man-made fibre industry. 'Regulator equipment', which is essentially produced on 'one-off' lines to satisfy the individual customer, is now the most profitable of the company's activities (despite the unstable nature of the business owing to the trade fluctuations which characterise the textile and man-made fibre industry).

In 1966, the company became a subsidiary of Brown's Ltd, Doncaster, but the family nature of the business still continued and the founder's personal influence was still felt. Shortly afterwards, however, David Robinson returned to his prime interest – research and innovation – when he became Managing Director of the separate company, Robinson Research (Lake District) Ltd, which had been formed just before the link with Brown's. David Robinson continued as Chair of the Board of D.J. Robinson and Company Ltd, however.

The departure of David Robinson from the Leeds factory was the end of an era, and he was replaced as Managing Director by the former General Manager/Sales Director of the company, George Taylor. The other members of the Board of D.J. Robinson and Company, in addition to David Robinson and George Taylor are Robert Hughes (who has been with Robinson's since 1966 and is the Financial Director/Company Secretary) and two Directors from Brown's Ltd. It should be noted that apart from Brown's financial interests in the company (Brown's now own 75% of the ordinary share capital), D.J. Robinson and Company Ltd continues to operate very much as an autonomous 'family' concern.

The last three decades have seen rapid expansion at Robinson's. The range of electronic instruments produced (general instrumentation products and regulator equipment) has now reached eighty different types, the number of employees has increased from 157 in 1980 to 483 now, the capital employed is £20 million and the annual turnover, which in 1980 was approximately £300,000, is today over £10 million, producing net profits of £2 million.

This rapid expansion has not been based on a long-term planned programme – like Topsy, the firm has 'just growed',and the company still retains many of the characteristics, both good and bad, of a 'family business'. Details of the present organization structure, and labour force, are shown in Appendices A and B.

2. The Human Recource Function

At present, the company has no human resource office, let alone a human resource department. The various human resource functions are carried out as follows:

Recruitment

Each individual Head of Department is responsible for recruitment and is expected to advertise for, interview and engage, any new employees which are required. This procedure applies to all recruitment, both 'works' and 'staff'.

As regards sources of recruitment for shop floor vacancies, many positions are filled on a 'word of mouth' basis. The company has strong contacts with the local Job Centre, and anyone sent along to the company is generally recruited. Management, administrative and clerical vacancies are normally advertised in the local or national press.

Personnel Records

These are kept by the Accounts Department, essentially for wages purposes (i.e.details of starting dates, leaving dates, absenteeism, holidays, tax details etc). The application forms of new employees are also retained by the Wages Department.

Training

Three young men are receiving craft training under an Engineering Industry Group Training Scheme, and they are granted day-release facilities for this purpose.

Wages and Salaries

These are administered by the Wages Section of the Accounts Department, under the overall responsibility of the Financial Director. Changes in rate or salary must be approved by the Financial Director.

Industrial Relations

Throughout the company's history, relationships have been conducted on a personal and 'paternalistic' basis, unhampered by rigid and formal lines of communication. The company is not a member of an employers' association and has not at any time considered joining. It refuses to recognise trade unions as negotiating bodies for employees but has no objection to its workpeople joining a union if they so desire. In fact, the percentage of employees who are trade unionists has recently increased to about 40% following intensive recruitment campaigns by two unions, the GMB and the AEEU, among white collar as well as production workers.

It has always been company policy to follow National Wage Agreements however, and rates of pay are always at or above average for the district.

Day-to-day relationships between management and employees are still conducted on a personal and informal basis. Employees with a problem or grievance can freely, through their supervisor, arrange an interview with the Works Manager. When a large group of employees has strong feelings about a particular matter, an unofficial spokesman to the management sometimes emerges, although it is not uncommon for a group of a dozen or more operatives to rush to the Assistant Works Manager's office with a particular grievance.

Employees who are members of trade unions often inform their branch of any grievances they have, and the District Official of the union then contacts the company's management by letter or phone. Such 'complaints' have been increasing in recent months, particularly in relation to the company's handling of disciplinary matters. The company deals with such matters exclusively by letter or phone. In the past year, two former employees who were dismissed for contraventions of works rules have been successful in claiming unfair dismissal at an industrial tribunal.

Health and Safety

At present, health and safety matters are two of the many responsibilities of the Works Manager.

Two supervisors deal with first aid. Any welfare problems are generally handled by the employee's Supervisor.

A contributory Pension Fund is provided for monthly staff employees only, and is administered by the Finance Director's department.

A canteen is provided for all employees to use, and is under the general control of the Finance Director.

NOTE: GMB = General Municipal, Boilermakers and Allied Trades Union

AEEU = Amalgamated Engineering and Electrical Union

Appendix A

ORGANISATION STRUCTURE – D.J. ROBINSON & CO. LTD.

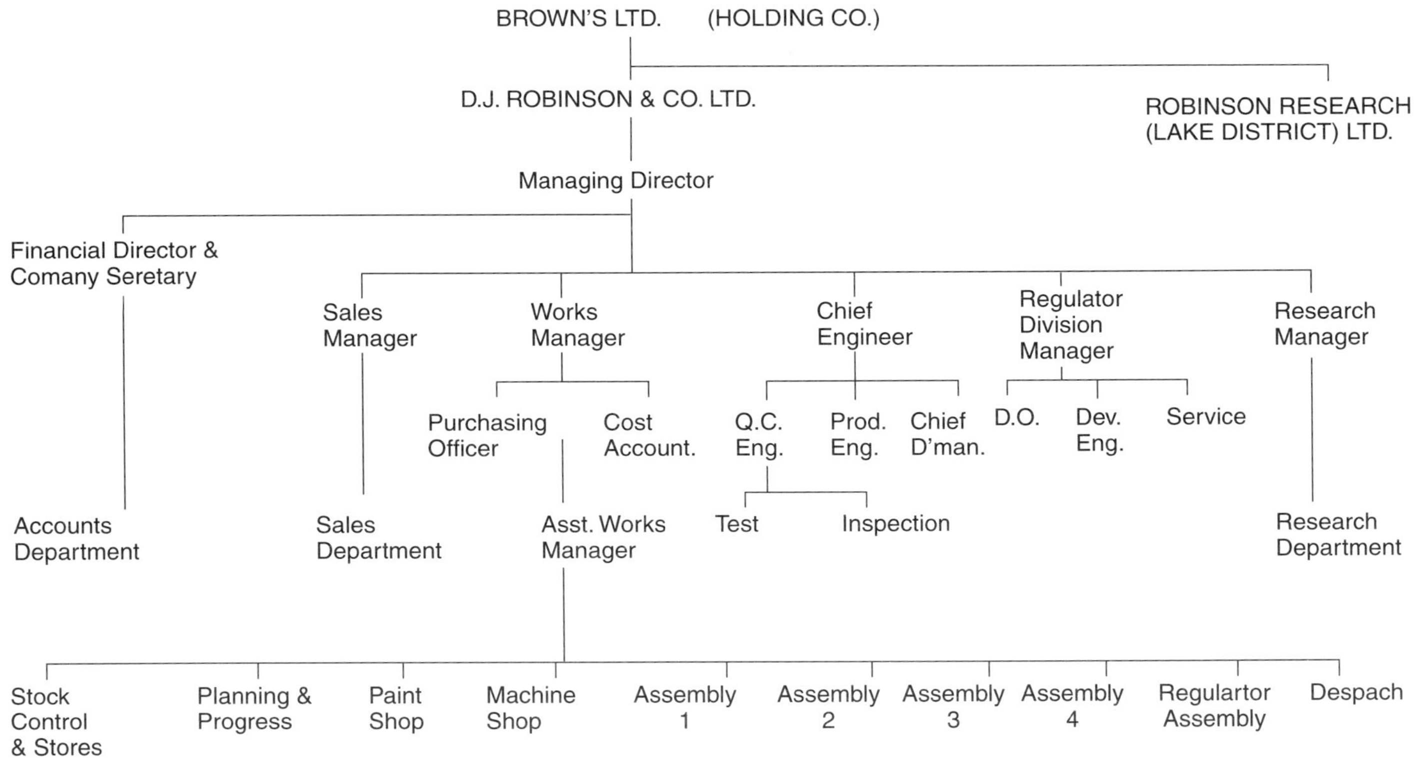

D.J. ROBINSON & Co LTD. LABOUR FORCE

Management/ Admin	Sales				Works		Engineering			Maintenance & Transport	Canteen	Total
	Sales Office	Sales Reps.	Sales Serv.	Sales Reg.	Dir.	Indir.	Insp.	Test	Dev. & Drawing			
16	53	12	17	5	202*	69	34	26	25	21	3	483

* a very high proportion of which are female operatives on small assembly work

Chapter 2

Human Resource Planning

John Lawler

Objectives

- to outline the purposes of human resource planning
- to examine the role of human resource planning within the management of people at work
- to examine the factors which influence human resource planning
- to consider human resource planning within an organizational context
- to discuss the process and focus of human resource planning
- to outline the methods traditionally used in human resource planning

What Is Human Resource Planning?

Human resource planning could be regarded as one of those activities within organizations which people largely take for granted. Its effectiveness is not often apparent. It is usually in cases where human resource planning has not been given sufficient attention or priority that its importance is recognised.

Essentially human resource planning is concerned with getting the right people in the right place at the right time. By this we mean that the requisite number of people with the appropriate skills, experience and aptitude are available for the organization's purposes at the time that the organization needs them in order to progress its strategic plans. The issue is not merely one of quantity – will we have the right number of people? – but predominantly one of quality – will we have the right skills and experience available to us? In times of rapid development which see the development of new technologies, new methods and new ideas, acquiring staff with highly specialised and rare skills may become increasingly difficult and expensive. If organizations rely on a reactive approach to staffing they may find the quality of staff they require expensive or impossible to attract and may well lose competitive advantage. Hence the importance of human resource planning in the overall management of people at work is not to be underestimated.

The Development of Human Resource Planning

Traditionally, the planning of future staff requirements has been known as manpower planning. In some organizations this term continues to be used. The development of a new name, human resource planning, can be seen in different lights. The increasing use of the term may be seen as a change in name only – a fashionable new label which indicates that the organization wishes to maintain an up-to-date image both within and outside its own boundaries. Other than a change in name, the traditional activities undertaken under the name manpower planning are maintained. Alongside the desire to be fashionable may be the recognition that the term is sexist and therefore should be rejected.

Alternatively, the new term, human resource planning, may highlight the need to review the traditional approach to the management of people within the organization. The term manpower planning has connotations of a certain mechanistic calculative approach to the management of people at work. This new term may be a further development in the trend towards effective human resources management and away from traditional personnel management. The emphasis is now being placed on effective management of people with a more strategic, rather than administrative, emphasis.

Those functions which support the development of effective HRM in organizations may need to be reviewed and their importance reinforced. The adoption of the human resource planning term may serve to do this and may also emphasise planning for future human resource needs is not the mechanistic series of arithmetical tasks it may have traditionally been seen as. Undoubtedly there will be organizations who have adopted the new terminology without any identified change in their practice. However, to treat the general use of the term solely as being a cosmetic change, would be to ignore the increasing need to treat current and future human resources in a different way to promote organizational effectiveness. The adoption of the new term associated with the effective management of people gives a clear signal to those within the organization that changes are occurring in the way in which human resources are regarded in the organization.

It is important at this stage to state that, as with effective human resource management generally, human resource planning cannot be viewed as a separate distinct function within organizations. The effective management of people requires forward planning and consideration of individual development alongside present and future organizational requirements for human resources. Thus it is important to stress the need for human resource planning to be seen as integral to the continuous management of people, and not to regard it as a separate or discrete function which can be separated totally from other elements of managing people at work.

The role of manpower planning can be viewed within a human resource planning framework. Bramham (1994) makes an important distinction between manpower planning and human resource planning which is worth further consideration. This distinction is that one signifies a purpose and the other a process. By this we understand that manpower planning seeks to use quantitative means to identify future demand and supply of staff. Human resource planning indicates a method of managing staff which seeks to motivate and develop individuals so that they are equipped to respond to the organization's future needs. Following this argument we can see that human resource planning has not superceded manpower planning, but that they overlap and both need to be accommodated. Manpower planning does need another name but the need for its function still exists.

In this approach we can see the value of manpower planning as attempting to add some hard data to an area which is often considered to be at the 'softer' end of management techniques. Added to this is the constant struggle for certainty in an uncertain world. Thus, in attempting to forecast demand and consider how this can be reconciled with supply, manpower planning makes a necessary, and to some extent brave, attempt to provide some regulation in an intrinsically unregulated area of organizational life. The argument which adds weight to the role of manpower planning is that too often managers, and personnel managers are included in this, are too concerned with operational matters to give sufficient attention to longer term planning. Bramham summarises this:

> *"There is a tendency to recruit today the employees they need today; little or no thought is given to tomorrow's needs. (Indeed management knows so little about personnel requirements that it tends to recruit and train what was needed yesterday, for it has often not determined what today's requirements are, let alone tomorrow's)."* (Bramham 1994, p156)

With the focus in today's organizations on increasing change and uncertainty and with managers being exhorted to 'thrive' on chaos, the role of such human resource forecasting may appear less relevant than ever. If things are changing at such a rate, why should managers try to think about tomorrow? There are two obvious responses to this. One is that the role of forecasting may paradoxically be enhanced rather than diminished in time of uncertainty. Even if forecasting cannot be entirely accurate, some attempt at understanding trends and demands may put the organization in a better position than would relinquishing any attempt at trying to forecast and adopting a reactive stance only. Again Bramham has a simple analogy for demonstrating this argument:

> *"The good navigator uses scientific method in applying his knowledge and skills, within the limits of the equipment available, in order to establish first his position and then his best course and speed, with a view to arriving at a chosen destination by the most suitable route. From time to time during the voyage he will take fresh readings; calculate what action is necessary to compensate for hitherto unforeseen changes in wind, current and weather; and adjust his course accordingly. If the wind changes dramatically the navigator is not likely to abandon compass and sextant, go below and pray to God to get him to port. He is more likely to apply his knowledge and skills to a reassessment of his position and course as soon as this is practicable"* (Bramham, 1994, p 157)

Thus some attempt at planning is always justified even in the complex area of human resources.

The second response to continuing and accelerating change is to look away from recruiting for *jobs* and to look towards recruiting *people* who are flexible and whose skills and potential skills are wider ranging. Thus as people are recruited who are able to develop their existing skills, and indeed are able to acquire new skills, the organization will be better able to cope with changes in their own demand for skills in due course. In this way managers strive to maintain some element of control over their human resource management processes, rather than forever reacting to events dictated to them by external forces. There are those who will always argue that in uncertain environments planning can consume valuable time which is much needed for other managerial functions. Bramham makes the point that events occur which involve managers in making decisions, whether these are foreseen or not. In undertaking some human resource planning there is no certainty that the decisions reached will be the best, but the probability that good decisions are reached is heightened by the planning process.

> *"Decisions which affect the future (graduate recruitment, building new factories) are made whether or not planning takes place. The choice is whether to be systematic in making decisions about the future or whether to be swept along by events"* (Bramham, 1994 p. 158)

The distinction between manpower planning and human resource planning is noted by Bramham. In doing this he also emphasises the symbiosis between human resource planning and human resource management more generally. Human resource planning in this respect is difficult to distinguish from good human resources management – it is not necessarily a part of HRM but it may even be the same thing.

> *"Manpower planning belongs therefore more to the areas of control, the technical aspects of matching supply and demand and general numerical analysis. Planning of human resources deals more with the management of culture and of employees as individuals whose creativity, adaptability and enthusiasm are seen as essential elements in organizational continuity and growth" (Bramham, 1994, p.164)*

To highlight the importance of the role of human resource planning in organizations: there is an increasing reliance on human assets at work and also increasing financial costs are required to maintain the correct profile of those assets. This indicates that future requirements cannot be left to good fortune accompanied by an optimistic view that the labour market will provide. Managers need to be aware of the imperative to plan now for future human resource needs within the organization.

The Organization and its Environment

The overall environment in which all organizations operate is changing perhaps more rapidly today than ever before. Change is perhaps more radical and more frequent and organizations need to plan for those changes which are predictable and to become more fluid and flexible in order to deal with those changes which are less predictable. The environment is complex and different elements will have different impact and importance at different times for different organizations. Given this complexity there is clearly the temptation that perhaps it is better not to invest time and effort in trying to predict the unpredictable and a more reactive approach to human resource planning is advised. It may be more useful, however, to try to consider what elements may be more predictable and attempt some planning rather than being quite unprepared for the future in whatever form it presents itself. Figure 2.1 details the important elements within an organization's environment which may impact on human resource planning. Changes in any part of this environment may suggest or demand changes to the human resource profile within the organization.

Environment Factors Influencing Human Resource Planning

Internal Factors	**External Factors**
Size	Demographic changes
Structure	Labour market
Strategy	Market changes
Culture	Education/Training
Technologies	Economic climate
Stability	Stability

Figure 2.1.

Internal Factors

The degree of stability within the organization will impact on the demand for staff. By stability we mean such factors as: the consistency of the organization's strategy, the routine use of the same technology, the stability of the workforce, the consistency of organizational size. Is the organization pursuing a strategy consistent with that pursued over its recent history? If so, its future human resource requirements may well be in line with those presently in demand. What of the future – has the result of this strategy been increased market share or the development of new markets? If so, what impact does this have on staffing levels and the skills and experience which are required within the organization? What of organizational size – have there been any major changes such as take-overs, mergers, redundancies? These all have implications for human resource planning.

External Factors

Again these factors have implications for planning how to use people at work. Changes may demand some response from the organization or, alternatively, planned changes within the organization may need to be considered in the light of external factors. The implications of external factors become obvious when one considers the growth of new industries and examples such as the rapid development of software houses in the 1980s. The labour market had only a limited supply of trained personnel available. There was no rapid growth in the number of computer-literate graduates in the labour market, therefore such organizations could not hope to address a shortfall in supply by traditional means, such as increased advertising or more attractive benefits packages than competitors. Situations such as this demand alternative and creative remedies which, in this case, included the identification of another group of potential employees with relevant aptitudes, rather than with existing skills who could be trained in the use of computer programming skills. In this case such organizations began to employ language graduates as an alternative source of human resources, having identified their language aptitude as being relevant in a different work context.

Other external factors are important, such as the present climate of employee relations and wider social changes as reflected, for example, in the changing work patterns demanded by employees. Here we can consider the demand for flexible career paths to allow for career breaks to rear children or care for other relatives. Wider changes in the market may bring other people with relevant skills onto the labour market. Changes in technology may render certain current and valued skills within work obsolete. In the case of relocation or the development of greenfield sites, local factors such as other work opportunities, education, leisure and housing facilities may have an important bearing for human resource planning. Whilst at first glance they may appear peripheral to the major concerns of the organization, without due consideration the company may find itself lacking the requisite levels of staff with the appropriate skills, if it cannot attract people into the geographical area.

Beyond these factors there are also other factors such as economic and political stability to take into account along with issues such as current educational policies and the skill levels of those entering the labour market for the first time.

We can see, therefore, that consideration of the wider environment is an important element for effective human resource planning. The environment needs to be scanned continuously, as is also the case for strategic business considerations. In this case, to plan for what can be predicted and to identify what may not be wholly predictable. In this way the organization is more likely to be prepared for change as and when it occurs, with a view to maintaining its competitive edge, through effective human resource management.

Operational Context

In the competition for scarce skills and experience, a major element for some organizations is its size relative to that of other organizations in the same or similar industries. In some respects the organization itself may be very powerful within its own immediate environment and this can have important implications for human resource planning, for example, the organization's power to attract staff. In the case of, say, IBM at one time certainly if not now, they may have been able attract and retain staff more easily than any of their smaller competitors. Their good business name, their reputation for providing a challenging work environment, their ability to provide good pay and conditions and to provide a career structure are all important factors in recruiting and retaining employees. Their competitors had this to contend with in their own search for employees.

Another important aspect of the operational environment which is worthy of consideration is the training role that one organization may have, beyond its own operations, within its industry as a whole. Two UK organizations exemplify this: the BBC and the NHS. Each organization is very influential in the areas of broadcasting and health care respectively. They each have a continuous demand for professional and trained staff to meet the demands of their own markets. Each employs significant numbers of those staff and each operates in an area of work which is continually developing and changing. Again, each is recognised as providing high standards of education and training within its own field. However, neither organization operates a monopoly. As each organization is developing and as technological innovations occur, they must ensure as far as possible, that there is sufficient labour available to meet their own demands for trained staff. If they were to rely on the open labour market to supply the requisite staff they may find that the necessary skills are not available in sufficient quantity to meet their needs at any particular time.

To prevent a critical shortfall in labour, each organization has developed, consciously or otherwise, a role as trainer for the industry. This is not to suggest that no other training is available, but that the training role they adopt is crucial for the continuing supply of the necessary skills for the industry as a whole. Thus they are ensuring that a pool of appropriate skills and aptitudes is maintained for them to draw on in the future. Some of this future demand for skills will be predictable whilst a considerable area of uncertainty remains. Maintaining a substantial pool of labour enables the organization to guard against the worst aspects of future uncertainty. Thus the training role of such an organization will differ from the training role of others in the same sector. In the latter case, training will be aimed at developing people for immediate and future predicable demand within the organization itself. The 'trainer for the industry' role is a guard against unexpected shortages in supply of labour both for the organization itself and for others in the field. The organization which adopts this role regards the investment it places in training, not necessarily for their own future use alone, as worthwhile in ensuring its continuing success overall.

The Mechanics of Planning

Levels of Planning

Conceptually, we can see human resource planning as being addressed at three distinct levels: the overall or national level, the organizational level and the operational level. At the national level, we are considering issues such as major demographic changes, national education and training policies and the extent to which such policies prepare young people for the world of work. Individual managers can expect to have little impact at this level in influencing policy for the benefit of their own company. Changes in these areas are likely to take place over the longer term and most organizations are in reactive positions here, that is, they regard those recently graduating from formal education or re-training as having achieved certain standards, but not necessarily as having the skills required for their own organization. There may be an inherent conflict between educational objectives and the skills needed by work organizations. There are, however, attempts to develop the links between education and work in order to address any conflict that is apparent between educational objectives and strategies and industry requirements (CBI, 1988).

At the organizational level, both the demand for and the supply of skills, experience and aptitudes needs to be aggregated in order to provide an overall picture of requirements in the organization and in order to utilise people's resources to greatest effect and with greatest efficiency. For example, demands for skills and expertise in one part of the organization may be addressed by the transfer or relocation of people already within the organization. At the operational level, the focus is likely to be on more immediate requirements. Thus the time scale of activities and of forecasts will alter with each level. The organizational level still has an interest in monitoring the effectiveness of each operational process in its role of integrating activity to pursue overall organizational goals.

Human Resource Planning Methods

There are a number of mechanistic processes which are recommended as aids to human resource planning (Torrington and Hall 1989, Cascio 1991, O'Doherty 1994). Again it is important here to acknowledge the seductiveness of these techniques. In themselves they present no easy resolutions to the uncertainties of future demand and supply of people at work. They may be seen, misleadingly, as being highly reliable and as providing clear direction for the future. It is not the methods themselves which result in good decisions, it is more *how* they are used. Thus the information they provide needs to be assessed within the framework of other information as detailed earlier. That strategic context includes information relating to external and internal environments. Additionally, it is also relevant to repeat a well worn cliché, that any information system is only as good as the information which is collected in the first place – 'poor information in, poor information out'. Thus information which relates to other elements of the human resource management process, such as that relating to appraisal, may in itself be incomplete or ambiguous or questionable in some other respect.

The methods available to assist in the human resource planning process are numerous. Those detailed below are intended to be indicative of the approaches available and do not represent a comprehensive list. These approaches need to be considered within the overall framework of a system of Analysis, Planning, Implementation and Review as detailed in figure 2.2. The value of considering these activities within a framework is that it emphasises the continuous nature of the planning process. It is

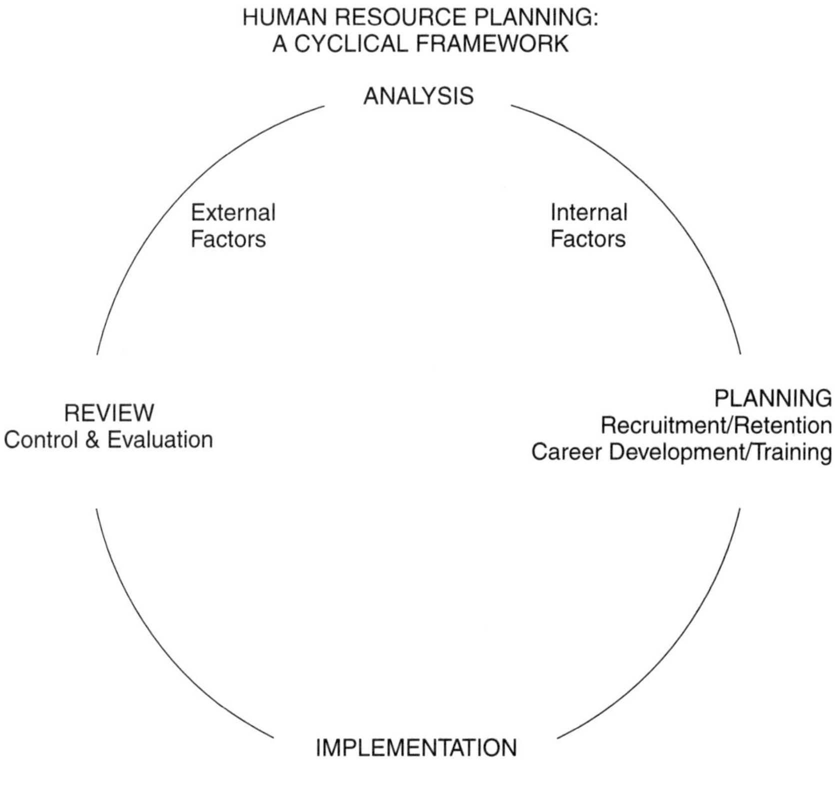

Figure 2.2.

only by maintaining this dynamic element that it is likely to be effective.

Each stage in the cycle may involve several elements.

1. Analysis

At this stage elements within the external and internal environment need consideration. These include issues such as: the state of the labour market, demographic changes, competitor behaviour, new technologies etc. Internally, important factors are: strategic objectives, employee profiles, organizational structure, career patterns etc. Information such as this provides the basis for the development of forecasts and thence decisions.

2. Planning

This stage involves plans for recruitment and induction of new staff, possible redundancies of staff in some areas, (re-) training and career development. Again, each element of this stage needs thorough consideration and the establishment of clear objectives.

3. Implementation

This is an obvious common sense stage. However, plans need translating into action if they are to have any impact. Thus, at this stage, targets need to be formalised and sufficient resources need to be made available to carry out all the activities listed at the planning stage. In addition, other processes, particularly those involving information systems and monitoring, need to be established in order to enable the next stage to be undertaken effectively.

4. Review

At this stage the organization considers whether its plans have provided the desired results. Information is gathered to analyse how the plans are progressing, what has and has not been achieved and the reasons for both of these are examined. Here the reconciliation of supply of, and demand for, labour takes place. Any shortfalls in supply can be investigated and alternative approaches taken to address them. Thus, if a certain set of skills is not directly available on the labour market steps can be taken to try to address that shortfall through, for example, retraining within the company or subcontracting the work or, ultimately, reviewing strategy. In other cases demand may fall short of current supply within the company, in which case reconciliation involves the redeployment of staff or redundancy. In this case, plans will need to be made very carefully, to identify specifically where any over-staffing lies, how redundancy is to be implemented and what the implications of these steps will be for the company, in both the short and long term.

The nature of human resource planning is such that it must be a cyclical process. Once demand and supply are reconciled, the ways in which human resources are utilized will be monitored against strategic plans and alterations will be made over time, in some cases to strategy, in others to human resource processes, to maintain the balance of supply and demand. Thus, information gained at this stage leads to both evaluation and control, with plans being made to address any deficiencies or difficulties. This in turn leads back to the analysis stage.

A cyclical model such as this perhaps oversimplifies the process. Each stage is not necessarily discrete and often elements of each stage may be happening concurrently. The importance of the model is that it demonstrates the need for the process to be dynamic and continuous.

In addition, there are other methods which can be used to assist this overall cycle. It is important at the analysis stage to consider the stock of workers currently available and the trends in people joining, leaving and moving within the organization. Here we are dealing with qualitative and quantitative data. We will want to know the numbers of people currently employed and their positions. We will also want to know general factors such as age and absenteeism rates, and more specific factors such as experience and skills, and again more operational elements such as performance and productivity rates. From information such as this we can draw a picture of the current situation.

In combination with strategic information regarding future needs for skills, aptitudes and so forth, we analyse the gap between future demand and the current situation. Furthermore, from considering information on recruitment trends, wastage rates, due to retirement, dismissal, or departure to other organizations, and career moves within the organization, we can also estimate the extent to which future demand is likely to be met from within the organization. This process itself in an organization of any size can be a major undertaking and different information may emerge for different parts of the organization.

Analysing Stocks and Flows

As a basis for any human resource plan, the organization needs to know its current stock of human resources – what skills are available now in the organization and in what quantities? This information provides only a snapshot of the situation which will provide inadequate information by itself. More useful information can be gathered by considering both the stock and the flows of skills and experience. This needs to be carried out to provide general information for the organization as a whole and also to provide information at the departmental level, in order to ensure that sufficient skills and experience are being maintained and developed in all parts of the organization.

Continuing analysis of stocks and flows has the benefit of enabling human resource plans to be monitored and also helps in both the allocation of work and in the assessment of productivity. Over a period of time, analysis of stocks and flows can provide rich information for the organization to assist in its strategic planning. Identification of turnover levels of staff in general, and in particular positions is important, as is the recognition of certain career patterns. Having established a baseline of information and standard turnover and wastage rates within the company, irregularities or changes in those patterns can be investigated, providing useful information in advance of any crisis in staffing.

The analysis of stocks and flows begins with establishing wastage rates for the company. This identifies the numbers of people leaving, for whatever reason, as a proportion of the number of employees as a whole. Many obvious factors lead to people leaving, such as: retirement, redundancy, ill-health, disability and even death. They may leave more of their own choosing, for example, to enhance their own career or for other personal reasons. As a starting point for generating this information, a simple wastage rate can be calculated for the company. This is arrived at through establishing for any particular period:

$$\frac{\text{numbers of staff leaving}}{\text{average number of staff}} \times 100$$

Clearly the usefulness of this information is limited as it does not distinguish one part of the company from another, nor does it indicate the reasons for leaving, nor yet the nature of the staff who have left. This needs further investigation. Similar calculations can be done at departmental levels to give a more precise picture of movement in and out of the company. The company may also wish compare wastage rates of those who have left voluntarily with those whose who left less through their own choosing. In this case, calculations can be made for each group, that is those leaving voluntarily as a proportion of numbers employed and those leaving for other reasons as a proportion of numbers employed.

Calculations such as this give a picture, which can be regularly updated, of the overall stocks and flows but again this information is limited. It does not give information on the nature of the stock of employees within the company. To gain more information on this the company can develop an idea of how stable the workforce is through considering another dimension, namely the length of service of people within the company. To do this we can develop indices for people with varying lengths of service, for example people with one, five or ten year's service within the company. Thus we calculate:

$$\frac{\text{numbers of staff with x year's service}}{\text{numbers of such staff employed last period}} \times 100$$

We can also use this dimension in looking at leavers. This gives us an idea of the extent to which the service profile within the company may be altering. Again, if these calculations are done singly, the resulting information is no more than a snapshot. If the calculations are done regularly, we have more useful information as trends can be identified and compared with plans and remedial action can be taken if necessary. Length of service may be an important factor in some organizations, but again this information may answer some questions whilst provoking more, such as how are skill levels changing within the company? Matrices can be drawn up to look at skill levels and comparisons between departments can be drawn as illustrated in figure 2.3.

Such information can provide necessary information for planning future work allocation, likely future recruitment and training needs, succession planning and so on. There are many other such calculations which can be usefully undertaken, such as looking at

Category of employee	DEPT 1	DEPT 2	DEPT 3	DEPT 4
Managerial				
Professional or Skilled				
Supervisory				
Unskilled				
Clerical				

Figure 2.3. Type of leaver by department.

wastage rates, or length of service, in particular jobs or at particular levels. This information can highlight important issues, such as high turnover in particular age brackets or within specific departments which may need further investigation. This data is valuable but is limited in its usefulness because it is largely numerical and does not provide any idea of qualitative issues. In order to make this information more complete, such calculations can be augmented by collecting other data through using, for example, exit interviews. These can give a clearer idea of why people are moving and whether they may be taking valuable skills and experience with them, which might have been retained in the company had certain steps been taken.

Analyses such as the above can become evermore sophisticated, especially with the assitance of computer modeling. Companies are thus provided with the ability to consider movement rates across jobs in the organization and consider career and promotion patterns within the company, alongside information on those leaving the company entirely. Computer models can be used to test hypothetical sutations for which the company may wish to make some plans, for example, the implications of a freeze on promotions, the knock-on effects of the departure of a particular team or cohort in the company, the reduction in the number of new recruits. All these factors can be modelled for their short and longer term implications.

The development of information on this basis enables models to be developed which chart progress through particular posts. One such model is the Markov chain (see Figure 2.4), here used within the context of a medical hierarchy. This can be used to identify patterns of movement and to estimate the effect of any change in any of the elements, for example if promotion at a certain level is no longer available, or if recruitment dries up at certain levels, we can estimate the implications of this for other parts of the system and draw up plans to reduce the difficulties which arise.

We have not developed here a sophisticated and accurate predictor of the future. Rather we have organised information in such a way

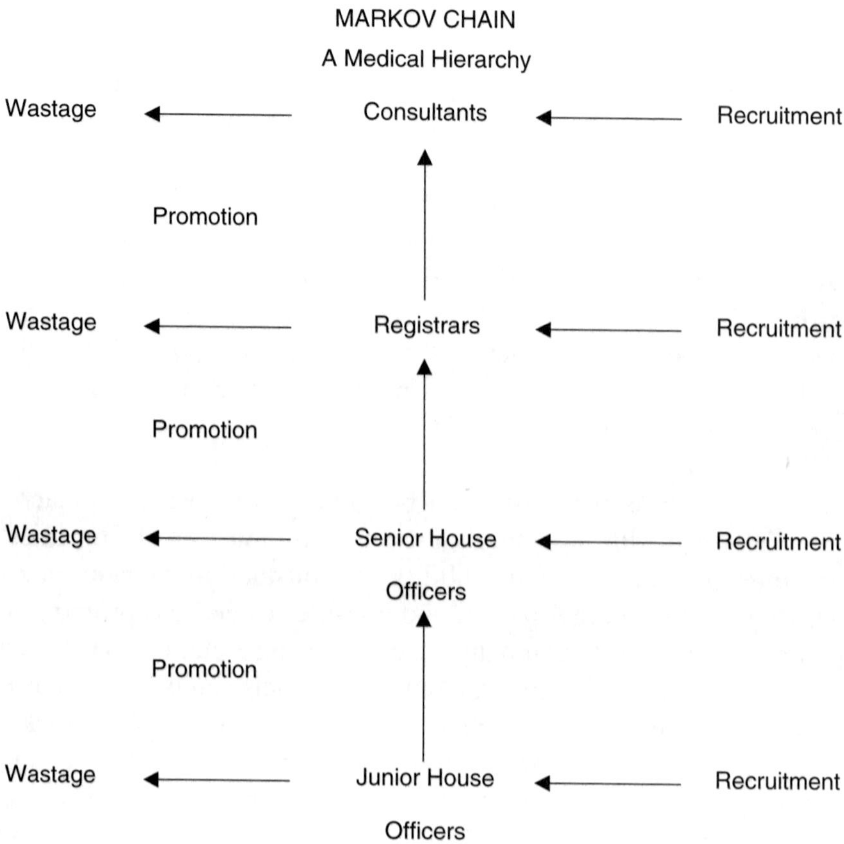

Figure 2.4.

as to see the implications of present trends and to highlight areas which need managerial attention if the organization is to be able to meet its objectives. Managers then have the choice, as with any forecasting system, between a number of actions. In this case the choices include looking at the possibilities of training, recruitment, transfer, redundancy etc. Building on this principle, we are now witnessing the development of more sophisticated computer simulations which attempt to manipulate many uncertain factors which have human resource implications. These enable managers to consider the implications of any of a range of probable and possible changes within the external or internal environment of the organization.

It is crucial that each of these processes or models is transposed from being a paper exercise, or a theoretical model , into a practical system. In order for this to happen, Cascio (1991) points out that any effective system needs to have the confidence of those who use it and, to gain this, must have the following characteristics:

- it must be founded on good quality information bases
- it must result in high quality decisions leading to effective action plans
- it must be practical to implement, that is, the organization needs to be able to put its action plans to work effectively.

Without the above conditions, any human resource planning is likely to be at best irrelevant and at worst seriously misleading.

Beyond statistical approaches and simulations, there is clearly the need for subjective views on the part of managers, who will have a more detailed appreciation of the operation than any simulation can provide. Thus in areas which are difficult to estimate, such as motivation and work satisfaction, the manager's subjective impression is important in developing a full picture. Additionally, methods such as Delphi technique are presented as being as relevant for human resource planning purposes as they are for other areas of planning (Cascio 1991). In this method, judgements are made by a number of independent, experienced people, drawing on information made available from all relevant sources. The information from them is aggregated and summarised and fed back for another round of evaluation. The advantage of this approach is that, through several iterations, an estimate will be developed which attracts consensual approval. In this way information receives evaluation from a number of sources, without interpersonal dynamics providing a barrier, and results in a broader guide for managers' decision-making.

Through techniques such as these, we can see the development of a more detailed picture to support human resource decision-making. All such techniques ultimately provide assistance to managers in their search for answers to human resource planning questions. The techniques do not in themselves, provide the answers.

Human Resource Planning – is it Feasible?

We have seen that there are a number of approaches to the issue of human resource planning. Writers such as Bramham (1994) argue that human resource planning is a new development which focuses on the strategic level of the organization. Its function is to consider many, if not all, elements of human resource management and to evaluate the extent to which these support the organization's strategy. Human resource planning must include elements of traditional manpower planning such as the more systematic, calculative elements upon which it has built its reputation. Other writers such as Sisson (1994) question the extent to which manpower planning was ever widely practised. He points out that such mechanistic processes were more suited to times of greater stability and that if ever there was a 'golden age' of manpower planning, it has passed. This approach acknowledges the theoretical value of planning for future demand of people at work and the argument that this process is most effectively aligned with strategic planning in organizations. There is however the question of the extent to which organizations conduct their strategy development in a linear manner, which allows the incorporation of other planning processes alongside. If strategy is developed more through a political or incremental process, the role of human resource planning alongside that is more problematic.

Additionally, we can see that strategic planning processes themselves may not be as common in organizations as theory might suggest, in some cases organizations may have no identifiable strategic planning process (Goold and Campbell 1987).

Even in cases where strategic plans do exist, their operational implications may be open to different interpretations. Thus strategic objectives which refer to percentage growth in productivity, or increase in profit, or increase in market share make sense on paper but their human resource implications could be many and varied. Sisson also argues that the short time scales within which most managers operate inevitably mean they have little incentive to develop any human resource planning on a longer term, more systematic, basis.

Sisson also argues that many of the planning processes in organizations are not clearly understood and an assumption of comprehensive rational planning systems is ill-founded. If this is indeed the case, the argument for human resource planning at a strategic level is still convincing in theory but does not appear to give sufficient regard to the complexities and uncertainties of organizational life. In spite of the growth of information technology and the access to increased information which this presents, there is still a lack of full understanding of the many processes which impact on effective human resource management. To assume a rational integration of all information in order to make reliable forecasts may be mistaken.

This perhaps presents a pessimistic or fatalistic view of the role of human resource planning but these points are important in demonstrating that human resource planning is not a panacea for an organization's ills, nor is it a mechanism to ensure a predictable and trouble-free future. This is not to suggest that the task is so complicated that it should be ignored entirely. Bramham's suggestion that in uncertainty, any planning and estimating is better than none, still holds true. The point to remember is that such systems themselves need to be dynamic and flexible and that the assumptions on which they are based need constant review to prevent such processes becoming obsolete and, worse still, misleading.

Summary

- Human resource planning is concerned with the ways in which future demand for skills, abilities and experience within the organization can best be met.
- Human resource planning has a focus both within the organization and externally.
- Human resource planning has close links with all other human resource management processes and is seen as being an integral part of effective HRM.
- Many factors both internal and in the external environment impact on the focus of human resource planning.
- Organizational strategy, structure and size all impact on the focus of human resource planning.
- The planning process draws on a range of techniques to assist in drawing up the most appropriate plans. It is a cyclical and dynamic process.

References

Bramham, J. (1994) *Human Resource Planning* (2nd Edition). London: IPM.

Cascio, W. (1991) (4th Edition) *Applied Psychology in Personnel Management.* Englewood Cliffs: Prentice Hall.

Confederation of British Industry (1988) *A Strategy for the Development of an Industry-Education Partnership.* London: CBI.

Goold, M and Campbell, A (1987) Strategy and Styles Decision Making. Oxford: Blackwell.

O'Doherty, D. (1994) 'Towards Human Resource Planning?' in Beardwell, I. and Holden, L. *Human Resource Management.* London: Pitman pp.118–156.

Sisson, K. (1994) *Personnel Management* (2nd Edition). Oxford: Blackwell.

Torrington, D. and Hall, L. (1989) *Personnel Management: A New Approach* (2nd. Edition). Hemel Hempstead: Prentice Hall.

Further Reading

Bramham, J. (1994) *Human Resource Planning* (2nd Edition), London IPM.

O'Doherty, D. (1994) 'Towards Human Resource Planning?' in Beardwell, I. and Holden, L. *Human Resource Management* London, Pitman pp.118–156.

Sisson, K. (1994) *Personnel Management* (2nd Edition). Oxford: Blackwell.

Torrington, D. and Hall, L. (1989) *Personnel Management: A New Approach* (2nd. Edition). Hemel Hempstead: Prentice Hall.

Questions

Discuss the arguments for human resource planning within the context of increasing environmental uncertainty.

'Human resource planning is manpower planning under another guise' Discuss this statement.

Examine the factors which influence the focus of human resource planning at work. In what ways might this focus alter?

Case

You are human resources manager of a large hospital trust. You have a specialist micro-surgery unit whose main work is with car accident victims. The unit is experiencing a considerable rise in demand for its services due to new techniques and the specialised skills of the medical staff.

This is the only unit within the county and demand is already exceeding your unit's capacity. With the growth of internal markets within the health system you find that you will be able to generate enough income to employ extra staff in the unit over the next two years, if you can respond to the increased demand.

- What steps would you take to try to respond to this growth in demand for services?

- Might anything have been done earlier to deal with this increase?

Chapter 3

Recruiting and Selecting People

Alistair Ostell

Objectives

- To outline the strategies of selection, placement and training and their uses in recruitment and selection
- To describe the phases and activities of a comprehensive approach to selection indicating the roles of personnel or HRM specialists and line managers
- To identify the main differences between competency-based and traditional approaches to selection
- To discuss the criteria used for the evaluation of selection procedures

After completing chapter 3 you should be able to:

- distinguish between the strategies of selection, placement and training and explain their appropriate use
- design an outline selection procedure which is suitable for a specified purpose
- evaluate the relative merits of the different predictors typically used in selection procedures, including competency-based ones
- describe the roles of personnel specialists and line managers in selection procedures
- discuss the problems of evaluating selection procedures and to identify appropriate criteria for evaluation purposes
- explain why competency-based approaches to selection have become popular and will be particularly relevant to many organizations in the future

Introduction

Recruitment, selection and placement are the activities concerned with finding suitable people to fill job vacancies within organizations. Since one of the most important factors which determines the success of an organization is the quality of the people it employs it is obviously crucial to establish effective ways of conducting these activities. In many organizations, particularly small ones, such activities are often conducted in a blinkered manner, just concentrating upon finding an appropriate person to fill an existing vacancy. However, if an organization is to obtain and utilise effectively the employees it requires on a long-term basis, its approach to personnel selection needs to be guided by a more general strategy for the management of human resources within the organization as a whole.[1]

Studies of personnel specialists reveal that they usually have a major role in conducting selection activities. It is thus necessary for them both to understand the conceptual basis of selection and to be able to design and implement appropriate selection procedures within their organization. This chapter describes the phases and activities of a comprehensive procedure and discusses the criteria by which such a procedure can be evaluated. It also explores how the emphasis upon competences and the changing nature of organizations is altering typical approaches to selection. First, however, some of the reasons why personnel selection should be viewed as one aspect of a broader human resource management policy are considered.

Human Resource Management and Personnel Selection

The need for effective selection and placement procedures arises from the simple fact that people and jobs differ. People vary considerably not only in their physical characteristics such as size, weight and strength but also in such psychological characteristics as intelligence, motivation, skills, temperament and goals. Because jobs also vary in terms of the attributes people must possess in order to do them, it is important to find the right person for the job if it is to be performed well. It is important, however, to view this process in terms of the broader human resource needs of the organization over the longer term.

The Changing Nature of Organizations and Their Environments

In order to achieve corporate objectives, organizations may have to expand or contract, to diversify or rationalise products (or services) and to modify or replace existing technologies for new ones. All such changes have implications for an organizations' workforce in terms of employee numbers, their levels of education, skills, mobility and so forth.

It is also a fact that organizations exist within a social-political-economic environment which can have a strong impact on the ways they operate. Changes in employment legislation and industrial relations during the last fifteen years have led to the erosion of restrictive practices and to a requirement for many employees, both to acquire more skills and to be more adaptable in their use. The same requirements for multi-skilling and flexibility in employees has also arisen in the past decade as organizations have attempted to match the economic competitiveness of their rivals, particularly from overseas.[2]

These facts mean that, from a management of human resources perspective, organizations need to identity the numbers and kinds of employees that will be necessary to achieve short and longer term corporate objectives, and to determine when these employees will be required. In establishing these facts it is important to take into account the influence of the environmental forces already mentioned and projected changes in them, together with factors such as employee turnover and promotion rates and the availability of relevant people in the labour market (see Chapter 2). These data as a whole should provide the focus and direction for selection procedures.

Selection as a Two-Way Process

For the sake of convenience we tend to describe the selection process from an organizational point of view, ignoring the fact that individuals are also choosing between organizations and jobs, thus making selection a two way process.[3]

This fact has two important implications. First, it highlights the need for organizations to market job vacancies in a manner which will attract the best candidates, especially when there is a limited supply of qualified people. Second, it emphasizes the need to offer job applicants who will occupy key positions (see Competency-Based Organizations below) a rewarding role in terms of job satisfaction, remuneration and genuine career prospects. The marketing of jobs in an attractive manner can create problems for selectors, however, because applicants who want particular jobs will often manage information about themselves to create the most favourable impression possible. Certain facts will be omitted, others will be exaggerated or even invented. Thus selectors need to collect pertinent information and to make discriminating judgements about job candidates. It is not always easy to see beneath the facade of competence and enthusiasm which an applicant may present, but it is essential to do so if the organization is not to end up with employees whose performance is mediocre.

The Costs of Poor Selection

The selection process is the point of access to an organization and, as such, it is a crucial aspect of human resource management which, if not treated seriously, can prove costly to the organization. When an unsuitable candidate is appointed to a job the organization not only incurs the immediate direct cost of poor performance but various indirect costs as well. For example, the employee may need further training, or the motivation of this person's colleagues might suffer if they have to undertake increased work loads. Conflict between employees and increased absenteeism can ensue and eventually an unsuitable candidate might have to be transferred or even dismissed with all the additional costs of finding a replacement. The following description of a selection procedure concentrates mainly on conceptual and procedural issues but it assumes that the whole selection process is guided by the human resource management policies and strategies of the organization.

A Comprehensive Selection Procedure: The Traditional Approach

The typical definition of selection – finding the right person to fill the right job – emphasizes the aim or objective of this activity but does not give any indication of the processes by which it is achieved. Yet without an understanding of the essential tasks entailed, it is not possible to develop flexible selection procedures. Instead people will tend either to trivialise the importance certain activities or to adhere slavishly and blindly to unnecessary practices, often with mediocre results, when more simple and efficient procedures might be available.

The crucial tasks in personnel selection are to accurately *predict* the future job performance of applicants on the basis of matching information about them (e.g. past work record, education, personal characteristics, etc.) against the known requirements for particular jobs and then to *decide* which applicants are most suitable for these jobs. Thus selection is a probabilistic process and errors are always likely as there is often insufficient information about applicants to make predictions with confidence, and the decisions of selectors are frequently subject to bias. In order to minimise errors when matching applicants with job vacancies, two things are required: an accurate and detailed model of the kind of person(s) being sought, known as a person specification, and pertinent, reliable information about applicants, collected through such means as application forms, references and interviews. If these are not available to selectors there is little chance that a selection procedure will be effective, no matter how complicated or sophisticated it might appear to be.

There are two common approaches to matching people and jobs, similar in many ways but with quite different emphases. *Selection* adopts a job-centred approach: it starts by defining the essential activities of a job, from this the requirements (experience, personal characteristics, etc.) a person must have are determined, and people are selected according to how closely they match these requirements. *Placement* utilises a person-centred approach to filling job vacancies. It involves hiring people on the basis of their general suitability for joining the organization rather than for a specific job. New employees typically undergo a period of training during which time the most appropriate job is identified for each one in the light of his or her particular attributes. This approach is frequently used when selecting school leavers or graduates who have little if any previous job experience.

A third approach to matching people and jobs is used when there are relatively few, if any, qualified people available to fill the vacancies. In this case people (who are considered to be suitable candidates for the jobs) are first *trained* to do the job. Those who are successful in training then form the pool from which people will be selected as required. Two notable examples of this approach are the selection of astronauts by NASA and the identification of deep-sea divers for oil exploration work in the North Sea.

For the sake of simplicity the following discussion will concentrate on selection rather than placement, although many activities are common to both approaches. The usual phases included in a comprehensive procedure are listed in Figure 3.1 together with the main activities associated with each phase.

PHASES	ACTIVITIES
DEVELOPING A PERSON SPECIFICATION	*Job analysis:* conduct a systematic analysis of a job to identify the specific tasks it entails and how they should be performed. *Job description:* write a full and accurate statement of what a job entails using a job analysis, indicating the activities/ responsibilities of any incumbent and expected standards of performance. *Person specification:* using the job description, develop a statement of the 'requirements' (e.g. education, experience, personal characteristics) any applicant must possess in order to do the job to the expected standards.
RECRUITMEN T	*Advertise* the job in an attractive manner through the appropriate media, providing sufficient information to attract suitable applicants and to deter unsuitable ones. *Application form:* design a form to be completed by applicants which will provide the essential biographical and other data needed to determine their suitability, distribute copies to applicants with additional information about the job.
SCREENING	*Use* the 'topping and tailing' method to eliminate from further consideration applicants who lack appropriate qualifications, or who are too highly qualified, based upon data from application forms and perhaps reterences, psychological tests etc. The screening process may be extended over several stages, eliminating further applicants at each stage. Draw up a short list.
SELECTION	*Test* applicants using valid and reliable psychological tests known to predict 'requirements' in the person specification. (These tests may be used to aid initial screening). *References:* obtain 'structured' references from referees on the suitability of applicants for the job. (Could be obtained for initial screening or after the interview). *Interview* applicants on short-list to: check and clarify information already collected; obtain additional information from face-to-face encounter; answer questions; influence applicants (possibly) by persuading them of their suitability or otherwise for the job. *Decide* which applicant(s), if any, is (are) suitable by matching information obtained from the application fom, tests etc., with the requirements of the person specification, looking in particular for evidence of both the *capacity* and *willingness* to work to the required standards. The 'objective' information (e.g. educational qualifications, past work record) should be given the greatest weight when making the decision.
INDUCTION AND TRAINING	*Induction:* arrange an appropriate welcome and familiarisation with the organisation for all new employees. *Training:* the systematic management of the work activities of new employees, when necessary, so that the information, attitudes, technical skills and other essential behaviours needed to perform their jobs effectively are acquired.

Figure 3.1. Phases and Activities in a Comprehensive Selection Procedure.

The exact position of certain activities (e.g. psychological testing) in the overall procedure can vary, as indicated by the broken lines (– – – –) and the number and scope of phases in a selection procedure will differ according to the type and level of job involved. The most thorough procedures go beyond making initial selection decisions and are also concerned with subsequent training (see Chapter 8) and even later appraisals of job performance (see Chapter 10). Information gained from these later phases can then be used to evaluate the success of selection decisions. Similarly, information from any phase can be used to evaluate the activities involved in the previous phase and to guide decision making in subsequent phases. For instance, information gained during the selection phase can be used to evaluate the recruitment and screening phases and also to guide the development of induction and training programmes. The sequence of phases (➡) and the interchange of information about phases (→) are identified by arrows in Figure 3.1. The selection of most employees is a joint activity undertaken by representatives of line management and the Personnel or Human Resource Management function. Some indication of their respective roles during each phase of a selection procedure is given below, although their exact roles will vary from one organization to another.

The Conceptual Phase: Developing a Person Specification

A crucial part of any selection procedure is the initial conceptual phase of determining the nature of a particular job, the kind of person most suitable for it and how that person can be recognised. This work is frequently skimped, perhaps because the information seems too obvious, but failure to do it adequately may mean that the remaining phases are pointless, no matter how carefully conducted. The activities entailed in this conceptual phase are detailed below.[4] They may appear easy to do; in practice, however, they can be quite difficult. It is for this reason that they are usually made the responsibility of someone in HRM who has had specific training in this field. The advantages of training are normally offset, however, by ignorance of what the job entails. Such information is best supplied by a successful incumbent of the job or by his or her supervisor. Thus if the conceptual phase is to be performed adequately it normally requires close cooperation between HRM and line management in order to end up with a useful person specification for a job.

Job Analysis

Job analysis is any systematic procedure designed to provide information about the specific tasks involved in doing a particular job and how these tasks should be performed. There are many ways this information can be obtained. For example, employees can be observed doing the job, or they might be interviewed and asked to describe what the job entails. Sometimes employees are required to keep a diary so that the range and frequency of the different things they do can be identified.

A number of standardised techniques of job analysis exist which can, in theory, be used to describe most jobs. These tend to be useful only for lower level jobs, however, and less formalised approaches are generally necessary to capture the significant aspects of many managerial jobs. A reason for this is because managers' jobs are less determined by specific technical skills, requiring people to possess various interpersonal skills as well. Whereas there is normally one correct or ideal way for performing a technical activity, interpersonal activities such as motivating subordinates, conducting interviews and running meetings can be performed in a variety of ways with similar success. Thus, to analyse many managerial jobs, methods of identifying the *more successful ways of performing* tasks, particularly interpersonal ones, are required. A technique which lends itself to this approach is Flanagan's *Critical Incident* technique which can, in fact, be used for analysing any kind of job.[5] The aim is to identify specific behaviours that are particularly important (i.e. critical) to the successful performance of a job, rather than to simply identify the tasks involved. The merits of this approach are that it tends to ignore the more trivial details of jobs and, by concentrating upon behaviours rather than tasks, it provides a better idea of the kind of person best suited to the job (also see *A Competence-Based Approach to Selection* below). In practice, a sound strategy for conducting a job analysis would be to employ a variety of approaches and to collect information from a number of sources in order to obtain a comprehensive picture of that job.

Job Description and Standards of Job Performance

Once a job analysis has been completed, it should be written up in the form of a job description, which is a full, accurate and precise statement of what the job entails. The job description should define the overall purpose of the job and list the specific activities required of any incumbent. As it is often less easy to list the specific activities of a managerial job than one on the shop floor, descriptions of the former frequently emphasize the *responsibilities* instead of the activities of the incumbent.

It is also important to identify the *standards of performance* expected of a person for each activity listed in a job description, as standards might vary depending upon the importance of a particular activity to that job. For instance, while a technical draughtsman will be expected to achieve very high standards for drawings, less will normally be expected in terms of interpersonal and administrative skills; whereas in the case of a manager the reverse might be true. These standards are the *criteria* which provide the focus for predictions, and selectors have to decide whether an applicant will meet these standards if appointed to the job.

Person Specification

A person specification is a statement of the 'requirements' (e.g. experience, education, skills, personal characteristics) a person needs to possess in order to achieve the standards set for the activities/responsibilities listed in the job description. Inferring what these requirements are from a job description is by no means easy for some jobs. Once again this process tends to be easier for lower level jobs, where technical skills are paramount, than for managerial jobs where interpersonal skills are also important. Thus, it is easier to determine the requirements for a lathe operator than to say what they should be for a marketing manager.

A number of writers have suggested ways of structuring the items in a person specification under set headings. Two well known approaches, the seven-point plan of Alec Rodger and the five-point plan of J. Munro Fraser are summarised in Table 3.1.[6] Such plans should be viewed as useful tools for directing thinking and not as rigid frameworks. It is important to guard against the assumption that there is one ideal type of candidate suitable for a job, whose requirements can be detailed exhaustively, when this stereotype has not been, and perhaps cannot be, validated. It is usually true that a range of candidates would prove suitable for a job as long as each possesses certain critical requirements and does not possess other unacceptable characteristics.

One problem of approaches similar to those above is that they do not indicate the *relative importance* of the different requirements. Thus, an alternative way of organising a person specification is to group the requirements into essentials, desirables, undesirables or disqualifiers. *Essentials* represent critical requirements a person *must* possess, and there are usually few of these; *desirables* refer to experiences, attainments, personal characteristics, etc. known to *aid* learning or job performance; *undesirables* include experiences or attributes known to cause difficulty to other people on the job (e.g. someone who smokes) but must not be illegal (e.g. racial characteristics); *disqualifiers* represent experiences or attributes known to be directly related to failure at a job (e.g. certain medical conditions). Of course it is possible to combine both approaches as illustrated in Figure 3.2. This specification is a summary of one produced for the secretary to the chairman of a medical products company which has dealings with overseas clients.

Note: the terms job specification and person specification are interchangeable. The former is possibly used more frequently than the latter but is, to my mind, misleading as it implies requirements of a job, rather than of the person doing that job.

Table 3: Two Plans for Organising the Items in a Person Specification

The Seven-Point Plan (A. RODGER)	*The Five-Fold Grading System (J. MUNRO FRASER)*
1. *Physical make-up:* health, physique, appearance, bearing and speech	1. *Impact upon others:* physical make-up, appearance, speech and manner
2. *Attainments:* education, training, qualifications, experience	2. *Acquired qualifications:* general education, vocational training, work experience, qualifications
3. *General intelligence:* fundamental intellectual capacity	3. *Innate abilities:* general intelligence, natural quickness of comprehension and aptitude for learning
4. *Special aptitudes:* mechanical, manual dexterity, facility in the use of words or figures, talent for drawing, music	4. *Motivation:* the kinds of goals set by an individual, his consistency and determination in following them up, his success in achieving them
5. *Interests:* intellectual, practical-constructional, physically-active, social, artistic	5. *Adjustment:* emotional stability, ability to stand up to stress and ability to get on with people
6. *Disposition:* acceptability, influence over others, steadiness, dependability, self-reliance	
7. *Circumstances:* domestic circumstances, age, mobility	

Predictors

A question which has to be answered at this early stage is: how will selectors recognise suitable candidates for particular jobs? If the person specification requires someone who can work in difficult circumstances (e.g. long and unpredictable hours), ways of identifying such a person must be established. What is required are sources of information, known as *predictors,* which will indicate whether an applicant possesses the requirements detailed in the person specification. Bearing in mind the tendency of applicants to manage the information they present about themselves, it is necessary to look for predictors which will

PERSON SPECIFICATION		
Job Title:	SECRETARY TO CHAIRMAN Job. Des. No.	
Requirements: (Disqualifier = Dis; Essential = E; Desirable = D; Undesirable = Un)		
PH YSICAL: health, physique, appearance	good physical health, no recurring illnesses pleasant, neat appearance strong regional accent smoker	E E Un Dis
EDUCATION/ QUALIFICATIONS educational and vocational attainments; general abilities; skills and intelligence	shorthand: 80 w.p.m. minimum typing: RSA II minimum at least 'O' level English or equivalent medical shorthand	E E E D
SPECIFIC APTITUDES/ SKILLS verbal,numerical, clerical, mechanical, conceptual, abililty to learn/develop	able to produce high quality work when meeting tight deadlines reliable, accurate memory knowledge of medical terminology capable of developing appropriate filing systems good word processing skills	E D D E D
EXPERIENCE: duration,range, etc.	wide experience of office practices minimum five years office experience experience of operating as a P.A. experience of dealing with overseas customers etc.	E D D D
ADJUSTMENT/ SOCIAL SKILLS: emotional stability; personal and interpersonal qualilies/skills	shows initiative and self reliance able to deal with a wide range of people in a tactful and sensitive manner able to manage 'crises' without becoming disturbed does not require a high level of social contact with other employees	E E D E
MOTIVATION: kind of motivation required for job; nature of rewards it offers	places importance on achieving high standards of accuracy and presentation has a commitment to high ethical standards satisfied to work within this role without looking for career advancement	E E D
CIRCUMSTANCES: age, mobility, location, domestic factors	possesses driving licence and willing to use own car during office hours when necessary able to work normal office hours without interference of domestic commitments probably in the age range 35–50	E E D

Figure 3.2. Example of a Person Specification Form.

provide reliable evidence of whether an applicant both can (i.e. has the *ability* to) and will (i.e. be *motivated* to) do the job to the required standards.

A well recognised principle in selection is that past performance predicts future performance, thus predictors should be used which provide evidence of what a person has achieved in previous jobs. In the case of school leavers and graduates with little or no previous job experience, it is important to examine their educational and social experience for evidence of the ability (or potential) and motivation necessary for a job. The traditional predictors used in selection procedures are references, application forms/biographical data, interviews, psychological tests and samples of work performance. All, or most, of these predictors are used routinely within many selection procedures. Each should only be used, however, if it provides specific, reliable information regarding the suitability of an applicant for the job. The final activity of the conceptual phase is to determine which predictors will be employed in the screening and selection phases.

Recruitment Phase

Recruitment is the process of attracting suitable candidates to apply for the jobs available. It involves deciding upon the most appropriate sources of candidates to approach and the best ways of approaching them.

Sources

The main source of applicants for jobs fall into two categories, those internal to the organization, including employees looking for sideways appointments, as well as those aiming for promotion, and sources external to the organization. The latter category includes government employment agencies (Job Centres, Professional Executive Register) and private agencies such as secretarial bureaux, schools, colleges and universities, groups contacted by direct advertising such as through trade magazines and journals, and finally private contacts.

The advantages of using internal sources for appointments are obvious – an internal applicant is generally well known to the organization and the costs of advertising, recruitment and training are much reduced. The disadvantages of internal appointments include the failure to inject new blood into the organization and the possibility of causing friction between existing staff, several of whom may be applicants for the same job. The merits and demerits of external appointments tend to be the reverse of those for internal appointments.

Attracting Applicants

The primary means of drawing the attention of candidates to jobs and persuading them to apply, is through well prepared advertisements placed in local or national newspapers and trade and professional journals. Determining the content, layout and presentation of advertisements is a skilled job which organizations may sub-contract to a professional agency, rather than run the risk of producing copy which either does not attract applicants to read it or fails to stimulate them to make enquiries about the job(s).

When individuals follow-up advertisements and enquire about jobs, their interest needs to be maintained and even increased. This can be achieved in several ways. The usual method is to send out additional details about the job and perhaps an attractive brochure describing the organization, together with an application form. Some organizations also provide a contact person within the organization who can talk to enquirers in a knowledgeable way about job.

The processes of recruitment and screening are sometimes best undertaken by external agencies. When an organization only has a small Personnel Department and/or lacks any individuals with real expertise in selection methods and/or is heavily overworked, it can be cost-effective to employ recruitment consultants, particularly if they specialise in certain sectors of the labour market (e.g. computing, finance, electronics). Certain consultants, known as head hunters, may also be employed by organizations when there is only a limited number of suitable people for a specific job (usually a very senior appointment). These people are probably already well established in another organization and it will require direct and discreet contact with them to establish their possible interest in a new appointment.

The time, effort and costs entailed in the recruitment phase of a selection procedure will vary, as with all other phases, according to the number, level and type of vacancies which have to be filled. Most activities in this, and indeed the screening phase, will be undertaken by personnel specialists who will probably want to consult line management about the best sources for obtaining applications and for information regarding trade or professional journals.

Screening Phase

Many people who apply for jobs are simply not suitable and the numbers of applicants frequently exceeds the vacancies available, so that it is necessary for selectors to screen all applications. *Screening* is the process by which candidates are eliminated from further consideration because they do not possess the essential requirements for the job, or because they possess certain disqualifiers. Thus the purpose of screening can be described as *eliminating failure.*

The predictor used most frequently in screening is the application form, but references, scores on psychological tests and a preliminary interview might also be used. (See Figure 3.1). It is often possible to screen out the majority of applicants simply by checking whether they fulfil the basic age and educational/technical requirements for a job, or achieve a particular score on a psychological test. Other applicants will be eliminated after more careful inspection of their application forms, perhaps because their prior job experience is inadequate or unsuitable. For more senior appointments, the screening phase will be divided into several sub-phases spread over a period of time (returning the application form, completing a psychological test, attending an initial interview). Different applicants will be rejected at each sub-phase if they fail to meet the relevant criteria.

A form of screening, often forgotten, yet which is important for all jobs and even mandatory for some, is *health screening.* The purpose of such screening is to ensure that employees are fit to do particular jobs and that the jobs will not adversely affect their health. It is also to preclude people from certain jobs where their health problems could, for example, be hazardous to the manufacturing process (e.g. in the food or medical products industries). Screening is often restricted to problems of physical health although it is of more prognostic value to also assess psychological health.[7]

The end product of a screening process should be a short-list of candidates all of whom appear to be reasonably suitable for the job, and who will proceed to the selection phase.

Selection Phase

Selection was described earlier as a process of predicting the future job performance of applicants on the basis of *matching* information about them with the requirements in a person specification, requirements which are believed to be related to successful performance of the job. Thus, whereas screening can be defined as the process of *eliminating failure,* matching might be described as *identifying success.* That is, the qualifications of those applicants who are not eliminated during screening are matched with the requirements of the person specification in order to find the best fit, as this person is the one who is likely to be most successful at the job. Screening and matching are not just different ways of describing the same activity, however, because the attributes of a person which might predict failure at a job are not necessarily useful for predicting success. For example, high anxiety-proneness and low intelligence will be good predictors of failure for many jobs, but low anxiety-proneness and high intelligence will not necessarily predict success. This is because there is not a linear relationship between scores for these attributes and success or failure at a job. Thus, screening and matching are complementary processes in a selection procedure.

Of all the devices available to selectors, the interview is the primary and often the sole predictor used (in conjunction with an application form) during the selection phase.[8] As it involves the only face-to-face encounter between applicants and selectors, it is probably best used after data from all other predictors have been collected, so that they will be available for checking and further exploration during the interview. Therefore the value of several other predictors will be considered first.

Application Forms and Biodata

Application forms can be particularly vaulable sources of information to selectors for two reasons. First, they (should) document an applicant's prior record, in terms of educational qualifications, work history and other experience which is relevant to the job in question, and as "past performance tends to predict future performance", these data are very pertinent to decision making in the screening and selection phases. Second, because of its standardised format, an application form provides *comparable* data for all applicants, thus simplifying the decision making process. Applicants who submit *a curriculum vitae* (C.V.) should also be encouraged to complete an application form as they might omit from the C.V. (knowingly or otherwise) certain information which is important for predictive and comparative purposes.

The potential value of an application form can be lost, however, if it is poorly designed. Forms which look unattractive, are complicated, difficult to complete and unnecessarily intrusive about an applicant's personal life can deter individuals who would be suitable for the job from applying. A well designed form can encourage people to apply by providing a clear and sensible format to help them structure their answers. It should collect information which is relevant for predictive and comparative purposes and, as far as possible, avoid questions which will prove offensive to applicants.

A problem selectors often experience with application forms is knowing how to assess the sheer volume of data they contain. At the initial screening stage it is important to check whether candidates meet the essential, objective requirements for the job as detailed in the person specification (e.g. educational qualifications, technical skills). The majority of candidates can usually be rejected after such a check. Next, it is useful to examine a candidate's prior record for *discontinuities, trends and explanations.* Discontinuities refer to unexplained gaps in a candidate's educational or job history, often indicated by dates which are not perfectly consecutive, and which might need to be explored during an interview. Trends are particularly important to identify; for example, do frequent job changes represent career progression or simply career change, is there evidence of early achievement in a job followed by steady decline, or vice versa? Any consistency in trends should be a good predictor of future behaviour. A well designed application form will ask applicants to outine why they changed jobs, or how their prior experience is relevant to the job for which they are applying. Explanations given can provide useful insights into a candidate's beliefs and goals.

The use of biographical facts (biodata) about job applicants (e.g. age, qualifications) which have demonstrable validity in predicting work performace for particular jobs has grown recently.[9] The importance of such predictors, if valid ones can be found, is that they considerably simplify the decision making process. When used alone, however, biodata have limitations: they are probably only suitable for relatively low level jobs, certain valid predictors (e.g. sex/marital status) are not legally acceptable and many biographical items only retain their predictive validity for short periods of time.

References

It is probably most useful to take up references prior to interviewing applicants, as the references can then be considered at the interview stage. Unfortunately, this is not always possible as some applicants are reluctant to let their employers know that they are applying for another job. Thus an organization might take up references only after interviews have been conducted, in effect to confirm or refute tentative selection decisions. To avoid such problems as breach of confidentiality, it is important to obtain the permission of candidates to take up references at a specified point in time.

References are one of the most controversial sources of data about applicants and are seen by some as little more than worthless pieces of paper. This is because references tend to convey selected opinions of referees rather than wide-ranging factual data about applicants. In part this problem originates with the selectors who often fail to provide adequate guidance to referees concerning the information required. A referee who is the current or past employer of an applicant is, potentially, one of the most valuable sources of information about that applicant. He or she can be properly utilised by being asked to complete a *structured reference* – essentially a series of questions which requests primarily factual information about the applicant's performance, successes and problems, and future potential. It is useful to collect at least two references, in case there are conflicts of data and opinion. References are sometimes very revealing through the information they omit, therefore it is often useful to follow up references with a telephone call to a referee who will almost certainly provide more detailed and accurate information verbally than in written form.

Psychological Tests and Inventories

Psychological tests and inventories are standardised instruments designed to measure individual differences in some aspect of human knowledge, attitudes, interests, personality traits or skills. They can take the form of written, verbal or performance tasks and be completed either with or without time restrictions. The best known of these instruments are probably intelligence tests and personality inventories. The use of the words test and inventory is not arbitrary: a *psychological test* is one for which individual questions have right or wrong answers, whereas answers to the items of an *inventory* simply reflect differences in individual preferences, habits and beliefs and there are no right or wrong answers.

There are literally thousands of tests and inventories and it is easy for an untrained person to be rather gullible about their value. Many of these instruments are acutally of little use, because they do not possess the characteristics of a worthwhile test or inventory. A worthwhile psychological test or inventory should be both a *valid* and *reliable* instrument. The former term is difficult to define but, technically speaking, it is a measure of the strength of relationship between a test/inventory score and whatever that score purports to assess (determined using statistical tests of correlation, the stronger the correlation the more valid is the test). In other words, validity is concerned *with how* well a test measures what it purports to measure. In a selection context it is the *predictive validity* of an instrument which is particularly important. When a test has high predictive validity, differences in test scores can be used to accurately predict differences in the *future* job behaviour of applicants. Reliability refers to the consistency of the results obtained from testing (again assessed using measures of correlation). A test is reliable when individuals obtain similar scores upon repeated completion of the same test over a period of time, or for equivalent versions of a test.

For a test or inventory to be of use it is also essential that normative data exist which indicate the average score achieved by individuals from a specific group (males, females, graduates, engineers, doctors etc.) and some measure of the distribution of scores for each group. For example, the standard deviation is a well-known statistic which is easy to calculate and from which it is possible to determine the range of scores within which 67%, 95% or 99.9% of a specific group fall. The significance of a person's score can only be assessed in the light of such data which will relate the performance of that individual to the performance of others. Finally, it is also crucial that whatever a test or inventory measures, it is *relevant* to predicting the future job performance of an applicant. It is a waste of time and money to collect information if it does not have predictive value for selection purposes.

Broadly speaking, psychological measurement devices fall into three categories: achievement tests, ability and aptitude tests and personality and interest inventories. Research to date has demonstrated that tests tend to have moderate to good predictive validities whereas inventories tend to have low predictive validities when used in a selection context.[10]

Achievement Tests. These tests assess a person's level of achievement in some specific area. They might be concerned primarily with assessing knowledge (e.g. university examination) or skills (e.g. driving) or both. Educational and professional examinations and tests to assess the results of industrial and occupational training fall into this category. The results of such tests are frequently used as predictors in selection procedures.

Ability and Aptitude Tests. Tests of aptitude are concerned with assessing whether a person has the capacity (potential) to acquire particular skills. In order to determine aptitude, individuals are usually given tests of fundamental abilities which are believed to be essential prerequisites of the capacity to acquire skills. As these so-called fundamental abilities are themselves partly products of prior learning, the distinctions between achievement and aptitude tests and between ability and capacity are, at times, more apparent than real.

Tests of general intelligence are the most well known tests of mental ability, but tests of more specific abilities such as verbal and numerical skills, perceptual abilities (tests of vision and hearing) and psychomotor skills (eye hand coordination) also exist. Most of these tests are relatively easy to administer and personnel specialists can be trained to use them in a relatively short period of time. They can be useful predictors, particularly when a job applicant lacks a prior work history.

Personality and Interest Inventories. These instruments hold a particular fascination for some individuals, who feel that through such inventories they will learn deep things about themselves or others. Generally, the view is inaccurate and derives from a misapprehension about the nature of personality inventories. Two points are important to remember about inventories First, inventories tend to be *transparent,* in that it is often easy to infer the purpose of a question, thus making it possible for people to distort their answers in order to create more favourable images of themselves than are actually true. Few people, for example, will honestly admit how prone to anxiety they are in social situations. Second, inventories tend to have low predictive validities in a selection context, a fact which partly reflects the transparency of these instruments and partly demonstrates that personality traits, such as 'dominance' and 'extroversion' are less important in determining job performance than are specific abilities such as problem-solving skills.

Although psychological tests and inventories may not be particularly useful as selection devices for many jobs, they can be valuable screening devices, identifying candidates who fail to meet certain criteria which are considered essential in the person specification, or who possess disqualifiers. Reputable tests and inventories are normally available only from a limited number of sources (e.g. National Foundation for Educational Research) and to appropriately qualified and trained users.

Work Samples

The foregoing predictors do not directly sample actual behaviours which will be required for successful job performance, instead they provide signs of what a person can do.[11] Thus, correspondence between the predictor (e.g. psychological test) and the criterion (job behaviour) is limited. A work sample is a specimen of some aspect of an applicant's work behaviour which is relevant to the job for which he or she is applying, so that the correspondence between predictor and criterion is close and its predictive validity is usually higher than that for a sign.

A work sample can be obtained in two ways. The first is to utilise existing samples of an applicant's work. For instance, academics might provide copies of recent publications and graphic artists or photographers could supply their current portfolios. As long as such samples are pertinent to the job for which a person is applying they can be immensely valuable predictors. One important limitation of an *existing* work sample, however, is that it is not always clear who produced it. It is necessary to clarify, for example, whether an academic actually made a substantial contribution to an article or simply polished the original manuscript supplied by an assistant. Another limitation of (almost any) work samples is that they indicate what a person can do (i.e. *ability*) but not what the person will do (i.e. *motivation*), if appointed to the job.

The second form of work sample is one that an applicant is required to produce during the selection process. For instance, a typist might be required to retype a corrected draft of a letter, and a heavy goods vehicle driver to complete a series of manoeuvres with an articulated vehicle. For these kind of tests it is important that there are standardised ways of scoring performance and appropriate norms for experienced and inexperienced workers. A complication with this form of work sample is that some applicants might become apprehensive of being evaluated and consequently obtain atypically poor results, nevertheless, work samples tend to have good predictive validity.

It is more difficult to create realistic work sample tasks for many managerial jobs: assessing the complex sequences of behaviour entailed in decision making, chairing committees and managing other people. Various exercises have been created for this purpose, however, including in-basket decision making exercises, different types of group discussion or group problem solving, self-presentation tasks and so on. These exercises tend to have lower validities when predicting future job performance than work samples involving psychomotor tasks such as typing and driving.

The Interview

The interview is the most widely used of all selection devices and is also one of the most controversial. It represents the only protracted face-to-face encounter between an applicant and the selector(s) and it has three main purposes. First, to check data already obtained about an applicant through references, the application form, and so on. Second, to allow selectors to utilise the unique information they gain from a face-to-face encounter (in combination with that obtained through other predictors) to draw valid inferences about the suitability of applicants. Third, to provide an opportunity for the selector(s) to influence directly an applicant's choices. The interview is an opportunity not only to question applicants but also to discuss the job and the organization. Good applicants may receive several job offers and the impression they form of an organization during the interview can be an important determinant of their final job choice.

The interview is also the time when line management take a crucial role in the selection process, as it is they who will make the final selection decision for their departments. Here a difficulty arises. Interviewing is a skill (actually a higher-order skill embracing a number of component skills) which can only be developed through training and practice, yet line management (and sometimes members of the Personnel or HRM function) have often had little if any training at interviewing or opportunities to practise what skills they have. Even a well designed and conducted selection procedure can founder at this crucial stage if the interviewing and subsequent decision making are handled poorly.

Research into interviewing has revealed that the judgements of untrained interviewers frequently differ for the same interviewee and generally have low predictive validity. This is because the typical faults of untrained (and otherwise poor) interviewers include failing to prepare adequately and not structuring interviews in a sensible and consistent manner, failing to obtain appropriate information from interviewees and drawing biased inferences about interviewees, thus leading to poor selection decisions.[12] Each of these problems is examined briefly below.

Preparation and Planning. A common mistake of experienced interviewers is to assume that their skills are sufficient for them to get by with little or no preparation. Yet preparation is crucial. It begins with a statement of the objective of the interview: to determine whether any of the short-listed applicants is capable and willing to perform the job to the required standards. The person specification provides the model for each applicant and it is important at this stage to decide what information it is necessary to collect in order to determine how well applicants fulfil this. Certain information from the application form or references might also need further clarification. To aid preparation it can be useful to develop an interview form with the items from the person specification listed in one column and a summary of the information known about the applicants with respect to each item in adjacent columns. In this way the missing or ambiguous information for each applicant becomes obvious. Specific questions can then be prepared, unique to an applicant, which need to be asked, along with the more general questions asked of all applicants. The purpose of developing a structure is to ensure some standardization of the interview, so that specific topics dictated by the person specification are covered and adequate time is given for applicants to ask questions about the job and the organization.

During the opening phase of the interview it is crucial to establish a good rapport, helping applicants to feel at ease and encouraging them to participate fully in the interview. There is no single way to do this but a friendly approach, attentiveness to the comments of interviewees and providing them with an opportunity to talk about a straightforward issue early on, will help considerably. The middle phase of the interview is devoted to the careful questioning of applicants (see below) and it is important to be flexible here, ensuring that topics are covered but not necessarily in any fixed order. It is also important that interviewees are given the opportunity to ask questions and to express points of view, however, they should not dominate the interview to such an extent that the selectors fail to collect the information they need. Before closing the interview, the interviewer(s) should check that all the important questions have been covered and give the interviewees an idea of how and when they will learn the outcome of the selection process.

Collecting Information. Information about applicants is collected through observing them and asking them questions. Much has been written in recent years about what can be learned from an interviewee's posture, gestures and dress. The average interviewer, however, cannot reliably interpret most of these aspects of an interviewee's behaviour. Nevertheless, it is usually easy to identify nervous candidates and those with little poise in the interview, who are often easily embarrassed by straightforward questions.

The bulk of information is collected through the careful questioning of applicants and listening to their answers. The emphasis on listening is vital as the questions asked of an applicant should not simply reflect the topics on the interviewer's *pro-forma* but also should be contingent upon the applicant's answers. This is only possible through careful listening.

The essence of effective data gathering during an interview is skilful questioning.[13] Three of the most useful question types which need to be used are *open* questions, *probing* questions and *closed* questions. Open questions take the form "Tell me about …", "How do you feel about …?". They encourage the interviewee to talk because the questions cannot be answered properly with a "Yes" or "No" type response. If the interviewer simply sits quietly after posing the question, or prompts a brief reply with a "Please go on …", "Tell me more about …", interviewees speak readily if they have anything to say. The probing question is often the least used of these three question types. It takes the form "Please elaborate upon …", "Tell me exactly what happened …", and it is intended to focus the interviewee upon a specific aspect of an answer he or she has given and to elaborate upon that answer. It is the probing question which frequently distinguishes the ignorant from the knowledgeable, the charlatan from the genuinely competent applicant. Closed question are those which require simple, frequently one word answers. They take the form "How old are you?", "When did you graduate?", and are ideal for checking facts and for collecting precise information about specific issues. Interviewers can stifle an interview, however, if closed questions are use repeatedly. Such questions can be very effective when used in conjunction with open and probing questions. Open questions get interviewees to talk in general terms; probing questions focus their answers on particular issues; closed questions dot the 'i's' and cross the 't's'.

Two other important question types are comparisons and hypotheticals. *Comparisons* take the form "What are the relative merits of A and B?". "Would you prefer X or Y?" and, as long as the 'pairs' are realistic, such questions can expose the beliefs, values and goals of applicants. A *hypothetical* question, such as "What would you do if …?", requires applicants to think about a new topic or situation and can be useful for revealing knowledge, beliefs and probably reactions, but only if the question is realistic and framed within the experience of the applicant.

The kind of questions to be avoided are *leading* and *multiple* questions. The former are phrased as follows: "You do agree that …?", "You would be willing to … wouldn't you?". Such questions suggest to the interviewee what the interviewer wishes to hear and many interviewees will simply agree with the implied answer although their private view might be different. Multiple questions, "How did you find your time at university and what did you do … perhaps you would also mention …?", should be avoided because they can be confusing and an interviewee may simply answer the question he or she prefers so that a critical question could be overlooked.

It is important to focus questioning on the past experience and behaviour of an applicant, not simply on his or her views, as a person's reaction patterns provide some of the most reliable predictive information about him or her. For example, a researcher might be asked "Tell me about the most difficult phase of the project", or "Please describe how you handled the problems" and so on. An interview has been described as "a conversation with purpose". This could be misleading because in normal everyday conversation comments and questions are often deployed simply for the purpose of developing and reinforcing social relationships, whereas within an interview they are used to make the interviewee think and provide detailed statements about specific topics. These two forms of skill are not interchangeable, which is why "good conversationalists" are often poor interviewers. Questioning skills are not easy to develop and it requires considerable practice for them to be used effectively.

Interviewer Biases. Whereas an interviewer's questioning skills determine the quality of the information obtained during an interview, it is the interviewer's *judgements* about that information which determine the quality of the final selection decisions. Bias in the inferences and judgements of interviewers is one of the main reasons why the interview can have poor predictive validity.

There are several well recognised judgemental errors which interviewers often make.[14] One is to *stereotype* interviewees, that is to inappropriately assign to each a character which is wrongly thought to describe members of a group (social, ethnic, religious, political) to which that person belongs. If that character does not approximate closely to the person specification for the job then the applicant is deemed unsuitable. Another common error has been described as the *halo effect.* This occurs when an interviewer judges a characteristic of an interviewee very favourably and then generalises that judgement to the person as a whole ("If he was in the Guards he must be suitable for the job"). The 'horns effect' reflects the opposite kind of judgement ("I don't think she can handle this job as she does become rather emotional at times"). *Contrast effects* also influence judgements when several applicants are interviewed in sequence. In this case an interviewer tends to see an average interviewee as being better or worse than he or she really is when the interviewee has been preceded by a series of poor or good applicants. Many judgemental errors exist and the problem for an interviewer is that these errors are often so deeply embedded in his or her thinking that it is difficult to recognise them. This is why formal interview training can be particularly helpful as it should provide a person with useful feedback about such errors.

The 'Structured' Interview. Structuring is obviously a matter of degree. For some researchers the *structured interview* is one in which all candidates are asked the same predetermined questions about how they would handle aspects of a job. These questions often focus on particular job situations derived using the critical incidents method and candidates' answers are assessed against a predetermined list of responses which represent effective, through to ineffective, performance for these situations.[15] In many ways such interviews are little more than verbally administered pencil-and-paper tests. They tend to have good predictive validity for specific jobs, but constructing the interview protocols is a time consuming process. Because the protocols are job specific, different jobs obviously require different protocols. Each of these has to be validated, which can be a costly process.

Some Additional Points. When interviews are criticised as selection devices it is actually a sloppy way of saying that *interviewers* fail to prepare and conduct interviews and make selection decisions in a skilful and objective manner. Once interviewers develop and utilise such skills, the interview can become an effective selection device.[16]

As noted earlier, it is sometimes true that line management lack the training and experience to be consistent and effective interviewers. One practice which can help to combat this problem is that of conducting *panel* interviews. A panel interview will nornally involve three or four interviewers, including one or two from HRM and one or two from line management. The advantage of such an arrangement is that it allows the interviewing load to be shared, each interviewer discussing with interviewees those subjects about which he or she has most expertise. It also permits the interviewers to check for judgemental biases by sharing their impressions with each other before reaching a final decision.

Board interviews are a particular form of panel interview which are often less satisfactory than one-to-one panel interviews. A Board is often large and composed of people who represent various parties interested in the selection decision but not affected by it. With so many interviewers, each can ask only one or two questions so that topics are not explored in any depth or in a coordinated manner and judgements of applicants are necessarily superficial, based on obvious characteristics (e.g. poise, articulateness), rather than on more important determinants of work performance and past work histories.

Assessment Centres

Assessment Centres refer to procedures for determining a person's suitability for appointment or promotion, not to places! These procedures assess many different attributes/behaviours of a job candidate, utilising a variety of predictors and a number of assessors. The aim is to be more comprehensive, more job-related (using work samples and signs) and more objective (consensus of judgements across independent assessors) than is true for traditional methods.[17]

There is a growing use of assessment centres in Britain, particularly by larger organizations. Assessment takes place over a period of days, usually in a residential setting where assessors directly observe individuals working alone or interacting with others in task and social activities. Judgements about the suitability of candidates for jobs have relatively high predictive validities for well designed assessment centres. This improvement is gained, however, at relatively high cost to an organization in terms of time, personnel and direct expenditure.

The Selection Decision

Some selection decisions are straightforward, as one applicant stands out from the rest as being most suitable. It is more usual, however, for there to be several suitable candidates, each with slightly different strengths and weaknesses. This often poses a problem for selectors who are unsure about how to weight and combine the different pieces of information into an overall judgement of a candidate. It is crucial at this point to keep the person specification in mind and to distinguish between essential and desirable requirements. Due emphasis should be given to each candidate's past record and to any significant trends in that record. Unless this is done the biases in judgement described above often result in inappropriate criteria being advanced as reasons for selecting or rejecting applicants. It is also the time when deliberate biases, such as political considerations, come to the fore and applicants can be rejected not because they are unsuitable for the job but because their appointment might prove inconvenient for a selector. The value of a panel interview, particularly one comprised of representatives of line management and personnel specialists, is that it is possible for the two functions to bring their separate perspectives to bear upon the final decisions, thus helping to expose and counteract the less deliberate biases in judgement. The end product of the decision making process is usually a rank ordering of candidates according to their suitability for the job. The best candidate is offered the job and one or two others are held in reserve in case the first candidate withdraws. The key processes in a selection procedure which have been described in this section and which result in the final selection decision are summarised in Figure 3.3.

A Competence-Based Approach to Selection

During the 1980's competence-based approaches to selection grew in popularity both in America and the United Kingdom. As a result the word 'competence' is now common parlance in many organizations although the meaning and usage of the term varies significantly.[18] This emphasis on competences is not peculiar to selection methods but is also the basis of recently developed training qualifications such as the National Vocational Qualifications (NVQs). Proponents of competence-based approaches to selection argue that they are much more effective at predicting occupational success than the traditional approach reviewed above. To evaluate this claim it is necessary to answer three questions: what is a competence-based approach; in what

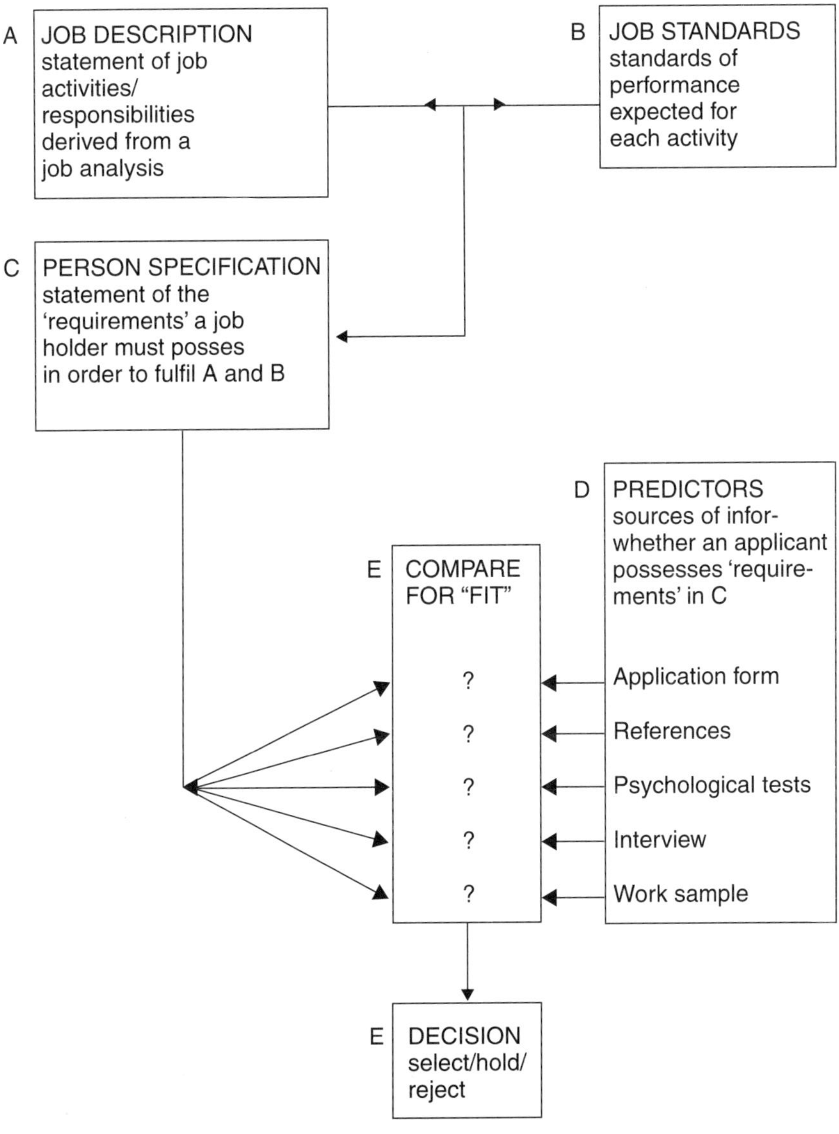

A, B and C are products of the initial conceptual phase of a selection procedure (i.e. developing a person specification). In the subsequent recruitment, screening and selection phases predictive information (D) is collected, compared for 'fit' (E) with the person specification and a decision (F) is made.

Figure 3.3. Key Processes in a Selection Procedure.

ways is it different from the traditional approach to selection; and do these differences have real merit?

The Competence-Based Approach

The origins and development of the job competence assessment (JCA) movement in America can be traced back to the work of psychologist David McClelland and his associates, who worked for a consultantcy, McBer and Co. In a contraversial article, McClelland argued that traditional predictors (eg intelligence and ability tests) had poor predictive validity for occupational success and needed to be replaced by competence-based predictors.[19] McClelland did not define 'competency' precisely, but a job competence has been defined more recently as "... an underlying characteristic of an individual that is causally related to criterion-referenced effective and/or superior performance in a job or situation.". The idea of a 'threshold' competence has also been introduced as an attribute which is essential to performing a job but is not causally related to superior performance.[20] Competences can be motives, traits, the self-concept, knowledge or skills.

Competences are identified through a *Behavioural Event Interview,* using Flanagan's Critical Incident Technique, in which people are asked to identify the behaviours which they used when they handled events at work successfully. This approach can be used for any job but it is typically used for managerial positions. It focuses on competences which enable a person to perform the technical aspects of a job (eg patience, endurance), or which concern *unstructured'* tasks (eg problem solving) and the *interpersonal* aspects of jobs (eg sensitivity to others), for which there is not a single right way of performing. Such competences complement rather than replace the specific technical knowledge and skills needed for particular jobs which are typically listed in a traditional person specification.

A competence analysis for a specific job should detail the criteria which define effective or superior performance, identify the key competences required to achieve these levels of performance and provide behavioural indicators for each competence identified. Analysis of candidates' answers during a Behavioural Event Interview indicates whether or not they possess the required competences. In theory the competence-based approach brings greater rigour and relevance to the conceptual phase of selection by establishing empirically the key attributes and behaviours necessary for superior performance. The traditional approach often infers attributes when a person specification is being developed and these inferences may reflect the biases of selectors. The emphasis upon *superior* performance also tends to be missing from the traditional approach and the choice of predictors can be very stereotypical. In practise, however, the two approaches overlap considerably and are often merged. This is particularly true in the case of Assessment Centres. Nevertheless, traditionalists continue to criticise strongly the efficacy of competence-based approaches to identifying occupational success, arguing that only ability and aptitude tests have been shown to have predictive validity.[21]

The controversy over the relative merits of competences versus ability and achievement tests as predictors is essentially an empirical matter but one which will not be resolved easily. Nevertheless, the popularity of competence-based approaches seems destined to grow for two reasons. First, because of their perceived relevance in identifying behaviours critical to success and second, because of the changing character of many organizations over the past few decades.

Competence-Based Organizations

Several trends are noticeable in the ways many organizations in western economies have changed over the last twenty years or so, as they have attempted to cope with the challenges of global competition, particularly from low wage economies. There has been a move away from mass production industries, with an increasing focus upon knowledge-based and service industries (eg software companies, consultancies, insurance and financial services). Many organizations have become less bureaucratic and mechanistic and more organic. These changes are reflected in flatter hierarchical structures with consequent wider spans of managerial control, reduced numbers of employees who are expected to be more efficient and productive thus requiring multi-skilling, greater flexibility in working practices and team working, often supported by improved technology. A consequence of these changes has been the tendency for distinct jobs and secure, well-defined career paths to disappear throughout many parts of organizations.

Another consequence of organizations having to contend with and adapt to changing (global) market forces and 'revolutions' in technology is that greater emphasis is now placed on finding individuals or groups who can make an important contribution to the success of an organization. First, core competences (critical knowledge and skills) which are not job specific but are needed by such individuals if they are to help an organization gain or maintain competitive advantage over the longer term, are being defined. Then individuals with these competences are identified or developed within the organizations, or recruited by them. Some of these individuals will become future 'key' players for the organizations. Thus, in such cases, selection policy is becoming much more strategic and developmental instead of focusing simply upon specific, narrowly defined jobs which have traditionally determined the career paths of individuals.

It is contended that these trends represent, or will come to represent, a fundamental shift towards competency-based, rather than job-based, organizations.[22] Such a shift will place a considerable onus upon those responsible for the recruitment and development of staff to establish comprehensive, predictively valid selection procedures and effective policies of staff development, which will meet the changing human resource requirements of their organizations over the longer term. Competence-based methods clearly have a key role in these areas.

Evaluating a Selection Procedure

It is not unusual for organizations to expend a considerable amount of time, effort and money in designing and implementing a selection procedure, and then not bother either to validate or evaluate it in any systematic way. The terms validate and evaluate are frequently confused and misused so it will help to clarify their meanings. *Validation* is concerned with the question "To what extent has this procedure achieved the results it was designed to achieve?", whereas *evaluation* is concerned with answering the more general but equally important question "Is this procedure worthwhile?".

There seem to be two main reasons why validation and evaluation are ignored. First, it can be personally threatening for those who design and/or conduct selection procedures to have their efforts assessed. Second, it is extremely difficult to validate and evaluate such procedures because their results often cannot be isolated from the influence of other factors. For example, the obvious criterion to use for validating selection decisions is the future work performance of new employees. Their work performance, however, will not only reflect their ability and motivation at the time they were selected, but also the influence of numerous other factors which come into play once they join the organization, such as training, the management style of supervisors, changing promotion prospects, etc. Nevertheless, unless a selection procedure is evaluated there is no way of knowing in what ways the procedure might be improved.

The criteria which are typically used to *evaluate* selection procedures, whether traditional or competence-based, include those of validity, reliability, fairness, social acceptability, administrative convenience and cost effectiveness. They are discussed briefly below. Each criterion can be applied to some element (e.g. the interview) or to a phase of the procedure, or to the procedure as a whole.

Validity and Reliability

In a selection context it is the predictive validity of a procedure which is crucial. This entails an assessment of whether the decisions made by selectors result in the appointment of individuals who prove to be competent and motivated employees. If predictive validity is low, an attempt should be made to identify where the invalidity lies. Is it, for instance, because useful predictors are being ignored (e.g. work samples), or are the selectors unable to draw valid conclusions from the data available to them?

It is, of course, crucial that selectors can make predictively valid decisions time and again. In other words, their decision making should be reliable as well as valid. Reliability is a measure of the consistency of decision making. If the quality of the graduate intake into an organization proved highly variable from year to year it would probably reflect unreliable decision making, rather than changes in the quality of the graduates. In order to improve the procedure it would be necessary to identify why decisions proved unreliable. It could be that different people are used as selectors in different years, some being consistently good and others consistently poor in this role.

Fairness

The purpose of a selection procedure is to *discriminate* the good from the poor applicants. It is also a legal requirement of any selection procedure that this process is fair. Fairness in this sense means that the procedure should not debar any individual or group of people from being selected on the basis of criteria which are irrelevant to successful job performance. Employment law relevant to selection has been revised considerably in the past two decades (e.g. Sex Discrimination Act, 1975; Race Relations Act, 1976) so that it is now unfair (i.e. illegal) to avoid selecting people to jobs on the basis of their race, skin colour, nationality, ethnic origins, sex or marital status, unless it can be demonstrated that any of these criteria are relevant to job performance. Sex status would be considered valid grounds for discrimination when determining the membership of certain religious orders but would not be accepted normally as a selection criterion for doctors, engineers, nurses or teachers.[23]

At present it is possible to discriminate against job applicants on the basis of their age, religion (except in Northern Ireland), past criminal record and political beliefs without behaving illegally. Such discrimination, however, is viewed by many people as being *unreasonable* (although legal) and is therefore becoming less socially acceptable. Human resource management policies in the field of personnel selection must obviously take account of current legislation and social values. It could prove detrimental in many ways to an organization if (by accident or design) its selection policies were found to be illegal and/or socially unacceptable.

Social Acceptability and Administrative Convenience

In an effort to improve the validity of a selection procedure it is possible to introduce features which prove counter-productive. An example could be the over-reliance on psychological tests as predictors, which might deter potentially good employees from applying for jobs. It could also complicate unnecessarily the administration of the procedure if applicants had to present themselves for several sessions of testing and if the scoring and interpretation of the tests was a time consuming process. Thus it is always useful when designing a selection procedure to consider the likely impact of any aspects of the procedure upon applicants and those responsible for conducting the procedure. Features which are not essential and which are likely to be socially unacceptable or administratively inconvenient ought to be avoided.

Cost-Effectiveness

Many improvements in selection procedures are only achieved through the use of additional resources (time, effort, materials, personnel), all of which incur a financial cost for the organization. Just as potential improvements in the reliability and validity of selection decisions need to be weighed against the criteria of social acceptability and administrative convenience, so potential or actual improvements should also be weighed against the financial costs involved. This is not always an easy calculation to make and requires an estimate of the value to the organization of any particular appointment. As a general rule, when the predictive validity of decisions is already high, then increased expenditure of time, effort and other resources will only result in marginal improvements and therefore will not be cost-effective. If the predictive validity of decisions is only moderate, however, then it is reasonable to expect that the costs of additional time, effort and so on will be more than offset by the financial benefits which will follow from an improvement in the quality of the selection decisions.

Conclusion

One of the most important factors which determines the success of an organization is the quality of the people it employs, so it is crucial to establish effective recruitment and selection policies. Personnel specialists play a major role in recruiting and selecting people for organizations, therefore it is necessary for them to: understand the conceptual basis of selection; be able to design, implement and evaluate selection procedures within their organization; and be aware of important developments in recruitment and selection techniques as they are relevant to the needs of the organization.

Selection procedures can range from brief, simple low-cost ones, to lengthy and comprehensive procedures which are very expensive to operate. For any procedure to be effective three things are required: accurate person specifications for each job; objective data relevant to the person specification for each applicant; selectors who are capable of making reliable and valid predictions about the suitability of applicants for jobs. However, the effectiveness of any selection procedure should not be taken for granted, each of its phases needs to be evaluated in order to identify whether and how improvements can be made.

Competence-based approaches to recruitment and selection seem destined to grow for two reasons: because of their perceived relevance in identifying *behaviours critical to success;* and because many organizations are now looking for adaptable people with core competences which are believed to be critical to promoting *organizational* success over the longer term, instead of simply identifying people capable of occupying rather narrow jobs and career paths. The growth of such approaches could re-focus significantly the aims and work of Personnel and HRM specialists.

References

1 D Torrington (1988), How does human resources management change the personnel function? *Personnel Review,* 17, (6), 3–9.

2 For a discussion of the changing nature of work and organizations see D Clutterbuck (1985), *New Patterns of Work,* Aldershot: Gower, and C Handy (1989), *The Age of Unreason,* London: Hutchinson.

3 P Herriot (1989), Interactions with clients in personnel selection. In P Herriot (Ed.) *Assessment and Selection in Organisations,* Chichester: John Wiley & Sons Ltd.

4 More detailed descriptions of selection procedures and processes can be found in: M Cook (1989), *Personnel Selection and Productivity,* Chichester: John Wiley & Sons Ltd, and M Smith and I T Robertson (1986), *The Theory and Practice of Systematic Staff Selection,* London: MacMillan.

5 J C Flanagan (1954), The critical incident technique. *Psychological Bulletin,* 51, 327–358.

6 J Munro Fraser (1978), *Employment Interviewing* (5th edition) London: MacDonald & Evans; A Rodger (1974), *The Seven-Point Plan,* National Foundation for Educational Research.

7 A Ostell (1986), Where stress screening falls short. *Personnel Management,* September, 34–37, for a discussion of aspects of psychological screening; M Lloyd (1988), The medical examination. *In* E Sidney (Ed.) *Managing Recruitment* (4th edition) Aldershot: Gower.

8 I T Robertson and P J Makin (1986), Management selection in Britain: A survey and critique. *Journal of Occupational Psychology,* 59, 45–57. Provides a recent review of the use of different predictors in selection procedures in British companies.

9 W A Owens (1976), Background data. In M D Dunnette, (Ed.) *Handbook of Industrial and Organizational Psychology,* Chicago: Rand McNally; R J Drakeley (1989), Biographical data. In P Herriot (Ed) op cit.

10 E E Ghiselli (1973), The validity of aptitude tests in personnel selection. *Personnel Psychology,* 26, 461–477; M Smith and I T Robertson, *op cit.* discuss the predictive validities of various predictors.

11 P F Wernimont and J P Campbell (1968), Signs, samples and criteria. *Journal of Applied Psychology,* 52, 372–376.

12 R D Arvey and J E Campion (1982), The employment interview: a summary and review of recent literature. *Personnel Psychology,* 35, 281–322.

13 P L Wright and D S Taylor (1994), *Improving Leadership*

Performance. (2nd edn), Englewood Cliffs, New Jersey: Prentice Hall (chapter 4).

14 F Landy and D A Trumbo (1976), *Psychology of Work Behaviour.* Homewood, Illinois: Dorsey Press (chapters 5 and 6).

15 G P Latham, L M Saori, E D Pursell and M A Campion (1980), The situational interview. *Journal of Applied Psychology,* 65, 422–427; T Janz (1982), Initial comparisons of patterned behavior description interviews versus unstructured interviews. *Journal of Applied Psychology,* 67, 577–580.

16 W H Wiesner and S F Cronshaw (1988), A meta-analytic investigation the impact of interview format and degree of structure on the validity of the employment interview. *Journal of Occupational Psychology,* 61, 275–290.

17 G C Thornton and W C Byham (1982), *Assessment Centres and Managerial Performance.* New York: Academic Press.

18 See articles in *Personnel Management* (1989), in June, July, August, September and November discussing the meaning of the term *competence* and reporting various approaches to assessing competences by different organizations

19 D C McClelland (1973), Testing for competence rather than for "intelligence". *American Psychologist,* 28, 1–14

20 See L M Spencer and S M Spencer (1993), *Competence at Work.* New York: John Wiley & Sons Ltd for the definition of competence and R E Boyatzis (1982), *The Competent Manager: A Model for Effective Performance.* New York: J Wiley & Sons Ltd for a discussion of *threshold competences*

21 G V Barrett and R L Depinet (1991), A reconsideration of testing for competence rather than for intelligence. *American Psychologist,* 46, 1012–1024.

22 E E Lawler (1994), From job-based to competency-based organizations. *Journal of Organizational Behavior,* 15, 3–15.

23 D Lewis (1983), *Essentials of Employment Law.* London: Institute of Personnel Management; *Butterworth's Employment Law Handbook,* 1984, 3rd Edition edited by P Waddington. London: Butterworth & Co.

Suggested Reading

L J Cronbach (1984), *Essentials of Psychological Testing.* (4th edition). New York: Harper & Row. (A good, comprehensive introduction to the nature and use of psychological tests with a helpful description of their use in a selection context.)

M D Dunnette (1966), *Personnel Selection and Placement.* Monterey, California: Brooks/Cole. (An in-depth approach to selection and placement, nevertheless, it is an excellent, readable text.)

M D Dunnette and L M Hough (Eds.) (1990/91), *Handbook of Industrial and Organizational Psychology.* (2 vols), Oxford: Oxford University Press. (An academic handbook, volume 2 includes a number of 'weighty' chapters on recruitment, selection, etc. Only to be tackled by those who want a thorough and academic grounding in the subject.)

P R Plumbley (1985), *Recruitment and Selection.* London: Institute of Personnel Management. (A helpful, general and practical book.)

P Herriot (Ed),(1989), *Assessment and Selection in Organizations.* Chichester: John Wiley & Sons Ltd (A useful collection of papers covering a wide range of topics relevant to personnel selection.)

Questions

1 Critically discuss the following statement: "Personnel selection is concerned with finding the right person to fill the right job".

2 Outline the criteria you would use to assess the suitability of a psychological test for use in a selection procedure. What are the strengths and limitations of tests as selection devices?

3 Discuss the view that interviews are so unreliable as sources of information about job applicants that they are not worth using in a selection procedure.

Case

W.A. WEAVERS LTD

Situation

W.A. Weavers is an established family company producing a number of woven materials for use in the furnishing industry. It recently developed a complex woven fabric, produced in narrow width pieces of different lengths, which has a variety of uses for implant surgery in humans. The fabric is patented and has led to significant advances in surgical techniques. Growing numbers of surgeons throughout the world are adopting the fabric for operations.

As a result of this development the company created a special 'clean room' plant to meet the exacting quality and hygiene requirements of the DHSS regarding the production of surgical implants. After weaving within the main factory, fabric lengths are washed, ironed and inspected within the clean room before being packaged into sterile containers. An appropriately qualified manager was appointed to oversee the operation of the clean room and adherence to DHSS regulations.

The fabric is very difficult to weave and, with the looms currently available, often has minor flaws which can be exacerbated by the sterilising processes. To combat these problems, W.A. Weavers transferred twenty inspectors from other product lines within the company to examine the finished fabric lengths. The major differences in their work are the more exacting standards set for the rejection of fabric lengths and the fact that the inspectors have to work in the sterile confines of the clean room plant wearing special overalls, footwear and headwear.

A year after the clean room plant was established, the inspectors' 'reject rate' for fabric lengths averaged 54% and the labour turnover for inspectors was 20%. A number of surgeons/hospitals from several countries, however, had returned items of fabric because of a variety of 'non-critical' flaws which made it more difficult to implant the fabric. Thus the reject rate for the year was actually closer to 60%.

W.A. Weavers replaced all returned 'reject' items of fabric free of charge, but realised that they must do something to improve the quality of fabric inspection if they were to maintain and develop their position in this new market. They were also concerned that the turnover level for inspectors was too high. The newly appointed Personnel Manager, Mary Brown, was asked to tackle both problems.

Action Taken by the Personnel Manager

Mary Brown discussed the problems independently with the Clean Room Manager and one of the Senior Fabric Inspectors. On the basis of these discussions it was obvious to Mary that a major cause of both problems was W.A. Weavers' inadequate selection procedures. The company was a rather old-fashioned family business and the selection of employees had never been a particularly sophisticated or informed process as far as Mary could see.

Thus, Mary decided to improve the selection procedure for these fabric inspectors. First, she obtained the job description for this position which the Clean Room Manager had written when the fabric lengths first went into production eighteen months previously. Checking through her files, she discovered two psychological tests which appeared to have face validity for the inspection tasks detailed in the job description. These were a Vigilance Test and an Item Discrimination Test.

Of the twenty inspectors originally employed, six had never had fabric which they had inspected returned, seven had had flawed fabric returned once, and seven had had inspected material returned on several occasions because of flaws. Four of the latter seven had already left the company and, on Mary's suggestion, the remaining three agreed to move to less demanding inspection lines within the company. Mary gave her two tests to the six inspectors with 'perfect' records and their scores turned out to be fairly similar. From these results, Mary determined a cut-off point for each test so that future applicants with scores below these points would be rejected automatically.

Due to a growing demand for the new fabric, Mary soon had to find five new inspectors as well as replacing the seven who had left or been transferred. She circulated details of the vacancies to local employment agencies and advertised in the local press:

> *Fabric Inspectors Required: W.A. Weavers has 12 vacancies for Fabric Inspectors. This is a responsible, well-paid job with promotion prospects and full company benefits. Previous experience desirable but not essential. Application forms from Ms Mary Brown, Personnel Manager.*

There were 104 applications, mainly from married women wanting part-time work and most of whom had no previous inspection experience. Of these 54 were rejected outright because they could not work shifts. The remaining 50 were invited in groups of 5–10 to "meet the company". This meeting entailed Mary giving them a short talk about the company and its products and then, without prior warning, giving the applicants the two selection tests. Only nineteen applicants bettered the lower cut-off points for the tests and these were invited for individual interviews but five declined the offer.

The fourteen remaining applicants were interviewed by Mary and the Clean Room Manager. Unfortunately, he could not attend several (five) interviews, so Mary's assistant joined her on these occasions. It was not easy to decide which of the applicants to reject as all seemed suitable candidates. Two female applicants were rejected eventually as they had been rather 'quiet' interviewees and Mary felt that they were perhaps too introverted.

The twelve new inspectors went through a particularly rigorous training programme which lasted for two weeks and after which each had a theoretical and practical test – all passed with flying colours. A year later none of the twelve have had any fabric which they have inspected returned, nor have any of the thirteen inspectors left from the original group. Only two of the new inspectors have left the company, although another two are complaining of the monotony of the job. The overall 'reject rate' for the twenty-five inspectors is 67%. In the light of these results, Mary feels well pleased with her new selection procedure.

Questions:

Study the above case and develop answers to the questions below, consulting other relevant texts if necesary. *The focus of your thinking should be primarily upon aspects of this case pertinent to the topic of personnel selection.*

- How justified is Mary's satisfaction with her selection procedure

- What criticism, if any, would you make of:

  (a) Mary's approach in designing the procedure?
  (b) The selection procedure itself?

Chapter 4

Rewarding People

Andrew Pendleton

Objectives

- To provide an overview of the main types of payment systems in use today
- To highlight the considerations managers should take into account when designing payment systems
- To evaluate incentive-based payment systems, and to identify the difficulties that often arise when these schemes are in use

Introduction

The determination and maintenance of a fair, equitable and effective pay system within an organisation is one of the most important and most difficult tasks facing human resource managers. Those responsible for designing pay systems have to strike a balance between a pay system which delivers satisfactory employee performance from an organisational point of view, and one which is viewed as fair and appropriate by employees and potential future employees. There has been a recurrent tendency for owners and managers to place more emphasis on the first of these, with the result that many a payment system has come to grief. If employees believe the payment system in use to be unfair they are unlikely to perform at their best. Indeed they may deliberately under-perform as a way of enacting revenge on their employer. Managers need to be aware of these possibilities in the current climate, where an emphasis on redesigning pay systems to enhance organisational performance has often gone hand in hand with a misplaced belief by managers that employee aspirations are secondary considerations. A further danger in the design of pay systems is the assumption that the pay system can be used as an 'automatic' mechanism or 'quick-fix' to harmonise organisational and employee objectives. It is often assumed that employee aspirations for additional financial rewards can be easily aligned with organisational concerns to improve the quantity or quality of employee performance, via the use of incentive systems. As we shall see, however, this both assumes that pay functions as a direct and straightforward motivator and that an apparent theoretical congruence between pay and performance can be operationalised in practice. Neither supposition should be taken for granted.

Designing a pay system, then, involves striking a balance between the objectives of employer and employee. In so far as it is unlikely that the objectives of the two will ever be identical, it is unrealistic to aim for a perfect pay system. Instead a system which minimises the problems often arising in the pay area may be the most that can be aimed for. Rather than relying solely on the pay system to generate commitment and secure control of employee performance, managers should use a range of other organisational mechanisms, such as employee participation in decision-making. With these observations in mind, this chapter reviews the main forms of payment system, and considers the costs and benefits which appear to apply to each. Most attention is devoted to the currently fashionable approach to employee remuneration, performance-related-pay, and it is suggested that the problems which tend to be generated by this approach to pay may well outweigh the benefits. Before turning to particular pay systems, however, we highlight some general considerations about the operation of payment systems which should be borne in mind by anybody attempting to introduce or revise a payment system.

The nature and objectives of payment systems

Remuneration is at the centre of the employee relationship, and a successful remuneration system is vital if an organisation is to achieve its objectives effectively and efficiently. Rewards may be paid in fringe benefits, such as company cars and share option schemes, as well as the wage or salary but usually the wage/salary is the main component of remuneration, (ie a shortage of suitable staff) may encourage organisations to increase wages or salaries to some groups of staff but not others. Whilst this may resolve the immediate problem of recruitment and retention, the danger is that this pay differential may lead to perceptions of unfairness among other employees and could detract from the motivational features of the pay system.

This example draws attention to the critical role played by employee conceptions of fairness in the operation of pay systems. Individuals judge their pay in relation to what others in the organisation or employees of other organisations receive. Research has shown that the point of reference is usually employees doing similar jobs either within the organisation or in the wider labour market.[1] If the pay system disrupts these relativities then employee dis-satisfaction is likely to result and the pay system will become ineffective in securing desired levels of effort and/or commitment. In the long term, with the development of large organisations and internal labour markets, as well as the development of 'fringe benefits', the notion of a prevailing 'going rate' in the local or national labour market for certain kinds of job seems to be in decline. Instead the points of reference for pay comparisons become more clearly situated in pay structures within the organisation. To put such comparisons on a more systematic and apparently rational footing, job evaluation methods can be used. Job evaluation systematically compares various features of jobs and, as Brown, Marginson and Walsh put it, "when correctly used, ... provides a means of maintaining and legitimizing a negotiated order. It provides a means for establishing criteria with which to assess the 'fairness' of relative pay, with implicit conceptions of fairness which are specific to the individual firm or bargaining unit".[2] However, in practice the objectivity of such methods is open to doubt as there will inevitably be a subjective, judgemental aspect to any comparative assessment of job characteristics.

A fundamental issue in the design of any reward system concerns the extent to which the rewards motivate those receiving them. A persistent theme among practitioners has been the efficicacy of marginal additions to pay to secure corresponding increases in performance. A central component of F.W.Taylor's 'scientific management', for instance, was the use of output-related payments as an incentive to employees to work in the manner desired by managers.[3] Other observers have been less convinced of the efficicacy of pay systems in this respect. Writers in the human relations tradition, such as Elton Mayo,[4] have suggested that the general state of management-employee relations could be a more powerful influence on employee performance (though the evidence from the Hawthorne Studies – the bedrock of human relations analysis – is by no means incontravertible on this point). Psychologists writing on this subject have indicated that the issue is somewhat more complex.[5] Even the simplest models of motivation, such as Maslow's 'hierarchy of needs',[6] suggest that the desire for status, recognition and creativity could be a more powerful influence on employee effort than pay. More complex models, as found in the expectancy theory approach, imply that pay can be a motivator in certain circumstances and for certain individuals7. The corollary of this, though, is that pay does not automatically function as a motivator and that the pay system should be treated with caution in this respect. It may be that the pay-off required by employees to meet organisational objectives is too great to be efficient for the organisation. An alternative perspective on the efficacy of payment systems is provided by Herzberg's two-factor theory of motivation.[8] Dividing features of working life into motivators and hygiene factors, the implication of his approach is that pay tends to fall into the category of hygiene factors. Potential additions to pay are likely to have weak positive effects on motivation but if the pay system is felt by individuals to be unsatisfactory then there may be a powerful negative impact on employee performance.

The balance of evidence suggests that the efficacy of the pay system as a motivator is limited, despite the intuitive appeal of a pay-performance linkage via the use of incentives. A further body of research findings suggests that employees trade-off effort against rewards – often referred to as 'the wage-effort bargain'[9] – deciding to accept below maximum levels of reward in return for less than maximum degree of effort. This phenomenon is often found where piece-rate systems are in operation. Employees regulate their degree of effort and output so as to secure stable, but not necessaraily maximum, earnings in the medium-term rather than the highest possible earnings in the short-term.[10]

A further issue in the design of pay systems concerns the role of employees themselves in the determination of rates of pay. It is arguable that this function should be the prerogative of managers: employee involvement in this process is likely to force remuneration to higher levels than is either necessary or efficient. However, there is a powerful counter-argument that giving employees' 'voice'[11] in the design of the payment system is more likely to lead to a system viewed as fair and satisfactory by employees. Since employee satisfaction with remuneration is of critical importance it is as well to give them, or their representatives, some input. Recent evidence suggests a declining number of managements who subscribe to this view. The incidence of collective bargaining over pay determination declined during the 1980s, especially in manufacturing. Whereas in the early 1980s some 70% of the UK employed labour force had their rates of pay determined by collective bargaining, by 1990 this had fallen to just over 50%.[12s]

This introductory review of the pertinent issues arising in the introduction and implementation of pay system suggests that the perfect pay system may be an unattainable goal. It is questionnable whether the pay system can be an effective tool for maximising output or performance. A more realistic objective, given the highly contentious nature of pay determination processes and outcomes, is to aim for a system which minimises problems and employee grievances. Managers may be better advised to employ a pay system which at least contributes to satisfactory performance, whilst using other mechanisms, such as employee involvement, to improve upon this. Unfortunately all too many organisations do not follow these strictures, instead viewing the pay system as a 'quick fix' to achieve organisational goals. In the following pages we outline the main characteristics of each kind of system, and assess the advantages and disadvantages of each. The suggestion in the analysis which follows is that those schemes which have the most ambitious aims tend to be those which suffer from the most drawbacks. Before turning to this, however, we discuss the methods and objectives of job evaluation.

Job evaluation

One of the key issues with any payment system, given the fundamental issue of fairness, is how to arrange the hierarchy of pay rates for different kinds of jobs. The set of techniques that may be used to determine how jobs are placed in a hierarchy of rates of pay is known as job evaluation. Job evaluation, as ACAS has put it, "is a method of determining, on a systematic basis, the relative importance of the demands of a number of different jobs in order to build an acceptable and equitable pay structure".[13] It does not determine the actual rates of pay as such, merely the relationship between the various pay rates in use in the organisation. Job evaluation grew considerably in the 1970s as firms attempted to rationalise their payments and industrial relations systems but during the 1980s the growth in firms adopting job evaluation slowed down considerably. By 1990 just over a quarter of workplaces with over 25 employers had a job evaluation scheme compared with just over a fifth a decade before.[14] The slowdown in the use of job evaluation appears to be related to reductions in union representation and shifts in the balance of power between managers and trade unions, especially in manufacturing workplaces. The need to demonstrate equity in payment systems was no doubt perceived as less pressing by many managers than in the earlier decade. Against this the onset of 'equal pay for equal value' – whereby female employees can claim pay comparability with demonstrably similar (in terms of responsibility, skills etc.) as well as identical male jobs – is likely to have had a countervailing effect, and probably accounts in large measure for the doubling of the incidence of job evaluation in public sector workplaces between 1980 and 1990.

Whilst job evaluation is an attempt to place pay differentials on a rational footing, some measure of subjectivity enters even the most analytical of schemes. For this reason most experts argue that employees or their representatives should be involved in the process of analysing jobs. By so doing managers are more likely to win the consent of employees to the final pay structure: employee involvement will facilitate the reaching of common ground on the more subjective aspects of the process. Job evaluation schemes can be classifed into two types: analytical and non-analytical. Non-analytical schemes are more subjective than analytical schemes since they do not systematically analyse the constituent features of jobs but instead compare jobs in their entirety. Thus these forms of job evaluation tend to reproduce existing informal evaluations of the comparative worth of a range of jobs. Within this cateogry there are three main approaches: job ranking, paired comparisons and job classification. The first of these compares jobs against each other, placing the jobs in a rank order of importance. The criteria used may include responsibility and skills required, and the exercise may be conducted using existing job descriptions. The paired comparisons approach is similar but is more systematic in that points are awarded for each job in comparison to each other job, in terms of comparative worth. At the end of the exercise the points for each job are added, with those jobs achieving the highest number of points being ranked highest in the pay structure. Finally job classification approaches the process in the reverse direction, creating a set of grades first and then attempting to allocate jobs to grades on the basis of the degree of congruence between grade and job definitions.

Non-analytical approaches to job evaluation have fallen out of fashion because of the degree of subjectivity associated with them. Even so just over one-third of job evaluation schemes take this form.[15] As noted above, there is a tendency for these methods to reproduce existing informal evaluations of the merits of particular jobs. There is thus the danger that pay structures based on these methods will incorporate existing prejudices about the worth of jobs. In particular there is a possibility that these forms of job evaluation will reinforce gender discrimination, with 'female' jobs being viewed as less worthwhile than 'male' jobs. The revision of the equal pay legislation in the 1980s, requiring that jobs of equal value (in terms of responsibilities, job content etc.) be paid equally between the sexes, has encouraged more systematic approaches to job evaluation. Use of a non-analytical scheme would not provide a strong defence against an equal pay for equal value claim taken to a an Industrial Tribunal by disgruntled employees.

The trend, therefore, is towards greater use of analytical approaches to job evaluation. Points rating is the most common type of analytical scheme, and is the method used in 45% of cases where job evaluation is practised.[16] In this approach a job is broken down into constituent factors (eg. skill) and sub-factors (eg. job knowledge, manual dexterity etc.). Each factor/sub-factor is awarded points on a pre-determined scale. The points are then added to give a final score for the job. There are a number of specific schemes embodying this approach, such as the Hay-MSL Method for analysing managerial jobs. The other main analytical scheme, found in around 15% of cases,[17] is known as factor comparison. This method analyses five components of jobs – mental requirements, skill requirements, physical requirements, responsibility and working conditions. Each job is ranked in relation to the others within each factor. The factor rankings are then considered together to form a job structure. It will be apparent that whilst both approaches attempt to use rational methods of comparison, they nevertheless rely on subjective evaluations to some extent. It is doubtful whether job components could ever be compared entirely objectively. This inevitable degree of subjectivity reinforces the point made earlier about the desirability of involvement of employees or their representatives in the evaluation process. Since employee beliefs about the fairness of pay structures tend to be critical to the success or failure of pay systems it is desirable for employee views to be incorporated into the process which determines how jobs compare with each other in the pay structure.

Time-based payment systems

There are two fundamental forms of payment system – those known as time-based systems where individuals are paid a standard rate for the job, usually expressed in the time spent at work, and output or performance-based systems where rewards are related to the degree or quality of effort expended. In practice, time-based systems are virtually universal in developed industrial societies. Most output and performance pay systems incorporate time-based systems with the latter providing the largest proportion of actual pay. In time-based systems the employee is paid a basic rate per hour, day, month or year for the actual time worked. This basic rate varies only with changes in the time worked, and does not relate to changes in performance and output. For manual workers payment is usually expressed in a sum per hour with the total wage determined by the number of hours worked each week.

By contrast, pay is usually expressed as a sum per annum for salaried workers with the employment contract stipulating the number of working hours required each week. In the case of manual workers it is common for the rate for the job to remain unchanged over considerable lengths of time, except for adjustments to meet increases in the cost of living. In salaried contexts, by contrast, it is common for workers to be situated on an incremental pay scale, usually according to age, qualifications and experience, moving one place up the scale with each year of service to the employer.

In time-based payment systems, then, reliance is placed on other elements of the organisational control system to achieve short-term changes in output or performance. As labour process analysts might put it, in these payment systems employers purchase labour power rather than an actual quantity of work as such. Other mechanisms of the management control system, such as disipline, work rules etc., will be necessary to convert this capacity to work into productive effort.[18] Whilst time-rate systems provide a weak incentive for employees to improve performance they have several advantages from a managerial point of view. Labour costs are easily predictable, and there is relatively little friction (compared with payment by results systems) between employees and managers over rates and levels of pay. Above all time-based systems are simple to administer. It is generally thought that the nature of the work to be performed will determine the suitability of this kind of payment system. Where tasks are complex and difficult to measure a time-based system is likely to be most appropriate, as it will be when output and performance requirements are fairly stable in the short-term. Conversely, when there are short-term variations in required output it may be thought appropriate to make use of an incentive-based system.[19]

Payment-by-results (PBR): piece-work

A persistent aspiration of many managers has been to use the pay system to improve performance, reflecting the belief discussed earlier that money can be used as an incentive. In the past such systems have been most commonly applied to manual workers, though there is some evidence of a slow but long-term decline. On the other hand there has been a steady increase in the use of performance-based pay systems for white-collar and managerial staff, albeit from a very low base, over the last fifteen years.[20]

The simplest form of payment by results is where output is directly related to payment. There is a standard unit of remuneration for each unit of output so that pay varies directly with output, such that if no output is produced no payments will be made to the employee. This form of simple PBR is now extremely rare and tends to be confined to 'sweat-shops' in the clothing industry and to home-work (which does not involve direct employment as such). It is far more common in most workplaces for a base wage to be paid with opportunities to supplement this by exceeding output targets. In one form a bonus per item is paid for each unit of output produced over a specified minimum. A more complex but nevertheless widespread system in manufacturing involves timing the typical length of time taken to produce each item of output. If the employee produces output in less time the employee is rewarded for the time saved. Typically the gains from time saved are shared between employer and employee. Usually piece-work operates on an individual basis but in principle group piece-work systems are possible: bonuses are paid to a group of employees on the basis of their collective performance.

The obvious advantage of piece-work appears to be that it provides an incentive for manual workers to maximise output so that a company can fulfill its order-book obligations in minimum time. In practice, however, there are a multitude of problems with the application of these kinds of system so that a system that may appear attractive in theory is certainly not so in practice. The fundamental problem is that it passes some degree of control over production and output to employees, whose interests are not necessarily the same as those of management and whose behaviour may not be determined by income maximising preferences. Furthermore, piece-work extends the range of issues over which there can be day to day conflict between employees and their managers. A classic participant observation study of piece-work by American sociologist Donald Roy in the 1950s found that workers adjusted effort levels to influence basic rates.[21] Where the timings for particular tasks were not generous (jobs referred to by Roy's colleagues as 'stinkers') the tendency was for workers to 'go-slow' in an attempt to force management to re-time the tasks more favourably. Conversely where making bonuses was relatively easy ('gravy jobs') workers tended not work at full stretc.h for fear that management would conclude that the timings were too generous. Furthermore the evidence suggests that workers choose not to work 'flat-out' to maximise earnings but to regulate their level of effort so that high but not necessarily maximum earnings are secured. One variant of this is where employees illicitly store output produced on high effort days for submission to supervisors on days where they feel like expending less effort. Piece-work then seems to have the perverse effect of restricting output and weakening management control of production.[22] It also tends to discourage information sharing between workers and supervisors, and to generate and reinforce 'low-trust' relationships between them.

As the above suggests, piece-work tends to encourage repeated negotiations, both implicit and explicit, over rates of pay. A further problem arises in relation to interruptions to workflow resulting from, for example, a failure to supply raw materials needed for production, which leads to workers being unable (through no fault of their own) to achieve bonus earnings. Employees have a legitimate argument that they should not be penalised financially for the failings of others. This problem tends to be overcome to som extent by the negotiation of 'fall-back' rates, providing some (but not usually total) protection of earnings. Since there are potentially a multitude of ways in which production may be impeded there is a tendency for these additional elements of the pay system to proliferate, adding to the complexities of administering piece-work systems, as well as diverting supervisory and employee time away from production in the course of negotiating these.

It is clear that piece-work systems can diminish rather than enhance management control of production. Since employees secure some control of both pay rates and total pay, management lose some control of total pay bill costs. Control over machine utilisation is also diminished since at some times employees may choose to operate their machinery highly intensively, perhaps disregarding health and safety considerations, whilst at others the machinery may be under-utilised. Maintaining product quality can also be difficult since employees have an incentive to pass-off defective products as being of acceptable standard. This problem can be overcome to an extent by the employment of supervisors to monitor product quality but the relationship between workers and quality control staff is inevitably fraught.

Given these problems it is not surprising that there has been a long term decline, albeit gradual, in the incidence of piece-work in the UK. The New Earnings Survey finds that the proportion of male manual workers paid on PBR systems declined from 44% in 1979 to 35% in the early 1990s. The incidence of PBR among female manual workers also declined, though to a lesser extent and from a lower base. There was also a fall in the size of PBR payments relative to total pay, from 9 to 7% for both men and women.[23] Despite the problems with piece-work systems, however, many managers believe incentives have a role to play in manufacturing environments. ACAS suggest that piece-work may be appropriate when workflow is relatively regular, where work content tends not to change, where tasks are easy to identify and measure, and where individual work rate is largely under the individual's control. Conversely piece-work is probably inappropriate in complex, inter-related production environments where high levels of teamwork are required.[24]

Other forms of payment by results

Although the problems of piece-work are now widely recognised among both human resources and line managers, many nevertheless perceive the need for some kind of incentive system as a way of encouraging high levels of output and performance. One possibility is a *group incentive scheme* in which a collective bonus is paid to a work group on the basis of collective output. These tend to be simpler to administer than individual schemes and potentially foster team-work to an extent not generally possible with individual piece-work. Equally, however, basing payment on group performance can heighten intra-group conflicts if some members of the group feel that others are either idling or insufficiently skilled. Of course, much of the rationale of this kind of system is the encouragement of 'horizontal monitoring' by workers of each other, but this is not necessarily positive in its effects. Group pressures can stifle innovation whilst the capacity of group norms to restrict output are well known from the Hawthorne Studies. At the other end of the scale there is always the danger of a 'free rider' effect – since an individual employee's performance only makes a small contribution to the total there may be a temptation to go slow, relying instead on the efforts of other members of the team. Whilst it may be in the interests of the group as a whole to work at high levels of effort it is not necessarily in the interests of any individual to work harder.

This 'prisoners' dilemma' can characterise other collective forms of incentive scheme such as *gainsharing*. Gainsharing is an approach which bases bonus payments not on increases in output but on reductions in costs relative to other measures of performance. The gain secured by such a reduction over a period does not pass solely to the organisation but is shared with employees. The two best known plans are the Rucker Plan, which bases the collective bonus on movements in the difference between the wage bill and total added-value, and the Scanlon Plan, which bases it on the relationship between the wage bill and total sales. These schemes differ from other payment-by-results schemes in that they focus on value rather than physical output. As such they are an attempt to encourage employees to work more effectively rather than harder per se. They are therefore usually associated with initiatives to encourage teamwork and employee participation in implementing improvements to production and service processes.[25] They are thus associated with more co-operative patterns of worker-management relationships than 'classic' payments by result systems. As yet there is relatively little research evidence on the efficacy of these schemes, all of it emanating from the USA, but the findings so far suggest that gainsharing has a positive effect on productivity.[26]

An alternative to piece-work, popular in the UK car industry in the 1970s and early 1980s, is *measured day work* (MDW). The novelty of this system is that it is essentially a time-rate system but one incorporating a performance incentive. The intention is to secure the best of both worlds: the pay system retains the simplicity of time-rate systems but has a stronger incentive element than is usual for such systems. The essence of this approach to pay is that, using methods of work study and job evaluation, a typical and realistic level of output is identified. A set of pay rates are established to correspond with this. Employees as a collectivity are then given the opportunity to decide to produce higher levels of output in the medium term, for which higher basic rates of pay will be paid. Should production occasionally dip below this target, employees are not penalised by a reduction in pay. Should production levels consistently fall below the agreed targets, lower pay rates may be introduced. The benefit of MDW, unlike individual piece-work, is that the pay system is simple to administer with none of the computation of individual weekly wages using a multitude of rates. However, the disadvantage of this system is that it is complex and time-consuming to establish. There is also a perception among some managers that higher levels of output and performance would be achievable with a stronger incentive. Although MDW is not widespread, a similar system to MDW can be found in some large UK supermarkets. In these, check-out operators are expected to process a specified number of customers' shopping items per minute. The scanning devices used to record purchases also record employees work performance in this respect. Should an employee not always meet this target no penalties are imposed. However, if they consistently fail to reach them the operator can be moved to other tasks within the store, often attracting lower rates of pay.

Performance-related pay

The most striking development in pay and rewards in recent years has been the spread of performance-related pay, sometimes also referred to as merit pay, in both the public and private sectors. Unlike piece-work and other 'simple' PBR systems, performance pay is awarded on the basis of overall work performance, not just levels of output (though output may be one component of this). It is therefore much more qualitative in nature than other incentive pay systems. The corollary of this is that the assessment process is potentially more subjective. This subjectivity, given the importance to employees of fairness and equity, can give rise to severe problems in performance-related pay systems. There are a plethora of aims for performance- related pay systems (as will be shown shortly), but a general contextual factor behind its development has been the perceived growth in competition and the need to improve organisational performance in response. In the public sector, performance-related pay has been seen as a central mechanism for bringing about improvements in organisational efficiency and effectiveness, as well as responsiveness to citizens and consumers. The Citizens' Charter puts performance pay at the forefront of mechanisms to improve public services.[27] Growth in performance-related pay has been concentrated among managerial and white collar staff. Survey evidence indicates that the proportion of these employees receiving a performance component in their pay rose from 12 to 17% of men and 7 to 13% of women beween 1980 and 1990.[28] Around 40% of public and private sector organisations now use performance-related pay for at least some of their non-manual employees.[29] The proportion of the performance element in total salary has also risen, from 3 to 4% for men and from 1 to 2% for women.[30]

There are various ways of running performance pay systems. However, there are a number of core features characterising most schemes. Each year the performance of employees is appraised by their superiors. This appraisal may focus on output-related and quality of work targets, but typically the procedure is to assess how far the employee has met objectives set in a previous appraisal session. Ideally the process should focus on the employee's actual work performance, but there is always the danger that an employee's attitude to work and the organisation will colour the appraiser's perception of their work performance. In this way an element of subjectivity enters the process. In any case, the assessment of how far objectives have been met will inevitably involve subjective assessments, except where objectives have been expressed in strictly quantitative terms. It is common for the employee's performance to then be expressed as a grade. Typically, grading scales range from 'excellent' to 'unsatisfactory', from '1' to '5' or 'A' to 'E'. On the basis of this assessment the employee will usually be awarded a performance-pay supplement, but there is often no direct relationship between particular grades and particular levels of payment.

The performance pay element may be incorporated into the pay system in a number of ways. It is common in the public sector for existing length of service-related incremental scales to be retained in their entirety: good performers progress up the incremental scale faster than usual. Alternatively, there may be a bar at some point below the top of the scale with a good appraisal necessary to progress beyond this. An alternative system, introduced in the UK Health Service in the late 1980s, awards a percentage addition to usual salary. For general managers a very good performance secures 6%, a good performance 4% and so on, up to a cumulative maximum of 20% over any five year period. In these types of performance-related pay system it is usual for employees to receive their 'normal' increment and any cost of living increase each year, as well as any merit pay supplement. Far more radical are those schemes, as introduced in British Rail in 1988, which make increases in salary entirely dependent on merit. Satisfactory performers receive an annual cost of living award whilst poor performers may be denied this. In these schemes it is usual for the incremental points in each pay scale to be abolished. Instead there are minimum and maximum points for each scale with progression through the scale dependent on merit.

So far we have assumed that there is a fixed percentage or award corresponding to each level of merit but this is not necessarily the case. In some schemes the sum awarded will be dependent on the finance available to pay groups at sub-organisational level and subject to managerial discretion: if all other performers in a pay group are judged to be poor or average performers, the manager making the pay awards may decide to award a very high merit supplement to the very good performer. In British Rail's performance pay scheme in the early 1990s, for instance, pay awards in one grade for good performers ranged from 9 to 20%.[31]

The features of performance-related pay schemes depend to some extent on the objectives of those responsible for introducing them. The research evidence so far indicates a package of objectives behind performance-related pay schemes. Kessler suggests that performance pay has a number potential functions besides the usual objectives of recruitment, motivation and retention.[32] Performance pay may be used as a mechanism as part of a broader programme of change to organisational culture. The emphasis on performance may form part of an attempt to make organisations more dynamic and more performance and market oriented. It may also be part of a trend towards a focus on the individual in the employment relationship. This may be connected with a strategy to reduce the role of trade unions and collective bargaining in pay determination. In effect, performance pay decentralises pay setting to individual line managers, though unions may retain a role in the negotiation of minimum and maximum rates. Performance pay is therefore consistent with the trend towards devolving aspects of human resource management away from human resource to line managers. It is also consistent with an emphasis on financial control. By targeting pay awards on those believed to deserve them most, the impact of the annual pay round may be less than where there is a generalised increase in rates of pay for all employees. Even when the difference is negligible it is arguable that performance pay uses cash resources more effectively.

In theory, performance-related pay has a lot to commend it. It even appears to meet the important criterion of fairness in so far as those working most effectively should secure the highest rewards. For this reason employees may welcome the introduction of this form of payment system.[33] However, as is generally the case with pay systems, the problems arise in the implementation. The difficulties tend to revolve around the fundamental issue of fairness, and tend to arise from the level of subjectivity that inevitably colours the assessment process. The line manager's perception of the employee's performance may well differ from that of the employee. Furthermore, when appraising employee performance, managers usually try to assess the individual 'in the round': that is to judge individual performance in its entirety, not just on the basis of objective assessments of performance output. Once this happens, however, there is the danger that the line manager will be appraising attitudes as well as behaviour and performance. This introduces the possibility that managers will view attitudes similar to their own, or which appear to be highly positive towards the firm, more favourably than those which differ or appear to be more neutral. Thus favouritism or the 'blue-eyed boy' syndrome can creep into the pay determination process. The tendency of performance based systems to discriminate against employees who differ from the managers responsible for appraisal is well known. A recurrent complaint has been that women fare less well under performance pay systems than men. In the UK civil service scheme, introduced in 1987, the pay statistics "showed a remarkable, but consistent, pattern of men and women on the same grade, with the same seniority, being paid differently".[34]

The problem of fairness and subjectivity in the relationship between the appraiser and appraisee is compounded by variations in perceptions among other employees. Where an employee is widely perceived by his or her colleagues to be a less effective performer than the performance pay award would suggest, this can lead resentment and de-motivation among the others. This highlights a more general problem with performance pay systems: for the vast majority who receive satisfactory assessments, a perceived failure on management's part to recognise their efforts can be demotivating rather than an incentive to perform better in future. Meanwhile those good performers receiving good appraisal marks may well have performed well anyway. The potential for increased pay is likely to be only one motivator among several. Indeed it may not be a strong motivator anyway, especially as in most systems the sum of money available for performance pay is not that high (given that the large group of satisfactory employees will take the lion's share of the money available for merit awards). However, a complicating factor is that both the absolute levels and proportions of pay available to senior managers may be higher than for more junior managers. The reason for this is that it is common for the top levels of performance identified in appraisal criteria to include reference to achieving change, using initiative etc. which top managers have a greater opportunity to demonstrate than more lowly employees. There is a danger therefore that performance-related pay schemes will tend to give a disproportionate share of high rankings to more highly-placed managers. In British Rail's scheme in the early 1990s, for instance, it was found that 55% of top managers received a good evaluation compared with 23% of more junior managers.[35]

Overall it is difficult to avoid the conclusion that performance pay comes up against as many problems as more traditional incentive schemes. The issue of fairness is a recurrent one in performance-based systems, compounded by the diffusion of pay determination to a potentially large number of line managers. Consistency of treatment is extremely difficult to achieve in systems of this type. There are similar problems to piece-work in so far as performance pay can encourage low trust relationships. Performance pay can subvert the appraisal process because employees have an incentive to conceal work problems and to emphasize, possibly exaggerate, their achievements. Astute employees will also ensure that the objectives agreed at the beginning of the period will be easily achievable. Meanwhile some employees will no doubt fall foul of the appraisal process because their objectives are extremely difficult to achieve, or may be unmet through no fault of their own. Performance pay can also be bad for teamwork in so far as one individual may secure the reward for a level of performance which owes much to their colleagues or subordinates. By providing an incentive to employees to emphasise their own contribution relative to that of other employees, performance pay systems can introduce a measure of potentially divisive competition to work environments where co-operative working relationships are more appropriate. For these sorts of reasons performance-related pay, 'flavour of the month' in the late 1980s and early 1990s, had lost some of its appeal to managers by the mid-1990s.

Profit sharing and employee share ownership

Mirroring the spread of performance-related pay in the 1980s and 1990 have been a number of other performance-based supplements to pay. These are based, either directly or indirectly, on the profits of the firm, and are paid as profit share bonuses or as shares. The growth of these schemes, usually grouped under the umbrella 'financial participation', has come about because of supportive government legislation attaching tax breaks to each type of scheme. In fact, with the exception of France, the UK has a more supportive legislative climate for financial participation than any other nation in the European Union, and the number of schemes within firms is much higher than the European average.[36] By the start of the 1990s 55% of UK workplaces with more than 25 employees were covered by one or more financial participation schemes. (WIRS)[37]

There are four main schemes currently in operation in the UK. *Approved Deferred Share Trust* profit share schemes, introduced in 1978, allow for a portion of profits to be used to purchase shares in the company for distribution to all employees. The shares are initially held in a profit sharing trust before disbursement to employees. Employees are exempt from income tax on the value of the shares as a benefit from employment if they are retained in trust for five years. *Save As You Earn (SAYE)* share option schemes, introduced in 1980, allow employees to take out options to purchase shares in their company three, five or seven years in the future. Meanwhile they save the money required using the tax advantageous SAYE scheme. Any financial gains made from the difference between the option and selling price are liable to capital gains rather than income tax. This profit will be smaller than the tax allowance in most cases so most employees will not pay any tax on the gains from exercising and selling the options are in effect tax free. *Discretionary Option* schemes have operated on the same principle from their inception in 1984 with the difference that the company can restrict eligibility to employees of its choosing.[38] Usually they are restricted to top managers and for this reason are widely referred to as 'executive schemes'. The most recent, and in some respects the most interesting scheme, is *profit-related pay (PRP).* Introduced in 1987 this scheme is based explicitly on the recommendations of Harvard economist Martin Weitzman.[39] He argued that pay levels tend to remain unchanged even in recessions, with the result that firms had to respond to reductions in profitability by reducing employment. He suggested therefore that employment levels could be stabilised to some degree if pay could be made to respond more flexibly to changes in firm performance. PRP attempts to do this by identifying a portion of pay which can change in response to changes in company profits. To encourage the take-up of PRP, this proportion of pay is exempt from income tax.

Table 1 provides details of the incidence of financial participation schemes in the UK by the early 1990s. The motives for adopting financial participation schemes vary between types of scheme, but it is clear that both the potential income gains and the tax breaks available have had a powerful impact on the take-up of them. By far the fastest rate of growth in the 1990s has been experienced in

Table 1. The Extent of Financial Participation Schemes in the UK 1993

Scheme type	Number	Participating employees	Value per person
ADST	1076	740,000	420
SAYE	1153	590,000	3,200
Executive	5332	80,000	20,000
PRP (1994)	7039	1,794,000	n/a

Source: Inland Revenue Statistics 1994.

PRP schemes, primarily because of the extension of the tax break in 1991 to 20% of salary. By 1995 the coverage of PRP schemes had risen to 2.4 million employees, just over 10% of the employed labour force, and an increase of 600,000 employees since 1994.

The economics literature predicts that financial participation will have a number of positive effects on firm performance.[40] Most obviously profit sharing, in whatever form, should provide an incentive not only for employees to work harder but also to relax restrictive practices. Of course the 'free rider' problem referred to earlier may dilute the impact of group incentive schemes of this type, but it is arguable that if additional mechanisms, such as employee participation in decisions, are introduced alongside profit sharing, employees will have a greater tendency to cooperate. This cooperation may take the form of information sharing with management and supervisors, so that the latter are able to make better decisions. Further arguments in favour of profit sharing can be located in risk sharing: if a portion of employees' remuneration is dependent on performance, it is in their interests to work productively. It also provides an incentive to monitor the activities of other workers to ensure that they do not go down the 'free rider' road. Finally, it has been suggested that the additional rewards accruing from profit sharing will encourage employees to remain with the firm, thereby improving the stock of human capital within the firm. Besides these arguments, some also believe (the UK Conservative Government among them) that financial participation will weaken attachment to trade unions.

The evidence on the efficacy of financial participation is not definitive.[41] Overall there are indications, from both case studies of individual companies and econometric analyses, that the effect of profit sharing on performance is positive but that the magnitude of the profit sharing effect is weak. The balance of evidence suggests that gainsharing (discussed earlier) may have a stronger relationship with improvements in productivity.[42] In both cases there are powerful indications from the literature that these incentive schemes per se have little effect. What gives them their potency are other mechanisms of employee involvement, often introduced in tandem with them. Another way of investigating the impact of financial participation is employee attitude surveys. In the British case the evidence so far suggests that those taking part in financial participation schemes have slightly more positive views about their employer, but the direction of causation is not clear from most studies.[43] These surveys also suggest that the effect of financial participation on attitudes to trade unionism is very weak. Whether profit sharing schemes generally, and profit-related pay in particular, stabilise UK employment in the way that Weitzman predicted is not yet known. What can be asserted with some degree of confidence, however, is that financial participation schemes do not have the negative effects so commonly found with the individual incentive schemes discussed earlier.

Conclusion

This chapter has reviewed the main forms of payment system currently in use in the UK today. The main message that comes from a wealth of empirical evidence on the operation of these schemes is that those which are premised on providing individual incentives tend to be beset with problems in practice. Given these findings it is questionable whether it is worthwhile introducing schemes of this nature. The root problem seems to be that individual incentive schemes have the capacity to offend, on a day-by-day basis, employee conceptions of fairness. Furthermore, systems of this sort build in perverse incentives – to restrict output in piece-work systems and to set easily attainable objectives in performance-related pay schemes. Both types also tend to have negative effects on industrial relations and employee morale. These schemes are often introduced to bring about major changes in employee performance. The evidence suggests, however, that the pay system cannot be used as a 'quick-fix' of this type. The best that can be hoped for is that the pay system chosen is relatively problem-free: other mechanisms, such as employee involvement, are less fraught ways of improving employee performance.

References

1. See W. Brown and J. Walsh 'Managing pay in Britain' in K. Sisson (ed.) Personnel *Management: a Comprehensive Guide to Theory and Practice in Britain* (Oxford: Blackwell, 1994, 2nd edition).
2. W. Brown, P. Marginson and J. Walsh 'Management: pay determination and collective bargaining' in P. Edwards (ed.) *Industrial Relations: Theory and Practice in Britain* (Oxford: Blackwell, 1995)
3. F.W. Taylor *The Principles of Scientific Management* (New York: Harper and Row, 1947). See M. Rose Industrial Behaviour (Harmondsworth: Penguin, 1988) chs. 2–4 for a good discussion of Taylor and Taylorism.
4. See M. Rose *op.cit,* chs. 11–13 for a review of human relations and Elton Mayo's role in the development of this perspective.
5. See P. Wright 'Motivating People', this volume
6. See A. Maslow 'A theory of human motivation' in V. Vroom and E. Deci (eds.) *Management and Motivation* (Harmondsworth: Penguin, 1970)
7. See E. Lawler *Pay and Organizational Effectiveness* (New York: McGraw-Hill, 1971).
8. F. Herzberg *Work and the Nature of Man* (New York: Staples Press, 1966)
9. W. Baldamus *Efficiency and Effort* (London: Tavistock Institute of Human Relations, 1961)
10. D. Roy 'Quota restriction and goldbricking in a machine shop' *American Journal of Sociology* (Volume 67, Number 2, 1952, pp. 427–442). Lupton
11. A. Hirschman *Exit, Voice and Loyalty: Responses to Decline in Firms, Organizations, and States* (Cambridge, Mass.: Harvard University Press, 1970)
12. N. Millward, M.Stevens, D. Smart and W. Hawes *Industrial Relations in Transition* (Aldershot, Dartmouth, 1992), ch. 7.
13. ACAS *Job Evaluation* (London, HMSO).
14. N. Millward *et al, op.cit, pp.* 266–269.
15. *ibid.*

16. *ibid.*
17. *ibid.*
18. H. Braverman *Labor and Monopoly Capital* (New York: Monthly Review Press, 1974)
19. ACAS *Introduction to Payment Systems* (London: HMSO).
20. See Department of Employment *New Earnings Survey* (London:HMSO), various years.
21. D. Roy 'Quota restriction and goldbricking in a machine shop' *American Journal of Sociology* (Volume 67, Number 2, 1952, pp. 427–442).
22. In this respect Roy's view differs from that of human relations writers. He suggests that restriction of output is a rational economic strategy wheras Elton Mayo viewed it as an irrational failure to adapt to the correct factory norms. Michael Burawoy, who conducted research into workgroup behaviour in the same plant as Roy had done some twenty five years before suggests that employee participation in 'games' over the negotiation of piece-work rates functions to enhance management control of production: playing the game generates consent to the 'rules of the game'. See *Manufacturing Consent* (Chicago: University of Chicago Press, 1979).
23. See Department of Employment *New Earnings Survey* (London: HMSO), various years.
24. ACAS *Introduction to Payment Systems* (London: HMSO).
25. See D. Mitchell, D. Lewin and E. Lawler III 'Alternative pay systems, firm performance and productivity' in A. Blinder *Paying for Productivity: A Look at the Evidence* (Washington DC: Brookings Institution, 1990)
26. See M. Weitzman and D. Kruse 'Profit sharing and productivity' in A.Blinder *Paying for Productivity: A Look at the Evidence* (Washington DC: Brookings Institution, 1990)
27. The Cabinet Office *The Citizens' Charter* (London: HMSO, 1991 Cm.1599).
28. See Department of Employment *New Earnings Survey* (London:HMSO), various years.
29. M. Cannell and S. Wood Incentive Pay (London: Institute of

Personnel Management in association with the National Economic Development Office, 1992)

30. See Department of Employment *New Earnings Survey* (London:HMSO), various years.
31. A. Pendleton 'Performance-related pay in British Rail' in S. Vickerstaff (ed.) *Human Resource Management in Europe* (London: Chapman and Hall, 1982)
32. I. Kessler 'Performance pay' in K. Sisson (ed.) *Personnel Management: a Comprehensive Guide to Theory and Practice in Britain* (Oxford: Blackwell, 1994, 2nd edition).
33. Most Inland Revenue staff were in favour of performance pay in principle. See D.Marsden and R.Richardson 'Performing for pay? The effects of 'merit pay' on motivation in a public service' *British Journal of Industrial Relations* (Volume 32, Number 2, pp. 243–262). However, an investigation by Inland Revenue management some years into the scheme found widespread dissatisfaction with the scheme. See B.Clement 'Tax office pay system condemned by staff' *Independent* (5 April 1994).
34. L. Symons, quoted in M.Whitfield 'Civil servants claim sex bias in pay system', *The Independent* (4 September 1991).
35. A. Pendleton, *op. cit.*
36. M. Uvalic *The Pepper Report* (Brussels: Commission of the European Community, 1991)
37. N. Millward *et al, op. cit,* pp. 263.
38. The tax position of these schemes was changed in the wake of the Greenbury Report on executive remuneration in July 1995. Options introduced after this date became liable to income tax when purchased rather than capital gains tax when subsequently sold. Later in 1995 the position was changed again: executive options became liable to capital gains tax as long as the option price was not 'manifestly lower' than the market value at the time of taking out the option.
39. M. Weitzman *The Share Economy* (Cambridge, Mass.: Harvard University Press, 1984)
40. See M. Weitzman and D. Kruse, *op. cit.* See also N. Wilson

'The economics of participation: an overview' in *European Participation Monitor* (Issue 9, 1994)

41. M. Weitzman and D. Kruse, *op. cit.*
42. D. Mitchell, D. Lewin and E. Lawler III, *op. cit.*
43. L. Baddon, L. Hunter, J. Hyman, J. Leopold and H. Ramsay *Peoples' Capitalism: a Critical Analysis of Profit Sharing and Employee Share Ownership* (London: Routledge, 1989). S. Dunn, R. Richardson and P. Dewe 'The impact of employee share ownership on worker attitudes: a longitudinal case study' *Human Resource Management Journal* (Volume 1, Number 1, pp. 1–17).

Further Reading

W. Brown and J. Walsh 'Managing pay in Britain' in K. Sisson (ed.) *Personnel Management in Britain,* 2nd edition, Oxford: Blackwell 1994

I. Kessler 'Performance pay' in K. Sisson (ed.) *Personnel Management in Britain,* 2nd edition, Oxford: Blackwell 1994

A. Bowey and T. Lupton (eds.) *Managing Salary and Wage Systems,* 3rd edition (Farnborough: Gower, 1989)

Exam questions

1. To what extent do payment by results systems cause more problems than they solve?

2. Is performance-related pay a viable way of improving staff performance in public services?

3. Why do payment systems so often fail to live up to the expectations of those introducing them?

CASE STUDY

Bradford Pollution and Energy Group (BPEG)

Background

BPEG is composed of a group of scientists who provide advice and undertake research on pollution and energy problems. It operates as a consultancy and has contracts with clients who approach it for help with specific problems. Clients include local government, manufacturing companies, service organisations and small businesses. The work is highly varied with a number of cross-cutting teams working on several contracts and projects at any one time. The projects vary enormously in scope, interest, complexity and duration.

Typically, BPEG employees have worked in universities and in research functions in companies before coming to work for BPEG. All BPEG employees are paid on incremental salary scales based on age: workers of the same age on the same pay scale receive the same salary. There are two salary scales: one for research and technical staff and one for clerical and secretaarial employees.

Labour turnover has traditionally been low but in the last year has tripled among the research staff. There are rumblings of discontent, and it is feared that turnover will continue at high levels. The human resources management committee has conducted exit interviews with all departing staff. A common theme arising in these interviews is that the leavers felt that the organisation failed to recognise the efforts and commitment of research staff, and that there was little recognition that some projects were far more demanding than others, often requiring research staff to work weekends. Some departing employees argued that there was no incentive to volunteer for more complex projects. However, boredom quickly set in on the more routine and straightforward jobs. Some of the younger research staff also complained that they were paid less than senior secretaries.

On the basis of this information the human resources committee has decided that the current pay system needs to be reformed to provide a greater incentive and greater rewards for good performance.

Task

You are the coordinator of the human resources committee and have to develop an appropriate pay system for BPEG.

1. Which of the following appears to be most appropriate in this case

   i) gainsharing
   ii) performance-related pay
   iii) a profit sharing scheme?

2. What are the advantages and disadvantages of each system?

3. Is reform of the pay system the best way to resolve the problems currently faced by BPEG?

Chapter 5

Managing Diversity at Work

John Lawler

Objectives

- to outline the different aspects of diversity at work
- to explore the factors which raise this as a management issue
- to discuss the implications of diversity at work
- to discuss traditional and more recent approaches to managing diversity
- to outline the factors behind positive management of diversity
- to consider managing diversity as part of the human resource management process

Introduction

Approaches to effective management in organizations repeatedly change and develop and new management issues and approaches to organizational success appear with increasing frequency. One of the human resource management issues which is beginning to receive more attention is that of managing diversity. In the US this issue has received attention both in academic circles and in work organizations, both commercial and public sector for a few years now. In Europe the issue is less extensively developed and is yet to join the mainstream of topics within the Human Resource Management field. It is important to consider the extent to which this is a topical fad as opposed to a serious human resources issue and, if it is a matter to be taken seriously, what are the factors which make it important for managers. Beyond that, we also need to ask what does 'managing diversity' mean and what are its implications for managers?

Influential Factors

Repeatedly organizations are faced with change – the scale and frequency of which are ever increasing. There are several major forces for change within organizations which highlight the area of managing diversity as an important issue for consideration, by both academics and practising managers. In short these factors can be listed as follows:

- internationalisation of the firm
- need to promote effective working of disparate work groups
- customer demand
- development of global markets
- increasing awareness of individual difference
- changing legislation and social attitudes
- changing work patterns
- increasing development of different segments of markets
- need to reflect and respond to local communities

We will consider these issues briefly and consider how they contribute to the importance of the effective management of diversity.

Internationalisation of the firm and the development of global markets.

Over recent years we have seen many organizations branch out to become involved in geographical areas far beyond those which they occupied in the early stages of their lives. In some respects these developments reflect strategic changes, which in turn are influenced by factors such as: different local economic factors; increasingly sophisticated technologies, including information technology; relaxation of legislation barring entry to markets and the lowering of political barriers, which may have prevented expansion and co-operation in the past. In response to these factors, organizations have developed in much broader geographical areas than was previously the case. Joint ventures, mergers and take-overs now mean that many large organizations operate globally. To this extent organizations may now have bases in various countries, each with their own national culture. Their own workers and managers may have very different work practices and perceptions about organizations, management and life in general from the ones which prevail in the organization's country of origin.

One option in these circumstances is to try to impose a way of operating which represents the methods in the original country. There are considerable difficulties in doing this – not least that of maintaining control from a distance and dealing with the resistance of the workforce in the host nation to the imposition of a 'foreign' organizational culture. Thus the prime difficulty may lie in coercing this new workforce to operate at a minimally acceptable level. Trying to develop the potential of the workforce may be very far down the list of management priorities. Similarly, the huge array of market opportunities and the potential for further segmentation of existing markets require a broader understanding than traditionally has been the case. Employing people with specialist knowledge of these market needs, and of customer perceptions in each of these different locations, clearly gives the organization a potential competitive advantage over other operators.

Promoting the effective working of disparate work groups.

Related to the internationalisation of the firm, we are increasingly witnessing work groups made up of people with very different cultural and work backgrounds. There are many barriers to effective communication and co-operation which may result from this and which stand in the way of effective organizational operation unless they are managed effectively. It is possible that some synergy can be developed through assisting the effective integration of the difference experiences which each individual brings to the work setting.

Customer pressure

Organizations are increasingly predicting, or already responding to, the rise in pressure from customers for those organizations which provide them with goods or services, to have a workforce which represents the customer profile. Thus, Reebok have attempted to develop a workforce more representative of some of their loyal customer groups (Griffiths, 1994). Similarly, Kibazo (1994) describes the clients of some consultancies as demanding racial diversity among the consultancy teams they wish to use.

Increased awareness of difference

In recent years there has been increasing recognition of the different characteristics of individuals. There is understandable dissatisfaction with the notion of successful nations and companies imposing their models of behaviour on other less powerful players. Additionally, there is an increasing recognition, socially and politically, of the potential to be offered to the wider community from groups previously regarded as less powerful within the status quo. This increasing awareness of difference means companies must now reconsider what they offer to specific groups, such as ethnic minorities or women, both in the roles of as employees and consumers, potential or actual.

Changing legislation and social attitudes.

Related to the points above, changing attitudes have led to changing employment legislation, such as the UK Equal Opportunities legislation, which has outlawed practice which was once seen as being acceptable in some quarters, such as discrimination on the grounds of gender or race. In addition to this we are witnessing changing expectations from the workforce, who expect some of the other roles they fulfil in life to be acknowledged by their employing organizations. Thus we have seen the development of maternity and paternity leave, carers leave and so on. Issues such as flexible work arrangements were not considered until recently as being within the mainstream of employment practice. Now both employers and employees are seeing the potential benefits of developing work flexibility. As a result, the issue is being given more earnest consideration.

Reflecting and responding to local communities.

In addition to utilising people with specialist knowledge of the requirements of customers within particular segments of markets, organizations which seek to recruit people from their local communities need to be conscious of the particular profile this presents, and more aware of the different opportunities and challenges presented by this potential workforce. There may be compelling reasons, beyond the purely commercial, why the organization should seek to have a workforce which is representative of its local community.

In some cases the need for taking effective strategies for managing diversity may be more pressing than others. The Los Angeles riots in 1992 had clear roots in ethnic tensions, and in a city with a widely diverse population and continuing unrest, organizations may have felt the need to take effective steps to manage the diversity within their own workforces and within their own communities more quickly and seriously than in some other contexts.

All these factors suggest that if the organization wishes to maximise its potential, it has to maximise the potential of its employees and of its environmental opportunities. The development of skills for managing divesity is increasingly being accepted as an effective way of achieving this.

Refocusing Human Resources Management

As organizations are faced with increasing competition, the need to focus on the company's human resources as the source of competitive advantage becomes more pronounced. How do we bring about this advantage in practice? How do we realise the potential of our staff? We have seen the growth of ideas which seek to promote individual development and which seek to encourage the development of improvements to the work process by such approaches as TQM, semi-autonomous work groups and the use of terms such as 'empowerment'. Yet organizations still struggle to realise the full potential of the people they employ. The issue may be whether we concentrate on developing the existing skills which our organizations value and maximise the benefits of them, or whether we review our approach and look for different ways of utilising our people at work – looking for something qualitatively and quantitatively *different* from our staff.

This approach involves a challenge to the orthodox ideas of unitary approaches to management. It involves a recognition of our human assets in a quite different way from that which has held sway in many organizations traditionally. A major part of this process is recognising the difference which exists within our staff group and within our potential staff group. This signifies a considerable shift from the perspective that many organizations may have of their employees.

It is traditional to see the staff as an homogenous group which should be managed with the accent on conformity – standardised job practices, employment packages, standardised reward systems and so on. Conformity is expected and rewarded. Such conformity may be reinforced by other processes, such as structured induction programmes. So the initial step of acknowledging difference among the group of staff in any organization is in itself problematic. Once this recognition of difference is made, we may see new ideas, new practices and new commitments to organizations develop. What is required is a wider range of approaches to managing people at work, through a recognition of difference and the search for, and implementation of, new perspectives, practices and ideas. This calls for a refocusing of human resource management beyond standard methods to include a wider perspective.

Elements of diversity: social and functional divisions

When we consider what constitutes diversity in organizations it is tempting to try to categorise the major factors which identify differences of experience, background, culture and so forth. The danger with this is that the more we consider difference along each of these dimensions, the more difference we uncover. Not only do we find that each dimension has a greater depth than we may have realised at first, but we may also find that other dimensions of difference emerge. In order to make some sense of the complexity, we need to make the distinction between visible and less visible elements of diversity – race, gender, physical disability and age are all largely visible elements – educational attainment, previous work or life experience, sexual orientation, personal values and belief systems are much less so. In the final analysis, the degree of difference is infinite. Is this issue, therefore, too complicated to consider? It may be that in many respects this has been seen as being the case and the reaction has been to develop a unitary approach to these issues – again to consider and emphasise commonalities and to ignore or minimise differences.

However, if we are to acknowledge that there are gains to made, both within and outside individual organizations, through considering difference, at what level should we begin, and from which perspective should analysis itself take place?

Social divisions

We have noted the potentially endless nature of developing categories of difference. Nevertheless, as a starting point it may be useful to consider difference initially looking at major social divisions in our society which, as organizations are part of society, are likely to be replicated within work. We can identify these major divisions as differences of gender, age, race or ethnicity and physical ability.

Alongside these major categorisations we also have issues such as sexuality or sexual orientation, which is receiving increased attention, and social class, which is receiving less high profile attention currently. What we are focusing on here, is not a detailed sociological debate over the problematic nature of each of these areas of difference, but more on the major factors which contribute to difference of experience. From that, we can investigate the implications for work organizations and how this diversity can be managed effectively.

We can begin this exploration initially by concentrating on differences on the basis of gender, age, ability and race. The bases of each of these differences differ themselves, as do the way they have been recognised, or not, in legislation and in human resource management practice. Indeed, we might see that each of these sources of difference, as identified here, have different implications for human resource management and, more widely, for the organization of work and other roles. Organizations have made progress in their recruitment and employment of women and minorities, as is described in summary elsewhere (Torrington and Weightman, 1994). However, the underlying impulse behind this progress in many organizations is, apparently, grounded on feelings of social justice and fear of legal recriminations rather than a recognition of the potential for competitive advantage.

This past decade has seen a major growth in the literature dealing with women in organizations and with women in management (e.g. Marshall 1984, Dix 1990, McDougall and Briley 1994). Given the disregard for this topic over many years, this move must be applauded and encouraged. The literature cites evidence of an imbalance in work positions, showing there to be fewer women than men in the higher echelons of organizational hierarchies. Reasons are also cited as to why this situation may have arisen over generations, and steps outlined which both men and women need to take in order to address this imbalance, again in the favour of organizations, women and social expectations more generally.

The growth of interest in women in work organizations is interesting, especially as it grew alongside an interest in the issue of race in organizations and in management. The literature on women, as mentioned, has grown hugely, whilst there remains a relative paucity of information which addresses the issue of race in organizations and, more particularly, race in management. One might speculate on the reasons why the issue of women in management appears to have created greater attention than the consideration of race in organizations. There are, no doubt, many factors behind this and the interrelationships of those factors goes beyond our remit here.

Functional divisions

In addition to social divisions, within organizations another obvious difference is that which results from the individual's training and experience of fulfilling a certain function within the organization's structure of work activities. Thus, in relation to the issues which face an organization currently, we might expect an accountant to have a different perspective from that of, for example, a design engineer. Are differences such as these worthy of further discussion? Herriot and Pemberton (1995) believe that if we are to consider the value of difference within the workplace, then differences such as these are of fundamental importance. They not only believe that this element of difference is of prime importance in taking organizations towards a successful future, but that these differences need to be reflected right through the organization, especially at board level. They criticise organizations for having groups of board members with very similar experiences, education, skills and perspectives which do not best equip them to deal with a turbulent environment.

> *"Boards have to make sense of an inherently ambiguous business and organizational context. Yet they perversely seem set on perpetuating themselves in their own image"* (Herriot and Pemberton 1995, p. 10).

These writers detail an aggregated profile of 30 major UK companies by sector, and point to a remarkable homogeneity within organizations in each sector in terms of variables such as age, gender, education, work experience and so forth. Whilst there is the argument that boards need to be united and stable, this conformity at board level does not present a picture of creativity and innovation, rather one of continuing momentum which may be suitable for certain environments but certainly not for all. To what extent are these companies ignoring the potential contribution of others, within their own organization, who may be able offer different perspectives and contribute new ideas? Jackson et al (1991) suggest that diversity on the board provides companies with competitive advantage, in spite or because of a higher turnover of personnel at that level. Herriot and Pemberton (ibid.) also point to other studies which add substance to this view, that in terms of performance and the ability to adapt to change, companies with diverse board members tend to do better that those lacking such diversity. It is important to recognise at this stage in researching the issue, that results so far are limited and much more needs to be done. Nevertheless results such as these challenge traditional thinking about continuity and stability at board level.

In some ways the issue of managing diversity is perhaps not as novel as some might think. There are clearly examples of organizations with largely homogeneous work forces. Most organizations, especially towards the end of this century, appear increasingly more heterogeneous, not necessarily in terms of gender, race and so on, but in other ways. These other ways have been acknowledged for many years as being areas which represent different interests, different perspectives. In this respect we are referring to divisions more readily accepted as presenting certain management challenges. There are the divisions present after mergers – who belonged to which company; there are pre-restructure and post-restructure recruits, different functional interests; different geographical locations and focuses. Managers may be more accustomed to responding to these challenges than to those presented by the issues we have considered thus far. Nevertheless, some of the same management skills are called for in integrating the different aspirations and interests of these diverse elements, as are necessary in facing the new challenges of managing diversity.

The choices facing managers in these situations are: whether to integrate cultures; whether to promote one dominant culture at the expense of another or whether to try to keep cultures separate to run in parallel, as it were. None of these is the easy option, but the integration of different cultures is the one which offers most hope to individuals who are part of the new organization or the entire unit. It offers more hope because it acknowledges their own needs and interests and they can identify with the company's intentions, which sees the promotion of individual development alongside the development and effectiveness of the organization.

Implications of Managing Diversity

An element of major importance when handling the issue of managing diversity, is that we are dealing with changing the perceptions of a large number of people, and with customs formed by many years of habit. This issue is relatively straightforward to describe but to put into practice effectively may be quite another matter. We are not dealing here with a new management technique which can be applied once it is understood. Effective management of diversity requires a change in attitude in many respects. We realise that changing behaviour is one thing, but new practices which require changes in attitude may be more difficult to effect.

The long-standing attitudes which need review are those stereotypes we all carry with us, regarding how we expect other people to behave, the roles we expect them to adopt and the abilities we expect them to have or to be able to acquire. To suggest that people have great untapped potential is one thing, but to suggest that this potential may involve them doing and saying things which we not have expected, using our old stereotypes, may be quite another.

Personal Bias

Similarly, our personal bias affects the ways in which we judge other people. We all gain impressions about people in the first few moments of meeting of them, or even of learning about them before having met them. In many respects this is a skill which we use to negotiate our way through the complexities of everyday life. To make quick judgements about people may be of little risk if our relationship is to be very short, for example, in our exchanges with shop assistants. If we are to establish a longer term relationship with someone, basing our approach to them on a stereotypical view of them is much more risky. It damages our chances of forming an effective relationship in the first place and does not allow people to develop their potential. Our society is littered with examples of behaviours and attitudes associated with certain stereotypes. Stereotypes are based on characteristics such as age, gender, race, physical abilities, regional accents and so on. Not only that, but we see within organizations stereotypes which are also functionally based. We can all conjure up stereotypical pictures of salespeople, accountants, administrators, personnel managers. The challenge posed by recognising diversity is a challenge to those stereotypes. In order to develop a more accurate view of people we need to be able to enter a dialogue with them and to find out from them what experiences they have which can be utilised at work, what motivates them, what values they hold, what their limitations are. This can only be done through investing time with people, which managers may have regarded traditionally as being a luxury, given the other demands of work. In order to manage diversity effectively it is crucial for managers to be able to get to know their staff and to manage relationships and behaviours, rather than to rely on predicting behaviours, based on stereotypes.

For some people this required change in attitudes may mean a review of their deep-seated beliefs about other people – beliefs to which they may have adhered throughout their lives, beliefs which may be both conscious and unconscious. In much of the management literature we read about the need for culture change within organizations and the ways in which this change can be brought about. Here we are talking about the need for managers to review their own belief systems, their own stereotypes, their own perceptions, and not merely to expect others to follow their lead. Managers are sometimes accused of jumping on the latest management bandwagon, trying to implement another new technique to increase organizational effectiveness. In this case any cosmetic attempt to recognise diversity, that is superficial recognition of the importance of the issue without effective support for it throughout the organization, is likely to be resisted strongly. Any half-hearted change will result in staff feeling let down, or losing what trust they have in their managers. We must acknowledge, therefore, that some organizations will want to take on board the issue of managing diversity for different reasons. Some will want to be seen as 'doing the right thing' and, to this extent, any progress will be limited because of the fashionable nature of their involvement. When they encounter problems in implementing any real change, the true nature of their interest in the area will become apparent to all. Others will, on the other hand, genuinely wish to make progress in the way they manage diversity and will genuinely value the diversity with which they are presented or which they have sought to promote.

Culture

The issue of culture is critically important to managing diversity. It is important to distinguish between organizational culture and individual cultural background. To some extent the ‘managing diversity’ case is contrary to that presented in some approaches to managing organizational culture. In these approaches we are led to believe that it is important to encourage individuals to commit themselves to the organizational culture, to emphasise the aspects they hold in common with other staff members. Employees are encouraged to integrate themselves with the dominant organizational culture. The ‘managing diversity’ approach is to encourage individuals to express their own cultural experiences, and for the management to integrate all these varied cultural experiences for the mutual benefit of the organization and its employees. Thus the emphasis is not on denying or changing individuals’ own experience of culture but on the organization adapting to the varied cultural experiences present within its own boundaries. This constitutes a quite different approach from those which advocate the development of management-led, imposed culture.

In recognising the issue of managing diversity, there may be a belief that the issue centres on managing a diverse set of people with diverse needs, experience and so forth. We must not lose sight of the other significant element in this issue, that is the diversity within management itself. We need to recognise that we are not reviewing the management of people alone but are also reviewing the managers themselves. When we talk of people realising their full potential this means that some of those people will aspire to management positions themselves. We need to be thinking therefore, in any organization which takes the issue of managing diversity seriously, of the profile of future managers. This means we are thinking about a management profile which reflects the diversity within the organization. Thus we should expect to see greater numbers of, for example, black people and women in management positions. This again underlines the fundamental nature of the management of diversity – it is not something which is done to the workforce, it signifies a change throughout the organization.

So, then we need to consider individual development in two ways. Firstly, by recognising difference and the particular experience which individuals bring to their jobs and, secondly, by considering what particular skills, expertise and perspectives non-traditional managers will bring to management. In this respect we are reflecting on managing diversity and managing by diversity. We also need to consider the changing social framework within which organizations operate.

At the wider social and political level, legislation exists in the UK, and in many other countries, which now makes discrimination on the basis of ethnic origin, gender and physical disability, illegal. There are also moves in some countries to introduce legislation to control discrimination on the grounds of age. Reviews of the effects of this legislation (for example, Torrington and Weightman, 1994) indicate that some change has resulted in many organizations, but that the scale of change is not great. In order for change to be more pronounced, changes are needed both within organizations and in their wider social environments. Changes in the latter include different child care arrangements, for example facilities for pre-school aged children and for after-school care. There also needs to be change to pensions provision, to allow for more flexible working over the span of an individual's career. Other developments, such as flexible working hours, career breaks and job sharing schemes need to be broadened in their scope if more people can genuinely have equal opportunity in the workplace. Whilst change has been introduced through legislation, individual organizations may have other internal adaptations to make in managing diversity.

Organizational Flexibility

Much organizational activity, as described in organizational analysis literature, is concerned with the search for certainty – the need for predictability. The implications of managing diversity are that there is a need to acknowledge the complexity and unpredictability of much of the organization's activity, environment and staff behaviours and needs. The old assumptions, based on the ideas of proponents of mechanistic approaches to management, are increasingly being brought into question. Writers such as Handy (1991) point out the discontinuities in organizational life and organizational operations and the need for increased flexibility across all areas of organizational activity. This is unlikely to be brought about through increasing systematic approaches to management, but more by the adoption of more organic and flexible means of organising work and ways of utilising people at work.

This increased flexibility must be brought about by many changes, to structure, to staffing and so on. To have real and lasting impact, all these changes must be related to broader organizational strategy. Efforts to recognise the diversity which faces organizations, however, appear rarely to be linked to broader strategic goals (Hall and Parker, 1993). They are typified, rather, by local programmes or initiatives which address elements of the issue, for example, how do we recognise issues relative to ethnic minorities or women, and so forth.

Hall and Parker believe that the organization needs to develop its own flexibility and that this should properly be incorporated into strategic goals. In this way these fragmented programmes can be seen as being related to strategic objectives and can perhaps be co-ordinated in order to promote greater effectiveness across the organization rather than being isolated in separate parts of the larger whole.

A related issue is the argument that organizations need to develop employees' engagement at work and employers need to acknowledge the whole of the individual's life interests, demands and experience, rather than consider them only on the basis of the role they occupy within the organization at that time. We are therefore considering not only current skills and abilities and the need to develop people for their future career moves, but also the wider interests and identities they have and the ways in which these can be incorporated into an effective management approach which increases individual commitment to work. In this way individual identities and individual differences should be encouraged rather than suppressed as is traditionally the case. So we need to consider people as men and women, old and young, white, Asian and Afro-Caribbean and so on and also to acknowledge their different roles in and beyond work. Such roles are those of parent, carer and so on, which again are given little opportunity for expression within traditional organizational climates. The overall thrust of their argument is that greater engagement at work results in greater work performance. They see flexibility as being a means to this end.

This can be argued not from the position of humanitarian work practices or from the perspective of political correctness, but from the point of increased organizational success. Hall and Parker (ibid.) argue that increased flexibility and the consequent increase in engagement within the organization results in several important benefits – these include decreased turnover of staff (and subsequent savings on recruitment and induction), greater morale, improved productivity and decreased absenteeism. McEnrue (1993) describes the benefits for organizations in her survey, which had developed positive approaches to managing diversity, as being considerably in excess of those detailed in the academic literature and other publications. It must however be borne in mind that the starting point for individual organizations will be different and that some will already have attempted to bring about these improvements in organizational operations, perhaps through other means, whilst others will be at the starting point in dealing with these issues. Thus such improvements need to be seen as being relative to the organizations success in managing diversity to date through other means, and not sold as guaranteed consequences of such approaches.

Nevertheless, the argument proposed here is that increasing flexibility is a fundamental and strategic way of dealing with all these issues under the same initiative. Initiatives in this area in the USA have resulted not only in greater employee stability but also in increasing co-operation among work groups and greater organizational creativity. European initiatives are also beginning. Organizations such as Digital (Walker, 1994), Xerox and Procter and Gamble (Roosevelt Thomas, 1990) Grand Metropolitan (Herriot and Pemberton, 1995) Wellcome (Mahon 1989) and Corning (Hall and Parker, 1993) are all cited as organizations working towards greater flexibility and co-operation, through the recognition of managing diversity as an important strategic issue. More recently Midland Bank, Littlewoods and W.H. Smith have been cited as developing more positive programmes (MacLachlan, 1995). The impact of these programmes needs further research and scrutiny, but the initial evidence supports making further progress in this area of human resource management.

Promoting flexibility at work raises important issues, such as equity internally. The move towards individually negotiated packages of pay and conditions rather than the traditional collective arrangements may remove this as a problem. The benefits of this approach are that they are in line with tailoring rewards to individual motivational needs. In attempting to allow greater flexibility how should this be allowed? Should it be incorporated into basic work conditions? Should it be seen as a benefit for workers, as a reward, as a public relations instrument? Alternatively should it be seen as a factor within changing organizational design to allow for increasing unpredictability through this greater flexibility? Such arrangements as the latter are in line with the future forms of organizations as predicted by such writers as Handy (1991) with his view of the 'shamrock organization' as being suited to the need for consistency matched with flexibility.

Traditional Approaches to 'Difference' in the Workforce

There is a variety of ways in which organizations have deal with 'difference' in their workforce. Considering positive ways of using this difference to advantage is more recent. We can outline three major approaches which perhaps typify the response to managing difference in the workforce generally.

1. Denial

The first response is to ignore any difference – to deny that there is any difference among the work group which has any bearing on organizational performance. A slightly more advanced response is that whatever difference there is, will have little impact and people will have to adapt to the predominant norms in the organization, or they will have to leave. This is the assumption that difference does not have to be 'managed' but that a natural process is underway which will produce a resolution of any contradictory attitudes or behaviours.

2. Assimilation

The second response is that of assimilation. This process accepts some responsibility for the management of difference the employing organization. Assimilation assumes that some differences exist and that these need to be combined into an homogeneous culture within which every one operates and thinks in a similar way, espousing the values and behaviours of the dominant organizational culture. The management of this process may involve structured induction programmes, development programmes which recognise difference but which emphasise commonalty among the staff and which promote organizational identity above any other. Additional conformity of behaviour within work is valued and rewarded.

3. Diversity as a Specialty

The third response is that which recognises and appreciates difference and which makes allowance for the different experiences and needs expressed by the minority group, however that is defined. Thus, the experience and expertise which this group has is, in itself, valued. The organization of work becomes structured to incorporate this specialist area of knowledge. Examples of this are to be found in organizations who employ a minority of, for example, Asian workers. Though they may be employed to do mainstream activities as other employees are, any issue which appears to have an Asian dimension to it, is assigned to them and they become 'experts' in the eyes of their employers. They are also seen as representing the views of that group of workers within the organization and, possibly, beyond its boundaries. In some respects, this specialism is appreciated and runs parallel to, and in support of, the organization's main functions.

The first response is likely to be relatively unconscious. It represents a lack of recognition of the issue of difference. The second and third responses indicate some managerial recognition and the identification of courses of action designed to minimise any predicted disruption.

These latter two, assimilation and specialism, are described by Herriot and Pemberton (1995) as the 'vindaloo' and 'nouvelle cuisine' approaches to diversity. The vindaloo approach, assumes that, regardless of the many mixed ingredients within the organization, they will all be rendered the same because of the maintenance of the one dominant organizational culture – the vindaloo spices make all the constituents of the meal taste the same because of the overpowering influence. Organizations may pursue the vindaloo approach in attempt to control uncertainty, to maintain control over the behaviours of individual employees and through this to be able to predict behaviours, methods of work and results. In addition to homogenising staff, organizations pursuing this approach are likely, according to Herriot and Pemberton, to recruit clones of existing employees, thereby ensuring continuing homogeneity within the workforce. Similarly, one might expect this approach to recruitment in organizations which adopt the denial stance. In doing this, diversity within the organization is restricted – people who are 'different' are unlikely to join the organization in the first place.

The 'nouvelle cuisine' approach is seen to resemble that style of cuisine, in that delicate portions of this interesting and different experience are preserved and used almost decoratively. They question whether this food is to be looked at and admired or eaten. In organizational terms, these minority experiences may be preserved and used to demonstrate a certain socio-political awareness but they are not regarded as essential to fulfilling organizational objectives.

These approaches may be made in good faith. They do not necessarily suggest manipulation or prejudice and exclusion. They may be determined as courses of action because of ignorance of any alternative approach. Which clearly begs the question – well is there any other approach?

Valuing Difference

Continuing their culinary metaphor, Herriot and Pemberton point to the 'Sunday lunch' analogy as the way forward for organizations wishing to develop the potential of their diverse staff. They argue that the entire constituents of the traditional British Sunday lunch are necessary for it be enjoyed to the full. The lack on any one element – be it the Yorkshire pudding, the roast potatoes or whatever, limits the enjoyment of the meal as a whole. Thus all constituents of the meal, and all the diverse elements within the employee group at work, should be equally valued in order to use their contributions to the fullest extent – to provide the synergy for competitive advantage. Issues of diversity will be incorporated into all operations.

The basic premise of this latter approach is in some ways nothing new at all. These views encapsulate the notion that the manager's prime task, at whatever level, is to develop the potential of staff to the full. This cannot be done through adopting standard approaches to management which do not recognise individuality and, implicitly, individual difference. The problem in this, however, is that without adequate skills in people management, managers will always struggle, even with the best intentions, to develop their staff to the full. In this respect, is managing diversity nothing other than another dimension in the effective management of people? That again leads to the question of how able managers are in this area:

> *What (Xerox) discovered when it began to look at managerial behaviour towards minorities and women was that all too many managers didn't know enough about how to manage anyone, let alone people quite different from themselves"* (Thomas, 1990, p115).

The challenge facing managers at all levels, therefore, is whether they can equip themselves with the skills necessary to develop their staff and thus utilise this under-developed resource.

The Way Forward

In the case of managing diversity, as in other areas of management, there are guidelines which some managers may find useful (Roosevelt Thomas 1990). There is a danger, however, that this issue is seen as being separate from other management activities when, ideally, it must be woven into all aspects of the organization's culture. Thus guidelines for managing change, for implementing TQM, or for developing staff more generally, are equally applicable for dealing with this issue. Perhaps the question which needs to be added to all these various guidelines regardless of the particular issue is "How does this process contribute to using people to the full?" In that way it will remain on the agenda as it is continually addressed rather than being seen as separate issue. We must beware mechanistic guidelines which seduce us into believing that managing diversity can effectively be done by following a simple procedure. It is not a simple issue. It would be paradoxical to suggest that there is a uniform way in which to manage diversity. Nevertheless, some pointers may be of use in developing a culture in which diversity is utilised rather than ignored or minimised. Such pointers include the following questions:

Why are we doing this?

There may be several reasons. Is the organization interested in this issue solely because it sees it as a means of keeping its employment practises legal? Is the interest because the organization wants to improve community relations, or because it wants to learn and develop and it sees diversity as a means to added competitiveness?

Are we prepared for change?

If diversity is to be valued at all levels within the organization, there must be real change. The profiles of managers and workers at different levels will look different in time. This will provide real difficulties. In organizations which are traditionally white, male dominated or accountant dominated or dominated by another distinct group, accepting diversity means that this group will have to abdicate a certain amount of power in the longer term. This is easily said but is highly problematic. Herein lies a major difficulty in developing the effective management of diversity.

What are our assumptions?

It is important to review the assumptions the organization makes about its present and future workforce, particularly around the capabilities of employees and the resources which might be available for them to use those capabilities.

What are our processes?

The assumptions we have, permeate many processes within organizations. We need, therefore, to review our recruitment strategies, our motivational processes and our career structures, in order that they are broad enough to accommodate a range of individual preferences and talents. We must also guard against processes which may institutionalise certain discriminatory practices. Evidence is growing which suggests that some human resources practices may be structurally discriminatory in that they have in-built biases against certain groups (e.g. Alimo-Metcalfe, 1994). We need also to consider how effective our appraisal systems are, whether mentoring systems are effective and so forth. All human resource management systems are relevant.

What is our culture?

What behaviours and attributes are valued within our organizational culture? What practices reinforce this culture? We need to review whether the conditions exist to develop an awareness, appreciation of differences and a realisation of the potential value to individuals and organizations of this difference.

How do we support managers?

If managers are not encouraged to develop their own practice,and to develop new ways of managing their staff, they will be unwilling to try to manage diversity positively. They will be thrown back to denial or assimilation approaches. There is no 'best way' of managing diversity but managers need positive support in undertaking a change in approach.

Who are our development programmes aimed at?

Questions in this area focus on who is involved in the process of identified training and development needs. Are programmes designed and imposed from above or through some degree of consultation? Are there other ways in which a variety of views can be expressed and a variety of needs to addressed? Roosevelt Thomas refers to this as the 'special consideration test'

> *"Does this programme, policy or principle give special consideration to one group? Will it contribute to everyone's success, or will it only produce an advantage for blacks or whites, for men or women? Is it designed for them as opposed to us? Whenever the answer is yes, you're not yet on the road to managing diversity"* (Roosevelt Thomas 1990, p117).

Conclusions

The changing environment in which organizations operate, and the assumptions which may have been appropriate to past environments, are being questioned with increasing vigour. The traditional assumptions which underpin much organizational practice, both formal and informal, include notions such as the following: that white males make up the great majority of employees; that the general western economy is a largely unchanging process, and business must value and protect stability within that; that economically less privileged groups, such as women and minorities, should be allowed access to a wider range of employment opportunities because of public decency and that this needs to be brought about through enacting legislation and enforcing organizations to comply with it (Roosevelt Thomas, 1990). All these assumptions can be and are being questioned. Increasingly it is argued that it is commercial pressure and competitive advantage which indicate that organizations need to rethink their approach to employment of different people.

> *"women and minorities no longer need a boarding pass, they need an upgrade. The problem is not getting them in at the entry level; the problem is making better use of their potential at every level, especially in middle management and leadership positions. This is no longer simply a question of common decency, it is a question of business survival"* (Roosevelt Thomas 1990, p108).

These traditional assumptions and practices are deeply ingrained in the fabric of many organizations. In their search for continuing stability, these organizations may choose to ignore the forces which indicate a shift in approach. We will see over time, perhaps not a long time, whether organizations and their managers are prepared to rise to this crucial human resources issue.

Summary

- Managing diversity includes many different aspects including both divisions based on: gender, race, age, physical ability and also diversity of experience: education, work experience, functional specialism.

- Diversity and its implications, both inside and outside work organizations, is growing in its importance.

- Managing diversity will prove to be a significant challenge and calls for a re-appraisal of present managerial practices and assumptions, and of organizational strategies and cultures.

- Organizations are seeking new ways of responding to diversity and using it to advantage. Managing diversity should best be seen as integral to other human resource management processes and not as an 'optional extra'.

References

Alimo-Metcalfe, B. (1994) 'Gender Bias in the Selection and Assessment of Women in Management' in Davidson, M. (Ed.) *Women in Management: Current Research Issues.* London: Chapman.

Dix, L (1990) *A Chance for the Top: The Lives of Women Business Graduates.* London, Transworld.

Griffiths, V. (1994) 'Management: Outsiders Welcome' *Financial Times.* 18th April p. 10.

Hall, D.T. And Parker, V.A. (1993)'The role of workplace flexibility in managing diversity' *Organizational Dynamics* Summer pp. 5–18.

Handy, C. (1991) *The Age of Unreason* (2nd Edition) London, Business Books.

Kibazo, J. (1994) 'Workforce 2000 Implications' *Financial Times* 30th Nov. p. 8.

MacLachlan, R. (1995) 'Equality makes good business sense, says CRE' *People Management*. 26th Jan. pp. 9–10.
Mahon, T (1989) 'When line managers welcome equal opportunities' *Personnel Management* Oct. pp 76–79.

Marshall, J. (1984) *Women Managers: Travellers in a Male World* Chichester, Wiley.

McDougall and Briley (1994) *Developing Women Managers: current issues and good practice*. London: HMSO.

McEnrue, M. P. (1993) 'Managing Diversity: Los Angeles before and after the riots' *Organizational Dynamics*.Winter pp. 18–28.

Further Reading

Herriot, P and Pemberton, C. (1995) *Competitive Advantage Through Diversity: Organizational Learning from Difference* London, Sage.

Walker, B.A. (1994) 'Valuing differences: the concept and a model' in Mabey, C. and Iles, P. (Eds.) *Managing Learning* London, Routledge.

Torrington, D and Weightman, J. (1994) 'Equal Opportunities and the Management of Diversity' in *Effective Management* (2nd Edition) Hemel Hempstead, Prentice Hall pp. 223–237.

Roosevelt Thomas Jr., R. (1991) *Beyond Race and Gender* New York, Amacom.

Questions

Discuss the reasons why managing diversity should be regarded as an important issue in the management of people at work.

Outline the different elements of diversity which may influence performance in the workplace. In what ways can managers respond to the resulting pressures?

"Managing diversity is another trendy management topic. Managers need do no more that follow employment legislation" Discuss this statement.

Case

You are production manager for a medium-sized manufacturing company. You have recruited your staff traditionally from the local community and promote staff within the company whenever possible. The local community has changed over the past decade with many more inhabitants now from ethnic minorities. Your supervisors, white men and women, have all worked for you for several years. Many of your recent recruits are black, coming from ethnic minority groups. Some of your supervisors have complained that they are having difficulties with their staff – they won't do what they're told and their productivity does not seem to be as high as for previous groups of workers.

- What might be the causes for this situation?
- Suggest some possible approaches for improvement.
- What difficulties might be encountered if this issue is ignored?

Part Two

Employee Development

Chapter 6

Motivating People

Peter L Wright

Objectives

- To identify the major factors which determine levels of motivation at work.
- To show how an understanding of these factors and their interrelationships can help managers to influence levels of work motivation.
- To identify the steps which can be taken to enhance levels of job satisfaction within organizations.
- To demonstrate the relationship between job satisfaction and important organizational outcomes, such as levels of work performance, labour turnover, absenteeism, industrial unrest and citizenship behaviours.

Introduction

To be successful, organizations need the commitment of their employees. Two kinds of commitment are important. One is a commitment to the achievement of the goals of the organization. The other, which is particularly important in the case of employees who are making a significant contribution towards these goals, is a commitment to remaining a member of the organization, rather than taking valuable knowledge and skills elsewhere. Gaining such a commitment is no easy matter. This is particularly true today, when managers are faced with far-reaching changes in the age composition of the labour force, in attitudes towards work, in employment opportunities and so on. There is no simple set of rules which can be applied to achieve commitment within organizations. Rather, to be able to influence employees' work behaviour and attitudes, an understanding of what motivates and what satisfies people at work is required.

In this chapter, we will attempt to answer two main questions. First, what determines the levels of motivation and job satisfaction which people experience at work? Secondly, what effects do these levels of motivation and job satisfaction have on important aspects of their work behaviour, such as levels of work performance, labour turnover and absenteeism? The aim is not to provide a review of the whole field of motivation and job satisfaction. It is to lay the foundation for suggesting practical guidelines which can be used to influence motivation and job satisfaction and, through them, people's work behaviour.

Motivation and the Management of Human Resources

In general terms, motivation is concerned with the forces which instigate, give direction to and sustain behaviour. In other words, motivation is what arouses people into action, determines their goals and influences the vigour and persistence with which such goals are pursued. More narrowly, in organizational terms, the motivation to work can be defined as the willingness to expend effort on a particular task in order to attain an incentive or incentives of a certain type. This definition is a useful one from our point of view because it focuses attention on one of the key factors which influence work performance – the amount of effort the individual is willing to put into his or her work.

There are, of course, a great many other factors apart from motivation which influence levels of work performance. These include such things as whether the workers concerned have a clear understanding of the goals they are intended to achieve, their level of ability, the difficulty of the task, the feedback they receive concerning their performance, and so on (see Chapter 7). In effect, these factors put people in a position where they *can* perform the task to the expected standard. However, whether they *will* do so will depend upon whether they are sufficiently motivated to be willing to expend the effort necessary to perform the task and perform it well.

Thus, motivation is a vitally important subject both for managers in general and the Human Resource Manager in particular. It is important to managers in general because it can be a major influence on their subordinates' work performance, and how well subordinates do their jobs will in turn have a major impact on the manager's own effectiveness and how easy a managerial life he or she has. Therefore, all managers need to have a good general understanding of motivation in order to motivate their subordinates to do their jobs well. Motivation is an important subject to the Human Resource Manager for three main reasons. Firstly, like any other manager, the Human Resource Manager will need to motivate his or her own subordinates to work effectively. Secondly, a major part of the Human Resource Manager's job is the design, implementation and administration of human resource systems which have important motivational implications. Examples include incentive systems, performance appraisal, job evaluation, training, recruitment and so on. Some of these systems are intended to influence motivation directly in one way or another but, in each case, people's motivation will also influence the way in which they respond to the system. Thirdly, the Human Resource Manager needs a good understanding of motivation because he or she may need to advise senior management on the likely motivational consequences of actions which they may propose to take. For example, overlooking a popular internal candidate for promotion could have widespread adverse motivational consequences among his or her fellow managers, who may take the decision as a sign that their own dedication and loyalty might similarly be overlooked in the promotion stakes.

To function effectively in all these areas, the Human Resource Manager needs to have a good understanding of what motivates different people, what factors influence their level of motivation and what steps can be taken to enhance motivation or maintain it at a satisfactory level. Two main types of motivation theory have been put forward in an attempt to answer these questions: need theories and process theories. We will examine each in turn.

Need Theories of Motivation

Needs provide the force which instigates motivated behaviour in the first place. They produce a feeling that we lack something necessary for our physiological or psychological well-being and make us agitated, restless or dissatisfied until we do something to dissipate the need. Need theories of work motivation are based on the assumption that if we can identify the different needs which motivate human behaviour and discover how these can be fulfilled within the working environment, then we will have discovered how to motivate people at work.

A wide variety of different needs have been identified. In the late 1930s, Murray and his colleagues listed no less than twelve physiological needs, including the needs for air, water, food, sex, etc, and twenty-eight psychological needs, such as the needs for achievement, affiliation, recognition, dominance, power, autonomy, play, and so on. In the early 1940s, Maslow suggested that there were five main classes of human needs: physiological, safety, social, esteem and self-actualization. He further suggested that these needs formed a hierarchy, with physiological needs at the bottom and self-actualization at the top. If the lower order needs are unfulfilled, he argued, they will dominate behaviour but, once they are fulfilled, they no longer motivate and people work their way up the hierarchy to esteem and self-actualization needs. However, the research evidence provides little support for this idea, and in any case Maslow's original theory contained so many qualifications and exceptions that it is difficult to see how any clear-cut conclusions can be drawn from it.

An influential need theory of the 1950s was Herzberg's motivator-hygiene theory of job satisfaction. He argued that job satisfaction and dissatisfaction were caused by two entirely different sets of factors. Factors such as supervision, salary, interpersonal relations and working conditions, he said, did not influence job satisfaction. Improving them would decrease job dissatisfaction but would not produce job satisfaction in a positive sense. The only way to produce job satisfaction, and thus increase motivation, according to Herzberg, was to make the work itself more interesting and improve such things as opportunities for achievement, recognition, responsibility and advancement. This process of actually building into people's jobs greater scope for personal achievement and its recognition, more challenging and responsible work and more scope for individual advancement and growth, Herzberg called job enrichment.

The theoretical and practical aspects of Herzberg's work have fared quite differently as far as subsequent research is concerned. The motivator-hygiene theory has been evaluated in a great many research studies and the majority fail to support it. It appears that factors causing job satisfaction and dissatisfaction do not divide neatly into two separate categories, as Herzberg suggests. On the other hand, it has been shown that job enrichment can have beneficial effects on both the quantity and quality of work output.

In other words, the major weakness of Herzberg's theory was not in claiming that job enrichment could increase motivation, but in claiming that it was the *only* way to increase motivation.

Indeed, from the mid 1960s, there was growing acceptance of the view that early motivation theorists had greatly underestimated the complexity of human motivation. Not only are people motivated by a wide variety of different needs, they are also highly variable. Whilst each individual may have his or her own hierarchy of needs, arranged in his or her own particular order of importance, this order will vary from individual to individual, and even within the same individual over time or in different situations.

The importance of individual differences is clearly recognised in current approaches to job design. One example is Hackman and Oldham's Job Characteristics Model, described in more detail later, in which it is suggested that employees' reactions to enriched jobs will depend upon the extent to which they value the fulfilment of higher order needs. However, the role played by individual differences in the motivation to work has much wider implications for managerial practice. Quite simply, it means that no theory of human needs can tell us what motivates a *particular* individual or group of individuals. People differ, and what motivates one individual or group of individuals may not motivate another or may motivate them to a different extent. Motivation theories can undoubtedly be useful in identifying the range of human motives and explaining how they affect behaviour. But, if a manager wishes to know what motivates a particular individual or group, there is no substitute for studying that particular individual or group, and finding out what is important to them, and therefore what motivates their behaviour.

An understanding of people's needs, however, is only the first step towards predicting and influencing their work behaviour. Needs provide only a partial explanation of motivated behaviour. Knowing that someone has a need for money, for example, will not in itself tell us what he or she will do to fulfil this need. The response may be to work harder (if this will result in increased pay); put in for promotion; look for another, better paid job; take an additional part-time job; become apathetic because there does not seem to be any way of earning more money, and so on. Thus, predicting which particular course of action will be selected in any one situation requires more than an understanding of human needs. It also requires an understanding of the *processes* whereby these needs are converted into motivated behaviour. It is this subject which is taken up in the next section.

Process Theories of Motivation

The portrait of human motivation presented by need theorists is largely an emotional rather than intellectual one. People are motivated to fulfil their needs without apparently devoting too much thought to the process. Process theories of motivation represent an attempt to redress this balance. The emotional aspects are not ignored, but greater emphasis is placed on the role of cognitive processes than in need theories.

A variety of different process theories have been put forward. Most are partial theories, in that they attempt to explain only one aspect of the motivational process. Locke, for example, has concentrated on the effects of goals on work performance. On the basis of extensive research, he and his colleagues have been able to show that gaining commitment to hard, precisely defined goals produces higher performance than simply asking people to 'do their best'.

The importance of goal setting has also been recognised by proponents of Organizational Behaviour Modification, who base their approach on Skinner's learning theory. They suggest that a combination of precise goals, feedback on goal achievement and positive reinforcement for good performance, such as praise, will have a major impact on productivity. In one study where these ideas were put into practice, for example, it was estimated that the company saved $2 million over a three year period.[1]

Another partial theory is Adams' equity theory which is concerned with the effects of perceived fairness of rewards on work behaviour. According to Adams, people who believe that their rewards are unfair in relation to those received by others will take steps to restore a sense of equity. Based on this theory, it has been suggested that people who believe that they are underpaid will feel resentful and decrease either the quantity or quality of their output, whereas those who believe that they are overpaid will feel guilty and increase the quantity or quality of their output. The research evidence firmly supports the first prediction, and this has obvious implications for the Human Resource Manager. However, people who are overpaid do not always react as the theory predicts. Some may feel guilty and improve their performance, but others may restore feelings of equity in more convenient ways, such as changing their perception of their contribution or finding a more favourably rewarded group with which to compare themselves.

Apart from these partial theories, there is one process of theory of motivation which attempts to provide a comprehensive framework within which it is possible to explain most aspects of work motivation. This is expectancy theory and the remainder of this section will be devoted to describing this theory in some detail.

The first major expectancy theory of motivation was put forward by Vroom,[2] although later writers, such as Porter and Lawler,[3] have both added to and modified the original theory in certain respects. The main principles of expectancy theory are presented in diagrammatic form in Figure 6.1.

Variables in 'solid' boxes represent those included in expectancy theory itself. Those in 'dotted' boxes show how other concepts, particularly those from other motivational theories, can be incorporated within an expectancy theory framework. According to expectancy theory, the level of work motivation is determined by two main factors: value of incentives and effort-incentive expectations.[4] Incentives are anything which the individual may receive as a result of achieving a particular level of performance. They include not only positive outcomes, such as: more money;

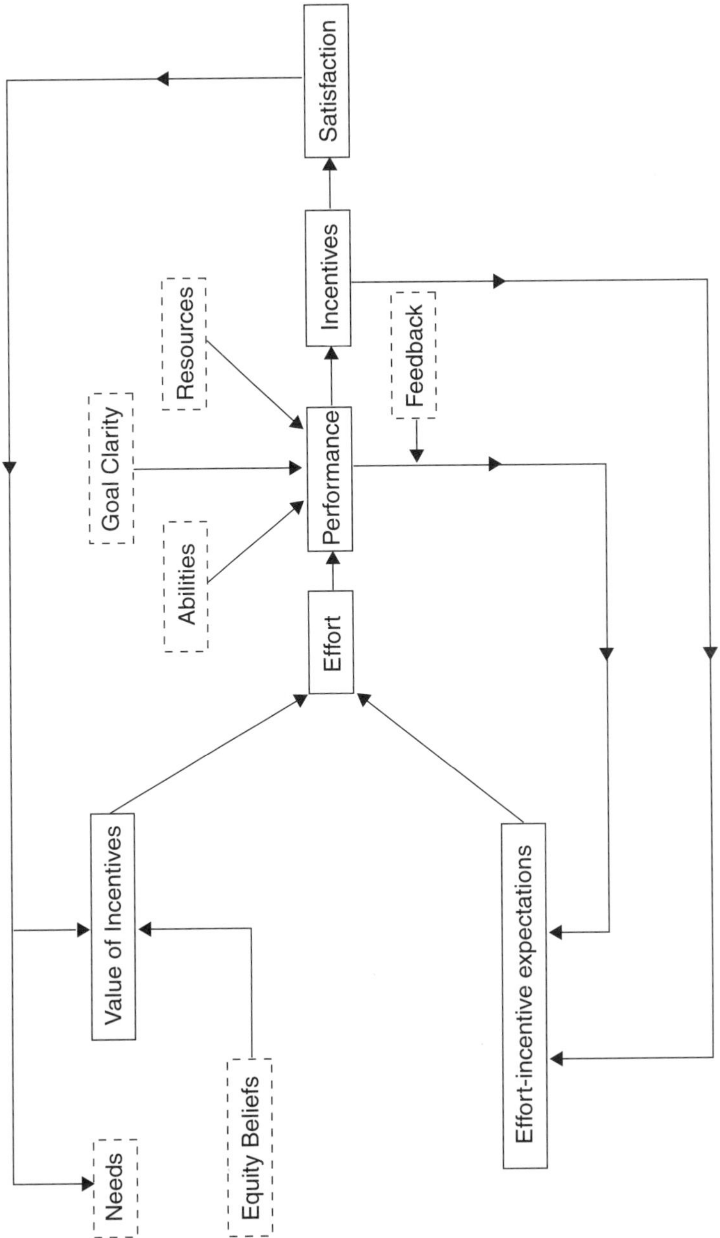

Figure 6.1. An Expectancy Model of Motivation and Job Satisfaction.

greater security; enhanced promotion prospects; social acceptance; a sense of achievement, but also negative outcomes, such as: loss of pay; damaged promotion prospects; social rejection; boredom; tiredness; headaches; loss of leisure time, and so on. These positive and negative incentives can be regarded as things which fulfil or prevent us from fulfilling our needs. Thus, just as people have different needs, the value of incentives will be different for different people. Some people may place a higher value on money, others on security, friendship, prestige, achievement, and so on.

Effort-incentive expectations refer to the strength of the individual's belief that he or she will receive, or avoid, such incentives by expending effort on a particular task. This is made up of two components. First, there are the individual's beliefs about the level of performance which he or she can reach, and second the individual's beliefs about the incentives which are likely to result from achieving that level of performance. According to expectancy theory, if any of these terms are zero, then motivation will also be zero. Suppose, for example, a sales representative is told that she will enhance her promotion prospects if she reaches the target of 500 units sold in each quarter of the following year. This will not motivate her if any of the following apply:

- her effort-performance expectations are zero. She does not believe that she is capable of selling 500 units in each quarter of the following year, no matter how hard she tries.
- Her performance-incentive expectations are zero. She does not believe that she would be promoted even if she reached the target.
- The value of the incentive is zero. She does not want to be promoted, but would prefer to continue as a sales rep.

However, providing all these variables are above zero, the individual concerned will be motivated and, the higher they are, the more motivated he or she will be and the more effort he or she will be willing to put into the task in question.

The amount of effort the individual puts into the task is one of the factors which will determine what level of performance he or she achieves. Other factors include:

Goal clarity The extent to which the individual has a clear understanding of the objectives he or she should be attempting to achieve with respect to the task in question.

Ability The extent to which the individual has the necessary knowledge and skills to perform the task well.

Resources The extent to which the individual has the equipment, support staff, raw materials, etc, necessary to perform the task well.

These factors, together with effort, will determine the level of performance achieved by the individual. Having achieved this level of performance, the individual will then receive certain incentives. Two broad classes of incentive can be distinguished: intrinsic and extrinsic. Intrinsic incentives are those which arise directly from the task itself, such as a sense of achievement, feelings of pride and accomplishment, satisfaction at a job well done. In effect, we award these to ourselves if we feel we have performed a task well. Extrinsic incentives, on the other hand, are those which are given to us by other people, and include such things as money, social acceptance, praise, promotion, and perks such as a bigger office or a named car parking space. Having received whatever incentives accrue from performing the task, the individual will then experience a certain level of satisfaction, which may be high or low depending upon the extent to which they match the individual's aspirations.

Thus far, we have assumed that the individual is doing the task for the first time. However, there are many tasks which we do over and over again. In so doing, we get first-hand information about how easy it is to achieve particular levels of performance; what incentives one actually receives for achieving these levels and how satisfying such incentives are. This additional information may in turn modify our original effort-incentive expectations, or our feelings about the value of incentives, thus affecting our level of motivation. To complete the model, therefore, it is necessary to build in various feedback loops to show that in many cases we are dealing with a cyclical process.

It is, however, possible to distinguish between two different types of feedback. In some cases, we may receive 'intrinsic' feedback from the task itself. That is, it is possible to assess one's own performance and obtain an accurate evaluation of the standard achieved, whilst actually performing the task, or immediately after completing it. Such information can obviously affect our beliefs about the amount of effort required to achieve a satisfactory level of performance, and this is shown in the solid feedback line from performance to effort-incentive expectations in Figure 6.1. Sometimes, however, it may be difficult to tell how well or how badly we are performing a task, or we may take actions which have repercussions of which we are unaware. Thus, we may not know whether we have achieved an acceptable standard of performance or, worse still, mistakenly believe that we have. In such cases, feedback from an external source of information can be very useful. This may come from the individual's immediate superior or a specially designed feedback system. Such 'extrinsic' feedback is shown separately in the dotted box in Figure 6.1.

Using expectancy theory, it is possible to analyse the effects of different incentives on work performance and explain why they have the effects that they do. The effectiveness of money as a motivator, for example, can be explained as a function of both its value as an incentive and the ease with which it can be linked with performance. Where a job has an output which can be counted (e.g. amount produced or amount sold), then it is possible to link specified amounts of additional pay to level of output, as in a piece-work system. Thus, there can be high expectations that improved performance will lead to additional earnings, resulting in increased motivation for people for whom money is a valued incentive.

Many jobs, however, do not have a single output which is easily counted. The Human Resource Manager is one example. Alternatively, the output may be under the sole control of the job holder. For example, a Production Manager whose department has a decline in productivity of 10% could be a poor performer, or someone who is coping magnificently with the adverse effects of a strike. In such cases, performance cannot be measured directly. Therefore, organizations wishing to relate pay to performance tend to give merit increases based on superiors' assessment or evaluation of performance in a personnel appraisal system. This makes the link between performance and incentives much more intangible. If the appraisees trust the judgement and objectivity of the appraisers, then the system may have the desired effect. On the other hand, if they believe that the appraisers are incapable of recognising good performance or that they give out merit increases on criteria other than performance, then this will undermine their effort-incentive expectations and their faith in the appraisal system. Thus, instead of motivating employees, the system may produce dissatisfaction, resentment and frustration.[5] Because of problems such as these, some motivation theorists have serious reservations about the value of merit increase systems based on human judgement.[6]

Turning next to social relations, this is an incentive which has high value for many employees, but it is not one which organizations can easily link to performance. The main source of incentives, such as a feeling of belonging or being socially accepted, is the work group to which the person belongs. They, not management, will decide what types of behaviour will be rewarded with social acceptance and, as the Hawthorne studies showed, the work group may use social control to hold performance down rather than increase it. Thus, attempting to improve social relations at work, e.g. by providing better social facilities, will not necessarily improve work performance. It may, however, improve job satisfaction which, as we shall see, may have other beneficial organizational effects.

Finally, there are the incentives which satisfy higher order needs.

Some of these, such as promotion and recognition, are extrinsic; that is, they are within the power of the organization or individual managers to give or withhold. Thus, they can be made contingent upon performance and, when used in this way, can be a powerful source of motivation for people who value such incentives.

Many of the incentives which fulfil higher order needs, however, are intrinsic. It is impossible to give someone a sense of achievement or the satisfaction of doing an interesting job. Nor is it possible to withhold such things. In effect, people award such incentives to themselves. All the organization or individual manager can do is to redesign the person's job so that it offers the opportunity to experience such things as challenge, responsibility, interest, achievement, and so on. On such jobs, however, there is a strong, natural link between performing well and receiving such incentives. One can only get a sense of achievement by achieving something; experience a sense of responsibility by behaving responsibly; or enjoy an interesting job by taking an interest in it. Thus, on intrinsically motivating jobs, people who value the fulfilment of higher order needs will monitor their own performance and reward themselves when they achieve what they consider to be a satisfactory level of performance. For this reason, they develop strong expectations that good performance will yield valued incentives, which explains why job enrichment can be an effective motivational technique for employees with strong higher order needs.

Research into expectancy theory has provided evidence that the basic central core of the model does have some validity. Early studies showed that a combination of value of incentives and effort-incentive expectations did predict job effort, but the correlation was relatively low, with an average of around 0.35. However, as Mitchell[7] points out, such studies did not actually test Vroom's model as it was originally formulated. Later studies, whose design more closely reflect Vroom's model, have usually produced much higher validity coefficients in the .50s and .60s.[8] Nevertheless, even correlations as high as this still leave a large amount of the variation in effort to be accounted for. Part of the problem is undoubtedly methodological. Variables, such as expectations, values and efforts are very difficult to measure precisely and accurately, so there could be large amounts of error involved in attempts to test the model.

However, it is unlikely that methodological problems alone are responsible for expectancy theory's failure to predict job effort more accurately. Another contributory factor is almost certainly the fact that the basic expectancy model does not include all the variables which influence effort. This has led expectancy theorists to develop more and more complex models, often incorporating concepts and processes from other motivation theorists, in an attempt to provide a more comprehensive explanation of the motivation to work. The fact that so many other theoretical concepts can so easily be 'grafted on' to expectancy theory is both one of its major strengths and major weaknesses.

It is a strength in that it allows virtually all motivation theory to be incorporated within one theoretical framework. Thus, the whole of need theory can be included in the model by making needs one of the major influences on value of incentives. Equity theory can be included by arguing that people's beliefs about whether incentives are equitable or not may also influence their value to them. Goal setting theory can be incorporated by assuming that goal clarity influences performance and, if targets are explicitly linked to promised rewards, this could affect effort-incentive expectations too. Finally, feedback can be incorporated into the model, either as intrinsic feedback, stemming directly from performing the task itself, or as extrinsic feedback from some external source.

Thus, expectancy theory serves the useful function of providing us with an overall picture of how the various different aspects of work motivation interrelate and interact with each other. Unfortunately, however, this does not make the theory able to predict levels of work motivation any more accurately, because all these additional concepts are also difficult to measure, and their precise relationship with expectancy theory variables is difficult to establish. This in turn makes it difficult to carry out a rigorous test of the model. Lawler and Suttle[9] comment rather sadly that, "at this point it seems that the theory has become so complex that it has exceeded the measures which exist to test it".

Furthermore, it is questionable whether even the more complex versions of expectancy theory include all the variables which influence human motivation. Expectancy theory seems to assume that people rationally work out their preferences and expectations (either consciously or unconsciously) in order to decide how much effort to put into a task. As Locke[10] points out, however, much of human motivation is not rational but is, instead, impulsive, emotional, neurotic or habitual, and no account is taken of such factors in expectancy theory. Whilst Locke's criticism is justified, it must be pointed out that this is also a problem for other cognitive theories of motivation, including his own goal setting theory. Irrational behaviour is, by its very nature, unpredictable. Certainly there are theories which can *explain* irrational behaviour after the event – psychoanalysis is a prime example – but such theories are notoriously bad at *predicting* what irrational behaviour will occur before it happens. It is arguable, therefore, that it is better to concentrate, as expectancy theory does, on the more rational aspects of human motivation, which are to some extent predictable and therefore controllable, rather than attempt to deal with the irrational aspects which, by their nature, are difficult either to predict or influence.

In summary, then, expectancy does not provide a final answer to the problems of work motivation. It does not include all the factors which influence work motivation nor, due to measurement problems, can it provide precise predictions of levels of work motivation. What it does do, however, is to provide a framework within which it is possible to identify the major controllable influences on work motivation and give some indication of how they are related. This makes it an extremely useful tool for the analysis of motivational problems. In effect, it provides a checklist of the factors which need to be taken into account when attempting to influence levels of work motivation. There may well be others, but unless *at least* these factors are taken into account, there is a danger that one of the key variables in a particular situation may be overlooked, and consequently an attempt to influence motivation will misfire. In Chapter 7, the motivational principles described in this chapter are incorporated into a checklist which is intended to help managers to analyse performance problems and identify potential solutions to them.

Job Satisfaction and the Management of Human Resources

Job satisfaction and its converse, job dissatisfaction, may be defined as the extent to which a person's general attitude towards his or her present job is either favourable or unfavourable. In addition to overall job satisfaction, it is possible to break down the person's attitude towards the job as a whole into more specific attitudes towards particular facets of the job, such as pay, supervision, security, social relations, working conditions, and so on.

From the Human Resource Manager's point of view, two main questions arise with respect to job satisfaction. What steps can be taken to improve job satisfaction and what effects does job satisfaction and dissatisfaction have on employees' work behaviour? We will examine each in turn.

Improving Job Satisfaction

Based on a review of research into job satisfaction, Vroom[2] suggested that the type of job which people typically find satisfying is one which provides "high pay, substantial promotional opportunities, considerate and participative supervision, an opportunity to interact with one's peers, varied duties and a high degree of control over work methods and work pace". Thus, one way to improve job satisfaction would be to attempt to provide jobs with the characteristics which Vroom describes. However, as Vroom points out, people differ greatly in their motives, values and abilities, and this is likely to have an effect on the type of job which they would find satisfying. Thus, providing the kind of job which would satisfy the 'average' or 'typical' worker would not necessarily satisfy everyone. Because of individual differences, different workers may experience different levels of job satisfaction within the same working environment. It follows that another way to approach the problem of improving job satisfaction would be to attempt to match the characteristics of the job to the needs of the workers concerned. Various different ways of achieving this end have been suggested.

Job Satisfaction Surveys

Not only may employees within a particular organization have needs which differ from those of the 'typical' or 'average' worker, but their perception of the extent to which existing job characteristics fulfil these needs may also differ from those of management. Thus, providing the type of job which management *thinks* would be satisfying to them may not in fact improve their jobs in ways which the workers concerned would find most desirable. In many respects, therefore, it would be useful to carry out a job satisfaction survey to discover which aspects of their jobs the employees themselves feel are least satisfactory, before making any changes. However, it should be noted that such a survey will raise expectations that things will be improved and, as is pointed out in Chapter 7, failure to act on the results of the survey could produce even lower levels of job satisfaction.

Individual Job Design

In many jobs, particularly at managerial level, the job content is to some extent flexible. This is sometimes seen quite clearly when a new job holder is appointed and does ostensibly the 'same' job in a quite different way from the previous incumbent. Certain core job activities may have to be performed, irrespective of who does the job, but outside these there may be many other activities over which the job holder can exercise some degree of choice. Such activities might include sitting on committees, liaising with other departments, carrying out special projects, attending conferences, and so on. Thus, managers who identify the preferences of subordinates with respect to such 'peripheral' activities, and take them into account when allocating them between subordinates, are likely to enhance their general level of job satisfaction.

Group Job Design

With more routine interdependent jobs, it is much more difficult to design jobs to suit individual needs. Nevertheless, it may still be possible to take into account the needs of the job holders as a group when designing jobs. In their Job Characteristics Model, Hackman and Oldham[9] suggest that certain core job characteristics produce favourable psychological reactions on the part of employees, and these in turn lead to beneficial work and personal outcomes (see Figure 6.2). They also suggest that the strength of the relationship will be moderated by the Growth Need Strength (GNS) of the employees concerned.

Employees with high GNS (those who value the fulfilment of higher order needs) are more likely to react favourably to enriched jobs than those with low GNS. The research evidence supports this conclusion. Higher levels of job satisfaction and work performance are found among high GNS employees than those with low GNS when jobs are high on the core job characteristics described in Hackman and Oldham's model.

Nevertheless, the model still has two limitations. It does not tell us what to do when employees on the same job have very different levels of GNS. If they do, then obviously a job designed to suit those with high GNS will be less satisfying to those with low GNS. The model also does not tell us what to do if the majority of the group has low GNS. It tells us how to enrich jobs to suit high GNS employees, but not how to design jobs which would be satisfying to those with low GNS.

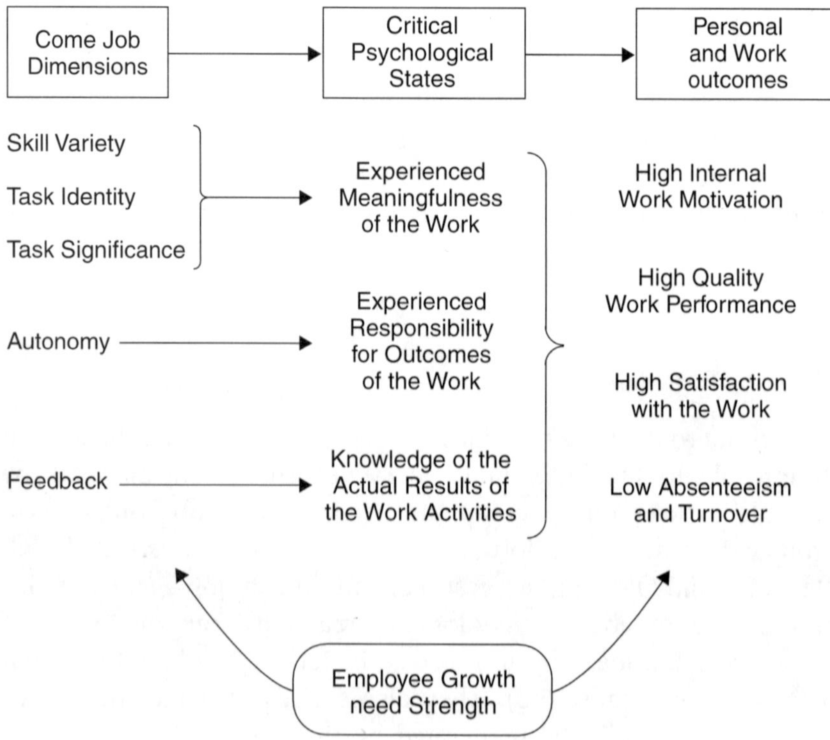

Figure 6.2. The Job Characteristics Model (from Hackman and Oldham, 1976).

Optional Work Systems

A system which would overcome the first of the above problems was introduced by Motorola in one of its departments. A group of sixty employees on an assembly line were given the choice of either remaining on the assembly line or moving to an enriched job where they assembled the whole product on their own. At first, only a few chose the enriched jobs, but eventually about half the employees moved over to the new method of production. Giving the workers the choice of the type of work they did appeared to have beneficial effects for both themselves and the organization. Absenteeism and labour turnover went down and product quality improved.

However, it must be admitted that this is an isolated example involving a relatively small group of workers. Running two parallel production lines would not be a practical solution for large scale production departments, particularly if competitors are manufacturing equivalent products cheaply using conventional production methods. Thus, in many cases, it may not be economically feasible to vary jobs to take into account individual needs. However, even if the job itself cannot be modified, there may still be steps which can be taken to provide a more flexible working environment.

Flexible Working Hours

There has been a considerable growth in recent years of 'flexitime' systems which allow employees to choose, within certain limits, the times at which they work. Typically, employees are expected to work a set number of hours in any one week, and there is a 'core' time during the day when everyone is expected to be present. Outside this, however, there is a broad time band within which the workers can choose the hours which they work to suit their own needs.

Cafeteria Wage Payment Systems

The conventional type of wage and salary payment system provides for a particular level of pay with standard deductions, benefits, holiday entitlements, and so on. However, this ignores individual differences between employees with respect to the types of benefits they would prefer to receive. Thus, some might prefer a straight salary with no deductions, apart from statutory ones, whereas another might prefer larger pension, health insurance, and so on, with their contributions deducted from their pay. Systems which allow employees a choice about such matters have been called 'cafeteria' systems because, like cafeterias, they allow people to select what they want from a range of alternatives rather than having to take a set menu. Research in the USA has shown that allowing employees to choose the type of benefits they receive, rather than imposing a standard system, can increase pay satisfaction without increasing the monetary cost to the organization. However, it must be noted that, because there are more statutory deductions in the UK, there is also less scope for flexibility in the way in which wages and salaries are paid than in the USA.

Flexible Leadership Styles

Modern leadership theorists tend to argue that there is no one best way to manage people.[12] The most appropriate leadership style will depend on the situation. Situational factors which determine the most appropriate leadership style include such things as the nature of the task, the amount of authority the manager has, whether the manager has all the relevant information, and the preferences of the subordinates. Thus, managers can, within certain limits, enhance the job satisfaction of subordinates by selecting a leadership style, e.g. directive or participative, task or person-centred, which matches the preferences of the subordinates concerned.

Selective Recruitment

So far, we have been considering ways of changing jobs or the working environment to match people's needs. However, there is another way of achieving a better fit between job characteristics and people's needs, and that is to select employees whose needs fit the jobs which the organization already has. The accurate identification of potential employees' needs during the selection phase is something which requires considerable skill (see Chapter 3). One alternative which has been suggested in recent years is the 'realistic job preview'. This gives potential employees a realistic description of the job, rather than the highly flattering picture usually given in job advertisements, thus allowing them to make a more rational decision about whether the job would be suitable from their point of view. Typically, realistic job previews reduce the number of applicants for a job, but those who do apply and are selected tend to be more satisfied and remain in it longer.[13]

Organizational Consequences of Job Satisfaction and Dissatisfaction

Job Satisfaction and Work Performance

Early theorists tended to believe that a satisfied worker would be a productive worker. However, the accumulated research evidence has shown that this is not necessarily so. Correlations between job satisfaction and work performance vary widely, but the average correlation has been found to be in the region of 0.14, a figure which Vroom described as being so low as to have little theoretical or practical significance.[14] Such findings are very damaging for theories like Herzberg's, which claim that job satisfaction leads to higher levels of productivity. However, they are quite consistent with expectancy theory. In effect, expectancy theory argues that it is anticipated rather than current satisfaction which influences performance. That is, a worker is motivated to expend effort on a task to the extent that he or she believes that this will result in obtaining valued incentives which will, in turn, give rise to feelings of satisfaction. Porter and Lawler[3] therefore argue that the way to improve performance is not to increase everyone's satisfaction and make everyone happy, but to ensure that the best performing employees are the most satisfied, by providing a strong link between levels of performance the incentives received.

Job Satisfaction and Labour Turnover

Studies of the relationship between job satisfaction and labour turnover have consistently found this relationship to be negative. As one might expect, the more satisfied workers are with their jobs, the less likely they are to leave them. There are, of course, other factors involved, a major one being the ease with which the worker can obtain another job. This will depend on such things as the state of the labour market and the extent to which he or she has skills for which there is high demand. Thus, a satisfied worker may move to what he or she believes will be an even better job, whilst a dissatisfied worker may remain in the same job because he or she cannot get anything better. Nevertheless, other things being equal, it does appear that increasing levels of job satisfaction does lead to lower levels of labour turnover.

Job Satisfaction and Absenteeism

Studies of the relationship between job satisfaction and absenteeism have produced inconclusive results. The relationship tends to be negative, but is very weak and variable. One recent review suggests that job satisfaction typically accounts for less than 4% of the variance in absenteeism.[15]

Thus, attempts to decrease absenteeism solely by increasing levels of job satisfaction appear unlikely to be particularly effective. A more promising approach would seem to be to attempt to *motivate* employees to attend work more regularly. This is the view taken by Steers and Rhodes.[16] They suggest that attendance motivation will be influenced by the following factors:

1. Work related attitudes, e.g. job satisfaction
2. Economic and market forces
3. Organizational control systems, e.g. rewards and punishments for attendance and non-attendance
4. Personal factors, e.g. family size, age, etc
5. Absence culture and work group norms

Steers and Rhodes further suggest that actual attendance also will be influenced by perceived ability to attend. This in turn will be influenced by:

1. Illness and accidents
2. Family responsibilities
3. Transportation problems

The full model is presented in diagrammatic form in Figure 6.3.

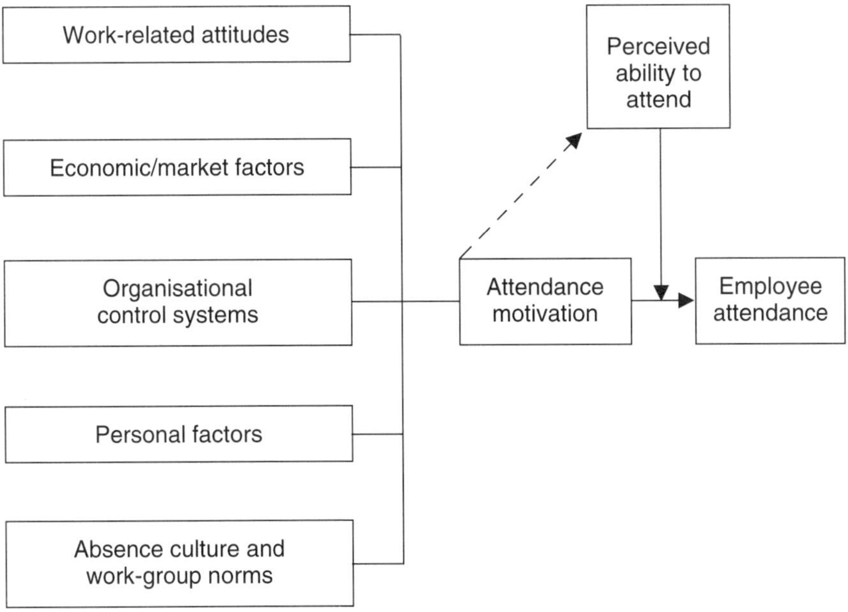

Figure 6.3. An Organising Framework for Understanding Absence Research (from Steers and Rhodes, 1984).

The major advantage of this model is that, like expectancy theory, it can be used as a diagnostic tool to pinpoint the key problems and find solutions. It may be that, in a particular instance, work attitudes are a major contributory factor in absenteeism and steps to improve job satisfaction are in order. In other cases, the problem may lie elsewhere and steps such as the introduction of rewards for good attendance, day care centres for children, a company bus or a company health programme could be more effective.

Job Satisfaction and Industrial Unrest

There has been surprisingly little research into the relationship between job satisfaction and industrial relations problems, such as strikes, go-slows, stoppages, working to rule, and so on. Common sense would suggest that dissatisfied workers would be more likely to take such actions but, apart from some research which shows that dissatisfied workers are more likely to join a union and more likely to vote for union representation, there is little or no firm evidence on this important question.

However, there is research which throws light on certain related types of behaviour. Dissatisfied employees are less likely to perform what have been called 'citizenship behaviours', such as helping co-workers, cleaning up the workplace and taking good care of company resources.[17] Conversely, they more frequently indulge in "non-compliant" behaviours such as complaining about the boss or the organization to outsiders, ignoring the boss, taking undeserved breaks, deliberately doing work incorrectly, and purposely damaging or defacing equipment.[18] On the face of it, this seems to contradict the conventional wisdom that job satisfaction and work performance are not related. However, citizenship behaviours are activities which are outside the employees' job as normally defined. Thus, they may benefit the organization as a whole but may not directly affect the employees' own output. Similarly, employees taking actions to the detriment of the organization may be able to do so without it affecting their own performance in any observable way. Indeed, it may well be that the whole point of such behaviours is to get one's own back on the organization *without being caught.* Thus, there may be hidden organizational disadvantages to high levels of job dissatisfaction, which are not revealed by conventional research methods because the individual's output on his or her own job remains apparently unaffected.

Conclusions

In this chapter, we have described the main factors which influence motivation and job satisfaction and how they in turn affect people's work behaviour. Because people vary so much in their needs, values, beliefs and expectations, it is impossible to suggest a single generally applicable solution to all problems of motivation and job satisfaction. What satisfies and motivates one person may not satisfy and motivate another. The principal aim of this chapter, therefore, has not been to suggest solutions to problems of motivation and job satisfaction. Rather, it has been to enhance the understanding of these subjects in order to enable Human Resource Managers and other managers to analyse such problems and identify more effective solutions for themselves. This is a theme which will be taken up in the next chapter when we shall be concerned with the question of improving work performance in more general terms.

References

1. E.J. Feeney (1972) Performance audit, feedback and positive reinforcement. *Training and Development Journal*, November, 8–13.

2. V.H. Vroom (1964) *Work and Motivation*. Wiley.

3. L.W. Porter and E.E. Lawler (1968) What job attitudes tell about motivation. *Harvard Business Review*, *46*, January–February, 118–126.

4. These concepts are given different names in different versions of expectancy theory. Valance, value of rewards, expectancy and effort-reward expectations are common alternatives.

5. See, for example, H. Thierry (1987) Payment by results systems: A review of research 1945–1985. *Applied Psychology: An International Review*, *36*, 1, 91–108.

6. See, for example, H.E. Meyer (1975) The pay for performance dilemma. *Organizational Dynamics*, Winter, 39–50.

7. T.R. Mitchell (1974) Expectancy models of job satisfaction, occupational preference and effort: A theoretical, methodological and empirical appraisal. *Psychological Bulletin, 81,* 1053–1077.

8. P.M. Muchinsky (1993) *Psychology Applied to Work*. Brooks/Cole.

9. E.E. Lawler and J.L. Suttle (1973) Expectancy theory and job behaviour. *Organizational Behavior and Human Performance, 9*, 482–503.

10. E.A. Locke (1975) Personnel attitudes and motivation. *Annual Review of Psychology, 26*, 457–480.

11. J.R. Hackman and G.R. Oldham (1976) Motivation through

the design of work: Test of a theory. *Organizational Behavior and Human Performance, 16*, 250–279.

12. P.L. Wright and D.S. Taylor (1994) *Improving Leadership Performance: Interpersonal Skills for Effective Leadership.* Prentice-Hall.

13. A more detailed discussion of many of these methods of matching the job content and environment to individual needs can be found in E.E. Lawler (1974) For a more effective organization – Match the job to the man. *Organization dynamics, 2*, Summer, 19–29.

14. Vroom, *op. cit.* For an extensive, more recent review, see M.T. Iaffaldano and P. Muchinsky (1985) Job satisfaction and job performance: A metal-analysis. *Psychological Bulletin, 97*, 251–273.

15. R.D. Hackett and R.M. Guion (1985) A re-evaluation of the absenteeism-job satisfaction relationship. *Organizational Behavior and Human Decision Processes*, *35*, 340–381.

16. R.M. Steers and S.R. Rhodes (1984) Knowledge and speculation about absenteeism, in P.S. Goodman and R.S. Atkin (Eds) *Absenteeism: New approaches to understanding, measuring and managing employee absence*. Jossey Bass, 229–275.

17. T.S. Bateman and D.W. Organ (1983) Job satisfaction and the good soldier: The relationship between affect and employee 'citizenship'. *Academy of Management Journal*, *26*, 587–595. C.A. Smith, D.W. Organ and J.P. Near (1983) Organizational citizenship behavior: Its nature and antecedents. *Journal of Applied Psychology, 68,* 653–663.

18. P.E. Spector (1975) Relationships of organizational frustration with reported behavioral reactions of employees. *Journal of Applied Psychology, 60,* 635–637.

Suggested Reading

For a collection of original articles and commentaries covering the whole field of work motivation and job satisfaction, see:

R.M. Steers and L.W. Porter (Eds) (1991) *Motivation and Work Behavior*, 5th edition. McGraw-Hill.

Questions

1. An understanding of human needs provides a necessary but not sufficient basis for influencing the motivation to work. Discuss.

2. To what extent has expectancy theory enhanced our ability to understand, predict and influence the motivation to work?

3. What are the implications of job satisfaction research for the management of human resources?

CASE STUDY

The Maintenance of Motivation

George is a 30 year old maintenance fitter. He takes considerable pride in his work, rightly considering himself to be one of the best fitters in the maintenance department. He gets on well with colleagues and, with bonuses, makes what he considers to be a reasonably good living. Nevertheless, he has been feeling more and more dissatisfied with the way things have been going at work recently. Whenever there is a 'tight' job to be done (one which is difficult to finish in the stipulated time) he or one of the other good fitters always gets it, whilst the easy jobs are given to people George considers idle or useless. George always manages to finish his jobs on time, so he receives the agreed bonus, but he resents the fact that he has to work harder for the bonuses than many of his colleagues who have what he regards as a very cushy life. When George complained to the departmental manager about this, he was told that they had to give some of the fitters the 'slack' jobs, otherwise they would never finish them on time, whereas they knew they could rely on George to finish even the most difficult job on time. George realised that the departmental manager was trying to make him feel better about the situation, but somehow it did not seem to work. However, George supposes he will just have to put up with it. There has been talk of him being promoted to foreman, but he is not sure he wants the job. He is sure he could do it, but he is not convinced any benefits would be worth the hassle involved.

How would you explain George's work motivation and job satisfaction in terms of the research and theory described in this chapter?

What effects do you think George's motivation and job satisfaction will have on his work behaviour?

Chapter 7

Managing Performance Improvement

Peter L Wright and David S Taylor

Objectives

- To introduce the context of performance improvement
- To explore the three stages of performance improvement:
  (i) identifying performance problems
  (ii) examining their causes
  (iii) identifying remedial actions for their improvement
- To expand on these stages through the consideration of different writers' approaches to performance analysis
- To provide a checklist to facilitate the analysis of performance problems and assist the identification of effective actions for performance improvement
- Briefly to compare the checklist 'bottom-up' approach to performance improvement with a 'top-down' organisational development approach

Introduction

A common theme which runs throughout this book is the identification of practical methods to influence the behaviour and attitudes of people at work. This concern can be seen in the different chapters on selection, training, motivation, staff appraisal, and so on. In order to deal with such topics in any depth, it is necessary to cover them in separate chapters, which may erroneously give the impression that such topics represent problems which can be looked at in isolation. Real life, however, does not segment itself as conveniently as the chapters in a book, and material from all these chapters may be relevant to the solution of a single real-life problem. The aim of this chapter is to present an integrated scheme for the analysis of performance problems which draws together material from many different aspects of Human Resource Management.

Maintaining and, where possible, improving the level of performance of subordinates is a major aspect of the manager's job. It is particularly important where the subordinate's performance falls below expected standards, but a significant contribution to organisational effectiveness can also be made by finding ways to improve the performance of people who are already performing their jobs satisfactorily. Furthermore, although there are exceptions, many of the methods which can be used to bring unsatisfactory performers up to standard can also be used to make satisfactory or good performers even better. Thus, whilst we use the term 'performance problem' for the sake of convenience in this chapter, it is worth noting that the term 'opportunity for development' would be equally applicable in many cases.

The Three Stages of Performance Improvement

In order to improve performance at work, whatever the current level of performance may be, three steps are necessary. The manager concerned must define precisely what aspects of performance it would be beneficial to improve, discover the reasons why performance is not satisfactory or not as good as it could be, and identify effective actions which can be taken to achieve the desired improvement in performance.[1] If any of these steps are omitted, then the attempt to improve performance is unlikely to be successful. If the performance problem is incorrectly defined in the first place, then much time and effort can be wasted attempting to solve the wrong problem. If the real reasons for the problems are not understood, then an inappropriate solution to the problem is likely to be chosen, such as trying to motivate someone who lacks the ability to do the task well in the first place. If effective actions to solve the problem are not identified, despite increased understanding, beneficial effects are unlikely to occur in organisational terms. The individual may know *why* his or her performance was unsatisfactory, but not have a clear idea of *what* to do to improve it. We will now examine these three steps in more detail.

Identifying Performance Problems

Where performance is obviously unsatisfactory it will be relatively easy to identify that a performance problem exists. Quantity or quality of output may be below laid down minimum standards. Costly mistakes may have been made. There may have been complaints from other members of the organisation, or from people outside the organisation, such as customers, clients, suppliers, government inspectors, and so on. On the other hand, it is less easy to identify potential areas for improvement when performance is satisfactory or good. Unless there are some obvious minor blemishes, a review of the employee's performance as a whole may be necessary. In an appraisal interview, for example, there will typically be some form of review of the employee's 'strengths' and 'weaknesses' (although we would not recommend the use of the term 'weakness' in the interview itself) which may reveal areas for further development. In yet other cases, an area for improvement may not even relate to the individual's present job, but may be concerned with knowledge or skills the individual may need for some future job or to cope with new developments such as changing markets or changing production methods.

However, identifying that there may be a need for performance improvement is not the same as identifying what it is. For example, the fact that a customer has complained about the arrogant manner of a sales representative may indicate that there is a performance problem, but it does not tell us exactly what the sales representative did to produce this impression. It could be any one of a number of things, such as accent, manner, style of dress, the use of particular words or phrases, and so on. Telling the sales representative to be 'less arrogant' will have little effect if he or she is unaware of the source of the problem. Thus, it will be necessary to identify precisely what the problem is before trying to solve it. Furthermore, even if we know what the problem is, this does not tell us whether it is worth spending time and effort trying to solve it. Both these points will be taken up later.

Causes of Unsatisfactory Performance

Early writers on work performance tended to assume that it was influenced by a relatively small number of factors. For example, Maier's[2] much quoted formula, put forward during the 1950s, suggested that:

Performance = Ability x Motivation

This formula serves the useful function of drawing attention to two of the major factors influencing work performance. It also says something of the relationship between them. The fact that the relationship is multiplicative suggests that there is little point in attempting to increase someone's ability if their motivation to do the task is zero, nor in attempting to motivate someone who does not have the ability to do the task in the first place.

Nevertheless, there are clearly other factors, apart from ability and motivation, which influence work performance. If one were to have a major operation, for example, then the services of a highly gifted, highly motivated surgeon would be very desirable, but the presence or absence of sterilised instruments, a fully equipped operating theatre and a back up team of anaesthetist and nurses could also have a major effect on his or her performance. Hence, an addition to the Maier formula produced:

> Performance = f (Ability x Motivation x Resources)

Therefore, in an attempt to provide an even more complete picture of the factors influencing work performance, more and more complex formulae began to appear. For example, Campbell and Pritchard,[3] suggested that:

> Performance = f (aptitude level x skill level x understanding of the task x choice to expend effort x choice of degree of effort to expend x choice to persist x facilitating and inhibiting conditions not under the control of the individual).

This formula undoubtedly gives a more comprehensive description of the factors influencing work performance than Maier's, but it does have a number of drawbacks as a diagnostic tool. Its apparent complexity would tend to discourage managers from using it. It does not give any indications of the actions which might be taken to solve the problem once its causes have been identified. Finally, the mathematical nature of the formula is largely spurious. The variables listed undoubtedly do influence performance in some way, but they are extremely difficult to measure and the relationships between them are quite complex. For instance, having a high skill level may actually impair performance on a relatively simple task, because the individual finds the task boring and consequently may not be motivated to perform well. In practice, therefore, it is unlikely that one could use such a formula to predict effort simply by inserting precise numerical values for the terms on the right hand side of the equation. This can reduce the formula's acceptability to scientifically trained managers, who may take the view that because it cannot be used like a 'real' scientific formula, then the whole idea is bogus.

An alternative approach is simply to list factors influencing work performance. Several such lists have been produced, including those of Steinmetz (see Table 7.1) and Miner (see Table 7.2).[4] Such lists avoid some of the problems of the formulae described earlier, but they are not without limitations. For example, the practical value of Steinmetz's list is limited by the fact that it is quite long, and includes many factors that the manager can do little or nothing about, such as sex and senility. It also omits others which the manager can do something about, including lack of feedback. Similarly, relevant factors such as lack of clear targets and lack of feedback are omitted from Miner's list, despite its length. Furthermore, whilst both Miner and Steinmetz discuss methods of improving work performance, they do not link specific remedial actions to each of the suggested causes of poor performance. Thus their lists may help managers to have a better understanding of the causes of poor performance, but they do not provide specific guidance on what to do to solve a performance problem once it has been identified.

Identifying Solutions to Performance Problems

Mager and Pipe's Flow Diagram

Many of the problems outlined in the previous section were overcome by Mager and Pipe[5] by the use of a flow diagram (see Figure 7.1). Mager and Pipe suggest that the first step in analysing performance problems should be to describe the "performance discrepancy", i.e. the difference between someone's actual performance and his or her desired performance. Next the flow diagram suggests that the manager should examine the consequences of the discrepancy, and only do something about it if these are important. It then asks whether the cause of the problem

Table 7.1. Steinmetz's List of Possible Causes of Poor Performance

Managerial and Organisational Shortcomings

Lack of proper motivational environment
Personality problems
Inappropriate job assignment
Improper supervision
Lack of training
Failure to establish duties

Individual, Personal Shortcomings of the Employee

Lack of motivation
Laziness
Personality clashes
Dissatisfaction with job assignment
Failure to understand one's duties
Chronic absenteeism
Alcoholism
Mental illness
Chronic illness
Senility
Sex

Outside Influences

Family problems
Social mores
Conditions of the labour market
Governmental actions
Union policies
Climate

Source: Steinmetz (1969).

Table 6.2. Miner's List of Factors Leading to Ineffective Performance in Business Organisations

Intelligence and Job Knowledge
- Insufficient verbal ability
- Insufficient special ability other than verbal
- Insufficient job knowledge
- Defect of judgement or memory

Emotions and Emotional Illness
- Continuing disruptive emotion (anxiety, depression, anger, excitement, shame, guilt, jealousy)
- Psychosis (with anxiety, depression, anger, etc., predominating)
- Neurosis (with anxiety, depression, anger, etc., predominating)
- Alcoholism and drug problems

Individual Motivation to Work
- Strong motives frustrated at work
- Unintegrated means to satisfy motives
- Excessively low personal work standards
- Generalized low work motivation

Physical Characteristics and Disorders
- Physical illness or handicap, including brain damage
- Physical disorders of emotional origin
- Inappropriate physical characteristics
- Insufficient muscular or sensory ability

Family Ties
- Family crisis
- Separation from an emotionally significant family
- Social isolation
- Predominance of family considerations over work demands

The Groups at Work
- Negative consequences associated with group cohesion
- Ineffective management
- Inappropriate managerial standards or criteria

The Company
- Insufficient organisational action
- Placement error
- Organisational over-permissiveness
- Excessive span of control
- Inappropriate organisational standards or criteria

Society and its Values
- Application of legal sanctions
- Enforcement of cultural values by means not connected with the administration of the law
- Conflict between job demands and cultural values as individually held (equity, freedom, morality, etc.)

Situational Forces
- Negative consequences of economic forces
- Negative consequences of geographic location
- Detrimental conditions of work
- Excessive danger
- Problems in the work itself

Source: Miner and Brewer (1976).

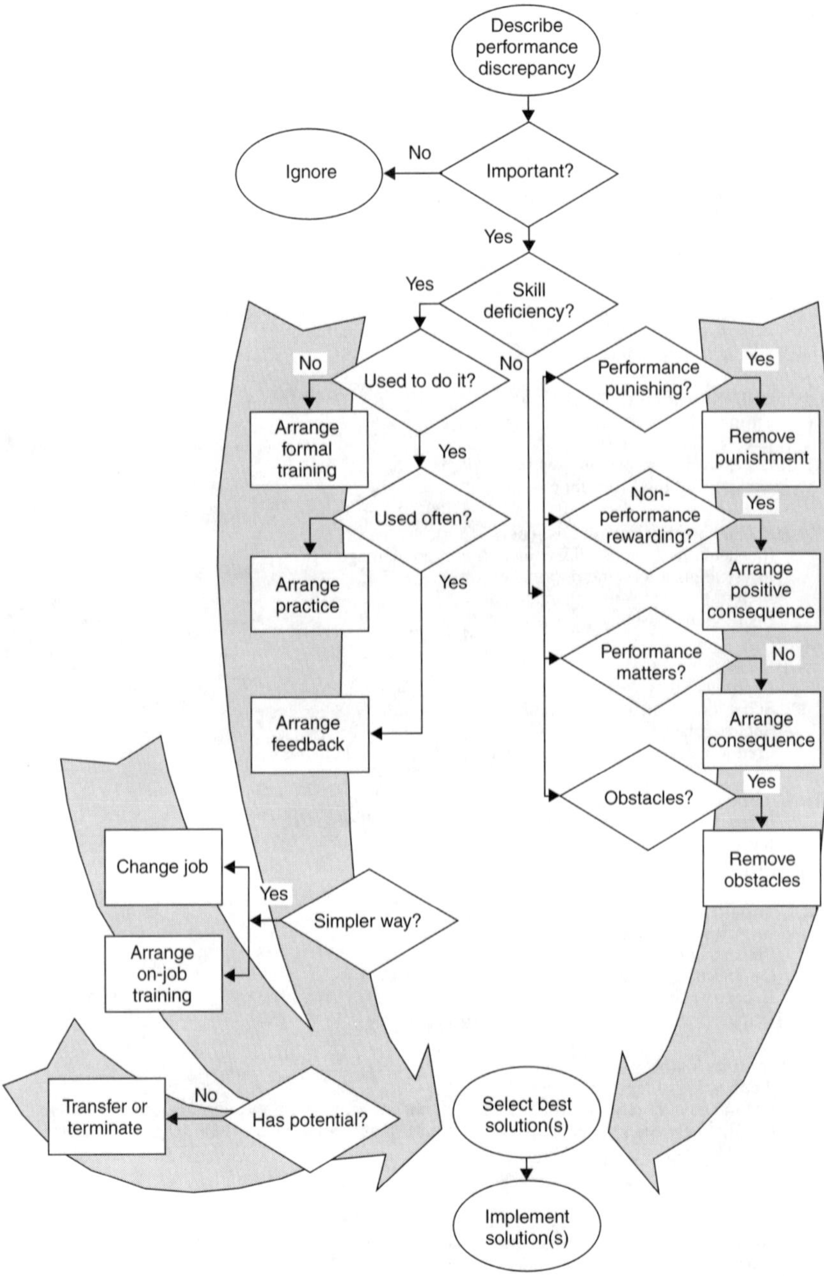

Source: Steinmetz (1969).

Figure 7.1. Mager and Pipe's Flow Diagram for Analysing Performance Problems.

is a skill deficiency. If it is, various questions are used to establish the nature of the skill deficiency and the remedial actions which can be taken in each case. If the cause of the problem is not a skill deficiency, then it is assumed that the problem is one of motivation or some obstacle preventing satisfactory performance, and again various questions are used to establish the specific cause of the problem and the remedial actions which can be taken in each case.

The major advantage of Mager and Pipe's flow diagram is that its step by step approach makes it easier to identify the precise cause of the problem, and the actions which can be taken to solve it. On the other hand, it does present a relatively limited account of the factors influencing performance, largely restricting itself to skills and motivation.

Taylor and Wright[6] attempted to overcome this problem by developing a revised flow chart based on Mager and Pipe's work, which included various additional causes of and solutions to performance problems. However, this rapidly became a very complex diagram, spreading over several pages. In this form, it would have been much too cumbersome to use as a convenient managerial tool. So they developed instead a one page checklist, which they felt would be easier to follow and easier to use in practical situations.

A Performance Improvement Checklist

The checklist grew out of our interest in manager-subordinate interactions in one-to-one situations, such as personnel appraisal interviews. It was therefore restricted to individual, rather than group or organizational problems. It also restricted itself to problems arising from the job itself. Subsequent use of the checklist, both as a training technique and in real life situations suggested that it would have been useful to include 'personal factors' as an additional cause of performance problems, even though the solution to such problems may in many cases be

1. What is the problem in behavioural terms? What precisely is the individual dolng or not doing which is adversely influencing his or her performance?
2. Is the problem really serious enough to spend time and effort on?
3. What reasons might there be for the performance problem (see column 1)?
4. What actions might be taken to improve the situation (see column 2)?

Possible reasons for performance problem	*Possible solutions*
Goal Clarity Is the person fully aware of the job requirements?	Give guidance concerning expected goals and standards. Set targets. MBO.
Ability Does the person have the capacity to do the job well?	Provide formal training, on-the-job coaching, practice, secondment, etc.
Task Difficulty Does the person find the task too demanding?	Simplify task, reduce workload, reduce time pressures, etc.
Intrinsic Motivation Does the person find the task rewarding in itself?	Redesign job to match job-holder's needs.
Extrinsic Motivation Is good performance rewarded by others?	Arrange positive consequences for good performance and zero or negative consequences for poor performance.
Feedback Does the person receive adequate feedback about his or her performance?	Provide or arrange feedback.
Resources Does the person have adequate resources for satisfactory task performance?	Provide staff, equipment, raw materials as appropriate.
Working Conditions Do working conditions, physical or social, interfere with performance?	Improve light, noise, heat, layout, remove distractions, etc, as appropriate.
Personal Problems For example, stress, substance abuse, family problems, etc.	Provide counselling if sufficiently skilled. Call in specialist helper.

5. Do you have sufficient information to select the most appropriate solution(s)? If not, collect the information required, e.g. consult records, observe work behaviour, talk to person concerned.
6. Select most appropriate solution(s).
7. Is the solution worthwhile in cost benefit terms?
   (a) If so, implement it.
   (b) If not, work through the checklist again, or relocate the individual, or reorganise the department/organisation, or live with the problem.
8. Could you have handled the problem better? If so, review own performance. If not, and the problem is solved, reward yourself and tackle next problem.

Figure 7.2. Checklist for improving work performance.

beyond the scope of the individual manager. A revised version of the checklist was developed which included this additional element.[1] This is presented in Figure 7.2.

The first step in analysing a performance problem is to *define the problem in behavioural terms.* That is, the manager should stipulate, as precisely as possible, what it is that the subordinate is doing or not doing which is adversely affecting his or her work performance. This helps to avoid one of the major pitfalls in attempting to improve work performance, that of defining a subordinate's performance problem in terms of personality defects, such as laziness, lack of confidence or arrogance. This is not to say that personality has no effect on behaviour. It undoubtedly does. However there are two good reasons for defining performance problems in terms of behaviour rather than personality. First, although personality influences people's behaviour, it is by no means the only determinant. The environment also has a major impact. Thus, people with quite different personalities may behave in quite similar ways when in certain environments, such as at a funeral service. Conversely, even though their personalities do not change, people often behave quite differently in different situations, for example, at a formal meeting compared with an office party.

The second reason is that, by the time we are adults, our personalities are relatively stable. Thus bringing about a change in personality is extremely difficult and is not something which managers have the expertise to do effectively, nor perhaps would it be ethical for them to attempt to do so. Thus, deciding that the problem is someone's laziness, lack of confidence, lack of foresight or aggressive nature renders the problem unsolvable. Further, we do not observe such personality traits directly. They are inferences based on the observation of behaviour. The individual has done, or failed to do, something to give us this impression of his or her personality, for example, sat around doing nothing when there was work to be done, failed to speak up in a departmental meeting or failed to order essential supplies on time. These rather more precise behavioural descriptions are much less complex to tackle. They are aspects of behaviour which a manager can probably get a subordinate to change if the right approach to the problem is used.

Having defined the problem in behavioural terms, the next step is to *ask whether the problem is really serious enough to spend time and effort on.* If the behaviour in question has little effect on the individual's work performance or that of others, then expending a great deal of time and effort in an attempt to change it would hardly seem to be an effective use of the organisation's resources. Of course, there may be times when we feel obliged to do so, for reasons of expediency. The organisation may demand compliance with apparently meaningless rules, or our immediate superior may insist on his or her own foibles being imposed on our subordinates. By the same token, however, it may be useful to examine our reasons for believing that a performance problem exists. It is all too easy to say something is bad for morale, bad for the company image, will upset people, or will give a bad impression, but will it? In some cases, such feelings may be justified but there is always the possibility that they are merely rationalizations designed to provide a justification for our own idiosyncratic beliefs or assumptions about correct behaviour.

Assuming the problem is seen as a significant one, the next steps are to *review the possible causes and then the potential solutions.* It is better to work through all the possible causes first, before thinking about solutions, because considering both causes and solutions together frequently results in premature closure of the problem solving procedure. Consequently, the quality of problem solving will be reduced. Evidence indicates that problem solving is improved by the following:

1. Defining the problem in ways that do not restrict diversity of thought (e.g. not defining the performance problem in personality terms but in terms of actual behaviour).
2. Creating conditions that enhance a variety of wide-ranging possibilities (e.g. using *aides-mémoire* to increase the number of factors considered, such as a checklist).

3. Postponing the evaluation (or judgement) of ideas for as long as possible, i.e. until the full range of possible causes have been considered.[7]

Goal Clarity

The individual may not know or may misunderstand the requirements of the job. For instance, the individual may not realise that a certain task is part of the job, may not know what standard of performance is expected, or may mistakenly place greater emphasis on one part of the job rather than another (for example, stressing quality of output when quantity is more important or vice versa, doing a preferred or easier task rather than a higher priority one).

If so, some guidance is necessary concerning the job requirements, priorities and expected standards. Depending on how the individual is likely to respond, such guidance may range from a quiet word pointing out that some aspect of performance is important, to a more rigorous goal setting exercise, say in a performance appraisal interview. Alternatively, if the problem is widespread, a more formal system such as Management by Objectives (MBO) for the unit as a whole may be appropriate. Research by Locke and his colleagues has shown that goal setting can be a highly effective method of improving work performance, particularly when combined with appropriate feedback.[8] Research has shown that:

1. Specific goals are more effective than ambiguous goals, such as 'do your best', or no goals at all.
2. Difficult but achievable goals lead to better performance than easy goals, with moderate goals in between.
3. Goal commitment is affected by expectations of success on the task and the rewards relating to success. However, it is not

necessarily affected by participation in goal-setting, although some recent evidence indicates that participation enhances feelings of self-efficacy.[9]

4. Feedback on performance, together with the necessary resource requirements (information, time, equipment, etc) must be provided by the manager and the organisation.

Ability

The individual may lack certain skills or knowledge required to do the job well. If so, and the individual appears to have the capacity to acquire such skills or knowledge, then some form of training or development may provide a solution to the problem (see Chapters 8 and 9).

Training and development are often seen as 'off-the-job' activities. Included in 'off-the-job' training are simulation techniques such as role-play exercises for the development of personal and interpersonal skills. However, there are tasks which can be set for training and development purposes which may be a mixture of on- and off-the-job task elements. Developmental assignments (setting a budget using available data from the present or past figures; drawing up a sales plan/advertising campaign etc) and other forms of simulated on-the-job training for management development (taking over a production unit for a period; chairing a committee, etc) are rarely used in a systematic way. Because they require a relatively large investment of time by the person's superior, they are not strongly supported. Coaching and mentoring suffer for similar reasons. There may be situations which arise due to changes either in the job (e.g. new technology) or in the person (e.g. reduced capacity due to an accident or changed personal situation) where training and development may be ineffective and we need to reconsider the task. This leads into the next item in the checklist.

Task Difficulty

Looking at the problem the other way round, the task may be too difficult for the job holder to be expected to perform it effectively. It may be more complex, involve more different aspects or shorter deadlines than the individual can cope with. Alternatively, the goals which the individual has been set, whilst clear, may be inappropriate. They may have been set at too high a level, or they may conflict. For example, the job holder may have been set high goals for both quantity and quality of output, either of which can be achieved, but only at the expense of the other. Thus, whatever the individual does, performance will be below standard in one area or the other. If it is decided that task difficulty, rather than lack of ability is the source of the problem, then simplifying the task or setting lower performance goals may be appropriate solutions. It is worth sounding a note of caution here, however. Taking work away from one person and giving it to another may just shift the problem along the line. Alternatively, simplifying a job too much, although it may solve an overload problem, may create an even worse motivational problem.

Intrinsic Motivation

The individual may not be motivated to perform well because he or she does not find the task rewarding in itself. That is, the job does not provide the interest, stimulation, opportunities for achievement, feeling of pride, etc which the job holder would like to experience. In order to provide such intrinsic motivation, it will be necessary to redesign the job in some way so that it provides more challenge, more responsibility, more intrinsically interesting work, and so on (see Chapter 6). However, because people have such a wide variety of needs, some of which cannot easily be satisfied within an organisational context, a manager should attempt to discover a person's immediate needs which are within the manager's or the organisation's power to fulfil. A manager is then more likely to allocate tasks and responsibilities which more closely match the employees' needs and hence increase the opportunity for improved work performance. A survey of 13 job enrichment programmes showed a median improvement in performance of 17%.[10]

Extrinsic Motivation

The individual may not be motivated to perform well because he or she believes that good performance will not be rewarded, or may even be punished, by other people, e.g. superiors, colleagues, customers, etc (see Chapter 6). Wright and Taylor[1] suggest that a simple 2x2 diagram may help in the analysis of the effects of extrinsic rewards (see Figure 7.3). To encourage good performance, the majority of items should be in quadrants 1 and 4. That is, good performance should result in many positive outcomes for the individual concerned and few negative ones, whilst the reverse should be the case for poor performance. Yet one often hears of good performers being punished and poor performers being rewarded. For example, conscientious employees may be given disliked and tedious tasks, because they are the only ones who can be relied upon to do them well, whilst "difficult" employees are not given disliked tasks because it is not worth the trouble this would cause. Similarly, poor performers may not be given difficult tasks because they would only make a mess of them. If the nature of the reward system is such that it does not pay to be a good performer, it is only to be expected that extrinsic motivation will be low. Under these circumstances, we suggest that the manager should examine all the rewards at his or her disposal – verbal recognition, more interesting work assignments, not being given last minute onerous assignments, time off, visits to conferences, salary and promotion recommendations, etc, and ensure that they go to the good performers rather than the poor ones. The research evidence indicates that rewards and punishments administered appropriately (i.e. contingent on performance) cause increases in performance. Conversely, administered inappropriately or not at all, they are likely to produce many dysfunctional effects, including declining productivity and feelings of inequity and dissatisfaction.[11] Where monetary rewards can be clearly linked to measurable levels of performance, this can have a marked impact on performance. A survey of 15 studies of payment by results systems showed a median improvement in performance of 35%.[10] However, care should be taken in introducing payment by results systems. Pay can be a powerful incentive for good performance but unless it can be directly linked to performance its influence will be severely restricted.[12, 13]

One area of performance, which senior management may wish to consider in relation to their own reward behaviour, is staff development itself. There are undoubted benefits for the manager who takes the time and trouble to develop his or her own staff, but there are also potential costs. For example, good subordinates may be lost through promotions and transfers, and there may be correspondingly less time to spend on the achievement of short-term goals. Thus, if senior management say they want managers to develop their staff, but actually reward more visible behaviours with easily measurable outputs, whilst ignoring staff development, then many managers will inevitably feel that it is not in their interest to spend much time on long-term staff development.[14]

	Good Performance	Poor Performance
Rewards	(1)	(2)
Negative or Zero Outcomes	(3)	(4)

Figure 7.3. Extrinsic Rewards and Work Performance.

Feedback

Poor performance may occur as a result of individuals not realising the need for improvement or, alternatively, they may be aware of their poor performance but be uncertain about how they might improve it. In both cases, the provision of feedback can influence the overall performance.

The first situation, a lack of awareness for the need for improvement, requires initially that the individuals are given some expected standards of performance. That is, some goal setting should be provided (see above under Goal Clarity). Once goals have been set, feedback relating to the achievement of the goals can be provided. In some cases goals may have been set, but, without feedback, personnel may believe they are achieving them. An example of this occurred at Emery Air Freight.[15] Employees believed that they were responding to customer enquiries within 90 minutes for nine enquiries out of the ten. The company introduced a simple feedback system whereby the employees monitored and logged their own performance. These records were periodically inspected by supervisors who gave praise for performance improvement (extrinsic reward) but simply ignored the results if no improvement occurred (zero outcome). The company used a similar self-monitored feedback programme for container utilisation and goods deliveries and the combination of goal-setting, self-monitored feedback and supervisors' recognition saved them approximately two million dollars over a three year period.

In the second case, where individuals may be aware of some aspects of poor performance but uncertain how to change it, some additional source of feedback will be required. This would normally be supplied by a trainer, mentor or the individual's manager. It is relevant to performance on multifarious tasks in which feedback is limited, or its implications difficult to discern, for the individual components which make up the task, but where an overall feedback measure will be available at the end of the task. Such tasks are also usually spread over a period of time, creating even more difficulty relating to the provision of feedback. Examples include selling, patient care, supervising, interviewing and training itself. Performance feedback tends to be given in overall performance terms – number of sales, patient recovery rate, employee productivity, employee satisfaction, performance improvement. However, assuming that overall performance measures indicate less than satisfactory performance, how does the individual identify particular aspects of performance which need to be improved? If, as noted above, the task is spread over a period of time also, even more difficulty may arise due to some aspects of performance not being recallable.

Two points are relevant for the provision of feedback for such tasks. First, feedback should be provided on each component, particularly in the early stages of learning. For more experienced individuals, besides giving feedback on individual components, feedback can be given on a combination or interaction of them in relation to the overall objective of the task. In addition, contextual influences which may also affect outcomes, such as individual customer requirements, individual employee differences, special patient requirements etc, should also be included and related to required performance. Second, any observed or noted discrepancy in performance of any of the components should be immediately raised with the employee to avoid longer-term problems or disasters.

Resources

The individual may not be able to perform well because he or she lacks the necessary equipment, staff, raw materials or support services. If this is the case, the manager will need to either provide the necessary resources or, in fairness, accept a lower standard of performance than otherwise might be expected.

The allocation of resources can be a source of conflict to individuals or groups. Resources are usually finite and, in allocation, one group's or individual's gain will be another's loss. Where the allocations are based rationally on company plans, groups or individuals are more likely to accept them even though they may be 'losers'. However, resource allocations are sometimes based on patronage or favour, in which case discontent may result and be manifested in a reduced level of employee cooperation.

Working Conditions

The individual's level of work performance may be impaired by adverse conditions, such as inappropriate levels of noise, temperature, humidity, interruptions, hours of work, and so on. As with resources, the manager will need either to improve working conditions, or accept a lower standard of performance than might have been expected.

There are legal requirements concerning minimum acceptable standards included in the Health and Safety at Work legislation. However, minimum standards rarely facilitate optimum work performance. In addition, working conditions may not only be important in themselves but may also indicate to employees the organisation's apparent concern for them. The employees' perception of this can affect their commitment to the company and perhaps, as a result, their work performance.

Personal Problems

The individual's work performance may have been affected by factors not directly concerned with work, for example: family problems, stress, substance abuse (alcohol, drugs, etc), lack of social acceptance, and so on. In such circumstances, unlike the cases we have previously discussed, there are no ready-made 'solutions' to the problem. Easing the person's workload may be appropriate as a temporary expedient, but obviously does not provide a viable long-term solution. Furthermore, telling someone how to solve their personal problem is not usually very effective. A solution which would work for the person giving advice may be inappropriate or unacceptable for the person with the problem. What the manager can do, providing he or she has the necessary skills, is to carry out a counselling interview. That is, allow the person to talk through the problem, and reach their own solutions, *without giving advice*. However, if the manager feels that he or she lacks the skills to do this effectively or the problem is too severe for the manager to provide effective assistance, then it will be more appropriate to call in outside help. This may come from specialist counsellors, either within or outside the organisation, or from groups such as Alcoholics Anonymous who provide help with specific types of problem. Given that occupational stress is a quite prevalent problem, it may also be worthwhile providing training in stress management for those managers who feel they would benefit from it.[16]

Identifying Specific Causes of and Solutions to Performance Problems

As we have seen, the same performance problem may have a large number of possible causes and solutions. Thus, if one of the main causes of a performance problem is outside the range of factors normally considered by the manager concerned, there is a danger that it will be overlooked, with the result that an inappropriate or less appropriate solution is selected. This is particularly likely to be the case when narrow, simplistic assumptions are made, such as "All poor performers are lazy" or "Performance problems can be solved by treating people with consideration and concern". Such assumptions undoubtedly match reality some of the time but, given the complexity of human behaviour, they also result in the manager being wrong much of the time.

The primary aim of the Wright and Taylor checklist, therefore, is to encourage managers faced with performance problems to consider a wider variety of options with respect to possible causes and potential solutions than they might otherwise have taken into account. It appears to have been successful in this respect. An experimental study showed that a group trained in the use of the checklist, identified significantly more possible causes and potential solutions when analysing a performance improvement case than did an untrained control group.[6]

Having generated such possible causes and potential solutions, however, the next thing which the manager must do to solve the problem is to identify from all these possibilities the most significant causes of the problem and the most appropriate remedial actions which can be taken. To do this, it may be necessary to gather further information. In particular, the individual concerned may have information which would throw more light on the problem and ideas concerning ways in which it could be solved. Nevertheless, even when the manager has collected all the available information concerning the problem, identifying its true causes and the most appropriate solutions may be no easy matter. This is a difficult enough task in itself, but it is likely to be made worse by the fact that it is often a source of conflict between superior and subordinate. As Mitchell and O'Reilly[17] point out, there is a tendency for people to a) think that their own behaviour is caused by external forces, whilst seeing that of others as being caused by internal forces, and b) attribute their successes to themselves and their failures to forces beyond their control. These two biases combined mean that superiors are likely to blame poor performance on causes within the subordinate (e.g. lack of ability, poor motivation, malice, etc), whereas the subordinate is likely to attribute poor performance to external factors (e.g. lack of resources, poor cooperation from others, overwork and, if pushed, lack of support from the superior).

Mitchell and O'Reilly suggest that one way to reduce the effect of such biases is to collect data on the consistency, consensus and distinctiveness of the poor performance. That is, the manager should ask whether the subordinate has performed the task poorly before (consistency), whether other subordinates perform the task poorly (consensus) and whether the subordinate has performed poorly on other tasks (distinctiveness). The greater the distinctiveness and consistency, and the lower the consensus, the more likely it is that the causes of the poor performance are internal. Conversely, the lower the distinctiveness and consistency, and the higher the consensus, the more likely it is that the causes of poor performance are external. Such rules are not foolproof. They assume that all the subordinates concerned are working under exactly the same conditions, and this may not be the case. For example, a manager might treat one of his or her subordinates quite differently from the others without being aware of it. Alternatively, an individual may consistently perform poorly, in comparison with his or her workmates, because the other members of the group refuse to cooperate with the individual, but help each other. Nevertheless, in many cases, the rules we have outlined will provide useful guidelines for analysing whether the causes of a performance problem lie within or outside the individual concerned. Furthermore, a knowledge of the biases which typically occur in such situations should also help the manager to counteract his or her own biases, and have a better understanding of the defensive reactions which subordinates often exhibit in relation to performance problems.[18]

If it appears that the problem is one which has its roots at the individual level, then it is necessary to decide which of the various possible causes are relevant in the case under consideration. A useful place to start is motivation. Mager and Pipe[5] suggest that a motivational problem exists when an individual who is not performing satisfactorily could do so if he or she had to. The question to ask, they suggest, is "Could the individual do it if his or her life depended on it?" If the answer is "Yes", then the problem is a motivational one. One point is worth noting, however. People may *claim* they would perform a job badly, because this is a more acceptable excuse for avoiding it than simply saying that they do not *want* to do it. A manager told us of a subordinate who said that he was dubious about taking on a routine administrative job because he would probably not be very good at it. The manager replied that he would give the subordinate the job for a year, and if he performed it well, would then take him off it. If, however, the subordinate performed the job badly, taking him off the job would deprive him of the opportunity to develop new skills, and he would therefore be left on the job. Thus, it no longer paid to be incompetent and the subordinate's doubts about his abilities suddenly disappeared. If subordinates claim lack of skill as a reason for not doing something, it would therefore be worthwhile to check, using the 2 x 2 diagram (Figure 7.3), whether there are not also sound motivational reasons for not *wanting* to do it. If there are, then changing the reward/punishment system or changing the nature of the job may be a more appropriate solution.

Similar problems may arise with respect to resources and working conditions. These are both a convenient focus for deeper more underlying motivational problems. It may be difficult for the individual to articulate things relating to the job itself which demotivate and dissatisfy. By contrast, it is easy to point to a low status company car or obsolete word processor as factors causing poor performance. In some cases, such things may be genuine sources of concern. In others, however, they may be symbols of a deeper dissatisfaction, and it is not unknown for people's dissatisfaction to get *worse* when given the improvement in resources or working conditions they asked for. They may have convinced themselves that such improvements would solve the problem, only to find that when they got them, the job was actually no better, and despair is the result. Thus it would be sensible, when there are complaints about resources and working conditions, to probe more deeply to find out whether there are other problems which might be the root cause of the complaint.

Identifying whether goal clarity is a problem is relatively straightforward. The manager can ask the subordinate what he or she thinks are the goals of the job and see whether the subordinate's perceptions match his or her own. Where they do not, then differences can be explored and resolved. This may not always help in attributing blame for past mistakes. One of the authors mastered very early in National Service the "What me Sarge, no Sarge, nobody told me Sarge" response, which can be quite difficult to break down or disprove. Nevertheless, clarifying goals for the future can, at the very least, ensure that this excuse will not work next time.

Similarly, feedback problems can be relatively easily identified by asking the subordinate what feedback he or she receives concerning levels of performance, how soon after the event it occurs, how useful it is, and so on.

This leaves task difficulty and abilities. These are, in many respects, opposite sides of the same coin. The task may be too difficult for the individual, given his or her abilities, or the individual's abilities may be insufficient to cope with the difficulty of the task. There is also the possibility that the individual finds the task boring because it is not difficult enough, and therefore is not motivated to perform well. Thus, such problems can be solved in a variety of ways, such as increasing the abilities of the individual, replacing the individual with someone of greater (or lesser) ability or changing the difficulty level of the task. The solution chosen will depend, at least in part, on the relative difficulty of these alternatives. For example, there is little point in deciding to replace the individual with someone more able, if such a person would be difficult to obtain or prohibitively expensive to hire.

Finally, if it is decided that lack of ability is the cause of the problem, it is still necessary to decide *why* the person lacks ability. As Mager and Pipe[5] point out, someone may lack ability because they never had it in the first place or because they used to have the ability but have become 'rusty'. It is therefore useful to ask whether the individual used to be able to perform the task well. If the answer is "Yes", the solution may be a refresher course, or quite simply an opportunity to practice the task more frequently, rather than a full training programme designed for beginners.

In this section we have concentrated on ways of solving a performance problem at the individual level. It must be recognised, however, that by no means all performance problems can be solved in this way. It may be, for example, that the individual is unable or unwilling to develop the skills necessary to perform the job satisfactorily or has needs which the organization cannot fulfil or cannot fulfil at an acceptable cost. In such cases the 'solution' may be to relocate or dismiss the individual, or at least suggest that he or she might be happier elsewhere. Alternatively, if the problem is a general one, in that similar performance problems arise with respect to other members of the organisation, then steps to solve the problem at the group or organisational level may be more appropriate. This might take the form of improving the organisation's recruitment and selection system or the introduction of some form of organisational development. The latter method will be taken up in the next section.

Solving Performance Problems at the Group and Organisational Level

A decision to investigate organisational and individual effectiveness usually arises when a line manager, Human Resource Specialist, or other key personnel, believe that an individual or group of individuals or the organisation as a whole, could be performing more effectively than they are presently doing. Our checklist approach is a 'bottom up' approach; that is, it initially looks at the behaviour of individuals in an attempt to improve their performance and, if this is unsuccessful, then suggests undertaking a more global investigation. An organisational development (OD) approach reverses this. OD specialists would tend to take a 'top down' approach, where diagnosis starts at the organisational level and works down to the individual level. Our reasoning in taking a 'bottom up' approach is that it may solve a problem with less disruption, and at a lower cost, than the 'top down' approach.

The OD approach, however, is likely to be more appropriate when it is believed that, although individuals may not be performing satisfactorily, tackling the problem at the individual level may be ineffective. This may be because groups of employees are exhibiting poor work performance or dissatisfaction. As a result, senior personnel may feel that unique individual variables are not the cause, but rather that more pervasive influences are affecting performance detrimentally, such as the work structure, organisational design or culture, inequitable reward systems, lack of cooperation between groups and so on. If this is the case, then attempting to solve problems at the individual level is unlikely to achieve success and a broader OD approach to the problem will be more appropriate.

As with the checklist approach to individual performance problems, an OD approach will follow the stages of diagnosis, intervention and evaluation. However, whereas an individual approach to problem solving is generally tackled by the job holder's line manager, OD approaches require the involvement of an OD specialist. Where an organisation has a professional OD specialist within its Human Resource management team, he or she will act as an internal consultant for OD problems. Where this is not the case, because of the broad range of special skills required for the application of OD, an external OD consultant will be required to assist the organisation through the change process. In this latter situation, some careful thought will be needed, both in appointing an external consultant and in applying OD techniques. The process of OD is usually both time consuming and expensive.

A second problem can arise in the problem solution stage. Some OD specialists have been criticised for their too rigid application of favourite techniques, such as sensitivity training, grid techniques or MBO (management by objectives), when other approaches may be more effective in overcoming the problem. Alternatively situations have arisen where key people within the organisation have believed that they knew what the problem was and have therefore sought a consultant to apply a particular remedy, even though their original diagnosis may have been incorrect. Another organisational factor relates to the acceptance of an OD specialist's recommendations. An organisation will waste both time and money, and perhaps exacerbate employee dissatisfaction if, after employing an OD specialist, it is unwilling to accept the diagnosis and recommendations generated or apply the interventions for inappropriate reasons. Several examples exist where this has occurred. One situation of increased dissatisfaction occurring among employees was experienced by a company which employed one of the authors. An initial agreement was made to feed back the results of a survey based on interviews and a questionnaire. On receipt of an analysis of the survey, senior management reversed its decision to feed back the results to the employees. As a result, dissatisfaction was expressed and the company experienced several serious production disruptions over the next few months. Consequently it is essential that an 'open climate' exists, or is willing to be accepted, for implementing OD activities.

Modern OD Techniques

All OD approaches are aimed at introducing planned change, based on preliminary diagnosis, to improve an organisation's effectiveness (see Chapter 14). Performance diagnoses can occur at three levels of analysis: the organisational level, the group (interpersonal and intergroup) level and the individual job level. Various factors are influential at each of these levels and, as a result, different OD interventions can be implemented depending on the problem(s) diagnosed. Table 7.4 indicates some of the major variables of influence under the headings of Unit of Analysis, Influential Components and Possible Interventions. Further details concerning many of these methods of organisational development can be found in Chapters 9 and 14.

Conclusions

In this chapter, we have attempted to show the wide variety of different factors, both individual and organisational, which can be involved in the solution of performance problems. We have also presented guidelines designed to help managers with the difficult

Table 7.4. Organisational, Group and Individual Factors in Unsatisfactory Performande.

Unit of Analysis	Influential Components	Possible Interventions
Organisational Level	Technological factors Organisational structure Data communication and feedback systems Organisational culture	Work organisation Quality-of-work-life programmes Structural design (division of labour) Function design (coordinaling functions) Survey feedback Organisation confrontation meetings Manpower planning; selecting, training and developing human resources; reward systems; goal setting Open systems planning Strategic planning Developing a corporate culture
Group Level	Task design – for interactions both between and within groups Group member attributes – demographic and other individual differences Group performance norms and expectations Interpersonal relationships within and between groups	Work design Team building Process consultation Johari Window Sensitivity training Survey feedback Selection, training and development Grid training MBO, goal setting, reward systems, quality-of-work-life Third party intervention Transactional analysis
Individual Level	Skill requirements Task meaningfulness Responsibility for outcomes Autonomy for working practices Feedback of job performance Individual differences	Job design, quality-of-work-life Career planning and development, training MBO, goal setting, reward systems Stress management Grid training, sensitivity training Selection see also Fig 7.2 – Checklist for Improving Work Performance

process of deciding which, from all the available alternatives, are the most likely causes and the most appropriate solutions. However, we did not present a flow diagram or checklist which would tell the reader how to identify the 'correct' solution to a performance problem. We have refrained from doing so for two reasons. First, it will be apparent that reaching solutions to performance problems is often not a clear-cut matter. In many cases, it involves gathering information from a variety of sources, including the subordinate concerned, weighing the evidence and coming to a considered judgement, rather than working through a series of simple yes/no questions. Second, there may be several different actions which can be taken to solve the same problem. Some may relate to the organisational environment and some may be things the individual can do. As we have noted, the subordinate may wish to blame the problem on the environment whilst the boss may be tempted to blame it on the subordinate. However, there may be no need to choose between the two. The sophisticated manager may, in effect, say to the subordinate: "You, as my subordinate, have every right to expect that I do my best to provide you with a working environment which will enable you to do your job well. On the other hand, no one can expect that an ideal environment will exist all the time. Therefore, I, as your boss, have the right to ask you to develop your abilities so that you will be able to perform the job well, even in less than ideal circumstances. Now let us see what we can do to achieve both these objectives". In other words, rather than looking for *the* solution to a performance problem, it will often be more appropriate to attempt to develop a balanced package of remedial actions.

References

1. P.L. Wright and D.S. Taylor (1994) *Improving Leadership Performance,* Second Edition, Prentice-Hall.

2. N.R.F. Maier (1955) *Psychology in Business,* Harrap.

3. J.P. Campbell and R.D. Pritchard (1976) 'Motivation theory in industrial and organisational psychology', in M.D. Dunnette (ed) *Handbook of Industrial and Organizational Psychology,* Rand-McNally.

4. L.M. Steinmetz (1969) *Managing the Marginal and Unsatisfactory Performer,* Addison-Wesley.

   J.B. Miner and J.F. Brewer (1976) 'The management of ineffective performance', in M.D. Dunnette (*op cit*).

5. R.F. Mager and P. Pipe (1970) *Analysing Performance Problems,* Fearon.

6. D.S. Taylor and P.L. Wright (1992) 'Influencing work performance: The development of diagnostic skills', *Journal of Management Development,* 1, 44–50.

7. D.M. Johnson (1972) *A Systematic Introduction to the Psychology of Thinking,* Harper & Row.

8. E.A. Locke and G.P. Latham (1984) *Goal Setting: A motivational technique that works,* Prentice-Hall.

9. P. Lorenzi (1989) 'Using self-efficacy to explain the effects of participation in goal setting', *Proceedings of the Midwest Academy of Management,* 46–50.

10. E.A. Locke, D.B. Feren, V.M. McCaleb, N.K. Shaw and A.T. Denny (1980), 'The relative effectiveness of four methods of motivating employee performance', in K.D. Duncan, M.M. Gruneberg and D. Wallis (eds) *Changes in Working Life,* Wiley.

11. P.M. Podsakoff (1982) 'Determinants of a supervisor's use of rewards and punishments: A literature review and suggestions for further research' *Organizational Behavior and Human Performance, 29,* 58–83.

12. L. Brading and V. Wright (1990) 'Performance-related pay', *Personnel Management,* Factsheet 30

13. A. Kohn (1993) 'Why incentive plans cannot work', *Harvard Business Review,* September/October, 54–63.

14. M. Sashkin (1981) 'Appraising appraisal: Ten lessons from research for practice', *Organizational Dynamics,* Winter, 37–50.

15. E.J. Feeney (1972) 'Performance audit, feedback and positive reinforcement', *Training and Development Journal, 26,* 8–13.

16. For a more detailed discussion of the nature of stress and its treatment at an individual level in organisations, see A. Ostell (1986) 'Where stress screening falls short', *Personnel Management,* September, 34–37; A. Ostell (1988) 'The development of a diagnostic framework of problem solving and stress', *Counselling Psychology Quarterly, 1,* 189–209; R. Karasek and T. Theorell (1990) *Healthy Work: Stress, Productivity and the Reconstruction of Working Life,* Basic Books.

17. T.R. Mitchell and C.A. O'Reilly (1983) 'Managing poor performance and productivity in organizations', in K.D. Rowland and G.R. Ferris (eds) *Research in Personnel and Human Resources Management,* Vol 3, JAI Press.

18. For a more detailed discussion of biases affecting perception and judgement, see Chapter 3 in P.L. Wright and D.S. Taylor (1994), reference 1 above.

Suggested Reading

A number of the references noted above can be recommended for further reading. Further details of the main approaches to performance improvement described in this chapter can be found in Mager and Pipe (1970) and Wright and Taylor (1994) Chapter 2, and useful reviews of the whole field are provided by Miner and Brewer (1976) and Mitchell and O'Reilly (1983). A more detailed account of the various factors influencing work performance than was possible in this chapter can be found in G. Dessler (1980) *Human Behavior: Improving performance at work,* Prentice-Hall.

Questions

1. What are the main factors which influence work performance? How would you decide which were the most likely cause of a performance problem?

2. What are the relative merits of Mager and Pipe's flow diagram and Wright and Taylor's checklist as means of analysing and solving performance problems?

3. Indicate how organisational factors can influence individual performance at work.

CASE STUDY

SALES PROMOTION

The Ed Brown Case

"He's gone too far this time", said Heather Caldwell. "He may be one of your best salesmen, but he is like a bull in a china shop inside the company. First he upsets Eastern region and now he has upset the Technical Department. You are just going to have to sort him out, Al". Al Phillips put the phone down. This was the third irate call about Ed Brown he had received in two weeks. Al was Central Region Sales Manager with Solent Oil and Cake, a leading manufacturer of animal feed, and Ed Brown was one of the three Sales Supervisors reporting to him.

The first irate phone call had been from Sam Turner, Sales Manager of Eastern Region. He claimed that Ed had 'poached' a major order from a customer in his region. Al mentioned this to Ed recently when they met briefly, but Ed responded angrily that he had got an order for the company and that was all that mattered, wasn't it? There was no opportunity to tackle the matter further then, and Al decided that he would discuss the problem with Ed during his next monthly visit to Ed's territory.

The second irate phone call was this morning. It was from the Technical Manager who complained that Ed had stormed into his office and arrogantly demanded an immediate analysis of a sample of animal feed for a major customer. When told that this might be difficult because of existing work schedules, Ed replied that the Technical Department was there to provide a service and not sit around drinking tea all day, tossed the sample on the desk and left. Al managed to placate the Technical Manager and even persuaded him to fit Ed's analysis in as soon as possible. However, the Technical Manager had obviously been angry enough to complain to Al's boss, Heather Caldwell, hence the third irate phone call.

Al is now faced with a dilemma. Ed and his sales team have one of the best sales records in the company. He is ambitious and has let it be known that, with his sales record, he is expecting promotion to Sales Manager in the near future. Ed is likely to resent criticism of his behaviour but, unless he mends his ways, he is unlikely to get promoted. SOC could then lose one of its best sales reps at a time when a major competitor is expected to launch a cut-price rival product. In the past, Al's policy of allowing Ed to get on with his job with minimum interference seemed to have paid off, but a serious discussion with Ed was now obviously called for.

Analyse the problems in the case study in preparation for an interview with Ed. Suggest possible reasons why the problems have arisen and the possible steps which could be taken to remedy the situation. Treat these as hypotheses which you could check out in the interview. Wherever possible, provide theoretical or research support for your proposals.

What do you think might be the causes of Ed Brown's performance problems and what remedial actions do you think might be taken to solve them? Treat these as hypotheses to be checked out later. Do not worry if some of them are contradictory.

Chapter 8

Training and Developing People

David S Taylor

Objectives

- To provide a definition of training and development
- To examine the effect of attitudes and policy on the status of training and development
- To explore the influence of training and development on productivity, recruitment and turnover
- To consider factors affecting training and development activities
- To view training and development within the human resource management function
- To describe a systematic approach to training and development for the non-specialist reader

Introduction

Human Resources training and retraining is one major approach used by work organisations to maintain and improve the competence of its workforce and increase its adaptability to changing organisational needs. It attempts to develop any combination of physical, social and cognitive skills in order to achieve new or more effective ways of behaving. The skills of a company's human resources are essential components for its success. Consequently, training and retraining, where implemented as an organisational development strategy, should be seen as an integral part of an organisation's investment plan. The organisation's human resources are the possessors of the skills and knowledge required to produce and develop the products or services provided by the organisation. The benefit to it of a highly skilled workforce is that it will be better placed to defend, maintain or increase its success in its market environment.

If we look at the role of human resource development in general there is a continuum of training and development needs to be fulfilled. In the short-term, new job incumbents need immediate training. Present incumbents may need retraining or additional training to fulfil short-term projects and departmental objectives. In the medium term, business trends need to be assessed to provide guidance for changing skill requirements. Career needs and succession planning will also need attention. In the longer term, any long-range strategic plans will need consideration for future skill requirements and human resource plans and these translated into training needs. Several aspects of this continuum are considered in other chapters. Chapter 2 is concerned with human resource planning which will influence longer term training strategy, and recruitment and selection (Chapter 3) is an alternative to training since, if people are available in the labour market with the required skills, then an organisation can choose whether to train or recruit. The previous chapter on Managing Performance Improvement indicates the importance of training as one potential short-term remedial factor. Training also impinges on the next chapter on Management Development and the broader organisational views expressed in Chapters 14 and 15. In order to avoid overlap, this chapter will look specifically at how training can be developed systematically to ensure that an organisation's human resources achieve the required knowledge, skills and abilities in an efficient and cost-effective way. It will begin by looking at the training context, followed by a description of a systematic approach to training. Three phases will be distinguished – the assessment phase, the training development phase and the evaluation phase. Since the chapter is aimed at the general reader, more emphasis is placed on the assessment and evaluation phases than on specialist training techniques relevant in training development.

The Training and Development Context

A Definition of Training and Development

Training and development can be defined as the systematic process concerned with facilitating the acquisition of skills, knowledge and attitudes which result in improved organisational performance. Several words are important in this definition. An emphasis on 'the *systematic* process' signals that the process should be a planned one, to fulfil some essential organisational requirement(s), based on careful information gathering. The definition includes *knowledge* and *attitudes,* as well as skills, to indicate that organisational performance involves more than just doing. Work is done in a context. An organisation has a culture based on its values, which will determine formally expected behaviours. In addition, there is likely to be an informal culture based on actual behaviours developed through social interaction. This context and how it is perceived by an individual will influence performance. Similarly, the work itself will involve varying circumstances, knowledge of which will influence how well the work is done. How well it is done will also be affected by an individual's *attitudes,* for example, the importance one attaches to the priority of tasks, the standards to which the work is done and the level of effort one is willing to invest. As noted in the previous chapter, without guidelines to indicate what is expected of them, employees will develop their own priorities and standards of performance.

Finally, the emphasis is on *improved organisational performance* rather than improved individual performance. Such an emphasis still includes concern for individual learning, but it broadens the context to relate it to corporate needs and strategies. It can encompass such important developmental activities necessary for future planned organisational changes. In addition, training and developmental activities related to succession planning can be based on human resource planning derived from corporate strategies.

Latham and Crandall[1] have pointed out that, over the past decade, the training literature has emphasised that training should be linked to an organisation's strategy. Brown and Read[2] argued that if UK companies took a strategic view of their training policies, the productivity gap between UK and Japanese companies would be narrowed. Hussey[3], who looked at management education and training, also emphasised the need for tying training directly to the achievement of corporate objectives. However, he expressed disappointment that this direct link was seen by only one third of his survey of UK companies. Very few managing directors saw training policy as an issue for them, but where top management did take an interest in training activities, spending was substantial and training programmes were relatively frequently revised to meet changing organizational needs.

The Status of Training and Development

A nation's view of the relative importance of vocational education and training is influenced by cultural factors. In Britain, for example, non-academic education and training have long been viewed as low status whereas in Germany the distinction between academic education and vocational education and training is emphasised less. Layard *et al*[4] have noted: "The British have always admired gifted amateurs. Except in certain well defined areas, like hard science, they have always stressed that character is more important than formal knowledge". This attitude is linked to the early identification of potential, a philosophy which Latham and Crandall[1] have noted emphasises selection at the expense of training. That is, by identifying people with strong potential for a job, we can minimise the amount, and therefore the expense, of formal training. To change to an attitude which encourages training requires a change from the belief that personality characteristics and potential (frequently based on stereotypes) determine effective job performance, to one that views individuals as more adaptable, versatile and developmentally more capable than stereotypic beliefs would indicate. This latter view, interpreted into an organisational philosophy, would emphasise a much more developmental approach to employees: identifying performance deficiencies and then correcting them through some form of training.

Such changes in attitude and practice are occurring in Canada and the United States. These are being influenced by legislation encouraging the recruitment and training of a culturally diverse workforce. It is likely that similar changes will also occur in Britain as a result of government legislation relating to equal opportunities, aimed at overcoming gender, racial or other minority group bias.

Government policy can also have a major influence on training activity. The tradition of apprenticeship has declined in Britain. A mixture of on- and off-the-job vocational education and training has been largely replaced by narrow organisation based on-the-job training. A probable influence on this has been the progressive abolition of the Industrial Training Boards that financed and encouraged vocational education and training. In Germany, the tradition of vocational education and training through a dual education system and apprenticeships has been maintained, with approximately 64% of the labour force having vocational and technical qualifications, compared to 26% of the UK labour force.

In France, vocational qualifications based on the craft level Certificat d'Aptitude Professionelle are held by approximately 40% of the working population. An emphasis on formal qualifications also influences the pay reward system, with pay in both France and Germany related to vocational and technical qualifications. In Britain the under-valuation of formal vocational and technical qualifications results in differential pay between different skill levels being substantially lower than on mainland Europe. Hence, there is little incentive value to individuals to participate in formal vocational and educational training, and, because of the high cost of youth pay to the employer, there is probably no incentive for them to increase expenditure through the provision of formal vocational education and training schemes.[5]

Training and Productivity

The question, 'does training improve productivity?', is not really a very sensible one. It does not require either research evidence or experts from industrial psychology to persuade us that a trained person will completely outperform another individual working on a trial and error basis. Training is essential for job performance and has a significant impact on productivity. However, people within organisations do ask questions, such as, 'does increased training result in increased job performance'? 'Will training beyond that required to provide basic skills make a company more competitive'? 'Does training have a positive effect on absences, turnover, accidents or morale such that cost reductions occur'? These are not unreasonable questions but the answers to them cannot be more than indicative. A problem of interpretation of such questions relates to the extent to which any changes that do occur are a result of the training only, or whether other features of the work environment are also influencing changes in job performance in a positive or negative way. Influential features can include changes in incentives, changes in supervisory practices and changes in job content. Only by carefully designing evaluation procedures for individual training courses, aimed at producing specific learning or skill changes, are we more likely to be able to make causal interpretations, as noted in the later section on the design of evaluation procedures. Nevertheless, we do need to look at what evidence exists, unless we are willing to accept a relationship as an 'act of faith'. Some senior managers and training officers do make training decisions on belief rather than systematic analysis. For example, knowledge of what other organisations are doing, particularly in relation to management training and development, may influence decisions in order to 'keep up with the Joneses'. Other training and development programmes may be introduced based on an idiosyncratic whim of a senior manager or because particular programmes are well advertised and marketed through training journals. So, is there any evidence that training and development activities influence a company's competitiveness, productivity or profitability? Certainly there is circumstantial evidence.

Peters and Waterman[6] examined the ten best performing US companies. They related the success to commitment to performance and to the development of the labour force. They suggested that, "… there were enough signs of training intensity to state that training was highly related to organisational excellence". They also noted that some companies encouraged a wide variety of learning which was not necessarily directly related to company activities.

Goldsmith and Clutterbuck[7], in viewing successful top British companies, concluded that training was a major contributing factor, "… both as a tool to increase efficiency and as a means of instilling the company's values into all its employees".

Galagan[8] in looking at the semi-conductor industry noted that, despite a dramatic reduction in profits between 1984 and 1985 in the industry, Motorola was nevertheless highly successful. Motorola related this to training and development and regarded their programmes as, "… an investment in the employees that pays off in terms of greater productivity, performance and quality". In a later article[9], Galagan reported on the success of the Arthur Andersen Worldwide Organisation and linked that success to its training policy and practices.

Finally, Deloitte, Haskins and Sells[10] found that the more successful companies, who show the best growth in output, profit, investment or people, are those that provide higher levels of training.

However, all these tend to report correlational studies or statements of belief, relating to the link between training and organisational success. One could equally propose the hypothesis that organisational excellence leads to increased training and development activity because successful firms can fund it more easily.

A study which supports the link between training activities and productivity compared 45 matched firms in Britain and Germany. Daly *et al*[11], found an average differential of 63% in productivity (ranging from 10% to 130%) between the two countries, favouring Germany. The authors of the inquiry concluded that much of the differential in productivity was attributable to skill factors achievable through training, both at the technical and managerial levels. This study was concerned with manufacturing industries in the metal-working sector. Two other sectors were also investigated[12, 13], the kitchen furniture manufacturing industry and garment manufacturing. In both cases, productivity was lower in the British firms and differences were attributed to training. Not only was productivity lower, but so was the quality of the goods produced.

In summary then, evidence does indicate that training can and does influence a company's productivity and hence its competitiveness and profitability.

The Influence of Training and Development on Recruitment and Turnover

There is some evidence from graduate employment[14, 15], that training and development activities influence graduate choice of companies. A lack of responsibility early in employment and the lack of a training and development strategy were viewed negatively by graduates. The four top-ranked factors which engineering graduates looked for in their choice of job and company were: challenging work, nature of the work, opportunities to use abilities and structured training.[14] Structured training became the top ranked deciding factor for graduates with more than one job offer.

In a survey in the South Hampshire region of employers in the mechanical, electrical and electronic sector, Jones and Goss[16] found that high training companies with an emphasis on the *development* of human resources were affected less adversely by skill shortages than low training companies who laid emphasis on the *exploitation* of human resources. They also noted that low training organisations inevitably lose their attractiveness to existing and potential labour and gradually lose their ability to retain and attract labour.

In a later study[17], they made a distinction between 'vocational' training and 'post-vocational' training. The latter category included companies which were involved in one or more of the activities of in-house supervisory training, in-house management development, external supervisory training and external management development. Companies not involved in any of these, but who were involved in other types of induction training and technical skills training, were classed as 'vocational'. They concluded that companies involved in 'vocational' training only were less likely to attract and retain suitable labour when compared with their 'post-vocational' competitors.

Finally, Blackburn and Hankinson[18] found in their sample of companies that firms undertaking formal training and development programmes had lower labour turnover rates than those which had no formal programmes. Such studies, in conjunction with those in the previous section, indicate that companies in which training and development is carried out as part of an organisational strategy are not only likely to be more productive and competitive, but are also likely to attract and retain high quality employees.

Factors Affecting Increased Training and Development Activity

It is interesting that although, when asked, almost all companies and their senior executives, will extol the importance of training, the reality relating to the investment in, and practice of, training is different, at least within Britain. For example, a report by Coopers and Lybrand Associates[19], based on an investigation of training activities and attitudes in British companies found, among other things, that "...except in some service sectors, training was not seen as an important contributor to competitiveness...and...few companies saw a direct link between training activities and profitability..." (p.4). One distressing finding of the study was the widespread ignorance of top management regarding the comparison of their company's training performance with that of their competitors in the UK, let alone overseas. The previously noted comparisons of British and German manufacturing companies support the view that many British companies do not view training as an investment which can influence productivity and competitiveness. Perhaps the best indicator of the perceived attitudes of some senior managers to training was the statement of several training managers and personnel directors relating to training costs, that ... "it was better that the full costs of their firm's training should not be made known to the board because, if it were, the board might wish to reduce it." (p.10). For most companies, it was only in the case of management training that some interest was expressed at board level. Companies which possessed a positive attitude towards training tended to be those for whom the impact of *not* training showed up rapidly, for example, in the service sector, where customer-staff contact influences customer loyalty, or in companies in which training is seen as an essential part of a general ethos of caring for, developing and retaining staff. In these latter cases training is seen as an *investment* rather than as a cost or *overhead* to be reduced when hard times occur.

Inhibiting Factors

Several factors can be proposed to account for why training suffers. A major reason may be that its value as an investment process is not apparent. Monetary investments can be assessed in terms of profit (or loss), bonuses, and so on. Investment in training and development activities can be difficult to assess in terms of their influence on organizational performance, particularly where training and development plans relate to medium to long-term goals. This is not helped by personnel involved in training who, understandably, are more often concerned with input factors (the training and development courses themselves) rather than output factors (the direct effects of the courses on company performance). As noted later, evidence indicates that companies and training personnel give little emphasis to the evaluation process. This indicates that training, other than perhaps induction and basic technical training, depends upon a belief in its effectiveness. Although top management is often criticised for its lack of support for training and development activities, without information and feedback from trainers regarding its effectiveness and its link to organisational strategy and goals, can they be fully blamed? A point noted by Torrington and Hall[20], based on survey data[21], notes that "…not all personnel managers have the thorough going commitment to it that their public statements indicate, especially when it is training and development outside the area of management development. This may well be because of the lack of interest by other managers, yet it has the effect that training is not always defended forcefully or promoted vigorously." ([20], p.405). If support for, and commitment to, training and development is not strongly given from the personnel area, it is unlikely that other senior managers are going to see it as a high priority area for financial support. The lack of national structures which induce companies to train can also influence the extent of training activities and its apparent status. Finegold and Crouch note that countries which follow a 'mixed system' of education and training, where academic education enjoys high prestige partially as a result of its exclusivity (Britain, Greece, Spain and Australia), tend to have lower participation rates in full and part-time education and training than either state-led (Japan, US, France and Sweden) or dual systems (Germany).

Supporting factors

National influences

A major supporting influence for training and development is the converse of the previous point. Institutional structures which *encourage* education and training will increase the extent of training activities. State influence through institutional structures can determine: (1) the routes available through the education and training system which determine the options available to individuals, (2) the roles, responsibilities and powers of each agent within the system, (3) the allocation of costs (grants/levies) for skills investment among the agents which act as incentives/disincentives affecting training and development decisions, and (4) the state's capacity to design and implement changes in the provision of education and training.[5] Different institutional arrangements relating to these variables will affect the quantity and quality of national achievements in education and training. For example, governments can determine the number of years of compulsory schooling. For training activities, they can influence contracts for apprenticeship schemes by specifying the need for off-the-job training and development as in Germany. Another example is the 1964 Training Act in Britain, which specified a system of levies and grants aimed at encouraging and funding sector-based (e.g. engineering, textiles etc) on and of-the-job training and development. However, the quality and quantity of education, training and development that occurs at the organisational level will be affected by other factors, such as the quality of the teaching staff, availability of resources, the efficiency and effectiveness of organisational systems and the management team, as well as governmental intervention.

Organizational influences

As noted earlier, a recurring theme from practitioners is the need to link training to organisational strategy. Organisational goals should influence training activities not only for such areas as product development, quality enhancement or changing marketing strategies but for any organisational changes. For example, Useem[22] noted that organisations that had downsized were "likely to place a premium on training new entrants, since they may be stepping into more demanding work settings" (p.422). It is also important that trainees, as well as their managers, are aware of and understand the link between training and the organisation's goals. As a result trainees are more likely to be committed to, and motivated for, training, since the learned skills will be seen to be valued by the organisation.

Pettigrew *et al*[23], from an analysis of their sample of 20 firms, distinguished between factors which drive, and those which sustain, training activity. According to them, the major initial trigger for training is technical change or product market developments leading to the recognition of a 'skill gap'. They note, however, that "other factors also need to be present to achieve effective and sustainable activity in training." They categorised these factors into four areas: business strategic; the external/internal labour market; internal actors, supporting philosophy, politics and systems, and external training stimuli and support, including funding. They note that where a sufficient combination of these factors apply, training activity will be influenced and sustained.

(i) *External influences*
Some external factors relating to government influences were covered in the previous section. In addition to these, both

customers and suppliers can influence a company's training activities; customers through a requirement for quality and suppliers through certificated training courses to ensure effective operation of their equipment, or correct use of their products. According to Pettigrew *et al*, external funding seemed to have little influence on most companies in their sample, in that the decision to train took precedence over whether costs could be defrayed through grants. Only a few companies who were low investors in training tended to consider the availability of grants early in the decision making process.

(ii) *Business strategic influences*

Where an organisation is making major technological or product-market changes, employees will require additional training and development in order to operate effectively in the new situation. That is, a 'skill gap' will exist between what employees previously did and what they will be required to do in the future. Training and development activities may be the only answer to overcome this skill gap, particularly if the skills required are new skills or if only a few people with relevant skills are available in the labour market. In the latter case, however, recruitment may be an alternative if only a very small number need to be recruited. Training and development activities will always compete with recruitment to some extent, where people with appropriate skills and experience exist in the labour market pool.

Two other strategic business circumstances have also been proposed to influence training and development activities. These are work redesign and downsizing. Useem, in his survey of 406 large American companies, found that "companies that had redesigned their work – whether through changes in the work process, increased employee involvement, or creation of a total quality program..." invested more both in entry level education and training, and employee development. Plant closures, staff reductions and other related downsizing activities led to increased investment in entry-level training. Pettigrew *et al* additionally suggested that reducing a workforce in an attempt to increase productivity, may lead to the need for the remaining employees to expand their skills, and therefore additional training and development activities will be required.

It is worth reiterating here, under strategic influences, that companies which integrate training and development activities within their strategy are more likely to attract and retain high quality employees. This in itself makes training and development in higher level skills more relevant and cost-effective.

(iii) *The external/internal labour market*

The skill gap between what employers want and what employees offer affects training and development as noted in the previous section. If no, or very few people exist with the required skills, training of company personnel will be necessary. On the other hand, if there exists a pool of people within the labour market with the required skills, as noted previously, recruitment is an alternative strategy. This will be a viable strategy, particularly where only a small number of people are required or where the training period is long and expensive. Internal factors which positively influence training and development were also noted in the previous section and include downsizing, problems of recruitment and retention and work redesign. Internal factors can also influence the level at which training and development is emphasised. For example, the introduction of team-working, empowerment and process re-engineering, has produced a downward shift in responsibility. As a result, more training is required at entry and lower company levels and less at supervisory and management levels. However, care must be taken to ensure that training and development activities occur at all levels. Useem notes a problem relating to training budgeting. He states that, "though training budgets are not strictly zero-sum, the evidence suggests that remedial and basic training for new employees, particularly prevalent among large and blue collar firms, may come at the expense of technological and managerial training for seasoned employees." (p.416).

(iv) *Management, culture and systems*
There is little doubt that a major critical factor for the implementation and maintenance of training and development activity is top management commitment.[23, 24, 25] Both Brown and Read and Hussey have argued that companies should take a strategic view of training policies and that these should be developed and reviewed by top management. By involving senior management in this way, their support for training and development activity will be increased. As noted earlier, Hussey points out that, where top management took an interest in training activities, spending was substantial and training programmes were regularly monitored and reviewed to meet changing organisational needs.

Pettigrew *et al* point out, however, that a positive culture for training is not itself sufficient. In addition, structures are required to translate the training philosophy into active training plans for individuals, otherwise a breakdown will develop between good intentions and their implementation. In his survey, Useem notes two company characteristics related to a company's management culture, which shape corporate education and training practices. These are: (1) the company's perceived innovativeness in human resource practices, and (2) its management resistance to change in human resource practices. He found that firms with innovative and less resistant management cultures invest more in the training of their main-line workers and also experience fewer problems in recruitment. He states, "if a better trained workforce is, or ought to be, a long-term company objective, the results indicate that an important facilitating change would be to enhance the value that management places on human resource strategies and innovations." (p.430). This reaffirms the important need for senior management to demonstrate a high level of commitment to training and development. Consequently, a major step in achieving an increased allocation of resources to training and development activities within industry and commerce is one which tackles the beliefs of top management. From within the organisation, those involved in training and development activities should be able to demonstrate to senior management the positive results and relevance of training. Linking training and development to corporate objectives will assist this process. From outside the organisation there is a need for state influence, through institutional structures, to encourage training and development activities at the organisation level.

The learning organisation

The concept of a learning organisation, though questionably anthropomorphic, is a captivating idea which has drawn a great deal of interest recently in the management literature. In some cases, as Garvin[26] notes, "… discussions of learning organisations have often been reverential and Utopian, filled with near mystical terminology". Nevertheless, the probable reasons for interest in this area relate to rapid changes in such areas as technological development, heightened worldwide competition and changes due to national and international political events, requiring organisations to develop a capacity for continuous improvement to remain competitive. From a training and development perspective, to develop and institutionalise organisational learning requires the creation of a culture of continuous learning for all employees. However, this in itself is probably insufficient, since its implementation and maintenance, like training itself, requires structures to translate the culture into policies and programmes. As in many similar areas relating to organisational development and organisational change, there is much written in terms of the qualities of the learning organisation[27, 28], but information relating to its practical achievement is less clear. For example, Garvin states, "learning organisations are skilled at five main activities: systematic problem solving, experimentation with new approaches, learning from their own experience and past history, learning from the experiences and best practices of others, and transferring knowledge quickly and efficiently throughout the organisation."

Some indications of factors impinging on these activities are given, but the problem of how to achieve them is less clear. Perhaps however, because of the wide range of differences between companies, prescriptive information for their achievement is impossible. Individual companies may need individual structures and mechanisms to develop and implement a culture of continuous learning. Again, however, as for the implementation and maintenance of training and development activity, senior management commitment will be a critical factor.

Training and Development within Human Resource Management

The Training Department has usually been viewed as an integral part of the organisation's human resource function. However, in small organisations, where no human resource specialist exists, training will be the responsibility of the owner. In medium and large organisations, however, with specialisation of functions occurring, the training function will exist as part of the human resource development area.

The argument for the close integration of training within Human Resource Management rests on the need to closely interrelate the various activities of recruitment, selection, development and training.

However, this does not necessarily require the training specialist to report either to the Personnel Manager or the human resource specialist. Alternatives include reporting to the Chief Executive or to a senior line manager. In areas where the impact of training or not training shows up rapidly, as in the service sectors, the Chief Executive may take a personal interest which requires the training specialist to report directly to him or her. This also serves to provide additional status to training.

Senior line managers may be responsible for training in those organisations where emphasis on training is given to a particular category of employees, such as sales. If training is restricted in this way, then the training personnel will usually report to the Sales Manager. This approach leads to the training being closely related to the needs of the department.

However, an important advantage in closely coordinating training and other human resource activities is that it results in more appropriate training, based on a coherent policy of Human Resource Management.

The training and development function

The training function can be seen to have two roles. There is a *reactive* role in which the training department provides the necessary expertise or skill in response to requests from line managers and supervisors. In this sense it is a service function, providing managers with support to help them fulfil their needs for an effectively trained workforce. The second role is a *proactive* one, in which the training specialists are involved in suggesting and, where necessary, implementing training, to fulfil not only short-term organisational needs but also longer-term corporate plans and strategies.

The reactive role stems from the responsibilities of the line managers and supervisors for the training and development of their staff. Each manager and supervisor is usually accountable to senior management for the performance of his or her staff. As a result they must bear the responsibility of identifying the training and development needs of their subordinates. In addition, the line managers will need to allocate time and resources for training, where resources may include space and equipment for internal courses. Finally, managers and supervisors should be responsible for the evaluation of the results of training in terms of assessing how their trainees subsequently perform in their job. In this situation, training is viewed as the responsibility of the managers and supervisors, with the training specialist performing the reactive role of assisting managers and supervisors in clarifying training needs, developing training courses and evaluating their success.

Having noted that, however, there are many managers who do not see training as their responsibility, not because of any logical or managerial reason, but largely because they have not considered training as a major influence on the achievement of their subordinates in organisational terms. The human resource management specialist may need to persuade line management of this – that basically training is their responsibility and the training function is there to advise and provide specialist assistance. Where the responsibility for training has been delegated to branch or division managers, with support from senior personnel and training specialists, it can be relatively easily established. One problem may arise, however. Line managers are often subject to relatively short-term objectives linked to productivity and profitability. This may discourage them from improving or upgrading their subordinates' skills through training, because they may not achieve output targets if personnel are off the job. To avoid this, devolved responsibility for training must be backed by senior management and the means to overcome the budgetary and time restraints must be provided.

Where training and human resource development is seen as a major source of investment by senior management, the proactive role of the training function will be easier to implement. For this proactive role, the training specialist needs to be involved at board level during the development of the organisational objectives; that is, its present and future needs derived from some form of strategic review. However, this has seldom occurred although, hopefully, the trend towards viewing training and development of all levels of employee, besides management, as a board level topic, will increase and add impetus to this involvement.

Training benefits and costs

It was noted earlier that many organisations perceive training expenditure as an overhead rather than as an investment. However, if training is to be viewed as an investment, it must lead to some identifiable return, like any other sort of investment. Consequently, what an organisation needs to know is, what are the benefits of systematic training and at what costs? It is difficult to identify *precisely* the outcomes from training. Training is one ingredient in the performance mix which is influenced by motivation, job design, equipment design, company policy, supervision and so on, as well as skill. Nevertheless, a systematic approach to training can achieve or influence the following:

- The speed of learning. Systematic training should achieve reduced learning time and higher skill levels, thereby reducing learning costs.

- Improved performance of existing employees. Job incumbents can, through training, up-date and improve their work performance. This should result in increased productivity through increased working speed, reduction in working errors, or both.

- Decreased supervision. A well-trained workforce should require less supervision and allow increased delegation. This releases management time for planning, organising and development activities.

- A more flexible workforce. Training can increase the range of skills of its employees so that, where acceptable, employees can cover for absent or sick colleagues or rotate jobs for various purposes, including that of increasing motivation levels.

- To ensure for succession. To prepare people within the organisation to fulfil its future needs for supervisory and managerial succession at all levels. This can influence turnover, since employees are less likely to leave if they believe that promotional opportunities are available.

- Improved company morale. An organisation which views training as an essential ingredient in caring for, developing and retaining its employees is likely to be one with high morale. It is also more likely to be receptive to change, resulting in increased flexibility in response to external situations.

To these may be added individual factors, such as self-fulfilment in achieving higher levels of skill, which will lead to increased self-esteem and greater job satisfaction. Also, at the national level, a country's international competitiveness and economic performance is significantly influenced by its skilled workforce and, as a result, its standard of living.

However, it must be remembered that although an organisation's positive approach to training can influence many of these factors, it cannot compensate for inadequate job design or poor supervisory and managerial practices leading to low motivation and morale.

It is relatively easy to measure the *costs* of providing training, but the problem, for which there exists no simple formula, is the measurement of the *financial outcome* of training to the organisation. This latter requires a cost analysis of some sort which attempts to estimate the effects of training on a company's profit statement. The costing of the provision of training involves calculating both fixed and variable costs. Fixed costs involve such things as capital and running costs of maintaining a training centre; the cost of the training personnel and equipment costs. Variable costs will be influenced by the number of courses run; equipment and materials used on a course; visiting speakers and so on. One could also include in the latter any costs incurred due to employees being non-productive during the period of their training, either through having to replace them or through lost production.

Once the costs have been determined, the problem is how to measure the economic results of the training to the organisation. In some situations, at the operator level, training costs can be compared with increases in productivity. For example, Jones and Moxham[29], in assessing the results of a new training system on sewing machinist skills, showed that the training resulted in:

(a) reduced training time to achieve a set standard (from 17 to 7 weeks);
(b) reduced labour turnover (from 70 to 30%); and
(c) increased output of about 30%.

A cost-benefit analysis can then be used to convert this into a financial statement.

The effects of training cannot always be so precisely identified, however, especially at the supervisory and managerial levels. Improving a manager's skills in staff development techniques would be seen as having longer-term rather than short-term results. In the longer-term, for example, it may be influential in reducing turnover, improving morale and reducing costs for management succession. In order to produce a cost-benefit analysis, however, what time scale do we choose, and on what do we base our 'guesstimates' relating to the monetary values of the outcomes? Nevertheless, if the investment value of training is to be demonstrated, estimates of the benefits in cost terms will be necessary. One needs to treat the figures with care, however. Figures, whether based on real or estimated outcomes, are often used out of context as 'hard facts'. It should be remembered that estimates are approximations and not certainties.

Earlier, in looking at the benefits of training, it was noted that organisations are not the only beneficiaries of planned training. In addition, benefits accrue to the individual and to the nation. This was earlier recognised in that, historically, individuals paid for their apprenticeships or, more recently, received low wages whilst serving them. Also recently, national funds have been available as an impetus to training. The Institute of Personnel Management proposed that learning costs should be shared by its beneficiaries in appropriate proportions, although without any real guidelines as to how this was to be calculated. Nevertheless, few would disagree with the proposition of shared costs. Since, however, employers are intimately concerned with profit, national pressure and incentives are needed to encourage them to train more. Because of the difficulties which can occur in carrying out cost-benefit analyses, the value of training as an investment rather than as an overhead may not always become apparent, especially if some of the returns on investment are long-term rather than short-term. Because of this, some form of motivation for training involvement needs to be stimulated at the national level.

We shall discuss additional approaches to the evaluation of training in a later section.

The training process

Training can, and occasionally does, develop without any real attempt either to establish whether the content is appropriate to the needs of the job holder, or whether the training methods are effective for learning that content. Frequently training, especially at the managerial level, is not based on an assessment of training needs. Training may be implemented because it is thought to be a 'good thing' or fashionable. Sensitivity, or 'T-group' training during the late 1960s and early 1970s was in this category.

Such 'fashions' will benefit some managers, by improving their communication skills and general understanding of people. However, it is rather like a shot-gun approach to target shooting. Inevitably some of the lead pellets will hit the target but a large number will miss. Even where training appears relevant to fulfil a perceived need, its success is frequently assessed on the basis of how much the participants enjoyed it, without any attempt being made to see whether it has actually brought about any real change in the employee's job behaviour. In an attempt to avoid or minimise such situations, it is essential to implement a systematic approach to training course development, the aims of which are:

- To increase the effectiveness of training by reducing learning time to achieve specified performance levels.
- To improve the job performance levels of present employees.
- To ensure for succession. That is, to prepare people within the organisation to fulfil its future needs for skilled manpower.

A Systematic Approach to Training

A systematic approach to training is one which is planned specifically to meet defined training objectives. This does not mean it is any more elaborate or expensive than unsystematic training. On the contrary, planned training is more likely to be cost-effective and because it is systematic it is more likely to be comprehensible to non-specialists and, as a result, to gain more commitment.

A systematic approach involves three major phases (Figure 8.1 below):

1. The assessment phase, which focuses attention on the training needs and training objectives of the organisation.
2. The training development phase, which is concerned with how the training objectives are to be achieved.
3. The evaluation phase, which attempts to answer two questions. The first is, "how far have we achieved our original training objectives?", and the second, "how valid were our original training objectives for the needs of the organisation?".

Each of these three phases can be further sub-divided as illustrated below in Figure 8.2.

1. The Assessment Phase

The assessment phase focuses attention on the training needs of the organisation, from which the objectives of training can be specified. It involves two main components: the identification of training needs and the specification of training objectives. Each will be looked at separately.

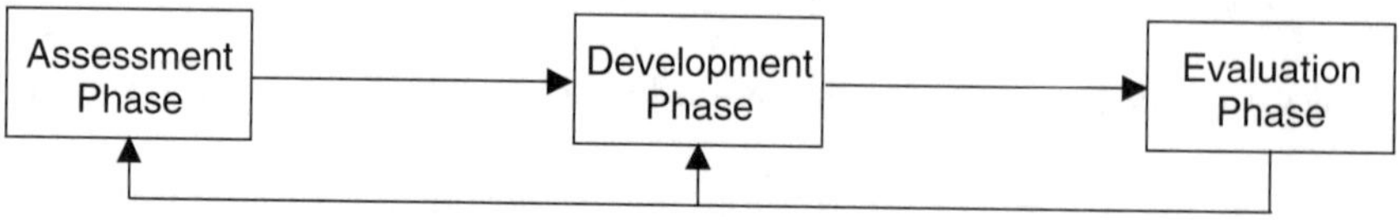

Figure 8.1 The Three Phaces of a Systematic Approach to Training.

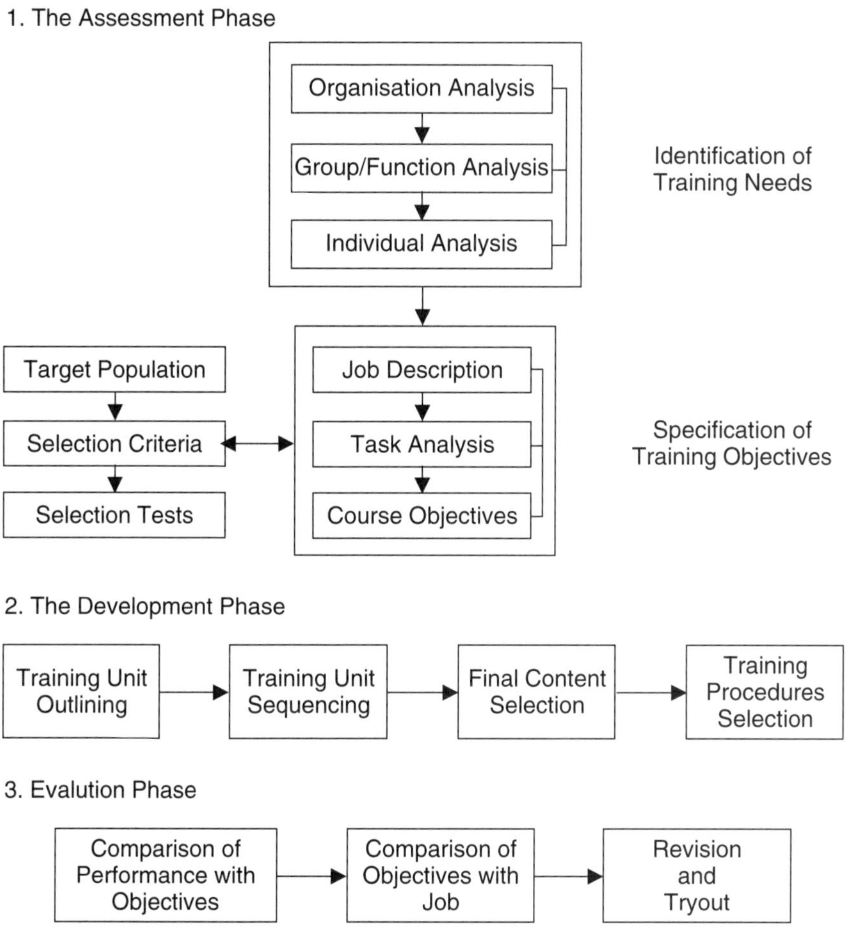

Figure 8.2 The Components of a Systematic Approach to Training.

The identification of training needs. Before the objectives and content of training can be specified, what training needs to be done, and where, should be identified. That is, the organisation must look at what is presently happening and what should or could be happening. Any differences between the two may give some indication of training needs. Of course it should be remembered that training is not the only influence on organisational success. Selection procedures, work design, resources and company policies concerning supervisory practices and payment systems, amongst others, can all influence organisational success. It is important to distinguish between the various causes of any discrepancies between actual and desired situations, otherwise incorrect solutions will occur that can create negative attitudes to training. Anecdotal evidence exists of many 'failed' training programmes where, in most of these cases, training was not the best approach to solve the stated problem. For example, low productivity being related to lack of skill when the reward structure, at worst, penalises individual effort or, at best, fails to reward it (see Chapter 6 on motivation). Another area involves situations in which, despite successful training, the newly learned skills cannot be applied on the job (for example, training supervisors in participation techniques which cannot be applied subsequently because of the nature of the organisation and expected role of the supervisor). A thorough training needs analysis may then highlight problems outside the training area which need to be solved before considering what training may additionally be required.

Training analysis can be carried out at three levels: the organisational level, the group/function level and the individual level. The three levels are interconnected and include some overlap. Analysis at the organisational level will often reveal training needs at the group level, which in turn will lead to training requirements for individuals. Similarly, an analysis at the individual level, for example poor sales performance, may indicate, at the group level, production problems of poor quality control, or at the organisational level, a product which is obsolescent, indicating a need for innovation.

An *organisation analysis* sets out to determine where, within the organisation as a whole, any training emphasis is required. Since organisations have limited resources, all organisational problems cannot normally be dealt with simultaneously. Consequently, one aspect of the organisational analysis is to determine priority, i.e. tackling those problems first, whose solution would provide the greatest organisational benefit. It is important in carrying out the analysis to state any deficiencies or problems as problems, rather than as perceived solutions. There is a tendency for managers to state organisational performance problems in terms of their solutions. For example, a reduction in sales might be expressed as 'a need to retrain our salesmen in more aggressive techniques'. That may be a correct solution but, on the other hand, it could be a problem of pricing policy, of an obsolescent product, or of poor quality. By stating the solution, further analysis or discussion is cut short. Providing training to achieve that solution may not eliminate the problem and a lot of money may be wasted in the process.

The importance and frequency of organisation analyses will be influenced by the context in which a company operates. The context can be seen as a continuum. At one end, organisations exist in a rapidly changing market, affected by frequent changes in technology, scientific discoveries or market conditions, for example in the areas of consumer electronics and computers. At the other end, organisations operate in a relatively stable commercial or technological environment, such as the banking or furniture manufacturing areas. The need for frequent analyses and the importance of those will be greater for organisational success in the former case than in the latter.

The contents of organisational analyses overlap with procedures which should normally be covered by the corporate planning and strategic review processes. These include reviews of organisational goals and objectives, of the company's strengths and weaknesses and of its human resource plans and skills inventory. Personnel records relating to strikes, turnover, absenteeism, accidents, productivity, customer complaints, and so on, may also be indicators of corporate or strategic problems. Consequently, the organisation analysis will probably involve discussion at board level and should include senior management from all the major functional areas, marketing, production, finance, etc.

The important objective of the organisational analysis is to decide whether the company is meeting its stated objectives. If it is not, the reasons for failure should be sought and the extent to which they can be influenced by training determined.

The *group* or *function analysis* involves looking at particular departments, functional areas or groups of people, to assess whether any of these require training. For example, sales training, training in production planning, training for computerisation in the wages and salaries department, or interpersonal skills training for middle managers, may all be possible outcomes from a group or function analysis. Here the achievement of departmental or functional goals is the expected outcome, including those relating to future changes in those areas. The latter includes not only changes due to technical or technological innovations and their implementation, such as the introduction of computers into production planning, but also personnel changes due to promotion and succession requirements. Indicators which may trigger a group or function analysis might include such factors as failure to achieve set objectives, observed shortages of expertise and skill, an ageing work group, or morale factors such as high turnover or absenteeism. However, as training plans are generally reviewed on an annual basis for budgetary reasons, the analysis at this level is likely to be reviewed annually.

Individual need for training, as well as being revealed by the previous two levels of analysis, can be assessed at the *individual level.* Indicators at this level might include: failure to achieve standard output, or any lack of success in achieving expected targets or, in the case of managers and supervisors, poor group maintenance, low morale, expressed dissatisfaction and high turnover. Besides production figures and other forms of direct information, such as complaints, information at the individual level can be obtained through performance review and development interviews. Potential reviews will provide information relating to succession planning and the needs of particular individuals for this.

Two types of approach to analysing training needs are probably apparent from the previous discussion. Firstly, the *General Survey* in which training needs are identified, usually through discussion between managers and supervisors. Problems which can provide a stimulus for discussion include failure to achieve organisational objectives or departmental targets. Changing operating conditions and changes in employee profiles may be other factors.

Although these surveys are usually verbal, through discussion or interview, they need not be and questionnaires can be developed to do much of the basic information gathering.

The advantage of some sort of general survey is that all, or most, managers and supervisors are being involved in the process of training from the beginning, with the probable result that they are more likely to be both cooperative and supportive of future training programmes.

The second type of information gathering source relating to training needs is the interview; either the performance review to assess individual performance, or the potential review to consider potential for promotion. It is important not to do both in the same interview for reasons discussed in Chapter 10.

The third method not previously mentioned in this chapter, although it is also relevant to selection processes (see Chapter 3), is the use of job description and task analysis techniques to explore both the detailed requirements of a job and the knowledge and skills required to achieve success in the job. The latter analysis will lead to a description of training requirements. Any discrepancy between these and the skills of the job holder will suggest the training needs of the individual.

From the research evidence available, it appears that a systematic analysis of training needs is seldom done. Without such an approach, however, it will be difficult for companies to integrate their training into their present and future corporate plans and business strategies. Training based on a sound analysis of needs is more likely to be valid and soundly based. It is therefore one of the most important stages in training course development.

Specifying training objectives. In some cases, the specification of training needs may describe the required behaviour change. However, this will usually be a rather general form such as, 'be able to carry out an appraisal interview', or 'improving typing skills', or 'be more effective in handling difficult patients'. Before developing the training programme, however, we need to know what the trainees already know and can do, and what they will need to know and be able to do at the end of the course. The difference between these two will determine the objectives and content of training. This applies equally to employees already in post and to those about to be hired. In the latter case, it is important to note that we can set our selection criteria at whatever standard we wish, assuming that we will be able to attract applicants. The more stringent our requirements, in skill and knowledge terms, the less training we will need to do. The level at which we set our selection criteria may depend upon what group of people we want or can realistically attract, that is, upon our target population. If no pool of people exists with the skills we require, or we would have difficulty attracting people with those skills, our target population may be school-leavers. If that is so, we might want only those with a GCSE pass at grade C in mathematics, in which case this would become part of our selection criteria. In the case of engineering apprentices this might enable us to reduce the amount of mathematics teaching required in the training course. At this stage there is an interplay between selection and training. Similarly, as a result of our assessment of training needs, we may realistically say that the probability of selecting people to carry out the job is low. In this case, we may decide to redesign the job in order to increase our chances of recruiting people who will successfully carry out the various tasks.

So, as a result of our assessment of training needs, we will be in a better position to decide whether or not training will be the best solution to achieve those needs. These decisions will influence our objective setting.

Assuming that we decide to go ahead with training and we know what the content of training will be, we need to specify the objectives. In specifying training objectives it is important to ensure that, wherever possible, they should be *observable* and *measurable*.[30] As far as possible, training objectives should state in the necessary detail:

- what the trainee will be able to do as a result of training;
- the normal operating conditions in which the behaviour will occur; and
- the standard of acceptable performance against which the trainees' behaviour is to be judged.

An objective which states that, 'at the end of the training course a manager will understand the process of communication' is inadequate. It fails to fulfil any of the three criteria. It may be adequate as a starting point for the design of training as a basis for discussion about the proposed content, but even then the use of the word 'understand' can be misleading. Will the manager in 'understanding' need to be able to design a communication system, or use one, or describe how it operates or, more likely, be able to communicate effectively to ensure that messages are received and acted upon in the way intended by the communicator? Consequently, the use of words such as 'know', 'understand' or 'appreciate' lacks precision. Instead, words such as 'solve', 'identify', 'perform' etc should be used.

The process leading to the specification of objectives will usually start with a job description. A job description will probably be held in personnel records. It is a narrative statement mainly describing the content of the job; any measures of performance, the conditions under which the work is done, and the position of the job holder in the organisational hierarchy. However, it does not provide details about the observable behaviour involved in doing the job. To achieve this, the job description is broken down into specific tasks, duties and responsibilities. These are then analysed to determine the knowledge, skills and, where appropriate, attitudes needed. This latter process is called task analysis. (It is worth noting that there is no single acceptable title for this analysis and it is referred to by names other than task analysis, such as job analysis and job specification).

The training objectives are then derived by comparing what the job requires in terms of skills knowledge and attitudes with the trainees' present attributes. For new recruits the total content of the task analysis will probably form the basis of the objectives, whereas for more experienced individuals this will be less so.

Specifying training objectives can be a time-consuming and difficult process. However it has two outstanding advantages. The first relates to the training itself. If a copy of the training objectives is given to the trainee prior to it, the total effectiveness of training will be enhanced. Secondly, well written objectives based on the three criteria noted earlier in this section will enhance and simplify the process of evaluation.

2. The Development Phase

Whereas the assessment phase is concerned with *what* one intends to achieve through training, the development phase is concerned with *how* one intends to achieve it. It involves taking the information generated through the previous analysis as the content and breaking it down into training units. These units should then be sequenced in such a way that learning is enhanced by ensuring some sort of logical order of content. That is, that each piece of provided information or skill occurs at the right time, so that it can be easily integrated with previous learning.[31]

When the content has been decided, the training techniques to be used will need to be selected. Should one use simulators, or real practice? How much lecturing content should there be, or would seminars be preferable? Would learning in groups, compared to setting individual tasks, reduce learning time? There are numerous training techniques and the final choice will depend on the skill to be learned, the cost of the different procedures (for example, simulation can be expensive, but so can real practice on sophisticated machines easily broken by trainees) and, of course, on what is available.

Other decisions to be taken by the trainer include *where* the training will take place, and *when* it will take place. In general, training can be carried out on the job, off-the-job or, as in the case of most apprenticeship training, both on- and off-the-job. On-the-job training involves instruction given usually by the employee's supervisor or a specially selected experienced employee. Most training is performed on the job. Techniques used include demonstration – commonly called 'sitting next to Nellie' – in which the trainee watches or is told how to carry out a task and then given a chance to do it; coaching, similar to demonstration and usually involving more guidance and counselling, and planned experience whereby, over a period of time, the trainee experiences doing different jobs in a planned way to develop the necessary skills through job assignments and problem-solving. Planned experience can involve the use of programmed instruction and computer assisted instruction. These techniques usually combine learning both on- and off-the-job by providing basic information regarding functioning, followed by on-the-job exercises to practise control. Off-the-job techniques are usually simulation exercises. They include equipment simulation (e.g. flight simulators) and situational simulations (e.g. business games, case studies and role plays). An important factor in off-the-job training is how well the skills learned in simulated situations transfer to on-the-job performance. For equipment simulation, usually the closer the correspondence between the simulator and actual equipment the greater the transfer. For non-technical skills such as problem-solving, interviewing and supervisory skills, an additional factor, that of a supportive organisational climate, can influence transfer to the job. Each approach has its value and their advantages and disadvantages must be considered in the light of the course content and the needs of the trainee. Factors which can impinge on the decision might include the safety of the trainee (the cost of breakdown due to incompetent control on both the organisation and on other employees) and the safety of others, such as the general public. Even where such issues are not relevant, in-company on-the-job training will only be the answer when sufficient time can be allocated for an instructor to provide the necessary amount of time and individual attention to the trainee, especially in the early stages of learning.

The issue of when training should occur depends on the status of the trainee. For new recruits, it will usually be immediately after recruitment in most cases. However, for those already in post, there is a need to consider when the training will best integrate with their work, with other training needs, and with the output or productivity needs of their departments.

A final point worth mentioning relates to the motivation of the trainees. New employees presenting themselves for training will exhibit varying levels of enthusiasm, ranging from a high level following a deliberate choice of jobs, to perhaps reluctance, where little or no choice has been involved. In any event, they will have already formed initial attitudes towards their training. Their early experiences on the training programme may or may not fulfil their early anticipations and as training progresses they will develop fresh attitudes not only about their chosen job, but also about the organisation they have joined. The way in which training is conducted, the behaviour of the instructors and other company personnel and the facilities provided, all offer cues from which the trainees will formulate their attitudes and motivation towards the company, their chosen job and their training. Motivation is also an important factor in training and retraining present employees. Their attitudes towards the company can be enhanced or damaged by the organisation's approach to training, which in turn can influence the success or failure of a training course. There is abundant anecdotal, as well as some research evidence, to indicate that training programmes can fail, whatever their technical merit, if they are autocratically developed and implemented. There is thus a strong need to involve people at all levels to solicit information and advice and to keep people informed of progress.

3. The Evaluation Phase

The final phase in any systematic approach to training is the evaluation phase. It is necessary for at least three reasons.

First, evaluation indicates the overall effectiveness of training in achieving what it set out to achieve, that is, whether it met its set objectives. This provides feedback for the trainers and may indicate areas for improving future training.

Second, evaluation information provides data which can be presented to senior managers, regarding the effectiveness of the training department's operations. From this, the senior managers can make decisions regarding the adoption and support of training activities. If employers and senior managers are to believe in the value of training and its relationships to organisational success, training operations should be justifiable in cost-effectiveness terms and evaluating training will provide a basis for this.

Third, the evaluation process can influence the trainees themselves. Letting trainees know that evaluation will occur is likely to influence their approach to training and their behaviour during training, especially if their success in learning the content will have some influence on their future positions within the company. As noted earlier, providing trainees with a set of training objectives will help them know what they need to learn, and giving them feedback on their progress is likely to have a motivational effect on their learning. Also, giving trainees an opportunity to comment upon the content of training and the techniques used may enhance their future attitudes both towards further training and the company itself.

This third point indicates that evaluation exercises will affect the nature of the situation. Observing and measuring trainees' behaviour will affect the behaviour if the trainees are aware of it. Asking trainees about their reactions to the course will polarise their thoughts and testing their learning will influence their efforts.

Having noted these three organisational advantages, evidence tends to indicate that evaluation is not given sufficient emphasis by companies and little notice is taken of the results. The evaluation that does take place is usually conservative and inaccurate. It is conservative because trainers are usually concerned about the ratings they receive at the end of a programme of training, since they could reflect badly on themselves and their efforts. Understandably they want good ratings irrespective of the effect of the programme on the trainees' learning. The ratings can be inaccurate because the type of evaluation, usually some form of questionnaire, is given to trainees who are usually on an end of course 'high'. They are therefore less likely to consider carefully the effect of the training on their future organisational behaviour. Also, the trainees themselves may be wary of making negative comments for fear of some form of retribution. As a result, they are more likely to criticise contextual factors like accommodation, organisation or conditions rather than the content and techniques of the training or company training policy. These factors negate the function of evaluation for the organisation, which is to ensure relevant training, to improve, where possible, the professional skills of trainers, and to provide senior management with information regarding the role of training in the corporate strategy of the organisation.

Following the question 'Why evaluate?' comes the question 'How to evaluate?'. As a feedback process it has three parts (Figure 8.3 below):

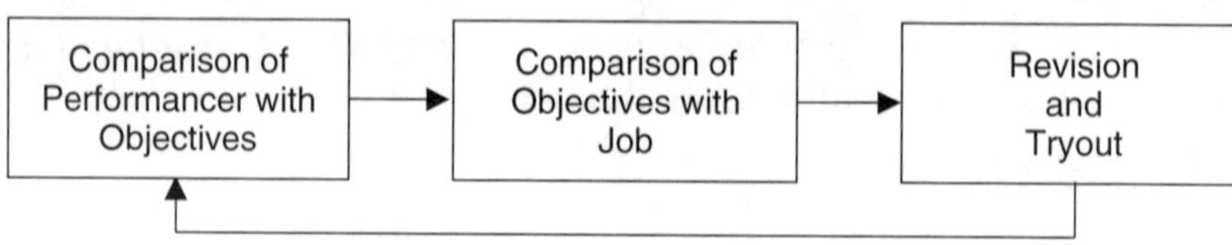

Figure 8.3. The Three Components of Evaluation.

In comparing what trainees can do differently as a result of the programme, with its objectives, trainers can assess how successful the training has been in achieving what it set out to achieve. This is termed 'internal validation'.

However, answering this question does not indicate the relevance of training to the organisation. If a thorough analysis of training needs has been carried out prior to the development of the training programme, and the objectives have been realistically based on those needs, it is likely that the training will be relevant. There are, however, examples of training having a zero or negative effect on job performance. For example, sales staff who, as a result of training courses, subsequently perform no better or marginally worse. To check this, it is necessary to measure subsequent job performance to assess whether the training has achieved the organisational needs for more skilled operatives, better sales people, or more effective managers. This has been termed 'external validation'. Were the training objectives realistically based on training needs and did training fulfil them? Validation is important because some overall measure of evaluation, such as an increase in profit or productivity, may be caused by other factors, such as changes in pay policy, supervisory practices, improved machinery or a change in market conditions. The term 'validation' is becoming less used and it is generally assumed under the broad umbrella of 'evaluation'. Nevertheless, the *processes* of validation must be performed if evaluation is to have any value.

As a result of validation and evaluation, indicators will emerge relating to training effectiveness. As a result, the content may need revision and the whole process of evaluation repeated. It should be seen therefore as a continuous process and not a single 'one-off' event.

The previous section implied that evaluation can occur at different points. The training literature usually distinguishes four *levels of evaluation.* These are the reactions level, the learning level, the job behaviour level and the organisational level.

The *reactions level* refers to the trainees' perception, opinions and evaluation of the training content and methods used and their feelings about the training staff and their presentation and behaviour. This information is usually collected by questionnaire, although interviews of selected trainees can also be used for depth of information. The information gained can provide a general view of the impact of the programme and also more particular information, where necessary, such as a comparison of its effect on younger, as compared to older, trainees, male and female, or any other distinguishing features between groups of trainees. Information can also be collected at different points in time. It may be that a trainee's view of the programme can change due to the events that occur over time. It has been noted already that an end of course 'high' usually occurs and trainees' reactions may change subsequently. It will be useful to check this by carrying out the evaluation at two points in time: immediately after training has finished and, subsequently, perhaps three to six months later.

Assessment at the *learning level* is concerned with measuring the extent to which trainees have learned the content of training – its laid down objectives. It may be related to a change in an individual's knowledge, skills or attitude. The assessment technique will depend upon what is being assessed. Tests of attitude will require numbered scales or ranking of importance. For knowledge, essay questions, multiple choice or 'true/false' questionnaires can be used. Skill learning, on the other hand, will require some form of performance measures, such as ability to handle difficult customers or perform a disciplinary or appraisal interview.

Again, tests can be performed at different periods of time, in this case usually to test retention of the learning. As a result of these, especially for little practised skills or techniques, it may be necessary to provide refresher courses.

It is expected that learning which occurs on a training course will be transferred to the work situation. For various reasons this may not always be the case and evaluation at the *job behaviour level* may indicate the source of the inhibitory factor. For operator tasks it may be easier to do this. Lack of transfer may well point to inadequate training content – poor teaching, low fidelity simulation or insufficient practice. However, for social, as in managerial and supervisor training, the reasons for poor transfer may be more difficult to pinpoint. Other non-training features may be influential here, such as the lack of reward or even negative consequences occurring as a result of implementation. A poor supportive climate may make implementation difficult.

Information relating to on-the-job behaviour changes can be achieved through various techniques, the most common being managerial and supervisory rating. However, others which could be used in the right organisational climate include rating by peers or subordinates. At the operator level, simple output figures may be sufficient, providing account is taken of any abnormal operating conditions which may be influencing productivity or output at the time the assessment occurs. Whatever form of assessment is used it is important that it should occur some time after the end of the training programme to allow for any adjustment period. This is particularly important when the training has occurred off-the-job. A 'sleeper effect' or time lag can occur between the trainees' learning and their demonstration of it.

Evaluation at the *organisation level* is an attempt to assess the effects of training on the overall functioning of the organisation. This can be demonstrated in numerous ways and some attempt to predict these should be made during the design of the programme. Indicators can include increased productivity, improved quality, reduced learning time and therefore costs, reduction in damage or errors, and those related to personnel criteria such as reduced turnover and absenteeism and improved cooperation.

These four levels can be seen to form a hierarchy, or continuum of effect. Training can fail at any of these levels. For instance, trainees may react well but fail to learn, or they may learn well but be unable to apply the learning. They may behave differently but without any effect on other people or the organisation. Consequently, evaluation should occur at all levels. If the job behaviour or organisational level is ignored we may be measuring only superficial changes, whereas if we fail to evaluate at the reactions or learning level, any changes that occur cannot be safely ascribed to training.

However, two major criteria for deciding the extent of evaluation are the cost of the evaluation process and the usefulness of the results. For example, a simple end of course questionnaire is relatively cheap but produces only low quality information, whereas quantitative data collected at all levels, though of great value relating to information gleaned, will be expensive in terms of costs and time.

The thoroughness and cost of the evaluation process will be influenced by the thoroughness with which the previous two phases have been carried out. The more thorough the assessment and development phases, the more observable and measurable will be the results and the more precise and simple will be the evaluation process.

The Design of Evaluation Procedures

A factor which may be apparent from the previous section is that a continuum of evaluation criteria exists, relating to the certainty of the inferred influence of a training programme on subsequent work performance. That is, we can assume a causal relationship between training and improved individual or organisational performance. Or we can assume an inferred relationship but be uncertain whether other factors, such as some form of better working conditions or improved supervisory practices, have made a contributory influence to the improvement in performance. The extent to which we can assume causality depends upon the design of our evaluation procedures.

In order to make causal inferences it is necessary to measure the knowledge, skill or attitude level both before and after training. In technical jargon, there is a need to use both pre and post-tests. There is also a need to use control groups, that is, groups of people of similar age, experience etc who do not experience the training at all or who only experience part of it. This helps to ensure that any differences which occur in performance cannot be ascribed to other variables which subsequently might affect work performance. However, this process is rarely carried out. The methodology requires a minimum number of people for many of the more sophisticated experimental designs. Rarely are the necessary number of trainees available.

Carefully designed evaluation procedures should not be

discouraged however and, whenever possible, the more sophisticated experimental designs should be used. Where this is not possible, it is still essential to collect data of some sort. Despite the view that simple pre-test/post-test designs are unacceptable because causality cannot be inferred, they do provide data which can help both to evaluate present courses and improve future ones.[32] Even a post-test on its own can provide data, albeit at a low level of sophistication, which can help course assessment. If simple designs such as the pre-test/post-test or post-test only are used, using the post-test at two points in time, such as immediately after the course and six months later, will enhance the value of the data collected.

A final factor which can make the design of evaluation procedures more or less easy is the sophistication of the measures which can be taken. For example, although at the operator level output changes may be measurable by the number of units produced, at the supervisory or managerial level it may be very difficult to enumerate changes in, for example, interviewing skills or participative management techniques. In these latter cases the performance changes may be only assessments by self, superiors, peers or, in rare cases, subordinates.

It is worth stressing that some data is better than none, but the more sophisticated the data the more sophisticated the inferences that can be made. Evaluation is an essential procedure, not only as a feedback device for improving training courses and their outcomes, but also because the information is essential to justify the value of the training department activities to senior managers and the organisation as a whole.

Conclusion

An organisation's employees are among the most important and expensive assets and their skills are essential for its success. Nevertheless, in many organisations, there is widespread ignorance among top management of their own training investment. In some companies it is not seen as a key element in the corporate strategy and the link between training and profits is not always recognised. As a result, training tends to have a relatively low status. To overcome some of these problems, training must be seen as an investment for an organisation and, as such, become of concern at board level.

To help this, training managers must themselves become more effective both at a reactive and proactive level. Close integration of training with human resource management policy is one requirement. Nevertheless, the basic factor which will improve the status of training is its proven success in creating a more skilled workforce which enhances the success of the organisation.

Training staff must prove the value of their training activities to the organisation and this is only likely if the training they provide is systematically developed, implemented and evaluated.

References

1. G.P. Latham and S.R. Crandall (1991) 'Organizational and Social Factors', in J.E. Morrison (ed), *Training for Performance: Principles of Applied Human Learning*, John Wiley & Sons Ltd.

2. G.F. Brown and A.R. Read (1984) 'Personnel and Training Policies – Some Lessons for Western Companies', *Long Range Planning*, Vol 17, No 2, pp 48–57.

3. D.E. Hussey (1985) 'Implementing Corporate Strategy: Using Management Education and Training', *Long Range Planning*, Vol 18, No 5, pp 28–37.

4. R. Layard, K. Mayhew and G. Owen (1994) 'Why We Need a Training Reform Act', in R. Layard, K. Mayhew and G. Owen

(eds) *Britain's Training Deficit: The Centre for Economic Performance Report*, Avebury, Ashgate Publishing Limited, Aldershot.

5. For information on and a comparison of different countries' approaches to education and training , see:
D. Finegold and C. Crouch (1994) 'A Comparison of National Institutions', in R. Layard, K. Mayhew and G. Owen (eds) *Britain's Training Deficit: The Centre for Economic Performance Report*, Avebury, Ashgate Publishing Limited, Aldershot.

6. T.J. Peters and R. Waterman (1982) *In Search of Excellence*, Harper and Row, New York.

7. W. Goldsmith and D. Clutterbuck (1984) *The Winning Streak*, Weidenfeld and Nicholson, London.

8. P. Galagan (1986) 'Focus on Results at Motorola', *Training and Development Journal*, May, pp 43–47.

9. P. Galagan (1993) 'Training Keeps the Cutting Edge Sharp for the Andersen Companies', *Training and Development Journal,* January, pp 30–35.

10. Deloitte, Haskins and Sells (1987) 'British Employers' Training Costs', *Works Management Journal*, August, pp 6–9.

11. A. Daly, D. Hitchens and K. Wagner (1985) 'Productivity, Machinery and Skills in a Sample of British and German Manufacturing Plants', *National Institute Economic Review*, February, pp 48–61.

12. H. Steedman and K. Wagner (1987) 'A Second Look at Productivity, Machinery and Skills in Britain and Germany', *National Institute Economic Review*, November, pp 84–95.

13. H. Steedman and K. Wagner (1989) 'Productivity, Machinery and Skills: Clothing Manufacture in Britain and Germany',

National Institute Economic Review, May, pp 40–57.

14. M. Killingly (1989) 'Manpower 2000: Critical to the Future of Engineering', Conference Proceedings, Southern Science and Technology Forum, University of Southampton, p.203.

15. P. Hawkins and I. Barclay (1989) 'Attracting and Retaining Engineering Graduates in the 21st century', in 'Manpower 2000: Critical to the Future' of Engineering Conference Proceedings, Southern Science and Technology Forum, University of Southampton, pp 194–202.

16. R.A. Jones and D.M. Goss (1990) 'Managerial Visions and Effective Training', *Industrial and Commercial Training*, Vol 25, No 6, pp 17–21

17. R.A. Jones and D.M. Goss (1991) 'The Role of Training Strategy in Reducing Skills Shortages: Some Evidence from a Survey of Small Firms', *Personnel Review*, Vol 20, No 2, pp 24–30

18. R. Blackburn and A. Hankinson (1989) 'Training in the Smaller Business: Investment or Expense', *Industrial and Commercial Training*, Vol 21, No 2, pp 27–29.

19. Coopers and Lybrand Associates (1985) *A Challenge to Complacency*, a report to the Manpower Services Commission and the National Economic Development Office, November.

20. D. Torrington and L. Hall (1991) *Personnel Management: A New Approach*, second edition, Prentice Hall (UK) Ltd.

21. L.E. Mackay and D.P. Torrington (1986) 'Training in the UK: Down But Not Out', *Journal of European Industrial Training*, Vol 10, No 1, pp

22. M. Useem (1993) 'Management Commitment and Company Policies on Education and Training', *Human Resource*

Management, Vol 32, No 4, pp 411–434.

23. A. Pettigrew, P. Sparrow and C. Hendry (1988) 'The Forces that Trigger Training', *Personnel Management*, December, pp 28–32.

24. K.N. Wexley and G.P. Latham (1991) *Developing and Training Human Resources in Organizations*, second edition, Harper Collins Publishers Ltd.

25. L.J. Mullins (1991) 'Successful Training – A Planned and Systematic Approach', *Administrator*, July, pp 4–5.

26. D.A. Garvin (1993) 'Building a Learning Organization', *Harvard Business Review*, July-August, pp 78–91.

27. P. Senge (1990) *The Fifth Discipline: The Art and Practice of the Learning Organization*, New York, Random House.

28. M. Dodgson (1993) 'Organizational Learning: A Review of Some Literature', *Organization Studies*, Vol 14, No 3, pp 375–394.

29. A. Jones and J. Moxham (1969) 'Costing the Benefits of Training', *Personnel Management*, April, pp 22–28.

30. R.F. Mager (1975) *Preparing Instructional Objectives*, Belmont, California, Fearon Publishers.

31. R.F. Mager and K.M. Beach (1967) *Developing Vocational Instruction*, Belmont, California, Fearon Publishers.

32. P.L. Wright and D.S. Taylor (1990) 'An Evaluation Package for a Small, One-Off Interpersonal Skills Course, *Training and Management Development Methods, Vol 4, No 3, 219–230.*

Further Reading

For a broad view of training and training techniques, any one of the following three would be appropriate:

R. Harrison (1988) *Training and Development,* Institute of Personnel Management.

I.L. Goldstein (1993) *Training in Organizations: Needs Assessment, Development and Evaluation,* third edition, Brooks/Cole Publishing Company.

K.M. Wexley and G.P. Latham (1991) *Developing and Training Human Resources in Organizations,* second edition, Harper Collins Publishers Inc.

For additional information in training approaches and techniques, two additional books are worth consulting:

J.E. Morrison (ed) (1991) *Training for Performance: Principles of Applied Human Learning,* John Wiley and Sons Ltd.

J. Patrick (1992) *Training: Research and Practice,* Academic Press Limited.

Questions

1. Describe the main characteristics of a systematic approach to training.

2. Why is a thorough and systematic analysis of training needs one of the most important phases in training course development?

3. Taylor and Company have appointed you as Training and Development Officer with the task of implementing training and development activities in this rapidly expanding company. Previously, training was largely provided on a reactive basis. How would you approach the task and what systems and procedures would you introduce?

CASE STUDY

MEADOWLEA DAIRIES

Meadowlea operates thirty dairies throughout northern England. They deliver milk, cream, eggs, yoghurt, orange juice and potatoes to households and shops on six days a week (double delivery on Saturdays, where required). Each dairy bottles/puts into cartons its own milk and cream, but buys in all its other products.

A general manager oversees the operations of each dairy with a management team reporting directly to her/him. The management team for each site consists of a production manager, a sales manager and a transport/distribution manager. In addition, an accountant and an engineer are located at five of the thirty dairies to provide services to approximately six dairies on a regional basis.

Usually, the general manager is promoted from within the group although a few have been recruited from outside the company.

Training of general managers involves having trainees go through all the main operations required for the successful running of a dairy. After a brief induction, the trainees have to spend six weeks on delivery rounds, to include both households and shops. They then spend two months in the production section, two months in purchasing/sales, two months in transport/distribution, two months with an accountant and one month with an engineer, ending up being attached to a general manager shadowing him/her on the job. The whole training period lasts for approximately one year.

Training has not been successful. Trainees have complained of boredom during the training period and, on taking up their posts, have indicated that the training did not adequately prepare them for the job.

As a result of this you, the group head of Human Resources, have been asked to do something to improve the training. What might be your plan of action?

Chapter 9

Developing Managers

Christopher Molander

Objectives

- To explore the strategic elements of management development and its links to corporate and HRM strategy
- To identify the ways in which managers learn
- To make clear where the responsibility for management development lies
- To outline the scope of management development activities

Introduction

In this chapter we shall describe the nature of Management Development (MD), challenging the common view that it is about 'sending people on courses'. This naturally leads on to a discussion of where the responsibility for MD lies in the light of current HRM thinking – with the line manager rather than the human resource department. There are practitioners in the HR field who would say that such a view has represented best practice for many years. Recently however, increased interest in HRM has led to a restatement of this important principle.

A model will be introduced to help the reader decide what type of management development activity is likely to be most appropriate in different situations. This will be followed by an analysis of the responsibility for MD.

An important element in the planning of effective MD is the identification and use of learning methods most appropriate to managers. We shall therefore explore the preconditions for effective managerial learning. Finally, the major types of development activity will be reviewed.

The Nature of Management Development

MD can usefully be described as 'a conscious and systematic process to control the development of managerial resources for the achievement of organizational goals and strategies'

At first reading this definition may appear vague. But its value lies in its generality. Organizations work in different environments and as a result have different cultures and structures and are faced with different problems. Not only is this true for any one organization in general, but within an organization, divisions and functions are faced with their own peculiar problems and have developed a climate and structure to meet their specific needs.

There can therefore be no one 'right' recipe for MD. It will vary from organization to organization, and indeed within organizations. As problems differ, so different managerial development efforts will have to be devised to cope with them. Management development activity, which will pay off in terms of improved managerial performance, will need to depend on an assessment of the prevailing needs experienced by management at a particular time. Hence, to do more than produce a very general definition might do more harm than good, since the identification in practical terms of the problems managers face is an important first step in planning development.

There are, however, a number of key words which the reader will do well to remember. Any effective management development effort requires to be part of a planned strategy – a 'conscious and systematic process' which has the clear purpose of helping managers meet 'organizational goals'. In other words random activities stemming from a multitude of objectives (for example, keeping training departments busy), and which are not necessarily in line with the climate and style of the organization, are likely to be at best a waste of time and money, and at worst positively harmful. Much of what passes for MD has the characteristic of randomness, and is sometimes controlled by individuals who have neither the authority nor the influence to ensure that there is likely to be an effective outcome of their efforts.

This risk is increased the further away planning occurs from the 'coal face'. Some of the largest and most prestigious organizations develop strategies without any significant line management involvement. The analysis of needs and the planning of initiatives have been left to experts who jealously guard their professional skills. The experts are mentally and physically far removed from the workplace. They have neither the knowledge to develop nor the power to implement 'tailor made' strategies designed to meet specific operating needs. Integrated and valid activities are likely to follow only from the closer involvement of line management in the whole process.

In general, management development activities can be focused at one of three levels; the individual, the group or the organization. The manner in which they are introduced by line management can either be prescriptive or consultative as indicated in Table 9.1. A number of examples have been given within each of the six possible boxes of types of development activity. Many more could be given, so the examples should not be taken as exhaustive.

The two dimensions of this table – the focus and style – are important to the understanding of the dimensions of MD.

Focus

It is commonly felt by managers that MD has for its purpose the change in behaviour of an individual – and indeed that is its objective. This change in behaviour may be brought about by providing managers with new knowledge, for example in some aspect of their profession, or by providing them with new skills, say in the area of 'human relations'. What is often overlooked

Table 9.1. Types of Management Development Activity

Style		Focus: Individual	Focus: Group	Focus: Organisation
Style	Prescriptive	E.G. General Management Courses Qualification Courses Some forms of Appriasal	E.G. Some forms of Team Building Project based learning Some forms of Management by Objectives	E.G. Some forms of Management by Objectives Some forms of Organisation Development
Style	Consultative	E.G. Counselling Coaching Needs analysis Career planning Specified experience Task related Courses	E.G. Analysis of problems Identificaiton of needs Role negotiation Action learning Some froms of Team Building	E.G. Organisation Analysis and Feedback

however, is that some behavioural change – better performance, different attitude to the job, greater useful output and so on can be brought about more effectively by changing the environment in which the individual works.

It is often the case that managers perform less well than they might, not because they lack the capacity or the inclination, but because there are constraints surrounding their role which either prevent them from behaving differently or encourage them to behave in the way they do. Take, for example, the behaviour of an individual in a team meeting. It might be said that X can be relied upon to be destructive at departmental meetings, and to engage in pointless argument some days and withdrawal behaviour on others. Does she need training in interpersonal skills? Or are there other issues which provoke the behaviour? A recent example of just this problem arose in a team meeting within an 0 & M unit. As a result of a team building exercise, it was discovered that the behaviour of the individual in question stemmed from a role clash with two other senior managers for whom the unit provided a service. This clash meant that she was unable to do a significant proportion of what she thought was her job, and others saw her as idle and 'biding her time' until she could take early retirement. Her behaviour in the meetings was much more related to the sheer frustration caused by the lack of job clarity than to any 'personal difficulty'. In this case, a restatement of departmental objectives and the accompanying re-definition of individual roles was sufficient to modify the observed behaviour.

The behaviour was symptomatic of a problem and not the problem itself. Dealing with symptoms is seldom helpful, The root cause remains, and one set of symptoms will often be replaced by another. It may be more effective to take as the target for change, not the individuals, but the circumstances in which they find themselves. Change the immediate 'environment' and the behaviour may change itself.

A second example may help further to make the point. Most organizations or divisions within them may be said to have their own culture or climate. By this is meant a set of assumptions about what is proper with regard to attitudes and behaviour at work. These assumptions and values are reflected not only in the way people behave but in the way they are managed. For example, many managers are apt to comment: 'What we need here are a few more self starters – people prepared to take initiative, to take risks and not just to live by the rule book, getting by without thinking'. In practice, however, the managerial style of the unit may be such as to reward precisely the opposite sort of behaviour. Risk taking, especially when things go wrong, may be followed by such retribution that the individuals concerned will 'keep their head down'. If they 'read' the organizational climate as one which rewards pedestrian rule-following behaviour, and which is disturbed by those who take initiative, then in their own interests they will naturally adapt their behaviour to fit perceptions of the climate.

Frequently, the organization's 'espoused' culture is at variance with the actual culture. Managers are quite capable of reading the culture for what it really is and adapting their behaviour accordingly. Why take risks when you observe that those who don't on the whole indulge in such creativity do at least as well, if not better than those who do? So the target for change of a management development effort may go beyond both the individual and the group and legitimately be seen as the organization itself. But the principle is the same. Behaviour in individuals may often be more usefully affected not by taking them as the target for change, but the culture in which they work. To many readers, this may seem far removed from MD as they know it. Indeed it is the case that some types of MD (operating at the organization – wide level) are akin to organization development. The relationship is symbiotic however, since MD is often the consequence of organization development activities.

Style

The second dimension in Table 9.1 is labelled 'Style'. Just as management development activities can produce change in behaviour by changing managers' immediate work groups, or the divisions or organizations in which they work, so change can be introduced prescriptively or as a result of consultation.

In recent years for example, many firms have attempted to introduce appraisal systems. Frequently the need for such systems is experienced not by potential appraisers but by the personnel department. Sometimes little or no consultation takes place with those who would have to appraise and still less with those who are about to be appraised. However sophisticated the scheme, months of effort can be wasted if managers lack the commitment to make it work. As a result many schemes have been abandoned.

Increasing interest is being shown in appraisal by line managers and there is marked evidence of a return to performance related pay. Such developments are symptomatic of the need to integrate personnel policy with the operating demands of the organization. An emphasis to be found in the principles of HRM as opposed to more traditional personnel management is the greater need to reward performance. This will lead to the introduction of more rigorous performance related appraisal systems, as well of course to more imaginative payment methods designed to win the 'hearts and minds' of managerial employees. The more traditional non-directive approach favoured by many personnel managers is likely to become less common.

Management by Objectives springs to mind as another obvious example of a technique often introduced in a prescriptive way. If the 'user' is not committed to the scheme, or if it is perceived as being out of line with the way the organization runs, then no amount of administrative effort will compensate. Many organizations have experimented with MBO; few can be said to have introduced it successfully, in such a way that it is still used, and seen as a valuable technique for improving motivation and performance. Later we shall say more about MBO. The purpose in mentioning it briefly now is to provide an illustration of prescriptive management development.

Any system of MD which is introduced without taking into account the expressed needs of the user or 'client' may be said to be prescriptive. It is by no means the case that all prescriptive introductions of management development activities are inappropriate. New employees, for instance, may require certain types of training and development and certain posts may require the possession of a particular qualification. In these cases prescriptive MD is appropriate. But where new ideas are being introduced, or the active involvement of those being developed is crucial yet uncertain, then prescriptive approaches are likely to be unnecessarily difficult to sustain – especially when the prescription appears to emanate from the personnel department.

In contrast, the consultative approach may have in some, though not all circumstances, more to offer. Appraisal systems, counselling, job rotation and career planning for example, require the active involvement of the manager being developed.

Who knows individual needs best – the manager or the boss? In all probability the one will have information which the other does not have. The boss may have a more detached view of the manager's strengths and weaknesses, and yet still be basing these views on limited and erroneous experience. Managers may be expected to have more reliable information of what aspects of the job motivate and those which do not; what they do well and not so well and of the direction in which they would like a career to develop. In such cases a consultative approach in which both the boss and the manager share information, identify problems and aspirations and mutually agree a planned development programme, is likely to be more appropriate. In other words, bosses who take their responsibility for developing their managers seriously will need to take account of the options open to them in deciding strategy.

A great deal of what passes for MD in business organizations may be said to fit into the top left hand box of table 9.1. It is prescriptive and aimed at the individual as the target for change. Indeed many managers when asked to define MD reply that, in essence, it is 'sending managers on courses'. Whilst individual prescriptive development has a real role to play, it can be overplayed. The initiation of other types of development activity which provide a thrust for change aimed away from the top left hand corner is timely.

The argument of this chapter so far has been based on the notion of choice. From it we can deduce three major possible ways in which change in the individual can be encouraged. The first type of general management development activity is based on the proposition that individual behaviour can be changed directly by the provision of training, for example, knowledge acquisition through job rotation and specific courses, or through feedback on performance. Here the target for change is the individual directly.

The second type of activity reflects the view that the individual's behaviour is a function of the values and attitudes held. If these can be changed, behaviour will change itself. This we may call the psychological approach. Team building activities which aim to clarify the group's objectives and to reduce the degree of conflict between members may in certain cases produce attitude change in the individual. Similarly, conflict between groups may be reduced by confrontation of difficulties and re-allocation of responsibilities.

A third approach is more sociological. The target for change is here seen to be the way in which work is organized and the structures set up to get it done. Work procedures can be more or less enabling or constraining. If the job itself offers little opportunity for taking responsibility, for example, it is little use exhorting managers to behave responsibly. Far more effective are changes in job content – not the amount of work to be done, but the quality of work experience which is offered.

If MD itself has been slow to become established much more so has this latter approach to it. The reasons are not difficult to appreciate. Approaches to change in work structure depend upon competent analysis and careful introduction. Matrix organization structures, for example, which encourage managers to use their skills wherever they are relevant, without too much regard for position and power are difficult to implement and manage, but they have been introduced to good effect within both the public and private sector.[1] In the private sector, changes in the procedures for getting work done have in the main been aimed at the shop-floor level – the many modified versions of 'job enrichment' and self managed work groups come to mind. But the principle is the same and can be implemented at any level. This principle is based on the observation that behaviour is symptomatic of the circumstances in which it takes place. Change the circumstances and individual behaviour will change.

All three types of MD might be going on at the same time, and with the involvement of all managers. MD is a major responsibility of any manager. It is not the exclusive preserve of the trainer. In particular, managers will need three basic attributes. Firstly, they will need the ability to analyse an organization, or at least their part of it and to diagnose accurately the root cause of presenting problems. Secondly, they will require a basic understanding of the techniques available for bringing about change in managerial behaviour. Lastly, they will need to exercise consultative and interpersonal skills for introducing change with the minimum of conflict and the maximum degree of commitment from others. It is hoped this book generally will encourage the manager to seek ways of developing these skills further.

The Responsibility for Management Development

Managers who have the professional responsibility for management development are usually located within the broader function of the human resource department. There are good practical reasons why they cannot achieve much on their own account. Organization development, management development and training professionals quite simply lack the authority. The writer has often sympathized with personnel professionals who, from a position in the middle ranges of management, have sought to move mountains. Guided by an 'inner light', nothing has seemed beyond their scrutiny. These are the managers who sooner or later lose heart. They move to other organizations, or long experience of frustration, failure and lack of organization commitment leads them unwillingly to accept reality. They become alienated from the job and sometimes from themselves. Change will only take place when those who have the authority (i.e. line managers) are motivated to bring it about. The increasing tendency towards the integration of management effort through greater concern for corporate planning and the declining role of the personnel department in implementing policy – as opposed to developing it – may increase the level of managerial motivation.

A policy making characteristic important for the management development professional is political acumen. Change is achieved more easily by working through people. This requires testing the limits of tolerance and working within these parameters. Certainly there is a problem of over acceptance of organizational constraints, but even the brightest trainers waste their talent by over-confrontation. The organization is a system, which has arrived at its present state through a mixture of external and internal pressures which makes its current structures and processes seem the most rational. Denial results in resistance. Where this denial is encountered, the organization is quite capable of by-passing the efforts of those who seek inappropriate change. Analysis of the political relevance and appropriateness of change is a strong weapon in the professional's armoury. There are other reasons why line managers should take the responsibility for MD beyond these tactical points. It takes us into well worn territory – the role of the human resource department generally. In Britain, as already in the United States, it is increasingly realised that the major responsibility for personnel administration must lie with the line manager. The term 'manager' implies managing people and their development. Managers should be encouraged not to pass over staff development to the HR Department, tempting though it may be for personnel people to seize the chance of 'empire building'! Managers' responsibility for their staff from recruitment onwards cannot be overstated. Managers who are used to being spoon-fed cannot be expected to develop responsible attitudes towards staff development. Strategically it is worth remembering what we have observed earlier: imposed management development systems (for example, some forms of appraisal) tend to be ignored or mishandled by managers who lack the commitment which comes from ownership of responsibility.

If managers are encouraged to develop their own management development priorities they will feel a greater sense of ownership. Such ownership is crucial to commitment. Without the necessary commitment there will be no action. This means that managers will express interest in different activities, and this will lead to a piecemeal organizational approach. So be it. The canons of ownership and commitment should override organizational concern for neatness.

Still relating to responsibility, there is one further point that should be explored with regard to the philosophy of MD. The more individuals have the responsibility for planning their development, the more they will learn, and the more they will be committed to undertake training and other developmental experiences. Perhaps most important, the greater the involvement by individuals in planning their own learning, the greater will be the chance that the training will be transferred to the job.

Care in the introduction of even the most enlightened development system is of the essence as many organizations have found to their cost. Bureaucratic methods of introduction will result in cynicism and inactivity. 'The medium is the message'. How MD is introduced speaks volumes to the employee about the real purposes which lie behind the introduction of change.

How Managers Learn

Based on the earlier work of Kolb et al,[2] Honey and Mumford[3] have identified four learning styles, which suggest that managers, along with everyone else, have different and preferred ways of learning:

Activists learn best when they are actively involved in concrete tasks.

Reflectors prefer to learn through reviewing and reflecting upon what has happened.

Theorists learn more effectively when they can relate new information to concepts or theory

Pragmatists learn when they see the relevance between information and real life issues and problems.

As Armstrong[4] reminds us, none of these four learning styles is exclusive; it is possible for a manager to be both a reflector and a theorist, whilst another might be both an activist and a pragmatist, or even a theorist and a pragmatist. Research indicates however that most managers have a preference for one method of learning over another.

One of the most important skills of MD specialists and managers then is to adjust their own approaches to the learning style of the trainees. In particular trainers must acknowledge their own preferred learning styles rather than making assumptions as to the best learning methods, based on their own preference.

It is likely that preferences will be related both to the type of organization in which the trainees work (for example local government rather than say a manufacturing company in the private sector). It is also likely that within one organization, managers with different work experience and professional backgrounds will prefer one learning style to another. The root cause of many training and development failures lies not in the lack of knowledge of the trainer but in the choice of an inappropriate learning medium.

The five preconditions for effective learning which follow should be read in conjunction with this important issue of delivery method.[5]

Goal Setting Develop learning opportunities which relate to the areas in which the learner has experience. Where there is an interest and a need to explore, training will be most effective. This is especially true of managerial skills. Successful skill training requires a high level of commitment on the part of the learner. The experience of many trainers suggests that 'problem based' training rather than more abstract generalized approaches is most effective. This seems plausible. There is in many managers a residual antipathy to the passive relationship of teacher and student reminiscent of school, in which there appears to be little direct relevance to the 'real world'. Every trainer will recall groups in which resistance to learning was clearly present. Working on the basis of expressed training needs presupposes careful job consultation or appraisal, from which training needs emerge.

Climate The adult manager will react better to a learning environment which demonstrates mutual respect between trainer and participant. Managers often object to being taught. A lecture for example, however accomplished the delivery, carries with it the implied message of the expert talking at the non-expert. The physical arrangement of the trainer 'up front' armed to the teeth with multicoloured OHP acetates with the learners facing him/her defines a relationship which is unsuitable for building on the knowledge the learners already have.

Implementation Most managers on development courses are already reasonably good at their jobs. They have had a great deal of experience. Their experiences differ. They are, as is the way with adults, quite capable of learning from each other. The learners are themselves an invaluable resource. When they express the need to know more, they are quite capable of finding answers for themselves. The word 'facilitator', although jargon, does at least express the promise of a more productive learning environment in which all the available sources of information are likely to be exploited.

Planning How the learning goals are to be achieved merits careful thought. As we have seen, each of us learns in a different way.

Training experiences which pay some attention to these differences presuppose a flexible approach, in which a number of different learning techniques may be going on at the same time, or at least within the same learning event. In every case, some discussion as to how the learning goals are to be achieved is a suitable beginning.

Evaluation Some form of evaluation of training is important in providing necessary feedback. What useful learning or experience the learners feel they have achieved is a prime source of such feedback. This information can be used for planning further activities as well as modifying content and methods of current training efforts. The process of involving participants in the evaluation process is important in demonstrating an 'adult' climate in which trainers and participants alike are involved in a 'learning community'.

The Organizational Life Cycle

Like human beings, organizations are constantly developing, so what might have been appropriate development techniques for organizations at one time might not be relevant at another. The notion of a 'life cycle' is a helpful concept in determining relevance.[6]

Many organizational analysts have over the years been struck with the analogy of the biological organism and the work organization. They have identified four or sometimes five stages in the organizational cycle and compared them to the biological cycle. Of course the analogy cannot be taken too far. Unlike the biological organism, the organization is capable of 're-birth', say for example as a result of takeover, a characteristic not given to mortals. Table 9.2 defines the stages in the cycle. They have been confined to those elements of most relevance to MD.

Birth Characteristic of the small entrepreneurial firm, much beloved currently by right-wing politicians. The entrepreneur has the vision and drive to start up an enterprise which is small enough for him/her to control directly. Although a high degree of risk is involved, division of labour and decision-making systems are rudimentary. The ownership of the risk has clear implications for managerial style which inclines to the authoritarian.

Growth Assuming the business survives, growth follows. Professional managers are employed who, whilst they lack the sense of ownership, are given a relatively free hand by the owner to develop the business. Many of the managers bring with them needed specialist skills to adjust structure and procedures to meet the demands of increased size. Because they lack the personal zeal of the owner and because there is already much to lose, the level of risk-taking declines.

Maturity This is the phase most closely associated with bureaucracy. Further increase in size leads to highly developed structures, normally based on functional differentiation. Sophisticated information processing becomes necessary to maintain growth. By now the entrepreneur has sold out and the business is run by professional, career-oriented managers, many of whom will stay with the company for a short time only. Change in the character of management is reflected in low risk-taking and a rule-oriented management style. Not all organizations easily make the necessary and continuous adjustments to the environment – changes in market, competition and so on. The very strength of the managerial style seen in the maturity phase can be a weakness. There is often a reluctance to respond to the need for rapid change. The pursuit of divisional and departmental goals may discourage the taking of an organizational view.

Decline In such cases decline may follow. Either the company does not see the need for adjustment to the environment or is incapable of making necessary changes to the product or service. There may be a diminution of role, due to changes in political attitudes of the government, without the emergence of a realistic alternative role (e.g., local government). Faced with a threatening

Table 9.2. Phases of the organizational life cycle

	Management Style	Planning and Control	Decision Making	Risk-Taking
Birth Phase	Power highly centralized	Informal structure	Crude inform-attain processes and decision making methods	Substantial risk taking
Growth Phase	High deleg-ation and freedom	Some forma-lisation of individual Functional organization	Initial develop-ment of information processes and decision making methods	Measured risk formal
Maturity Phase	High deleg-ation and fixed goals	Formal bureaucratic structure Highly developed functional basis of organization	Sophisticated information processing	Conservative, low risk taking
Decline Phase	Low deleg-ation and fixed limited goals Finance led	Highly developed bureaucratic structure Mostly func~tional basis of organ-isation	Limited inform-ation for control purposes	Very limited risk taking

environment, organizations in the decline phase tend to become intensely bureaucratic. At the same time, effective power is withdrawn so that it rests with the higher echelons of management only. Decision making processes are harnessed to the problem of survival There is an unwillingness to expose the organization to anything but a minimal level of risk-taking.

Management Development Implications of the Life Cycle

The professional should gear strategy to help develop those skills in managers which are appropriate to the growth phase of the organization. The direction of the strategy is suggested in Table 9.3.

Failure to relate objectives to a prior analysis of the development phase is perhaps the major cause of resistance amongst line managers. Day-to-day experience is perhaps a better basis on which to test the validity of proposed developmental opportunities, rather than a theoretical model of what organizations in general should be striving towards. Nonetheless, many of the well established development techniques stem from a time when Western society and its work organizations were in the maturity phase. Personal growth and organizational prosperity were seen as linked and equally attainable objectives. Some organizations are now in the maturity phase, but many could best be described as entering into post-maturity,

Some will perish; others will embark on the process of re-growth. Such a process requires different management structures and styles to those which were appropriate in the maturity phase. Managers will require a leaner, tougher, internal organization climate which emphasises individualism and personal responsibility, and rewards those who demonstrably contribute to the organization's financial stability. It is in this context that the prime objective should be to match the activity to the developing needs of the organization.

Over the last few months, in discussion with senior managers of three large organizations, the writer has heard the same thing: 'The training I've had in this company has been fine for me personally, but from the organization's point of view it's been irrelevant'.

There is a need today to build up processes and techniques which are relevant to entering a period of re-growth. The development of appropriate managerial structures and the identification and

Table 9.3. Growth phase and management development activity

Phase	*Activities*
Birth (Innovation)	No particular MD effort required. The organization is too small to allow of MD specialization. The entrepreneur will intuitively resist MD. He knows what he wants in others and will find appropriate colleagues. Available capital will be directed towards defraying start up costs and the development of new market opportunities, Managers will learn on the job. Development will be problem centred and self appropriated.
Growth (Expansion)	As the organization increases in size, the need emerges to develop a suitable structure based on differentiation. More refined financial controls will be required. Opportunities for individual development are still readily available. The critical role of the entrepreneur declines. Key MD activities: • Development of appropriate managerial structures • Identification and development of individual professional and managerial talent • Management succession and appraisal • Management by Objectives • Team-building
Maturity (Control)	Emphasis on growth is tempered by concern with monitoring achievement. This will encourage bureaucratic "sprawl" and bureaucratic skills are seen as important. Opportunities for individual growth limited to steady career development, often within one function. Identification with the organization decreases, with consequential decline in levels of motivation. The managerial "specialist" emerges. Key MD activities: • Interpersonal Skills Training • Autonomous managerial work groups • Management by Objectives • Counselling and Coaching • Appraisal • Committee (rather than Team) Skills Development
Decline (Survival)	The organisation becomes "finance led". This will have significant impact on organizational culture and management style, which will become more centralized and controlling. The level of bureaucracy will increase and middle managers will have less power. The problem of survival becomes paramount. The organization becomes reactive to external pressure. The level of motivation declines sharply. Key MD activities: • Political Skill Development • I Negotiations Skills Development • Assertiveness Training • Finance Skills Development • External Environment Control Skills

rewarding of individual and managerial talent is of paramount importance. Out of what appears to be desperation, some companies are returning to 'outward bound' methods which were in vogue at the end of the Second World War. In the writer's view, the problem of transferability of such experience to the workplace remains as big a problem now as it was then. There is a long way to go in the development of adequate responses to current organizational needs.

Apart from the problem of relevance, there is the practical problem of cost. Training budgets are among the first to be cut in periods of economic pressure. In the public sector, such cuts have been particularly severe. Initiatives which involve much more than petty cash expenditure are unlikely to survive here. It has long been argued that in times of economic depression, companies should increase their expenditure on the development of managers. They would then be in a good position to exploit market opportunities when the 'up-wave' arrives. Once the growth has begun again it is too late to begin identifying the need for increased managerial skill. This argument, though strong, has rarely proved convincing.

A feature of organizations in both the post-maturity and the re-growth phases is that the power of finance managers increases, companies become finance led. Managers whose careers have for the most part been within the financial world are not well known for their interest and concern in the application of training to management problems. For this reason also then, training will have to demonstrate its cost-effectiveness if it is to remain a significant item in the annual budget.

So there are three clear principles against which we can measure the likely success of MD in the forseeable future:

1 It must be relevant to company needs.

2 Ownership and commitment must be won through problem-centred development activities.

3 Cost-effectiveness must be demonstrated,

Let us look then at some major development techniques, bearing in mind that the user must decide whether they are appropriate at the time.

Potentially Effective Development Techniques

Competence-based development and development centres

There has been something of a mini-revolution in MD centred upon 'competencies' or areas of activity and behaviours which managers in a particular organization could be expected to perform competently. Armstrong[7] provides an example of a list of core competencies which a company has deemed to be an essential part of the equipment of their managers:

Strategic capability to understand the changing business environment, opportunities for product-market development, competitive challenges and the strengths and weaknesses of their own organization in order to identify optimum strategic responses.

Change management capability to identify change needs, plan change programmes and persuade others to participate willingly in the implementation of change.

Team management capability to get diverse groups of people from different disciplines to work well together.

Relationship management to network effectively with others to share information and pool resources to achieve common objectives.

International management to be capable of managing across international frontiers working well with people of other nationalities.

Such analysis has many potential benefits. It has obvious uses in the selection and appraisal processes as well as a basis for developing an MD strategy. Such analysis does however need to be behaviourally anchored – that is, what specific and observable behaviours will be used to assess whether managers are or are not demonstrating the relevant competencies in their work Development centres (like assessment centres an event and not a place) should be available to allow managers to examine and understand the competencies they require now and in the future. Feedback counselling and coaching by professional MD staff and trained line managers should be available to participants.

Self development

Increasing emphasis is placed in modern approaches to MD on the need for managers to take responsibility for their own development. Pedler[8] observes that 'any effective system for MD must increase the manager's capacity and willingness to take control over and responsibility for events and participating for themselves in their own learning'.

The process of self development leads to an increase in commitment and thus to speed of learning and to cost effectiveness. Moreover the development will be problem centred. Self managed learning groups, computer based training and interactive video can be used in this regard. The provision of feedback is essential to this learning process.

Management by Objectives

It is arguable that MBO is fundamental to good management. In the late 1960s and early 1970s it became a fashionable technique. Frequently abused, it was later to fall into general disuse.[9] It is now more properly used as an essential element in performance review or appraisal. Its use as a technique of management development is likely to grow along with the need to use managerial resources more effectively.

The basic process is threefold. The Managers discuss and agree with their boss the objectives of their job for a defined period (usually six months or a year). Specific goals or objectives are agreed in line with departmental objectives ('Key Results'). At the end of the agreed period, boss and manager jointly review actual performance against the agreed criteria. Strengths and weaknesses in the managers' performance are explored. Where appropriate, ways in which each can help the other to improve performance are reviewed. Key results are set for the next review period.

One of the major reasons for the early failure of MBO systems, apart from the obvious one that too much was expected of it, was that the technique was seen by many managers solely as a means of identifying shortfalls in performance and of tying people down to specific job descriptions. MBO was originally conceived as a participative technique. Its purpose was to encourage mutual exploration of problems and the development of action plans, using the subordinate as the major resource. There should be an underlying belief that participation in objective setting leads to a higher level of commitment and therefore better results. If targets are imposed on managers, the latter may become competitive, using energy to justify themselves in not meeting objectives and in attempting to negotiate the least difficult key results for the next review period in order to appear better than they are on the next day of judgement.

Properly handled, as an element in effective performance review, MBO is a powerful element in any MD strategy.

Performance Review

Chapter ten deals with this topic in depth. It is mentioned here mainly as a reminder that it is one of the most cost-effective techniques open to the manager who takes the development of employees seriously. In recent years, traditional types of appraisal have given way to more participative methods which are not so firmly anchored to rating scales. Most managers would accept that they have a duty to review the performance of the managers responsible to them, at least annually, and that they in their turn have a right to expect such a review from their own boss.

Performance review is essentially a two-way communication process, during which boss and manager have an opportunity to review the latter's performance in an atmosphere which is neither competitive nor punitive. It may well be that the manager can suggest changes in the behaviour of the boss or in work processes and systems which are causing problems. It is also important to bear in mind that the review provides an opportunity to explore successes as well as those behaviours which have caused the boss concern. As part of the review, targets and key results should be agreed. It is in this context that MBO has its place. It is now generally agreed that performance review should be separated from succession planning and from pay negotiation. The relationship between boss and manager in effective performance review is different to that normally found in negotiating relationships. The openness of the former should not be contaminated by the competitiveness of the latter. This is not to say that rewards are not important. Indeed, unless it is possible to reward desired behaviour – by salary increase, promotion, status changes and so on; there is little justification for expecting managers to maintain their efforts to improve performance.

There should be a clear link between performance review and salary adjustments. The emerging culture of many organizations is increasingly one which emphasizes the need for a greater link between performance and reward. In the NHS for example, pay is frequently related not only to an incremental scale but also to performance related bonuses in addition. But since pay and performance review involve different types of relationship, they should not be combined in the same session. In chapter six, the essential link between reward and motivation is explored more fully.

Interpersonal and Team Development Skills

Managers who plan and develop departments or organizations should recognize the varied leadership requirements of different positions. In particular, a crucial aspect of managers' responsibility is the development of appropriate management styles in those they manage. Whether the latter do develop them will depend greatly on the way they themselves are managed. Leadership skills can be learned. A major implication of situational theories of leadership is that managers will need to have the sensitivity to recognize what style is appropriate and when, and to have the flexibility to adjust accordingly. Readers should consult chapters six and seven for a more detailed discussion of contingency in this context,

Many training programmes are available which are designed to develop the interpersonal skills of managers. Such programmes are normally experience-based. That is, the participants have the opportunity to learn for themselves what impact they have on others and, by experimentation, to increase the repertoire of possible responses to differing situations.

The training materials developed by Hersey and Blanchard for example, are based on the identification of an individual's management style, with the use of personality profiles. Exercises, 'games' and role-playing may be used to offer the participant an opportunity to experiment with alternative forms of behaviour.[10]

Since individual managers spend most of their time working in small groups, it is not surprising that team development has become an important aspect of interpersonal skills training.[11] Programmes are readily available which help managers look at the behaviours which are necessary in effective teams, and to analyse their own preferred ways of behaving. Often with the help of a 'consultant', established work groups can learn to examine their strengths and weaknesses both in terms of how they work (clear purposes and objectives, efficient use of time, for example) and how the team members relate (listening skills, conflict management and leadership styles). Good team work is an important factor in obtaining and maintaining the commitment of individual managers to the achievement of individual and group goals. It is not always appropriate however. It is increasingly argued that managers, especially those who work in an organization at the post-maturity phase of the life cycle, need to develop a greater degree of assertiveness, (this is not the same as aggressiveness), and to become better negotiators. Help in the handling of change and conflict may be more important than the development of team skills. Several external courses are now available which focus upon these issues.

Coaching

Coaching is a process of systematically increasing the ability and experience of managers by giving them planned tasks, coupled with continuing appraisal. Management development professionals may well have a useful role to play in the development of coaching skills in line managers, but the activity itself can only be done within the context of the manager's job.

Coaching as an effective technique rests on six basic principles:[12]

- It is experience on the job which teaches most.
- The ways jobs are structured influences the amount of learning which takes place.
- The example of the coach influences the attitudes,behaviour and development of managers.
- If managers participate in the setting of their learning targets, they will be more committed to their attainment.
- Learning, in part, depends on knowing effort has met with success.
- Coaching is a continuing process.

Coaching minimally involves three basic activities; delegation, counselling and appraisal. It is in delegation that senior managers can most clearly exercise their ability as a coach. Effective delegation involves the setting of objectives; terms of reference and boundaries of authority and responsibility. Standards must be set and performance assessed, preferably in a quantifiable form. The action should always be in the hands of the learner. The skill of coaching depends on limited intervention, so that learners do not make too many mistakes and lose confidence on the one hand,

and so that they do not come to depend on their tutor on the other. The boss should encourage self-analysis of performance; but should be prepared, as a normal element in appraisal, to monitor performance against agreed success criteria.

There are two great dangers in delegation. The first is that the tasks delegated are themselves unlikely to provide much learning. Delegation of trivia will alienate rather than motivate managers. The second danger is that the boss will not use the experience as a training technique (i.e. follow it up with appraisal) but simply as a way of getting work done.

Mentoring

Mentoring[13] differs from coaching in that it does not normally involve a manager-boss relationship. An older manager unconnected with the department of the learner is usually involved. Mentoring is also about feelings and relationships rather than tasks.

Mentoring allows the learner to discuss emotional issues, which will include the expression of personal feelings with someone they can trust and respect. The gain for the learner comes from the sharing of the mentor's experience and knowledge of the organization.

In addition, mentoring provides a rewarding challenge for older managers to share in the growth of another manager.

Project Learning

Often referred to as 'action learning', it is said by some to be a highly important development in approaches to training.[14] The basic principles of action learning are that managers learn by doing real work, rather than being taught in a classroom, and that they learn from each other, rather than from management teachers. The role of the 'adviser' is to provide conditions in which managers may learn with and from each other.

Managers normally work in small groups of around four or five, meeting at frequent intervals over an extended period of time, perhaps six months or more. Managers individually bring to the group a work problem which they personally experience and which they are committed to resolving. There should be few limits as to what constitutes a suitable problem, but it must satisfy the criterion of ownership and be complex enough to require the shared energy of the group in exploring its dimensions and helping the manager find workable solutions. Factual problems, or problems not intimately related to managers' jobs, are not suitable. It is important that the members appreciate that as much learning for the individual members of the group can come from helping each other as from receiving help with their own problems.

Much attention has been given to groups made up of senior managers from a wide variety of different organizations. It is likely, however, that projects dealing with familiar problems in a familiar setting will be the most common. Whether a 'stranger' group or an 'insider' group, what is important is that the members have equality of status, otherwise the process of developing effective working relationships will be difficult.

The essence of action learning groups is that the learning process is self managed and that members share the responsibility for the learning of others as well as themselves. It might be appropriate to have an 'adviser' in the group from inside the company or an external consultant – whose function is to help develop effective working processes, rather than to get involved in substantive issues.

As with other forms of learning, individuals should have the support of their boss who, though not a member of the group, maintains interest in progress and in any specific outcome which may affect the working of the department.

Distance Learning

Sometimes referred to as 'open' learning, it may be defined as learning at a time and place to suit the learner. Some companies are reluctant to release staff to attend even a one week training course, so distance learning is an important and relevant initiative in training design.

Basically, distance learning depends on the development of learning packages which can either be bought from an institution such as a University (e.g. the Open University Business School), or a management training centre. They can also be developed 'in house'. They may involve the use of written material only, or a combination of written and audio visual material. Computer-based programmes linked via a modem to a centre have a great potential, alas as yet barely discovered.

However operated, any package should contain three elements:

1. Information in the form of lecture; guided and provided reading; case study exercises; video films and 'instruments' for self-appraisal.
2. Tutoring and counselling help, either face to face or via the telephone or through a computer link.
3. Self-help groups of learners engaged on the same programme.

The essence of distance learning is that it is student rather than teacher managed. It meets the basic requirements for effective training suggested in this chapter, as well as having the advantage of avoiding block release from work. It helps also to cope with the fears many managers have of going back to the classroom. Such learning is also relatively cheap, since most of the material can be used many times. It is sometimes imagined that distance learning is broad in scope. Whilst it is true that a manager may use this type of learning to obtain a degree in management studies, for example, there is nothing in the technique which prevents an application to more specific learning needs such as the personnel selection interview, or basic financial skills for managers,

Companies will need to do more than simply buy some distance learning packages. The manager's boss should be involved in the training, to ensure that it forms part of a coherent development strategy. His or her interest in progress will be an important element in the learner's motivation. It is also important that the boss provides opportunities for the learner to use the skill and knowledge learned. Research appears to indicate that face to face contact, either with a manager or tutor or at least with a small group of fellow learners, is an important element in maintaining motivation.

International Development

In the quest for greater market and product opportunity, many organizations have sought to 'globalize' their activities. This has come about largely as a result of changes in the world political climate, advances in technology, (such as computing and air travel) and the manifest need for greater cooperation between countries in order to share development costs.

The international manager requires core skills which are not only technical in nature, but which involve emotional maturity and the motivation to develop people skills – especially those of cultural flexibility, team building and motivation.

As Beardwell and Holden suggest, it is likely that some or all of the following techniques will be useful:[15]

- In-house cultural and language courses
- Overseas secondments for younger managers
- Tailored development programmes for host country managers
- Transferring host country managers to local offices
- Undertaking educational courses with an international base

Conclusion

The term 'management development' is generally employed to describe the use of any technique to develop managers. It includes, therefore, both education and training, together with planned on-the-job development and self-development by reading and study.

In this chapter, the point has been made that there is a good deal more to MD than sending people on courses. The success of MD efforts depends largely upon using techniques which are appropriate to the organization's growth stage and upon involving the learner in the planning and management of learning.

We have argued that the responsibility for MD must rest with line managers. It is their responsibility to develop subordinates and they are most likely to be able to provide the most effective development opportunities.

Early in the chapter we touched upon the role of the human resource department. It was argued that, except on rare occasions when personnel people may be expected to have the relevant knowledge (e.g. industrial relations legislation), the HR department should not play a direct role in MD activities. This is not to say that it does not have a role at all. It has a crucial one of encouraging managers to engage in effective development; in ensuring that finances and other resources are available; in the monitoring of training activities for cost-effectiveness and, perhaps most important, in encouraging top management to develop a clear and positive policy with regard to MD generally, which they then ensure is carried out. In the writer's view the relative ineffectiveness of many MD specialists and trainers can be accounted for by their eagerness to 'run courses' rather than to develop policies and systems for training which line managers will accept and implement and which are integrated with corporate strategy.

Such a view has been expressed by enlightened human resource professionals over the years. It appears that in Britain line management itself is becoming aware of the need to take greater ownership of MD strategy. This should allow human resource specialists to concentrate on what they should be good at: the development of *policy* and the monitoring of its implementation. The *processes* by which the policy is implemented should become the province of line management, aided if necessary by operating HR professionals reporting to them.

References

1. Refer to Chapter 14. Also read Davis, S.M. and Lawrence, P. (1977), *Matrix,* Wokingham, Addison Wesley

2. Kolb, D.A., Rubin, I.M., and McIntyre, J.M. (1974), *Organizational Psychology: An Experiential Approach, Englewood Cliffs,* New Jersey, Prentice Hall

3. Honey, P.A. and Mumford, A. (1989), *The Manual of Learning Opportunities,* Maidenhead, Peter Honey

4. Armstrong, M., (1995) Ch. 32 in *A Handbook of Personnel Management Practice* (5th Ed.), London, Kogan Page

5. Molander,C.F., (1986), *Management Development: Key Concepts for Managers and Trainers,* Bromley, Chartwell Bratt

6. Kimberley, J. and Miles, R., (1980), *The Organization Life Cycle,* San Francisco, Jossey Bass

7. Armstrong, M. op. cit. (Ch 34)

8. Pedler, M., Burgoyne,J. and Boydell, T. (1986) *A manager's Guide to Self Development,* London McGraw-Hill

9. For a discussion of the problems inherent in MBO, read: Molander, C.F. (1972), 'Management by Objectives in Perspective', *Journal of Management Studies,* Vol. 9, No. 1, February, 1972

10. Hersey, P., and Blanchard, K., (1977), *Management of Organisational Behaviour: Utilising Human Resources, Englewood Cliffs,* New Jersey, Prentice – Hall

11. A good basic account of the processes of team building may be found in: Armstrong, M. (1992), *Human Resource*

Management, Strategy and Action (Ch. 10), London, Kogan Page

12. Singer, E.J. (1979) *Effective Management Coaching,* London, IPM. (2nd ed). Although not recent, it is still an excellent account

13. Hunt, D.M. and Michael, C. (1983) 'Mentorship: A Career and Development Tool', *Academy of Management Review,* Vol. 8 No. 3

14. Revans, R. (1974) 'Action Learning Projects' in Taylor, B. and Lippitt, G.L. *Management Development and Training Handbook,* Maidenhead, McGraw-Hill

15. Beardwell, I. and Holden, L., (1994) *Human Resource Management: A Contemporary Perspective,* London, Pitman

Further Reading

Burgoyne, J.and Stuart R. (1991) 'Teaching and Learning Methods in Management Development', *Personnel Review,* Vol. 20 No. 3

Easterby-Smith, M. (1985) *'Evaluating Management Education', Training and Development,* Aldershot, Gower

Huczynski, A. (1983) *Encyclopaedia of Management Development Methods,* Aldershot, Gower

Molander, C.F. (1986), *Management Development: Key Concepts for Managers and Trainers,* Kent UK, Chartwell Bratt

Mumford, A. (1989), *Management Development: Strategies for Action,* London, IPM

Questions

1. What is meant by a 'systematic' approach to management development? Outline the essential elements of such an approach.

2. Under what conditions do managers learn best?

3. Distinguish between the responsibility of the line manager and the human resource specialist for the planning and implementation of MD activities.

CASE STUDY

Five Managers with Problems

Here are brief notes on five managers at different stages in their career with the group which you manage. The notes indicate such things as past and present performance, attitude to work and the organization…

Manager A

Manager A does an adequate and sometimes a very good job. She rarely shines however, either technically or managerially. She is now in her early forties and has been in her present job for nearly five years. She is a long serving member of the organization. She has always been very conscious of her position and status and takes every opportunity to indicate that she expects to move on to a more senior position. Her own direct manager is not so optimistic however, and sees it as unlikely that A will get much beyond her present level.

Manager B

Manager B has had a very successful career to date, both inside and outside the present organization. She has finally gained the senior position she has worked for over the years and has been in post for some six months. She is in her mid forties. She is finding that some of the technical requirements and the overall activity and time pressures associated with the new job difficult to cope with. She has been behind programme for most of the time. Also she is unused to managing a team with a wide age range and diversity of professional skills.

Manager C

Manager C has looked the same for many years, but he is not yet fifty. He has been in his present job for nearly ten years and is well known for not getting too involved. Everything is under control, done to time, and procedures are well tried and reliable. He never needs to take work home. He arrives at and leaves the office punctually. He is on good, if rather formal, terms with his staff and is calm and polite in his dealings with people from other departments. He is not interested in promotion and the only time that he gets upset is when changes are suggested in work procedures or his responsibilities.

Manager D

Manager D has only been in management for about eighteen months. He is something of a technical 'whizz kid' who produces high quality work all the time. He has a team of six specialists whom he treats as equals. He makes little attempt to run the team, contenting himself with sharing the work and helping people in difficulties. He has little time for administrators, and pays scant attention to returns and non technical paperwork. The work of the group, although good, is usually behind schedule.

Manager E

Manager E is a long serving member of the group and is still under fifty. He has a good record over the last ten years as a manager and is respected for it. In the last year, his absences have increased and his team have missed deadlines and generally given signs of low morale. He has always been active in local affairs, but this has never been allowed to interfere with his work. Only last week he has featured in the press, through his work with a local housing association.

Brief

The information about each of the five managers is obviously insufficient for you to make an analysis of problems with any degree of certainty. But read through the notes and suggest:

- Possible problems (if any) that these managers represent to the organization and to their immediate manager in particular.
- The possible range of approaches which could be used to deal with any problems.
- The development needs which each individual manager may have and how they might be satisfied.

Note This activity benefits from small group discussion, during which it is likely that a wide range of different perceptions of the five managers will emerge. This process might challenge some of your own preconceptions!

Chapter 10

Managing the Appraisal Process

Gerry Randell

Objectives

- To provide an historical overview of a process of management that has existed for a long time under the term 'staff appraisal' but has now been expanded and called 'performance management'
- To analyse the determinants of human performance at work so that appropriate diagnoses of what can be done to improve performance can be made
- To set out the conceptual, theoretical and practical problems of performance management
- To clarify the interactions between performance development and performance assessment
- To describe the place of career development in performance management
- To discuss the role of validation of human resource management
- To give guidelines about how performance management schemes can be designed and implemented

Introduction

Performance appraisal is the process by which individuals' work is observed, assessed, recorded, reported and discussed with the purpose of, somehow, improving the quality or quantity of work done, and maintaining or increasing the satisfaction the individual obtains from doing it. This somewhat simple definition obscures the enormous complexity of the process and the controversy that surrounds it.

In the past few years the complexity and controversy have been further aggravated by the trend in 'personnel management' to integrate the various practices, procedures and strategies of the profession into a seemingly more coherent system, and calling it 'human resource management'. Now the basic procedures of personnel management, staff appraisal, performance measurement, payment by results, merit rating and career development have all been pulled together under the term 'performance management'. Controversy rages about whether this is an appropriate way to go about managing the human resources of an organization.

What can be agreed is that appraising an individual's performance is a fundamental component of human resource management, as it is from this process that the data are generated for any systematic development of individuals, their training, their reward, their career path, the design of their jobs, their promotion, their dismissal, and even their early retirement. In addition, it is the source of information for plans and decisions to be made about the structure and management of the organization as a whole. It is therefore of the utmost importance to an organization to get it as technically sound as possible.

The key issues that will be considered in this chapter are the relationships between the main purposes of performance appraisal, which can be grouped as follows:

immediate performance improvement, performance related payment, the identification of potential for other jobs, and the validation of management procedures. The most controversial of these issues is relating financial reward directly to assessments of work performance, and this will be discussed later. The chapter will end with guidelines about the integration of performance management methods and how they can be implemented.

The History of Performance Management

It is not easy to decide what to do and how to go about improving the performance of people at work. There are many strategies that can be used. They range from what can be called the 'mega', when beliefs about the management of people are applied, to 'macro' systems, 'midi' techniques, 'mini' skills and 'micro' good intentions. Examples of these methods are set out in Table 10. The purpose of this table is to illustrate the history and the range of strategies that have been used by organizations over the years to improve performance at work beyond what could be achieved if people were just left to get on with it by themselves. Herein lies a moral. The inept application of banal concepts can detract from the 'natural' process of performance development that occurs with able and committed staff. To interfere with nature can be dangerous, so, before embarking upon a performance improvement programme, organizations should think and plan very carefully and guiding this process is a key function of the Human Resource Manager.

The assumption behind all the methods listed in Table 10 is that somehow or other they will increase corporate, team or individual performance and/or organizational morale and personal motivation. The management literature abounds with examples and cases that purport to give evidence of the effectiveness of these methods.[1] Some of the methods are cheap but difficult to apply; some are expensive and even inflationary; some are seen as threatening both to managers and managed; some are seen as undermining managerial authority; some are dangerous to organizational health when ineptly applied.

Table 10. Performance Management Methods

Since the dawn of managerial history, work organizations have sought ways to improve the performance of their staff in their jobs. Some examples of the methods used can be categorized according to how comprehensive and all-embracing they are to how instant, assertive and prescriptive, as follows:

MEGA (applying 'beliefs' to 'shake-up' the organization)

strategic human resource management; Business Process Re-engineering; worker participation; worker control; co-ownership; charismatic leadership; transforming management; exhortations for excellence; threats to survival.

MACRO (using 'systems' to build 'structures')

career development; Total Quality Management; work study; performance indices; Management by Objectives; job design; job rotation; job enrichment; merit rating; payment by results; job evaluation; Investors in People.

MIDI (developing 'techniques' to influence attitudes)

staff appraisal; supervisor training; managerial styles and grids; consultative committees; customer orientation; quality circles; Training within Industry; team building; ergonomics.

MINI (inculcating 'skills' to change behaviour)

counselling; coaching; interactive behaviour; interpersonal skills; schedules of reinforcement; Behaviour Modelling; group management; individual leadership.

MICRO (displaying 'good intentions' to obtain commitment)

concern for people; winning friends and influencing people; Transactional Analysis; One-minute Managing; empowering.

What can be observed in practice is that managers, consultants and academics tend to home in first on a particular category, from mega to micro, and then a particular approach within that category. Why this is done is perhaps more to due the particular backgrounds, experiences and personal philosophies about people and organizations, rather than any exact diagnosis based on a systematic analysis of what would be best for a particular organization at a particular moment in time.

This difficulty can be helped by looking at the history of performance management methods.[2] There have been very many well-intentioned, well-planned, well-designed projects in the past that have failed. There have also been many poorly conceived, ineptly designed projects that have succeeded. It could be that it is the *process* of performance management that is more important than the *content*. What is common to all the methods in Table 10 is that they all involve getting, giving and sharing information with people at work for the purpose of changing their, and the organization's, behaviour so that people are more satisfactory at their jobs and more satisfied with them. It is probable that it is this process that is central to, and crucial for, any behaviour change. It could therefore be argued that collecting information and using it to influence behaviour is certainly necessary and may be well on the way to being a sufficient method for identifying and overcoming the barriers for improved performance management. The problem with this conclusion is that it is just too simple sounding but, at the same time, its complexity and difficulty is underestimated by most managers, not the least because the process of changing behaviour, especially if it is significant, invariably releases anxiety, frequently anger, and often resentment. It is handling these emotions that makes the task even more demanding.

Organizational Diagnosis

Organizations that are trying to improve individual and corporate performance are faced with two main sources of difficulty. The first is concerned with information about the effectiveness and costs of the various sections and people in the organization; these can be called the *structural* problems. The second concerns the behaviour of the various groups and individuals in the organization, how they communicate, compete, conflict, achieve and feel about the organization. These can be called the *behavioural* problems. The biggest barrier to improving performance of and within organizations is mixing up these two sets of problems and using structural solutions to solve behavioural problems and attempting behavioural solutions for structural problems.

Clearly these two sets of problems and possible solutions overlap and interact, so it requires special effort and understanding to disentangle them. The advantage of putting in this effort is that the organizational problem becomes more clear and is therefore open to a more precise and effective treatment. It is sad to see organizations using so much managerial time and to solve effortse an inaccurately diagnosed problem. The history of management is strewn with many examples of such wasted effort. For example, of relevance to today, developing measures of performance for control or incentive purposes is a structural solution, when what is often lacking is the display of concern or appreciation for the work of individual members of staff, a behavioural problem.

Therefore, the first stage in changing the behaviour of organizations and people is making the diagnosis of what exactly is wrong, or inadequate, or inappropriate, and deciding what needs to be changed to ameliorate the condition. So it is an information gathering stage. There are two ways of getting this information and making the diagnosis. The first is to read the books and magazines on management, or go to conferences, or visit so-called successful organizations and see what is going on there, and decide from this 'survey' just what is needed in one's own organization. There is, of course, the chance that this may be a right decision, but there is higher probability that it is not. The alternative way is to gain information about what is really going on inside one's own organization, what groups and individual members of staff are actually doing and what they think should be done differently, and feed this into some kind of diagnosing/decision-making process. It is surprising to note that once this information has been surfaced and shared the structural or behavioural change solution is frequently obvious and, as a consequence, commitment to its application has been obtained through the information gathering process.

So what should the strategy be for improving organizational performance? The first stage has been signalled – use performance management to collect the information to diagnose just what an organization should be doing differently next – the *primary structural change*, and what individuals should be doing next – the *primary behavioural change.*

The next stage is to get these diagnoses turned into *appropriate* and *acceptable* 'treatments' or 'action plans' to which the staff of the organization are committed, i.e. influencing behaviour towards the achievement of structural and individual change. The next stage is to be ready to handle the emotional reactions that very frequently arise when trying to change anything or anybody – the resistance to change phenomenon. This can be achieved by providing an organizationally sanctioned occasion when organizational, managerial and individual changes in behaviour are discussed calmly, sympathetically, sensitively and, hopefully, effectively, with all those individuals and groups who will be affected by the performance management changes.

It must not be forgotten, as Table 10 implies, that some kind of performance management already goes on in all organizations. It can be seen to range from informal chats, where a manager makes a few 'helpful' comments about a member of staff's work, through discussing how well plans and objectives have been met and setting new ones, to instituting large-scale procedures like 'Total Quality Management' and 'Investors in People'. Examples of all these approaches can be seen throughout British work organizations and little agreement exists about what would be the best approach to this important area of human resources management. The confusion arises from a lack of understanding about the whole process of human resource development.

When the conceptual, theoretical and practical implications of performance management systems are analysed, the enormous complexity surrounding the process emerges. It is these difficulties which cause organizations to struggle with the problems of devising an appropriate scheme of staff development. From an analysis of the literature, research and observational studies of current practices in various organizations throughout the world, some general conclusions can be drawn. To impose some order on to the diversity of the difficulties, the analysis and conclusions will be grouped into Conceptual, Theoretical and Practical problem areas. However, it is stressed that, in practice, all these problem areas will be brought to bear simultaneously on a particular performance management system.

Conceptual Problems

The overall purpose of any performance management scheme should be to make an organization more effective through developing its human resources. In other words, staff development. Organizations can take many approaches to managing their staff and the need exists to evaluate, control, develop and predict the behaviour of staff by assembling information of their past, present and predicted future performance at their jobs. By any standards this is a mighty undertaking, something that is not likely to be achieved through a single system and at one 'sitting' between a manager and a member of staff. Of the four needs, i.e. the evaluation, control, development and prediction of work performance, only one – performance development – can directly improve the performance of staff at their existing jobs. The others, important as they are, can only increase the chances of better performance; they do not necessarily bring it about.

As a performance management scheme produces information collected from employees about how the organization should handle their capacity and motivation to work, it can be regarded as an aspect of Organization Development. Further, this information-based, rather than belief-based, decision making about organizational change should lead to decisions being made that have the commitment of the participants, rather than just tacit compliance. If, therefore, it is the policy of the organization to build up a more committed staff, then performance management should be regarded as a way of achieving it. This is where performance management also contributes to the corporate plan of the organization, by providing precise information to direct planning and change within the organization in the way it treats its staff. This aspect of human resources management is further elaborated in Chapters 2 and 15.

The meaning of the phrase 'staff development' also needs to be explored. Encouraging staff to 'work harder' and to gain more 'job satisfaction' are worthwhile intentions, but imprecise aims. In the final analysis, staff development should both add to people's capacity and their inclination to carry out their current job. If this does not happen then any staff development procedure is a failure.

Managers are expected to get a return from and, hopefully, improve upon the resources they are designated to manage. If they are responsible for the manufacturing, marketing or money resources of the organization they are forced to actively manage them. The nature of such resources is such that if they leave them alone the machines will corrode, the markets will be invaded and the money will be devalued; managers are therefore forced to apply considerable effort to guard and develop these resources. Modern management is also expected to do this through decision making on the basis of data rather than myth and belief. The opposite pressure applies to the management of people. If this resource is left alone it will grow by learning to respond to the experiences gained from the environment. It may not grow in the directions hoped for by the organization, but if the culture is basically benevolent and concerned, much of the growth will benefit the organization. Consequently organizations are inclined to take a passive approach to person management and let nature take its course. If the policy decision is made to actively involve managers in the development of the organization's human resources, then what is achieved must be more than what would have been gained by leaving people to develop themselves. This point is the basis for much of what is known as the dysfunctional outcomes of performance management procedures, where this gain over nature is not obtained.

Theoretical Problems

Behind the whole process of performance management are various theoretical assumptions about the nature of work, people, organizations, and even life itself. It is not the purpose of this chapter to survey all the relevant philosophical, economic and ethical issues. They are obviously of fundamental importance, but beyond the scope of this book. Nevertheless, they must at least be touched upon so that practitioners in this field are aware of the complexity of the problem. This point builds upon the issues of motivation and job satisfaction that were described in Chapter 6. The basis for the complexity is that work is an interaction between people and organizations, and the point of this interaction is known as Management. To start to understand just what goes on to make this interaction produce desirable outcomes, both to people and employing organizations, the notions about effective organizations, developing individuals, skilful management and the determinants of work performance need to be clarified.

So what is an effective organization? Is it one that has a high return on investment? Or is it one that gives a responsible service to society? Or can it be judged by the quality of working life it provides its members? Or shall this large question-begging statement be replaced by a simple view? For example, an effective organisation is one that learns, i.e. is adaptive, flexible, useful and growing? Chapters 5 and 14 in this book also touch on this view as it is one of the key concepts of Human Resource Management.

What, then, are developing individuals? Are they people who are continually adding to their capacity to do their job and experiencing growth in their motivation to do it? But just how do people learn, step-by-step or through flashes of insight? Can they be told to do such things or are they more readily obtained through a learning experience? What can be said with certainty is that people need precise information about what they should be learning for effective learning to take place. Giving a general exhortation to 'pull themselves together' and 'go off and work harder' is of little use. Similarly organizations need precise information about people's needs before they can add to the level of motivation. These observations raise the whole subject of learning and motivational theory which underpins most performance management and staff development activity. Although there is as yet insufficient general theory to prescribe what organizations should do, there is enough to indicate that which is appropriate to apply to the problem of designing performance management schemes.

What, then, are skilful managers? Are they those who are able to observe, check, get, give, share and use information about human behaviour at work; to achieve development both in the organizations for whom they work and the individuals who work for them? And to do this in a supportive way that aids understanding and tolerance of the difficulties involved in changing behaviour. This raises complex theoretical problems about the nature of human skills and implies that person management is a skill that, like any other skill, can only be acquired through practice and feedback. To learn a skill a person must first want to become skilful. A skill cannot be taught, it can only be learned. This is complicated for those skills where some kind of practice has already taken place, because then there is an 'unfreezing' problem, where a learner is helped to understand just how much more there is to learn. It is important at this stage not to undermine a practitioner's self-esteem. So managers must be helped to realise that it is no criticism of them personally to say that every manager has a lot to learn about how to manage their staff. As Wright and Taylor[3] so cogently display, it is just these interpersonal skills of gathering information, influencing behaviour and handling emotion that turn a manager into a leader. They argue that the attempt by organizations to increase the amount of that most elusive of all managerial attributes, 'leadership', within the organization, could well start with training managers in performance management skills.

What, then, are the determinants of work performance? How much of individuals' work arises from what is 'inside' them, e.g. their abilities or attitudes; or 'inside' the organization, e.g. the tools that they have been given, or the way they are managed? Disentangling the causes of work performance, then allocating causal contribution to each determinant is one of the great theoretical and methodological problems of organizational psychology. It is a long way off being solved and, this being so, gives another reason why naïve attempts at measuring what may appear to be causal factors, through simplistic rating scales, should not be lightly undertaken. The analysis of the history and content of what is now known as the 'Performance Management' component of Human Resource Management not only displays the split between structural and behavioural approaches, it also reveals an additional major dichotomy. This is between trying to manage performance through giving people 'learning experiences' or through giving them more financial reward. In the final theoretical analysis, no matter what the determinants are of work performance, there is always something, whether it is a change in the individual or a change in the work environment, that can be done that would improve an individual's performance on a job. It is the diagnosis of this that is the essential objective of any performance analysis and which should be the focus of any staff development scheme.

Practical Problems

The task now remains to consider how to establish an effective performance management scheme. Although the ideas presented above are simple, putting them into practice will not be easy. The first step is to accept the enormity of the problem and, like any enormous problem, the only way to handle it is to break it down into its component parts. It is a danger to design a performance management scheme that is so comprehensive and attempts to achieve so much that it can only be carried out by paragons of managerial skill! Such a scheme is administratively attractive but as it is to be used by ordinary line managers, who more often than not do not possess the range of the designer's technical and management competence, it is probably doomed to failure. There is also the ethical point that it is grossly unfair on people at work to evaluate their performance before attempts are made to help them to develop it. Further, it is incorrect to assume a direct relationship between performance at one level of work with potential for another. The most common practical error seen in the design of performance management schemes is the attempt to achieve performance development, merit rating and potential identification all in one programme. The most common theoretical error is the assumption that a merit rating policy, e.g. giving more reward for more work, necessarily improves the quality of individuals' work or their satisfaction. It could just be that they work harder at getting rated better to the detriment of the true effectiveness of their work or motivation. Consequently, it must be a carefully considered policy decision by an organization to link pay directly with performance through some kind of merit rating scheme. However, there are many other ways that managers can reward their staff and discrimination, precision and skill are required to manage a reward review system.

This raises, again, the controversial issue of relating financial reward directly to assessments of work performance. Even though the surveys indicate that the proportion of performance management schemes that include some element of linked payment or merit rating has remained static at about 40%, what can be currently observed, particularly in the private sector, is a growing swing towards performance related pay systems. This analysis of the basic conceptual, theoretical and practical issues of performance management enables some policy and operational recommendations to be made.

To give differential reward for different levels of performance requires performance to be measured. Performance does not need to be measured. As a large volume of work indicates, usefully summarised and progressed by Bailey,[4] it is extremely difficult to measure performance with any degree of accuracy or acceptability. It therefore follows that it is unwise to risk undermining the performance development component of performance management with an inept and distracting performance measurement scheme. This leads to the clear recommendation that performance development should be separated from performance assessment and, for the ethical reasons touched on earlier, the development should precede assessment.

1. *Performance Development*

   There is little doubt that an effective performance review system which results in commitment to changes in individual, managerial and organizational behaviour is the cornerstone of any performance management system. There is also little doubt that assembling information about the performance of staff for the purpose of improving it is both the responsibility and duty of all line managers. Only they have direct access to the main determinants of behaviour at work.

   An approach to making the performance review more systematic that is often advocated by many organizations, is through setting targets or some kind of objective. So-called 'management-by-objectives' has very wide support as a way of controlling and assessing the performance of people at their jobs. Unfortunately, when this technique is applied to performance management, it can have many adverse effects. The main one is diverting the discussion away from any precise issues of individual behaviour. This is especially noticeable when there is effort to agree quantitative targets rather than behavioural change. Then there is the problem of allowing for chance extraneous factors in the judgements made by managers which could affect the achievement of targets.

The most severe constraint on performance reviews is the ability of managers to carry them out. It is easy to design forms and relatively easy to fill them out. But to control subjectivity and to cope with the complexity of observing and changing human behaviour requires a great deal of skill and effort. Getting managers to obtain and apply these crucial aspects of interpersonal expertise is an enormous task. It should start by persuading managers that performance management is not about assessments or ratings, although these may have to come later on in the process. In the first instance, all it is about is diagnosing what an individual needs to know next that could add to their capacity for their existing job, i.e. a development step. Also, to diagnose what the manager should try to do next that would help the individual's motivation in that job, i.e. 'motivation growth'. Unless these two fundamental purposes are understood by managers and achieved through a performance review system, the whole process is a waste of time and effort.

The support system, or paperwork required for a performance review procedure need only be quite simple. In theory a blank sheet of paper should suffice. But, in practice, some pre-printed form that signals organizational sanction and support for performance reviewing would be useful for sending information, or such things as training needs, through to the appropriate departments. How well a form is completed is also a useful indicator of the effectiveness of the review and can impose pressure on managers to use the process properly. Whether or not there is a need for automatic 'sending in the forms', i.e. 'staff reporting', is a debatable issue and can form an interesting aspect of organizational politics! There is little doubt that the key advice in designing a performance review system is to 'keep it simple', both in content and practice. The crucial determinant of its success is the commitment of the participants to its principles and process. Therefore, any system or paperwork procedure must be seen as a support rather than a threat.

2. *Performance Assessment*

Measurements of work performance are required by an organization for many reasons. They are useful in work planning, in costing and for contrasts and comparisons. They can also be required to feed a differential payment system. A 'fair' and acceptable reward system is an essential requirement of any organization. The process whereby people are observed, have their performance assessed, are given the opportunity to discuss their assessment, and what that means in terms of their payment, is that part of performance management known as reward review. Chapter 4 reviews the issues surrounding wages and salaries and sets out the differences between assessing the worth of jobs, job evaluation, paying differential rewards for performances and merit rating. As Chapter 4 shows, the whole area of relative rewards is shrouded with cultural, historical and legislative factors. There is an important difference between job evaluation and merit-rating. Job evaluation is all about assessing the worth of the job a person is doing. As Chapter 4 explains, there is the implication of something absolute, fixed over time and separate from individual behaviour about job evaluation. Whereas merit-rating is all about the relative worth of one individual's performance with another, it is variable over time, and is very much concerned with individual ability and effort. Consequently, organizations can design the two procedures separately. However, in practice, it is not so easy to make a firm distinction, particularly when both systems are expected to make use of the same performance management data. An additional complication, which is most marked in those companies without a clear job grading structure within a job evaluation scheme, is when individuals perform so well that the organization loads more work, and perhaps responsibility, on to them over the review period, so the staff expect financial recognition for performance in what is in effect a new job. It is this overlap area between job evaluation and merit-rating which is the most demanding aspect of managing an organization's wages and salaries procedures, particularly on the skill of the manager, and the morale of the staff. So, using the appropriate job evaluation procedures is an essential part of organization management, whereas setting up a merit-rating scheme is not essential for developing an effective organization.

However, where the policy of the organization is to vary financial reward according to relative achievement or ability, information is required to feed this system. Consequently, the person responsible for the payment and perquisite procedures requires information that discriminates between individual performance so that these decisions can be made. The key issue here is devising and operating an appropriate scale, or scales, that allow for meaningful and acceptable discriminations between work performances to be made.

The history of rating scales of work performance is a long one. The two main approaches to this assessment problem are either to develop more dimensions of work performance and more elaborate scales for measuring them, or to stick to a single dimension rating scale of overall worth and then to institute procedures and training to control the subjectivity involved in its use.

The arguments in favour of a multidimensional approach are that they can cover a wide range of work outcomes, which can be given previously agreed relative weights, so the whole procedure appears more fair, comprehensive, thorough and even 'scientific'. Latham and Wexley[5] give a full account of this approach and provide useful guidelines for 'making the system work'.

The main argument in favour of the unidimensional approach is that the human brain cannot be beaten as an instrument for observing, assembling and analysing a wide range of imprecise, often conflicting, information and for quickly coming to a decision based upon it. The problem is to get the owner of the instrument to use these impressive facilities properly! The observation can be made here that university staff have used a 6 point unidimensional assessment scale for generations of students, First, Upper Second, Lower Second, Third, Pass and Fail'. It appears to work, even though mistakes may get made from time to time, but in the highly disciplined academic environment they are thought to be rare.

This unidimensional approach can be seen operating in many British companies who have deliberately ensured, over a long period of time, that the scale is used in a disciplined way by managers. It is this point that is often forgotten by designers of appraisal schemes. It is easy to design a rating scale of work performance, usually by a committee, issue it, and expect managers to use it. But, without a history of experience, understanding, care and commitment, the categories on the scale will be interpreted differently by the managers. Phrases like, "I only allow 1's to work for me", or "staff are not as good as they used to be – all I ever get are 3's", will soon indicate rampant subjectivity.

The human brain is not only a marvellous instrument for using information, it is also superb at misusing it. So, if a straightforward approach to quantitative assessment for a reward review is required, then the first step is to define a unidimensional scale, probably with 5 or 6 categories, described as operationally as possible, perhaps in the first instance with predetermined indications of what proportion of a department's staff should fall within each category. Then to put a great deal of effort into getting managers to control their biases and prejudices when using it. The effort should be more towards attitudinal training rather than skills training, as rating exercises only help managers to be more skilful in manipulating and misusing the scales for their own ends.

The key objective in this training is to bring about 'disciplined subjectivity' in the use of the scale, and this can take a long time. Even with a great deal of care and technical expertise, the use of quantitative assessment methods for discriminating between work performance and determining pay will cause an organization a large amount of trouble and take up a great deal of managerial time. The question will be raised as to whether or not it is worth it, particularly if it appears to be causing more alienation and conflict than motivation and commitment in the staff of the organization.

Once policy and practice in the two main components of performance management have been established, performance review and reward review, then the data generated can be used to diagnose the next stages in the process. This is where Table 10 can be used to structure a diagnostic process. The danger here is the tendency to go for the 'flavour of the month', and decide upon a method that is currently popular. Contemporary approaches to performance management, as assembled by Neale[6] and Armstrong,[7] would indicate that the next stage should be some system for succession planning or career development.

3. *Career Development*

Organizations have a continual requirement to identify and develop their future managers for the purpose of laying the foundations of effective performance in other jobs, i.e. forward looking performance management. Individuals want to know and understand how their career is likely to develop over time. To assemble and use information for predicting the future behaviour of people at work is probably the most technically complex and sensitive of all individual and organizational development activities.

A key issue is deciding over how long a period of time predictions are to be made. If attempts are made to make predictions beyond the 'next' job or promotion then information needs to be assembled at some 'central' point to help data based decisions to be made by a 'management development adviser'. This is now frequently done by means of some kind of 'assessment centre'. These are occasions when a member of staff is given a battery of tests, exercises, questionnaires and interviews aimed at eliciting their capacity and inclination for higher level jobs, and the possible directions for their careers. Fletcher and Williams[8] review the main issues involved and show how such activity abounds with technical and administrative pitfalls. Like reward review procedures, reviewing an individual's potential for other jobs does not necessarily add directly to the performance in their existing jobs. The existence of such potential review systems may 'keep staff at it', but they may also encourage looking too much at the future, so letting the present go by default. Obviously line managers are often asked by members of staff to express an opinion about their careers and potential and, as a result of such discussions, information may be generated of use to the potential review process. Whether or not a line manager should conduct the formal review of their staff's potential and possible career path is a difficult organizational decision to make.

The crucial theoretical problem here is just what of a person's capacities, inclinations, needs and experiences are predictive of higher level managerial behaviour. The technical problem is then assessing them. On top of all this is the problem of raising expectations in those people who are led to believe they have potential, and maintaining motivation in those who are given the impression they do not. This is a veritable quagmire for performance management.

The main practical issues in any potential review procedure are deciding who should enter it and then how the outcomes should be handled. The role of the line manager is critical. As a result of reviewing current performance the manager is best placed to form a judgement on whether or not an individual should be considered for another, possibly higher level job, and then to issue the 'ticket to ride' the potential review procedure, although the 'system' should not prevent individuals issuing their own tickets. Observations from the performance review are usefully fed into the potential review process, both qualitative and quantitative where available, preferably on a specially designed form rather than just photocopies of the performance review and reward review documents. This may sound like extra paperwork, but potential reviewing does not apply to all the staff all the time. Entering the potential review procedure should be regarded as a 'special ride', and not automatically undertaken on an annual basis. This is such an important, sensitive area of Human Resource Management, that it has to be initiated very carefully and thoroughly by a line manager. The 'central' assessment, evaluation, and decision making process can then be followed by, hopefully, highly competent 'assessors' so that the next task for the line manager is handling the re-entry back to day-to-day departmental work. For a 'high flier' this should not be too difficult; for the 'work-horse' this may be exceedingly delicate, and will again stretch the interpersonal management skills of a line manager to the limits. Consequently, all the paperwork and demands on a line manager should be, once again, aimed at giving help and support in this difficult aspect of performance management.

4. *Validation of Performance Management Procedures*

A further aspect of performance management which is frequently overlooked is the need to discover how well the organization's human resource management procedures are working, such as selection and training schemes. Data for this 'organization review' can be derived from existing performance management schemes but it is probably better obtained through special 'follow-up' reports of individuals' performance. This is the field of validation and is usually the province of independent or external researchers. Some organizations are setting up internal consultancy and personnel research groups, which are seen as independent enough to carry out the analysis of what may be very sensitive data. The key problem here is that of organizational politics. Many senior managers would appear to resent efforts to investigate whether or not they are managing their staff effectively. When they do they would not necessarily give their full cooperation for such data to be accumulated and analysed.

In the field of organization review the requirement to use all types and levels of measurement is paramount. The more precise and higher the level of measurement achieved, the more advanced the statistics that can be used.

Also, this area of personnel research can be used as a proving ground for performance measures that are needed in other areas, particularly reward and potential reviews. If they do not work here the only outcome will be that a few statistics will have been under-estimated. If incorrect measures are used in staff development, then a large number of alienated performances will be the outcome. The availability of staff and resources to devise performance measures, and to undertake follow-up studies within an organization, provides the opportunity not only to accumulate data on the effectiveness of personnel practices, but also to indicate the best ways to integrate them.

The first paperwork requirement of an organization review procedure is sound performance measures. Research over the past twenty years, culminating in studies at Bradford, published by Bailey,[5] has shown that some kind of behaviourally anchored scale, based on empirically derived incidents and dimensions, is possibly the best available technique to use. Although exceedingly time-consuming to produce, behaviourally anchored rating scales (BARS) can provide the foundation for quantitative approaches to organization review, and provide the source of validated measures of performance for the reward and potential reviews. The further point can be made that the standing of Human Resources Management will be determined by the quality of organization review statistics that are generated. At the moment 'HRM' has still to prove itself as a force in organizational management. The proof will follow the generation of high quality performance management validation data.

The Way Ahead

There is currently a great deal of discussion about integrating personnel practices in an organization within a strategic human resources management policy. This does not mean that all personnel practices should be run together, although bureaucratic tidiness and simplistic application of theory may be seen to imply this. On the contrary, effective human resources management means getting all the bits of practice as technically sound, administratively convenient and socially acceptable as possible, and as skilfully run as practicable. This means putting effort into controlling the possible contamination of each part by keeping separate the conflicting purposes and data. Energy can then be put into ensuring that the separate parts of personnel activity are integrated into a systematic whole. This is perhaps the key issue in Human Resources Management, obtaining integration at the 'macro' level without impeding the effective operation of the parts.

The above observations and the history and analysis of performance management given in this Chapter should provide sufficient evidence to encourage the separation, in practice, of performance, reward, potential and organization reviews. It is a key recommendation of this Chapter that the achievement of effective performance management is too important to risk the dangers involved in contaminating the information of decision making, by attempting to merge the four separate groups of purposes into a single, monolithic performance management scheme.

When the separation is so planned, each of the procedures can be developed as an independent exercise, sharing information where it is relevant. As the process of Performance Review is the only one of the four that can directly add to the development of an individual and an organization, then this is the one which provides the information base for worthwhile performance management schemes. If an organization really wants itself to be developed in this way, the following then need to be undertaken, probably in parallel, and possibly starting in this order:

(a) *Policy*

The first thing that needs to be done is to spread the key concepts, as set out above, of performance management around the organization, preferably starting at the top, so as to get managerial commitment, rather than compliance, to any systems or procedures that may be developed.

As a start, a 'Board Seminar' should be held. where the senior managers of the organization share their views about performance management and are helped to understand the concepts and practical implications of what could be effective performance management. If it is then agreed that a scheme is appropriate for the organization, the policy decision to apply time and resources to achieving it can then be made, and responsibilities allocated to bring it about within an appropriate time-scale.

Whether or not performance should be linked directly with pay is a very serious policy decision for an organization. There are philosophical, economic and practical arguments both ways. The decision should be based on information about the current condition of the organization, and in what direction it should go, rather than just on the philosophy and opinions of the most influential members of senior management. To get this diagnosis right is a crucial issue in the human resources management of any organization.

(b) *Training*

Concepts without the ability to apply them are barren. Perhaps one of the major weaknesses of management training is the tendency to teach information and let the skills go by default. Unfortunately, skills can only be acquired by people who want to learn them, so there is sometimes a major problem in 'unfreezing' managers from their personal view that they already have sufficient interpersonal skills to carry out performance management effectively. The fact is that half of all managers are below average in their level of skill to interact purposefully with their staff, and numerous surveys and research studies indicate that the average itself is rather low!

The 'unfreezing' process to encourage managers to acquire the skills of performance management can be achieved in various ways, but there are two main principles that could be applied. The first is the design and content of the skills training; the second is the sequence and timing of such training. Experiences in undertaking this work has shown that training courses in performance management skills[9] must be of at least two days' duration. The first day should aim to get across the main concepts and the notion that changing the behaviour of staff is a skill, nothing more, nor less. Then the practical work on the first day should demonstrate just how much of the skill there is to learn, and then display to each and every member of the course the precise aspect of their own behaviour which needs to be changed to increase their own level of skill.

The second day builds upon the first, giving supervised practice in the insights gained on the first day and, additionally, developing in the participants the ability for observation, self-analysis and self-tutoring. Such precision and experiences in learning can only be achieved through the use of skilled tutors. The availability and efforts of tutors is the key to the acquisition of skill in trainees, for it is essential that the practical work undertaken on the course is accompanied by exact and acceptable guidance about the trainees' performance, i.e. feedback. Without skilled tutoring the learning can not only be inefficient, it can also be dangerous to the further acquisition of the skills of performance management within trainees, who are either given a false feeling of confidence, or doubt that they could ever interact purposefully with their staff. Taylor and Wright[10] set out the issues in training tutors very thoroughly, and show how important this is.

To create acceptance of, and commitment to, the need for acquisition and growth of performance management skills, such training should start at the 'operating' top of an organization and preferably be concentrated within divisions of the organization rather than spread across levels. In this way a climate of understanding and a will to be skilful can be quickly achieved within working units, so that the skills are subsequently practised in a supportive environment. They will then be likely to grow rather than wither, and so become an established part of managerial behaviour.

(c) *Support systems*

As has been noted before in this Chapter, the main use for printed performance management forms is the overt organizational sanction they give to the expenditure of time and effort on the process. The design of the forms and other paperwork in performance management procedures is often seen as the end result of staff development schemes rather than a means of achieving increased 'performance' of both individuals and organizations. Consequently, as the above principles have explicitly stated, separate provision should be made to meet the needs of any merit rating, job evaluation, promotion or validation systems.

Once training arrangements have been made and introduced for the necessary skills to be developed in the organization, the need for pre-printed forms can be directed towards providing guidelines and support for the exercise of performance management skills, and to meet the secondary organizational need for a control procedure, to ensure that performance development and disciplined assessment has taken place. It cannot be stressed enough that forms should be designed to meet the needs of the line managers, to be precise and skilful, rather than seen as material for a records department.

(d) *The next stage*

No human resource management procedure should ever remain static and, in the light of practice and experience, it should be improved. Once the level of performance management skill in managers has been increased then the support procedures could be changed in accordance with the growth of this skill, so that even more effective performance development is achieved. If personnel policy decrees that a fast pace of development takes place, then refresher and advanced training courses need to be implemented. Problems will also arise with changes in the expectations of the individuals making up the organization, and with the rate of growth of the organization itself. These factors may lead to desirable changes in the performance management procedure. Therefore, the scheme will need to be monitored and changed in accordance with information about its effects and effectiveness.

Once the basic procedures for developing performance in the existing job, rewarding it, collecting information for promotion and career development have been established, then other aspects of performance management can be addressed. These basic procedures will then produce the data needed to diagnose which of the many other methods of improving performance listed in Table 10 should be used next.

Conclusion

This chapter has ranged widely over the many issues surrounding the concept of performance management. It has not put forward a set of proposals that would enable an instant performance management scheme to be installed. Instead, it has laid down the principles that should guide the design and implementation of a scheme based on a diagnosis of the immediate performance improvement needs of the organization.

Many managerial colleagues will have their own views about the meaning, purpose and practice of performance management. Some of them are difficult to shift and it may be unrealistic to suppose that a truly effective performance development scheme will be able to be achieved easily. The fundamental principles about the analysis, diagnosis and treatment of an organization's performance, that should guide the design and implementation of any scheme can be summarised as follows:

1. Performance management should be 'development led' rather than 'assessment led'. This means that managers should appraise their staff for the purpose of diagnosing what they should be doing differently next that would add to their performance in their existing job; and to discover what the organization should be doing differently for them that would add to their inclination to apply their capacity to their job. In the light of fairness and natural justice, this diagnosis and action plan should precede any assessment of a person's relative worth to an organization, and their potential for higher level work.

2. Performance management should be 'skills led' rather than 'forms led'. This means that early on in the process of, introduction of a new or revised performance management scheme, a start should be made to ensure that managers have the interpersonal skills necessary to interact purposefully and effectively with their staff.

3. Performance management should be 'line-management centred' rather than 'personnel centred'. This means that it should be designed and accepted as a procedure for helping line managers to develop their own staff better, rather than being a part of the personnel department's attempt to develop work and power for themselves. Clearly a delicate balance has to be established between the line managers' need for help and guidance in developing their own staff and the Personnel Department's need for information about employees. Achieving this balance is one of the essential features of Human Resources Management.

References

1. D.C. Wilson and R.H. Rosenfeld, *Managing Organizations,* McGraw-Hill, London, 1990

2. G.A. Randell, 'Employee Appraisal', in *Personnel Management: A comprehensive guide to theory and practice in Britain,* 2nd edition, K. Sisson (Ed.) Blackwell, Oxford, 1994.

3. P.L. Wright and D.S. Taylor, *Improving Leadership Performance,* Prentice Hall, Englewood Cliffs, N.J., 1984.

4. C.T. Bailey, *The Measurement of Job Performance,* Gower, Aldershot, 1983.

5. G.P. Latham and K.N. Wexley, *Increasing Productivity Through Performance Appraisal,* Addison-Wesley, Reading, Mass. 1981.

6. F. Neale (Ed) *The Handbook of Performance Management,* Institute of Personnel Management, London, 1991

7. M. Armstrong, *Performance Management,* Kogan Page, London, 1994

8. C. Fletcher and R. Williams, *Performance Appraisal and Career Development,* Hutchinson, London, 1985.

9. G. Randell, P. Packard and J. Slater, *Staff Appraisal – A First Step to Effective Leadership,* Institute of Personnel Management, London, 1984.

10. D.S. Taylor and P.L. Wright, *Developing Interpersonal Skills Through Tutored Practice,* Prentice Hall, Englewood Cliffs, N.J., 1988

Further Reading

The following books are easy to read, thorough, and contain many useful suggestions for implementing performance appraisal:

R.I. Henderson (1984) *Performance Appraisal,* (2nd edition), Reston Publishing Company Inc.

G.C. Anderson (1993) *Managing Performance Appraisal Systems,* Blackwell

C. Fletcher (1993) *Appraisal: Routes to Improved Performance,* IPM

Questions

1. What are the main issues that have to be covered when designing and implementing a staff appraisal scheme?

2. Compare and contrast a *development* approach to performance management with an *assessment* approach.

3. What is the role of *performance measurement* in staff development schemes?

CASE STUDY

The Sam Turner Case

It's time I did something about Sam Turner's performance at his job, thought Heather Caldwell, Regional Sales Manager of Solent Oil and Cake PLC, as she looked over the current sales figures. Sam is one of the three Sales Managers reporting to her. He was appointed to his present position just over a year ago after a successful period as sales supervisor. However, the performance of his area has not come up to expectations. Sam has achieved only steady sales, rather than the average increase of four per cent obtained in other areas. Two main aspects of Sam's work behaviour cause Heather concern.

First, he seems to spend more time in the office than other Sales Managers. The office is neat and efficiently run with well-used planning aids much in evidence. However, Heather wonders whether he is maintaining enough contact with key customers. For example, she is concerned about two of his major accounts, Smith's PLC and West and Sons. He has not visited either of them in the past year. This adds to Heather's workload because their buyers, old friends of hers, contact her directly. After having dealt with their enquiries, she has always sent copies of correspondence to Sam, hoping that he will take the hint and establish contact himself but, so far, they still come directly to her.

Second, labour turnover is greater in Sam's group than in any of the other sales areas. Four of his nine sales reps left last year, giving "frustration" and "poor pay" as the reasons. However, the most recent one to leave, an old friend of Heather, told her privately that she was leaving because she could no longer stand Turner's "overbearing attitude".

Heather will be seeing Sam next week for his quarterly sales review. Obviously, something will have to be done to improve his performance – but what, and how?

What do you think might be the causes of Sam Turner's performance problems and what remedial actions do you think might be taken to solve them? Treat these as hypotheses to be checked out later. Do not worry if some of them are contradictory.

Chapter 11

Managing Stress at Work

Alistair Ostell

Objectives

- To discuss different uses of the term stress and provide a working definition of psychological stress
- To describe the consequences of psychological stress for individuals and organizations
- To examine ways of measuring stress in the workplace
- To consider the main sources of stess at work
- To discuss individual and organizational strategies for managing stress

After completing chapter 11 you should be able to:

- List the three main approaches to defining stress and describe the key processes of an interactional model of psychological stress
- Identify how psychological stress manifests itself and ways in which it can be measured at work
- Explain the differences between a source, mediator and moderator of stress
- Compare the relative merits of the different strategies for managing stress at work
- Appreciate the importance of understanding the nature, causation and management of psychological stress to the process of managing human resources at work and to the design of jobs and the workplace

Introduction

The subject of stress is very topical and one which is intrinsically fascinating to many people. It is difficult to read magazines or newspapers, to listen to the radio or watch television without encountering the subject. However, for all this attention on stress and despite the fact that most people would claim to know what stress is, there seems to be little understanding of the specific psychological processes involved when people become distressed by events and circumstances. Yet, without this understanding, it is difficult for someone to know how to avoid, or to cope best with stress, either in themselves or others.

Stress in the workplace is a particularly important, contemporary issue. The ever increasing requirement for organizations to be more competitive by cutting costs and improving efficiency has produced numerous changes for employees. For example, they have often had to take on enlarged jobs with increased responsibilities, to become multi-skilled, accept flexible working, higher job mobility, performance-related job and remuneration contracts, and so on, while also faced with long-term job insecurity in some cases. Thus, the pressures upon many employees have never been greater. The direct and indirect costs to them of such circumstances are high and can result in deteriorating psychological and physical health, reduced job satisfaction, poor work relationships and, in some instances, loss of job. The costs to organizations are also significant in terms of poor standards of work, absenteeism, labour turnover, industrial relations problems, litigation regarding stressful working conditions, and increased health care insurance premiums. Therefore, it is of great importance that personnel specialists appreciate the nature of stress, its impact at work, how the Human Resource Management (HRM) function can help the organization to assess levels of work stress, and how individuals and the organization can best manage stress at work.

The next section of this chapter discusses different uses of the term stress and offers a working definition of psychological stress.

Subsequent sections examine how psychological distress can be recognized and the longer term consequences of stress. Sources of stress at work and how workplace stress can be measured are considered next. Then strategies for the management of stress at individual and organizational levels are explored. Finally, the topics of organizational crises and post-traumatic stress, and litigation and stress, are considered briefly.

Theoretical and Conceptual Background

A Definition

For the purposes of this chapter the following definition of psychological stress will be used:

> *A person is in a state of psychological stress when that person perceives and reacts to situations and events, whether real or imagined, in such a way as to tax unduly, or exceed, their resources for coping. Psychological stress is indicative of dysfunctional ways of thinking and acting which lead to an unsatisfactory person-environment, or person-self, relationship.*

Defined in this way, a person is described as being *psychologically stressed* when that person engages in certain ways of thinking and acting as they anticipate or attempt to cope with situations, or to manage themselves. These ways of thinking and acting are *dysfunctional* because they result, particularly when maintained, in *psychological distress:* disturbances in thought, emotion and behaviour which are disruptive to normal functioning but which are normally not sufficiently serious or enduring to be considered mental illnesses. In other words, these disturbances, sometimes known as stress reactions or stress responses (e.g. anxiety or depressive states, post-traumatic stress, protracted grief, preoccupation with failure), are not indications of organic disease processes, but of the failure of people to cope adequately with their work, social, domestic or personal circumstances.

The term stress has been used in various ways which can make the subject confusing, particularly for the lay person. In order to lessen this confusion and to appreciate why psychological stress has been defined as it has above it is necessary to examine briefly some commonly held views. The two most common views of stress are captured by the phrases "she is under a lot of stress" (the stimulus or engineering view) and "he looks really stressed" (the response or medical view).[1]

The Stimulus or Engineering View of Stress

The stimulus or engineering view sees stress as a load or pressure placed upon someone and strain as the outcome of attempting to cope once that load exceeds a certain point. Thus strain, in the form of psychological distress, is seen as the consequence of too much pressure. This view is a popular one, no doubt because it seems to correspond with experience and perhaps because it is felt to exempt people from responsibility for their mental, emotional and physical distress. Put differently, if these distress reactions were inevitable, given the pressures people had to cope with, then they escape any stigma associated with having the reactions.

The engineering view has several obvious limitations as it cannot adequately explain various facts. For example, a task which proves stressful to one person can prove stimulating or challenging to another. Further, a task which is disturbing to a person on one occasion might have little impact on another occasion. Thus, a manager will normally find it much more anxiety provoking to make a presentation to a group of colleagues, who are expected to be severely critical of the views expressed, than to make that same presentation to supportive and interested colleagues. Paradoxically for the engineering view of stress, people also exhibit distress reactions because the load upon them is too low! For instance, people become upset and protest about having insufficient work, or tasks which are too easy for them. Thus situational pressures alone are not an adequate explanation of the occurrence of distress states.

The Medical or Response View of Stress

The medical or response view of stress sees the phenomenon as a general bodily response to some environmental pressure or demand. Hans Selye was primarily responsible for advancing this view. He saw the stress response (called the General Adaptation Syndrome or GAS) as a universal and fixed pattern of physiological reactions which occurred whenever a person faced a stimulus which was noxious to body tissues. He subsequently argued that psychological events could also produce the GAS. This reaction pattern has been likened to an emergency response (initially evidenced by increased heart rate, deeper and faster respiration, the redirection of blood from the skin and various organs to the muscles, etc), mobilizing people so that they can take appropriate action to defend themselves against the noxious stimulus.[2]

The medical view is also of limited use in providing an understanding of stress, because the general physical changes it identifies in people facing so-called stressful situations can also be observed in people engaging in activities not usually thought to be stressful (e.g. taking exercise). Further, contrary to the views of Selye, the same situation can lead to quite different, disturbing psychological reactions in people (e.g. anxiety, or anger or depression) each of which is associated with different physiological reaction patterns. Thus, although Selye was able to identify a general response syndrome, it is not observeable in all situations which people describe as stressful, and its pattern varies from person to person and situation to situation when it does occur.[3] But, most importantly, this model does not account for why and when people experience psychological distress, whether they are facing demanding or apparently trivial situations.

The Interactional View of Stress

In order to understand how situations, whether apparently demanding or trivial, can result in people experiencing distressing psychological and physical states, an interactional view of stress is required. This focuses upon the *psychological processes* involved when a person notices, makes sense of and reacts to situations or events. The basic premise of the interactional view is that *situations of themselves are not intrinsically stressful; rather, people distress themselves by the ways they perceive and react to situations.*

Figure 11.1 portrays diagrammatically the interactional view using three overlapping circles. The largest circle represents a *person* who is the central point of reference in this model. *Situations* to which the person has to react are portrayed by the circle on the left. They can arise from external circumstances or events (e.g. of work, social or domestic origin), or from within the person (e.g. an individual's state of mind or health), hence the overlap of these circles. Situations are not taken at face value but are appraised in terms of their significance for the person, and of how to respond to

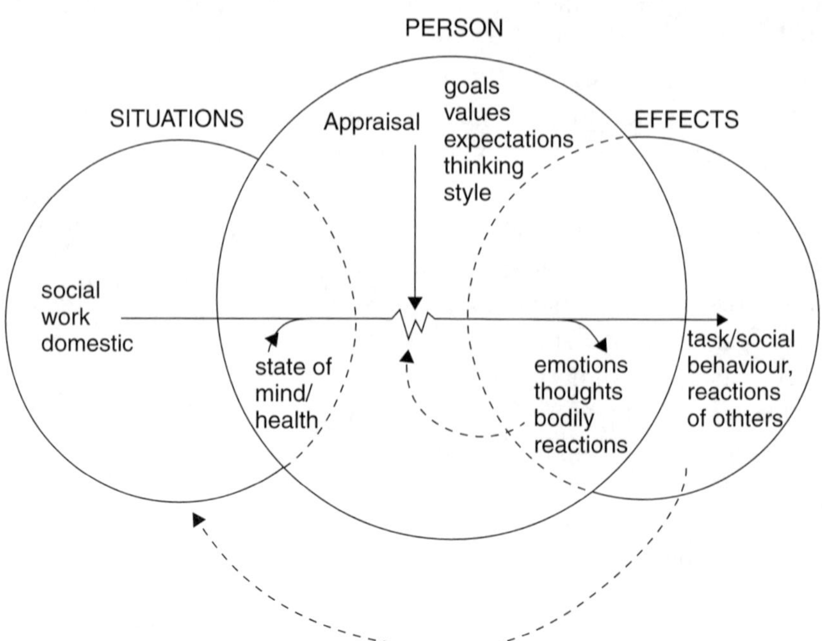

Figure 11.1. An interactional model psychological stress.

them. Various *effects* (the right circle), internal to the person, follow from the appraisal processes, including changes in thoughts, emotions and bodily reactions. Changes also occur in the person's overt behaviour (e.g. task performance, social interaction). The dotted lines indicate that these changes *feed back* affecting, on a continuing basis, both the person's reactions and the situation to which the person is responding, thus modifying the person-environment relationship. Because of this mutual influence and exchange between the person and the environment, interactional models are sometimes called *transactional* models.

Appraisal, Costs and Coping

Appraisal processes mediate a person's interchange with the world and two general kinds of processes have been identified: attributing *meaning or significance* to events, and then determining how to react in the light of these judgements. Lazarus has called these processes *primary* and *secondary appraisal* respectively.[4]

In order to attribute meaning or significance to an event people relate it to their goals, expectations and values, but not necessarily in an objective and dispassionate manner. Events or circumstances which are judged to be consistent with a person's values and goals, which meet expectations and offer valued opportunities, are appraised favourably and lead to positive emotions, thoughts and reactions. Some situations are appraised unfavourably, however, and lead to negative reactions (ie. psychological distress). Ostell argues that these situations are judged to be problematic in that there is a disparity between what a person wants to happen – or demands should happen – and what is actually happening, with no immediately obvious way of removing the disparity. Any situation can be a problem for someone if it is at odds with that person's values, goals and expectations. Yet it is not the disparity *per se* which proves distressing, but the perceived costs associated with the disparity. Six costs have been identified, which can be associated with problem situations, and which promote distress:

the perception of physical harm; utilitarian costs such as the loss of a job; self-disapproval due to the failure to meet own standards; social disapproval because of not fulfilling the expectations of others; the destabilising of a person's sense of social and cultural reality; and perceiving own values being violated by others. Thus, distress is not inherent in situations. but is a biproduct of people realising (or just anticipating) that a particular situation is problematic for them – their values and goals will not be realised and at significant cost to themselves.[5]

Psychological distress, however, is not an inevitable result of an unfavourable primary appraisal (i.e. defining a situation as a problem with significant costs). Much also depends upon secondary appraisal, that is, deciding how to respond to a situation. A person may recognize the costs posed by a problem, but view it as a challenge, plan how to respond in order to avoid the costs, or to create a positive outcome, and then take effective action. Another, who might lack the ability to change a situation, or is faced with an unchangeable situation (e.g. imprisonment), *actively accepts* these circumstances. Both cope (react) in a psychologically healthy manner, which emanates from constructive secondary appraisals, so that if psychological distress was experienced initially it is subsequently diminished if not dissipated.

Alternatively, a person who is capable of solving a problem might engage in *dysfunctional thoughts* instead, ruminating bitterly about the injustice of a situation (as they see it), blaming others for having caused their plight. Other people also *act dysfunctionally,* driving themselves relentlessly to achieve marginal and unnecessary improvements, or by taking on responsibilities which they can never fulfil, simply to impress others. These people are described as reacting in a dysfunctional manner because their thoughts (secondary appraisals) and subsequent actions result in them becoming mentally and emotionally upset and lead to them taxing unduly, or exceeding, their coping resources. *It is dysfunctional ways of perceiving and reacting to problems which distress people, more than the lack of technical competence, or of external resources, to handle problems.*

When people fail to handle problems effectively and their distress continues they tend to re-iterate the process of appraisal and reaction, often on a trial-and-error basis, until an acceptable solution is found and their distress is removed. Repeated failures at this process, however, can lead to even greater distress and to people behaving in very dysfunctional ways, further exacerbating the problem(s) and having a debilitating effect upon their psychological and physical well-being.

Stress and Culture:

An interesting question for the interactional view to address is whether any situations are *intrinsically stressful* to human beings? If not, why do people experience similar distress when confronted by the same situations, such as marital disharmony, bullying managers, high workloads, tight deadlines, and so on? It must be admitted that some circumstances appear to be intrinsically stressful, in that they impinge adversely upon the very core of a person's being, regardless of how that person thinks and reacts (e.g. acts of abuse, physical torture, and so on). Whether such acts are intrinsically stressful will perhaps always be a matter of contention.

Nevertheless, the reason why many people react similarly to everyday situations at work and home is largely because people within a particular society or culture share certain core values and beliefs about how to behave. They could also lack skills to handle certain situations because these skills are not normally inculcated (e.g. physical survival skills in an urban society). Thus, situations are problematic and psychologically costly precisely because they impinge adversely upon these commonly held beliefs, values and goals, and expose skill deficits. The stress is not in the circumstances per se but in the shared ways people perceive and react to these circumstances.

Conclusion

Some of the issues concerning the merits of these approaches to stress are fairly technical, nevertheless, it is important to have a broad grasp of them. The way stress is conceptualized can critically affect views about how to deal with it. Of the three main views examined, the interactional or transactional view gives most leverage in understanding the phenomena which constitute the field of stress. This view sees individuals as being central to the process of generating the distress they experience, while recognizing the (sometimes enormous) difficulties which situations and events can pose for people. It also acknowledges the importance of managing situations to help pre-empt or minimize psychological stress and any consequent distress that individuals might otherwise experience, a particularly important strategy in the context of stress at work.

Recognising Psychological Distress

It is frequently assumed that psychologically distressed individuals are easily identifiable through their appearance and behaviour. This is partly true as individuals who are furiously angry, seriously depressed, or trembling with anxiety, are relatively easy to identify. People who have been distressed for a period also look very fatigued and act as if they are not coping well. However, at work, most people believe it is not to their advantage to be seen to be distressed and therefore disguise their feelings and manage their behaviour, often over long periods, in order to appear as normal as possible. (This seems to be particularly true of stressed senior managers and directors). Further, stress states are not necessarily experienced as dramatic and disturbing, therefore, it is possible for people either to fail to monitor their reactions closely, or to suppress their experience of stress, so that they do not even recognize their own distress reactions!

Nevertheless, when people are not coping effectively with their work, social or personal lives, certain signs of psychological distress eventually leak out. The most obvious initial indicators are uncharacteristic, negative changes in mood, thinking and behaviour. The particular mood changes can vary widely from person to person depending upon the specific problems they are dealing with. Mood changes tend to be fairly transient, when they endure they are described as emotional states. In stressed people these states often take the form of recurrent irritability or anger. Anxiety reactions such as nervousness or panic feelings are common, and depressive reactions may emerge when problem situations are protracted and difficult to resolve. Guilt and shame are also distress emotions associated with people behaving in a way which contravenes their values (see table 11.1).

A stressed person's thinking tends to become preoccupied with the focal problem often making it difficult to, 'turn off'. Such preoccupation, coupled with the effects of emotional arousal, can result in a reduced ability to concentrate upon other issues, to retain information, to retrieve information from memory and to make decisions. Rumination, the process of endlessly, 'churning over' disturbing thoughts (e.g. 'blaming others' and 'refusing to forgive') about past events, also characterizes the responses of some people. Over time individuals often experience lowered self-confidence and reduced belief in their ability to cope. If work or personal circumstances deteriorate then self-condemnation follows, particularly in depressed people.

All these changes can be reflected in behaviour as well. People may become argumentative and quarrelsome or socially withdrawn. They tend to take longer over and make more errors in their work, so that 'double-checking', is frequent. They may rely increasingly upon palliatives such as cigarettes, alcohol, sweet foods, caffeine and even drugs (prescribed or otherwise) to help themselves cope. Increased absenteeism, particularly in lower grade jobs, often ensues and eventually people may (be required to) leave their jobs.

Table 11.1. Signs and Symptoms of Psychological Distress

GENERAL FEATURES

Definite *negative changes in mood, thinking and behaviour* which persist and are sufficiently definite for (most) people to recognise that they are psychologically distressed. These changes may escalate over time.

MOOD CHANGES

The most obvious sign is usually a change in mood. People are often described as *irritable* or *snappy*. Specific emotional reactions to look for include:

> **anxiety states, nervousness, panic states**
> **depressive feelings, sadness, apathy**
> **anger, irritability, resentment**
> **guilt, shame**

COGNITIVE CHANGES

Changes in cognition (thinking) are often only obvious, initially, to the sufferer. They include:

> **trouble concentrating, difficulty 'turning off',**
> **unduly forgetful, difficulty in making decisions,**
> **lack of interest in life, self condemnation,**
> **reduced belief in ability to cope**

BEHAVIOURAL CHANGES

People often attempt to disguise any changes in their emotions and thinking by managing their behaviour to appear normal. Nevertheless, changes to look for include:

> **increased errors at tasks, double-checking everything,**
> **argumentative and quarrelsome reactions, or perhaps**
> **withdrawing socially,**
> **ponderous reactions but often over-reactive when agitated,**
> **growing reliance on palliatives, increased absenteeism**

PHYSICAL CHANGES

The above changes are accompanied by physiological changes within the body, due in part to altered concentrations of different hormones secreted by the brain and endocrine glands, which can produce in a short time reactions such as:

> **irregular breathing, hyperventilation,**
> **increased and irregular heart rate, palpitations,**
> **sweating, poorer muscular coordination,**
> **headaches and migraines, dizziness, faintness,**
> **nausea, diarrhoea, frequent urination,**
> **reduced ability to 'resist' infections**

If these physiological changes are sustained it is believed that they play a role in promoting many diverse physical problems and illnesses (often through depressing, but sometimes through over-activating, the immune system) such as:

> **reduced ability to recover from infections,**
> **disturbed sleep patterns, diabetes,**
> **arthritis, cancer, irritable bowel syndrome,**
> **coronary heart disease, ulcers, hypertension,**
> **hay fever and allergies, asthma attacks, back aches,**
> **hyperthyroidism, chronic fatigue syndrome**

Impact and Longer-Term Consequences of Stress

The Individual

By definition, distress states are not enjoyable and result in a lessened sense of well-being for the individual concerned. Work performance generally suffers, as do social and intimate relationships, though psychologically distressed people often attempt to maintain their work performance at satisfactory levels through reliance on palliatives, the support of colleagues and friends, or the sheer determination not to give up. But, in doing so, they often simply tolerate or suppress their emotional distress, eventually at a cost to their health. This is because the disturbances in mental and emotional functioning described above are accompanied simultaneously by changes in bodily reactions. For example, the brain increases the secretion of various hormones such as adrenalin, noradrenalin and cortisol which serve to mobilize the body for action, but raised levels of cortisol also depress the immune system at the same time. If such changes are extreme, or become chronic, they can result in physical problems in any system of the body, including headaches and dizziness, heart palpitations and chest pains, hypertension, breathing problems, nausea, ulcers, inflamed muscles and joints, impotence, diabetes, diarrhoea, and so on. Recurrent illness through minor infections and slow recovery from infections, are typical of a depressed immune system (see table 11.1).

Why people experience *specific* physical problems and illnesses is not understood clearly. An explanation which is used frequently is the *diathesis-stress* model, which argues that each person has particular constitutional vulnerabilities which predispose them to certain disorders or illnesses when they become stressed. A number of other factors also contribute to determining the particular health problems people experience including: opportunistic infections contracted when immune systems are depressed (e.g. bacteria or viruses which are prevalent in the environment at a period in time), and behavioural response patterns to stress (e.g. heavy drinking leading to cirrhosis of the liver; smoking and lung problems).

Because of the natural resilience of the human body, some physical problems (e.g. ulcers, hypertension, coronary heart disease) may take years to emerge or become problematic, which is why it is staff in mid-life who often experience health crises, crises wrongly attributed to the effects of ageing rather than to the accumulating effects of not coping adequately with work and other problems. Thus, stressed individuals are ones whose entire beings are disturbed to some degree, whether they see evidence of and recognize it or not. Failure to correct this disturbance over the longer term leads to further deterioration in health, whether mental, or physical, or both, and can ultimately lead to early death through such problems as heart disease.[6]

The Organization

The impact of stressed individuals upon organizations is difficult to quantify precisely but is considerably greater than is often realised. It is manifest in poor job performance, disrupted work relationships, absenteeism and sickness leave through psychological distress and physical health problems, and eventually in labour turnover.

Figures from the Confederation of British Industry estimate that in the U.K. 360 million working days are lost annually through sickness, at a cost to organizations of £8 billion. The U.K. Health and Safety Executive suggests that at least half of these lost days involve stress-related absence.[7] Costs for stress-related labour turnover are more difficult to ascertain, but high rates of turnover not only disrupt work processes and relationships but also increase greatly recruitment, induction and training costs. Staff replacement costs are typically in the region of 50% to 90% of annual salary and can be considerably higher for senior executives.

The costs of stress related poor performance at work are also high. Staff who are psychologically stressed tend to take longer over tasks and make more errors; they may procrastinate or, alternatively, react impetuously, and make poor decisions; they fail to communicate, or do so inadequately; and tend to handle their staff ineptly. Stressed people can become obsessive and even paranoid in their thinking, refusing to work cooperatively with colleagues. Such performance, if widespread, will lead to low job satisfaction and poor morale among staff and, ultimately, result in gross inefficiency within an organization. The financial costs of such inefficiency cannot be calculated readily but are obviously high. This is particularly true in the case of senior executives or other people holding critical jobs where, for example, the failure to take decisions, or making poor decisions, could have disastrous consequences for the competitiveness or viability of an organization. The recent case of Robert Maxwell who, it has been suggested, was seriously mentally disturbed toward the end of his life, is a sobering example

Stress at Work: Sources and Causes

Sources of Work Stress

Work Factors

Research has indicated that work factors associated with psychological stress can be grouped into five categories:[8]

1. factors intrinsic to the job (working conditions, workload, travel, etc)
2. role in the organization (role conflict, role ambiguity, etc)
3. relationships at work
4. career development issues (job security, over/under promotion)
5. organizational structure and climate.

Work factors which are associated with psychological stress are often described as *sources* of stress. This is a potentially misleading term, as it could be interpreted to mean causes of stress. By and large they are not, instead they are best viewed as circumstances which, if at odds with an employee's beliefs, values and goals will prove problematic, and if the employee then reacts in a dysfunctional manner, as discussed previously, will result in psychological distress.

One important qualification, however, is that certain working conditions (e.g. noise, heat, repetitive physical actions leading to muscle/joint strain) can cause damage to the human body resulting in *physiological* distress which can then lead to psychological distress if employees find the damage difficult to cope with. No employer can afford to dismiss these effects lightly, as they are not only detrimental to employee health but have important legal implications for employers (see *Litigation and Stress*). Jobs need to be designed to avoid, or to minimise, problems arising from such working conditions.

Change Factors

To say that change is a characteristic of individual and organizational life is little more than a truism. Social and family life are disrupted regularly by change of one form or another whether through illness, bereavement, divorce, or job-related social mobility. Change is also increasingly essential to organizations as they attempt to contend with (global) competition and to assimilate developments in technology, particularly information technology. When organizations undergo a high level of change (restructuring, modifying working practices or culture, etc) high levels of psychological stress in (parts of) the organizations are quite probable. This is because all changes require people to make an adjustive effort, which is often demanding for them. Thus change is one of the most important job factors associated with psychological distress, and it is prudent to plan carefully for change so that it is conducted efficiently without provoking unnecessary psychological distress in employees.

Non-Work Factors

Poor performance at work can often be attributed to non-work rather than to work factors. When a person is confronted by the problems of a difficult divorce, or dealing with a dying parent or a sick child, financial difficulties, or conflicts with close friends, any distress they experience will often 'spill over' into the work setting and affect performance adversely. Life cannot be compartmentalized and the old adage, "Don't take work problems home or bring home problems to work", is, at best, short-sightedness. When non-work problems are the reason for poor work performance, sensitive and constructive support will help employees to cope more effectively and to restore work performance levels more quickly (see *Managing Stress at Work*)

A Special Case of Work Stress: Helping and Service Roles

Although stress is a phenomenon common to all occupational groups people occupying service roles, particularly professional helping roles, have been identified as individuals prone to high levels of psychological distress. The term 'professional helpers' includes such job roles as teachers, doctors, nurses, social and probation workers, therapists, police and prison officers.[9]

Professional helpers are distinguished from most other occupational groups in that they are dealing primarily with other people, rather than machinery, plant or systems, people with whom they often have fairly intense, repeated and perhaps extended contact, rather than brief episodes of interaction. Individuals occupying such roles have often been diagnosed as suffering from emotional exhaustion, depersonalization and feelings of decreased accomplishment. It has been proposed that these states are the result of a psychological process called *burnout,* brought about by unrelieved job pressure. A key mediating factor in this process appears to be intense job involvement, a vocational commitment to the job in many instances. Absolutist values also play an important role. A person holding such values is driven to meet certain standards of care, helping, or achievement, because these standards are seen as being right and appropriate, whereas anything less is unacceptable.[10]

Causes, Mediators and Moderators of Distress at Work

Causes and Mediating Causes

The discussion of psychological stress in this chapter views thought processes as *causes* of psychological distress and its longer term impact upon health. This occurs in two ways: directly, or indirectly, as mediating processes of the influence of other variables. In the first case, by thinking in ways which promote anger (e.g. anger at self for not achieving certain personal goals) or anxiety (e.g. hypochondriacal concern about personal health and longevity) a person causes his or her own distress. In the second case, if a person perceives, for example, external work situations as *problems with important costs,* these pereptions play a causal role by *mediating* the impact of the work situations upon the person, leading to distress and perhaps ill-health reactions.

Moderators of Psychological Distress

Whereas thought processes can be viewed as causes of distress, certain other factors seem primarily to moderate stress responses. That is, they tend either to augment, or to lessen, the strength of stress responses. For example, role ambiguity at work might not lead to distress reactions in emotionally stable employees, but could prove very distressing for emotionally reactive ones. If so, emotional responsiveness would moderate the impact of role ambiguity upon psychological health.

Factors which moderate responses to job demands and other aspects of the work environment include: demographic factors, personality variables, abilities and skills, preferences and expectations, and health-related behaviour. Two personality factors, and several other moderators of stress responses, are discussed briefly below.

The term *personality* refers to established and elaborated patterns of thought and action, which characterize a person and together distinguish that person from other people. Personality derives from the combined effects of genetic and environmental factors. It is usually described in terms of dimensions or traits, such as extroversion-introversion, dependent-independent, or impulsiveness, group mindedness and emotional stability. Research has demonstrated that people can be more, or less, prone to become psychologically stressed at work because of their particular traits, thus making them less, or more, suitable for certain organizational roles. This is too large a subject to explore in detail here but two examples can illustrate this point. People who score highly on the trait anxiety-proneness (variously described in psychological inventories as neuroticism, emotional instability, emotional reactivity) tend to suffer psychologically and physically when in particularly demanding jobs. Their emotional reactivity to certain situations is much higher than for people low on anxiety-proneness. Thus, although their work performance might be quite adequate, it is achieved at some cost to themselves. Conversely, psychologists have identified the *hardy* personality as one which is resistant to mental and physical distress when a person occupies a demanding role. Hardiness is a personality style reflecting *commitment* (a person's belief in themselves and the importance of their work and relationships), *control* (the tendency to think and act as if the course of events can be influenced) and *challenge* (the view that change rather than stability is the normative mode of life). Research findings regarding the moderating role of hardiness are mixed. Nevertheless, the implications of research findings into *moderating* traits for the selection and promotion of staff in organizations are clear: selectors need to make informed and judicious decisions in order to match people to demanding organizational roles in an appropriate manner.

Another important moderator is the nature of the *life events* a person is experiencing. If someone is faced with a high level of upsetting life events (e.g. relocation of job and home, separation from loved ones, birth of a baby and financial problems) on top of their normal work responsibilities, they are much more vulnerable to becoming stressed than when such events have not occurred. Similarly, people who are very tired physically, who perceive themselves to be working in a dangerous environment, or who have been ill recently, are often more easily and extremely disturbed by events. Awareness of their vulnerability in such circumstances allows people to take action to help themselves.

One of the most important factors which moderates stress reactions by buffering people against the impact of stressing events is that of *social support,* whether at home or work. Physical fitness and being well-rested also help lessen the impact of stressing circumstances.[11]

Measuring Stress In the Workplace

Behavioural Performance Data

Although there might be evidence of stress problems within an organization, there is often an understandable concern that bringing the issue of stress into the public arena will open a Pandora's box of problems which could otherwise have been avoided. This raises the interesting question of how it is possible to assess whether these stress problems are sufficiently severe to merit some kind of initiative on the part of the organization without making it a public issue.

In theory, all that is needed is to analyse organizational data relevant to the incidence and severity of stress problems. In practice, however, this is often difficult to do because the relevant data either have not been collected, or have been collected, but for reasons other than the assessment of stress problems, and are therefore less useful than they might be. The kind of evidence which could indicate the existence of stress problems is *deteriorations in behavioural performance data* for different departments in an organization. Examples could be:

- reduction in product quality
- unexplained increases in production time and in the incidence of plant breakdowns
- repeated and growing evidence of the failure to meet performance deadlines
- increases in client complaints about service quality

Line management would be the obvious source of these data, assuming that appropriate recording systems were being used. Evidence of stress problems might also be found in records of increased absenteeism, resignations and dismissals to which personnel should have access. More direct evidence could be reflected in the incidence and nature of stress-related medical complaints reported to occupational physicians, and in everyday anecdotal accounts.[12]

However, any data appearing to indicate a growth of stress problems would have to be interpreted with great caution as there might be plausible alternative explanations for those data. For example, during economic recession an increase in stress-related medical complaints could reflect changes occurring outside an organization (e.g. mortgage repossessions, family members being made redundant) rather than internal problems. Similarly, records indicating no increases in absenteeism or resignations might simply reflect the unwillingness of people, although stressed through their jobs, to leave an organization due to the unavailability of alternative jobs. Thus, at best, indirect evidence of stress problems must be treated as only being possibly indicative of stress. More unambiguous data are needed before firm conclusions can be drawn about whether changes in behavioural performance data are the result of stress problems. Such data might be collected through a stress audit, but this is inevitably a much more public process.

Stress and Health Audits

A stress audit is essentially a tool for assessing the prevalence, strength and nature of stress problems within part of, or throughout an organization. Audits are usually designed to assess:

- recent or current symptoms of psychological stress and medical illnesses using standardized scales
- work situations thought to promote these symptoms
- how employees attempt to cope with these situations
- non-work problems which could also lead to psychological distress

- psychometric tests and inventories might also be used to profile the ability and personality characteristics of (groups of) employees

The primary tools used in stress audits are questionnaires and interviews, but behavioural performance data might also be collected to cross-check the data obtained by these tools. Certain instruments, incorporating a comprehensive range of separate scales, have been developed which can be used in stress audits. The value of these instruments is that, if well constructed and used widely, they can provide comparative data across organizations and occupational groups.[13] A limitation of them is that they will not be tailored to capture the specific characteristics of an organization, any particular recent changes which have occurred in it and unusual problems which may have arisen. In order to do the latter it is first necessary to conduct exploratory interviews with a cross-section of staff to identify such issues, and then to design a stress audit incorporating the issues in order to assess their impact. A further limitation of stress audits is that they tend to focus upon what is promoting distress in employees, rather than taking a broader view by identifying what is promoting enjoyment and satisfaction at work (i.e. health). The author favours the latter approach – i.e. a *health audit* – as it provides a more balanced view of an organization and also suggests directions in which changes might be made.

Evidence indicating widespread elevated levels of psychological distress within departments or organizations needs to be compared with data drawn from other departments or comparable organizations, or epidemiological data from broader population samples, in order to provide a perspective and to assess its significance. For example, epidemiological data indicate that 20% to 25% of people in community samples are psychologically distressed on a chronic-intermittent basis, and that they account for 50% of the episodes of psychological distress in the sample. During a calendar year more than 30% of people experience a period of psychological distress lasting at least a fortnight.[14]

It is not sufficient, however, to know that employees report higher levels of psychological distress in certain departments or organizations than in others. What is also needed is an understanding of the work or other factors which promote that distress (and this is where interviews can often provide in-depth data beyond that obtained through questionnaires). Relatively high levels of reported distress during major company changes, such as relocation or restructuring, could be expected as a result of the disruptive impact of these changes. It would be much more revealing to find such levels in a particular department or organization which was not undergoing obvious changes, when comparable departments or organizations indicated more typical results.

Stress and health audits should be conducted by appropriately qualified professionals who have relevant experience, access to standardized psychological measures and the skills to analyse and interpret the data obtained. Such professionals would normally have at least a first degree or relevant training in the behavioural sciences. Most HRM functions would lack suitably qualified people.

Managing Stress at Work

The approach of organizations to stress related problems can be classified as *inactive, reactive or proactive.* The *inactive* approach either tends to ignore stress problems, because they are viewed as not being relevant to the work situation ("It is not the responsibility of the company to sort out his marital problems"), or sees them as evidence of unsuitability for that organizational role ("If she cannot take the heat, she should get out of the kitchen"). Such attitudes are best viewed, charitably, as extremely naive. A person's marital problems might stem in part from the demands of their work role, but even if this is not so the disturbing effects of these problems on the employee are likely to spill over into the work situation. Further, the approach of simply sacrificing people who find difficulties coping with certain aspects of their role usually takes little account of the opportunity-cost entailed. The cost of replacing basically competent, if not outstanding, individuals usually far outweighs the cost of helping them learn to cope better with aspects of their role which they find troublesome. Only if people cannot learn after appropriate help should they be relocated or replaced.

Reactive organizations are ones which respond when stress related problems have already had damaging or fatal effects upon staff. The death of fairly senior staff through stress-related heart disease, drink problems or by suicide usually sends tremors through colleagues who then determine to react to problems they have recognized for some time. *Proactive* organizations, knowing of the damaging effects of stress upon employees and upon the effectiveness of an organization as a whole, tend to develop comprehensive strategies both to help people cope better with their problems and to pre-empt unnecessary work-related stress.

The Nature of Stress Interventions

All stressed people have two kinds of problems to cope with:

1. *situations or circumstances* of whatever kind which they find problematic and psychologically stressful;
2. their resultant *distress reactions* (mental, emotional, behavioural) which, because of their unpleasant nature, become problems in their own right, ones which are often more difficult to cope with than the original problems.

Broadly speaking, organizations can employ two kinds of interventions for dealing with stress problems, which tend to have somewhat different objectives:

1. *personal change interventions* which focus upon improving problem solving skills and/or enabling people to handle better their distress reactions;

2. *organizational change interventions* which focus upon modifying organizational structures and practices in order to make work and the workplace more conducive to healthy living.

Interventions Focusing Upon Personal Change

Personal change interventions are attractive to some organizations because they are less disruptive and are considerably less expensive than restructuring an organization, or changing radically its policies and culture. More importantly, however, there are many jobs where it simply is not possible to remove the pressures and problems which result in work-related stress for employees. In such cases they must not only improve their job (problem solving) skills but also learn how to:

- avoid becoming distressed if possible (corrective strategies aimed at changing dysfunctional reactions)
- better manage their lives and circumstances so that they are able to endure demanding situations (buffering strategies making people more resilient to the damaging effects of psychological distress)
- relieve or dissipate distress states when they do occur (palliative strategies).

Another reason why individually-oriented change interventions are important is because the work performance of employees is often affected by personal and domestic problems arising outside of work. Such problems can only be addressed on an individual basis.

As there are numerous interventions focusing upon personal change, only the most commonly used ones will be discussed below.[15] The primary benefits of each are summarised in table 11.2. Most of these interventions would be conducted by externally based professionals. However, the Human Resource Management function might have in-house staff with at least a basic training in certain areas, for example, employee counselling. Experts would be called upon for dealing with more difficult cases.

Table 11.2. Effects of Different Kinds of Stress Interventions upon People

TYPE OF INTERVENTION	*EFFECTS OF INTERVENTION a*			
	Under-standing	*Palliative*	*Buffering*	*Corrective/adaptive*
Relaxation and related training	L b	H	M	L
Physical exercise	L	M	M	L
Stress awareness and lifestyle training	H	M/H	M	L/M
Promoting psychological health	H	H	H	H
Counselling	L/M c	M	M	H c

a: Indicates typical effects, much depends upon the specific 'design' and quality of 'delivery' of an intervention

b: Intervention promotes high (H), medium (M) or low (L) understanding of the nature of stress, palliative, buffering or corrective/adaptive effects

c: Counselling often focuses simply upon the problem a client brings to the counselling situation and its rammifications, not upon the broader context of life which will often be addressed in lifestyle and promoting psychological health training. Sometimes its corrective/adaptive effects will be narrowly focused

Relaxation and Related Training

Relaxation is one of the most widely used techniques of stress management and it is simple to understand why: it is easy to teach on an individual or group basis and most people experience an immediate if short-lived beneficial effect from it. Relaxation techniques are concerned with teaching people to dissipate muscular tensions and other reactions (e.g. acid stomach) they generate when psychologically distressed, and are thus symptom-oriented. In practice, the techniques have a useful palliative function, but do relatively little to help people stop generating the psychological and physical disturbances they experience.

Biofeedback techniques are similar in principle. They involve the use of instruments which provide a visual or auditory signal to indicate to a person how well they are learning to control a bodily reaction indicative of psychological distress. Again the techniques often do not address directly the psychological processes generating the distressing physiological processes which the person is trying to control: their impact is primarily palliative.

Relaxation training is sometimes used as the first step when people learn *visualization techniques.* These are a form of mental conditioning where people are taught, for example, to focus mentally upon a difficult situation and to imagine using suggested strategies for coping with it (e.g. imagining using certain techniques to manage anxiety in order to deliver a lecture successfully). When effective, this training can teach people to pre-empt distress arousal or to moderate distress reactions. The learning, however, is often situation specific and tends to not generalize to other problem situations.

Physical Exercise

Regular, moderate physical exercise has a number of beneficial effects upon mental and physical health. As a short-term strategy it can help a person by disrupting mental processes associated with distressing emotions and by burning up excess levels of certain hormones, such as adrenalin and noradrenalin, thus leading to symptom relief. As a longer-term strategy, regular aerobic exercise increases production by the brain of opiate-type substances, known as endorphins, which have analgesic effects and promote positive moods, thus having anti-depressant effects. Regular exercise can not only moderate the impact of distress reactions but also result in enhanced self-esteem. It is misleading, however, to think that these palliative and buffering benefits of exercise are comparable with the development of effective coping skills which can pre-empt distress arousal.

Some organizations, most notably large American companies, have invested heavily in providing sports and exercise facilities for their staff. The companies report reduced absenteeism, better employee health, improved work performance and other positive effects offsetting the financial costs incurred.[16] Such results are of considerable benefit to both individuals and organizations, nevertheless, it is obvious that a significant part of these benefits is simply a consequence of the improved health of employees, and has little to do with the alleviation of psychological distress states brought about by the failure to cope adequately with work or personal problems.

Stress Awareness and Lifestyle Training

Stress awareness courses concentrate upon helping participants to recognize signs of psychological distress, to appreciate its damaging effects and to identify sources of stress. Advice is usually offered about work habits (problem solving strategies, time management), about diet, exercise and hobbies as factors which, if handled appropriately, buffer people against the impact of situations which they find distressing, and also about palliative strategies for symptom relief.

Lifestyle training can be viewed as an extension of stress-awareness training and is basically geared toward educating people how to live in a more healthy way. It usually focuses upon issues such as smoking, alcohol consumption, diet, exercise, sports or hobbies, taking holidays, rest, sleep, and so on. Awareness courses typically last from half to a whole day. Life style training could be part of a stress-awareness course or perhaps a stand-alone one hour lecture or a one day session.

It is difficult to generalize about the value of these kinds of training because so much depends upon the specific content of the courses and how they are conducted. Generally, both kinds of course have a useful educational function which often provides participants with insights into their own behaviour, and some ideas about changing behaviour. If people adopt sensible strategies for healthy living they can palliate distress reactions. Equally important, being physically fit and well-rested moderates the impact of distressing situations, as people tend to be less reactive to them and more able to withstand any distress they do experience.[17] By definition, however, neither form of training does much to improve participants' skills at analysing and resolving their own stress problems.

Promoting Psychological Health

Training concerned with promoting psychological health goes beyond simply learning about buffering and palliative strategies for dealing with distress reactions and focuses upon helping people to acquire psychologically healthy ways of thinking and acting. Thus people are enabled to better handle work, domestic and personal problems because they have learned the principles and developed strategies for avoiding becoming distressed in the first place. Although stress awareness and lifestyle courses may touch upon these issues, they are rarely addressed sufficiently to promote widespread enduring changes in thinking and behaviour.

Psychological health training focuses upon teaching people to explore their reactions to specific situations, to recognise dysfunctional patterns of thinking and acting, to identify psychologically healthy alternatives, and then to implement these new patterns of behaving. What this training is doing is providing people with some of the knowledge and skills used by professional counsellors so that they become, in effect, more competent self-counsellors. Thus they are better equipped to deal with existing problems, and any associated distress, and to avoid becoming distressed by many future problems. Such training requires a commitment to change on the part of participants and a willingness to exert some effort to achieve this change instead of simply looking for 'quick fix' solutions. The results can be enduring and extend into all aspects of a person's life, promoting psychological well-being with its consequent physical benefits. Because this training goes beyond learning about buffering and palliative strategies it, of necessity, usually requires two or three days rather than a single day of training, but the results should justify both the financial investment and the personal effort involved.

Counselling

Interventions which have primarily palliative or buffering effects are not adequate for people who are really distressed by work and personal circumstances. What they need is focused, precise and fairly immediate help with their problems. This is best achieved through face-to-face counselling in most instances. Effective counselling should enable employees to explore and find ways of solving, or adapting to, their problems, and to manage their thoughts and actions more effectively, so that they learn to avoid becoming distressed, or to minimize any distress reactions they do generate. Thus, ideally, effective counselling should have pervasive, enduring, corrective and/or adaptive benefits.

Counsellors vary considerably in their training and approaches. What most organizations need are counsellors who can provide brief, problem-focused help which enables employees to deal with their problems and distress effectively and relatively quickly, rather than protracted therapeutic approaches attempting to rectify long-standing personality problems.

Counselling can be provided by in-house professionals, or by local externally based counsellors, or by organizations which offer a range of counselling services (e.g. helplines, telephone counselling, face-to-face counselling) through what is called an Employee Assistance Programme (EAP). The annual fee for providing an EAP is normally high (e.g. currently £25 to £40 per employee for a limited number of counselling sessions, typically 4 to 6), more costly than employing internal counsellors and much higher than local external counsellors. But EAPs often appeal to large organizations which have employees in a number of scattered locations not easily serviced by local counsellors. EAPs often offer a broader range of services than psychological counselling, including legal and financial advice.

Job and Interpersonal Skills Training

It is important to remember that work-related psychological distress sometimes arises when people lack, or fear they lack, the knowledge and skills needed to meet their job demands, or to cope with interpersonal situations at work. This can occur when employees are moved to new jobs, or when their work responsibilities and activities are changed, or when people and jobs have been mismatched through poor selection or promotion decisions. In such cases appropriate technical or interpersonal skills training is obviously needed.

Interventions Focusing Upon Organizational Change

Emphasizing a personal change approach to employee stress might be a way for an organization to avoid admitting any responsibility for contributing to the stress-related problems of employees. This would be highly regrettable (and possibly foolish from a legal point of view) if the problems could be avoided by reasonable alterations in some aspect of the external situation, such as changes in organizational structures, policies and practices. Changes of this kind do not improve a person's coping skills but, by removing or modifying circumstances which are often problematic for employees, can either lessen the likelihood of people experiencing stress or buffer people against the impact of demanding job situations.

Many organizational change interventions have been advocated. Although there is not space to consider them at length some deserve brief discussion for illustrative purposes.

Improving Working Conditions

In recent years working conditions believed to produce or be implicated in the physical and psychological health problems of employees have received considerable attention. These include the repetition of sequences of actions, or various activities, resulting in repetitive strain injury; regular and extended use of VDUs associated with the experience of headaches; the 'sick building syndrome' (as defined by the World Health Organization) characterized by employees suffering such symptoms as headaches, nausea, dizziness and fatigue during the working day, but not after they leave a building; different shift patterns of working and the various behavioural and health problems of shift workers.[18]

Improving the physical working conditions for employees could involve ergonomic solutions ranging from the redesign of jobs and equipment to changes in the design and construction of buildings. Some working conditions cannot be altered, except at considerable expense, and may only affect a relatively small proportion of the workforce. In such cases changes to the recruitment and selection policies of an organization might be needed (see *Causes, Mediators and Moderators of Distress at Work* and chapter 3).

Clarifying Selection and Promotion Criteria

Decisions to offer certain individuals particular jobs, or to promote them, are frequently a source of disturbance for others in organizations who might challenge, for example, the equity of the decisions. Such decisions can also frustrate a manager's plans for his or her own staff. These problems can lead to disruptions in working relationships and to team performance.

It is probably impossible for problems of this kind to be eliminated from an organization because perceptions of equity are so subjective and individuals' goals will often conflict. However, an organization can eliminate some of the distress which is generated by ensuring that the criteria for selection and promotion are clear and understood by staff and that organizational practise in this area conforms with stated policies.

Job Enlargement and Enrichment

Job enlargement and enrichment are approaches to the design of jobs which are concerned with making them more personally satisfying and involving for employees and therefore, in theory, less potentially stressful. Job enrichment approaches, in particular, design jobs so that they provide opportunities for individuals to experience greater autonomy, responsibility and meaningfulness through their work (see chapter 6). These conditions should promote a greater sense of personal control, a condition which is associated with feelings of personal health. Once again individual differences are important, as not all employees want a high degree of autonomy and responsibility in their jobs.

Lessening Requirements for Job Mobility

It has traditionally been an expectation for many jobs that employees will move from one location to another, sometimes in different countries, as part of their training and career development. Job relocation represents a significant demand for individuals in terms of coping with change, and is obviously potentially stressful for employees and their families. Relocation is sometimes a necessity if a person is to receive training, or wants advancement. However, policies requiring employees to relocate only when really necessary will reduce these potentially stressful demands upon many employees.

Career and Personal Development

In recent years, career paths have become much less predictable for employees, whether blue or white collar, and large numbers of redundancies have increased the competition for jobs and reduced the certainty of employment for people. Further, established careers are disappearing in some organizations so that individuals have to have more flexible expectations and be more adaptable in their approach to work and advancement than before (see chapter 3). These changes represent further demands upon people which are not always easy to cope with, especially for older people who have been used to more stable employment conditions. Organizations can contribute to a lessening of these potentially disturbing circumstances for their staff through clarifying career or advancement routes for employees, providing regular performance appraisals, training and re-training opportunities and supportive counselling when needed.

Promoting a Healthy Corporate Culture

Organizations operate in changing competitive, technological, economic, social and political environments. New problems are forever emerging and have to be dealt with, often with difficulty and sometimes stressfully for those involved. Organizational culture serves two primary ends: to help an organization solve these problems and achieve its goals; and to do so by creating a climate in which its members function effectively and, ideally, in psychologically healthy ways. It is arguable that the former end is frequently so dominant in the minds of those who shape the culture that the latter end is neglected, or not recognized for being potentially unhealthy.

Two examples illustrate the above point. The espoused values of many organizations today are 'achievement', 'competitiveness', 'excellence', 'success' and the like. These are perfectly proper values for an organization. However, if they are articulated in an all-or-none manner, any behaviour or outcomes which do not conform to these values are perceived as being second-rate and unacceptable. Employees caught up with absolute views of this kind make themselves immensely vulnerable to stress whenever their performance does not (or appears not to) meet these values, even although higher levels of performance might not have been possible! (See *A Special Case of Work Stress: Helping and Service Roles*). If organizations (and employees) articulated their values more pragmatically it would still be possible to achieve desired targets but without many of the costs incurred through stress.

Organizations with a highly autocratic management style tend to be characterized by such factors as poor communication, lack of consultation and employee involvement, motivation by fear more than by encouragement, and psychological distance between managers and subordinates. This style creates an organizational culture which suits some people but is more often resented and resisted. In most situations less autocratic management styles appear both more effective for achieving organizational goals and in promoting the healthy and constructive involvement of staff.

Choosing Between Interventions

New approaches to stress management appear regularly, some of which are promoted through the different media and are little more than gimmicks. In order to assess their merits, all interventions need to be evaluated against such questions as:

- is the intervention aimed primarily at informing and educating people or at developing their skills?
- does the intervention help people cope better with their problems, or with their psychological distress, or both?
- will the changes achieved through the interventions tend to be palliative and short-lived, or have longer-term buffering effects, or be corrective and enduring, or some combinations of these?
- how efficient is the intervention in terms of cost, time required to achieve its effect and ease of implementation and administration?

Although psychological counselling is usually the most powerful intervention for people who are really distressed and looking for help, other interventions should not be overlooked, particularly training in psychological health. Fortunately, the majority of employees in an organization are not in critical need of such counselling but, nevertheless, many could also benefit from psychological health or other forms of training.

Stress is such an individual phenomenon that it will *always* be possible for employees to generate psychological distress in any variety of ways. Therefore, the HR function, when helping an organization concerned to address the stress problems of its employees, should really consider what *combination* of interventions (personal/organizational change) it would be most appropriate to adopt.

Organizational Crises and Post-Traumatic Stress

During the past two decades a number of well publicised disasters have occurred which proved so disturbing for those involved that they were *traumatised psychologically.* These disasters include incidents such as the capsize of the Zeebrugge ferry, the Kings Cross Station fire, the Hillsborough Stadium disaster, the Bradford Football Stadium fire and the Piper Alpha oil rig disaster in the North Sea.

On a much more regular basis employees become traumatised by smaller-scale incidents or crises at work. Counter staff working in the branches of banks or building societies may be seriously distressed after a hold-up, fire brigade staff after removing badly charred bodies from a burnt out building, police after attending a serious motorway crash, employees working in the vicinity of an explosion at a chemical plant, and so on. Simply watching a disaster occur is enough to traumatise some people, and very often those who assist the victims of disasters or major crises become victims themselves.

People who are seriously distressed as a result of incidents of this kind experience such symptoms as intrusive recollections, recurrent dreams, or suddenly feeling the event was recurring, hyperalertness, sleep disturbance, concentration or memory impairment, and so on. These responses are sometimes called "a normal reaction to an abnormal situation". If treated relatively quickly and appropriately by trained people most symptoms disappear within about a month. If trauma symptoms persist without obvious remission the person is described as suffering post-traumatic stress syndrome. It is not uncommon for there to be a latency period of months before the syndrome becomes obvious. This can occur when people do not seek, or cannot find help and "grit their teeth and bear it". The syndrome is evidenced by a growing sense of isolation from others characterized by diminished responsiveness or interest in events, avoidance of activities that stimulate recollections of the traumatic event, and intensification of symptoms by exposure to such activities. Sleep disturbance, survivor guilt, concentration and memory impairment are common symptoms. It can prove considerably more difficult to help people overcome their reactions to disasters once their symptoms have persisted for long periods.[19]

When faced with disasters or crises organizations usually call on the services of individuals or groups, sometimes known as crisis counsellors, who specialize in helping victims of such incidents. Some organizations which face situations of this kind regularly, for example banks, building societies and the police, have their own in-house staff to deal with initial incident de-briefs and use external professional staff to handle the treatment of post traumatic stress cases.

Litigation and Stress

Background

Although stress is a psychological state generated by people as they perceive and react to situations, rather than by situations *per se,* this does not mean that the working conditions or life events that people have to contend with are immaterial to their psychological and physical health. Certain working conditions (e.g. involving life threatening circumstances) and life events (bereavement) prove very difficult to handle for the majority of people, and certain people, because of their particular personality characteristics, are especially vulnerable to becoming distressed in some jobs. Thus, employees often feel that they have legitimate compensation claims against employers for *personal injury* (psychological or physical) suffered as a consequence of job experiences.

The legal system within a country obviously has to make decisions regarding the reasonableness of these claims. In North America employers pay for these types of claims through a *no-fault* insurance system of workers' compensation. This guarantees the employee medical benefit and a proportion of lost wages, but usually leaves the employer immune from negligence suits and even more damaging costs. By way of contrast with North America, civil claims for compensation in the UK are *fault-based* requiring the employee to demonstrate employer negligence. It is perhaps for this reason that there has not been a comparable growth of work-related stress claims in the UK courts compared with that in North America, although matters are beginning to change.

Stress litigation within the UK is still novel. It is likely to increase, however, as a result of changes in the Health and Safety at Work Act of 1974 (HSWA 1974) and recent High Court rulings, particularly the *Walker v Northumberland County Council* case (see below). Since 1974 HSWA has imposed on employers a *duty of care* for employees to ensure that they do not suffer personal injury at work. Traditionally, personal injury claims have concerned:

1. *Physical injuries* such as accidents with machinery and equipment or incurred through contact with harmful substances when, for example, appropriate clothing was not provided.
2. *Diseases* caused by employees' work or work environment, such as asbestosis or pneumoconiosis.

However, HSWA does not contain *rules* with respect to work stress. But as a result of a recent European framework directive on health and safety at work employers are now required to evaluate the risks of mental stress problems associated with work.

The Nature of Personal Injury Cases

Broadly speaking, claims are made currently in the courts for three types of case: *physical-mental cases, mental-physical* cases and *mental-mental* cases.

1. Physical-mental cases: Such cases occur when psychological symptoms develop as a result of a physical injury or occupational disease (e.g. uncontrollable fear of heights after a fall off scaffolding).
2. Mental-physical cases: These cases arise when physical symptoms are believed to have developed from psychological stress (e.g. hypertension or stroke resulting from performing a demanding role over a protracted period of time).
3. Mental-mental cases: Mental-mental cases entail the occurrence of psychological symptoms consequent upon a person having been involved in a demanding job situation. Two kinds of demanding situations are distinguished:
   (a) *acute* situations, such as witnessing or being involved in a mentally disturbing event which results in further mental disturbance (e.g. post-traumatic stress reactions in bank employees after being threatened during a hold-up).
   (b) *chronic* situations, where an employee is subjected to difficult work circumstances over a protracted period of time (e.g. police officers, doctors, social workers).

Current Situation[20]

Physical-mental cases

In the UK cases involving personal injury with a psychological element are well recognized and have been won in civil courts at least since the turn of the century.

Mental-physical cases

Claims for *mental-physical* cases are often problematic when the personal injury is in the form of a disease or a medical condition which takes a significant period of time to emerge. First, the medical authorities and the legal sytem have to be persuaded that the condition actually exists. Second, establishing causation is difficult in such cases as alternative explanations for the physical problem(s) often exist. For instance, hypertension might arise as a reaction to work, to family problems, to diet or to all these factors. Repetitive strain injury (RSI) is a good example of these difficulties. A journalist employed by Reuters recently failed to win a High Court case against his employers because of the medical evidence they submitted questioning the nature of RSI whereas, a legal secretary with a City of London firm has subsequently received significant compensation after suffering RSI at work.

Mental-mental cases

The incidence of claims for *mental-mental* cases grew rapidly during the 1980s in the US and Canada. There has also been a similar, if less rapid, trend in the UK.

Acute cases: Claims for *acute* cases become very apparent following major disasters such as the sinking of the Zeebrugge cross-channel ferry, the Bradford Football Stadium fire, the King's Cross Underground fire and the Hillsborough Football Stadium disaster. Claimants are typically identified as suffering from post-traumatic stress syndrome for which substantial damages have been awarded on occasions. A fireman attending the King's Cross Underground fire who subsequently suffered deep depression was awarded £143,683 damages (*The Guardian,* 1993) but claims by policemen for the traumas experienced after the Hillsborough disaster have had variable results. Only officers who carried out rescue work in the pens where deaths occurred have been awarded compensation (*People Management,* May 1995).

It must be recognised that people can experience post-traumatic stress without being involved in a major disaster. Examples include bank staff involved in a hold-up, fire officers removing charred bodies from a building, police attending a serious motorway crash, and employees working in the vicinity of an explosion at a oil refinery.

Chronic cases: As far as employers are concerned the most significant recent developments in the field of stress litigation must involve *chronic, mental-mental* cases, and in particular the case of *Walker v Northumberland County Council* (*Accountancy,* January 1995; *People Management,* April 1995).

In brief, John Walker had been employed by Northumberland County Council as a social worker for sixteen years when he experienced a 'nervous breakdown' in November 1986. This followed several years during which his workload had increased considerably and the council neither provided additional resources nor restructured the department to help staff. Walker returned to his job in March 1987 advised by his psychiatrist not to take on his former level of job responsibilities. Walker's manager would not accept this but instead offered additional, albeit, temporary staff assistance. During September 1987 Walker took sick leave and subsequently experienced a second breakdown. In February 1988 he was dismissed on grounds of permanent ill-health.

A claim was subsequently made against Northumberland County Council for *negligence* in failing to provide a safe system of work. The High Court decided that:

1. Walker had a normal personality but had experienced psychiatric problems as a result of trying to cope with work pressures and these had terminated his career.
2. Walker's first breakdown was not *reasonably foreseeable* but the second was.
3. As adequate additional assistance was not provided to Walker the council had failed in its duty of care to provide a safe system of work.

Unison, Walker's union, is pressing for damages, which are yet to be settled, of the order of £200,000. Another important case of chronic, cumulative stress, involving a junior hospital doctor and Bloomsbury Health Authority has recently been settled out of court.

Implications of Stress Litigation Cases for Employers

There seem to be four legal issues which will determine whether a case of stress at work will lead to a successful personal injury claim:

1. *Stress-induced illness:* employees will need to establish that they have actually suffered a stress-induced illness and medical disagreement about conditions such as RSI indicate that this will not necessarily be easy.
2. *Causation:* it must be shown that a mental or physical illness was brought about due to stressful workplace conditions and did not result from some alternative cause, such as eating/drinking habits (for physical illness) or marital disharmony (for psychological problems).
3. *Foreseeability:* it must also be shown the employer could have foreseen that the employee's stress-based illness was likely to ensue from the workplace conditions.
4. *Reasonableness:* when the risk of a stress-based illness is foreseeable for a particular employee then an employer must take reasonable steps to satisfy the duty of care.

During recruitment employers often collect data on the personality of job candidates, past work history and so on, as part of their selection procedures. Employers, and particularly HRM specialists, need to consider whether they use these data appropriately. For instance, individuals vulnerable to stress should not be recruited to certain demanding jobs, and when individuals do evidence signs of work stress such data about an employee might help advise an employer about how to reasonably fulfil the duty of care.

Conclusions

Psychological stress, if it endures, is disturbing for those who experience it and its consequences can also be disruptive at work. It is important to be able to identify symptoms of psychological distress, and to understand the mediating and moderating psychological processes which result in such distress, if a person is to be able to cope with stress effectively.

There are numerous sources of stress at work. Major changes are often associated with higher levels of employee distress, and people occupying *professional helping* roles are particularly prone, as a group, to high levels of distress. The use of *behavioural performance data* and sophisticated *stress or health audits* can enable an organization to establish the stress levels of staff, to make comparisons of stress levels between departments, worksites and even different companies, and also to diagnose the main reasons for existing levels of stress or recent changes in stress levels.

In order to manage stress in the workplace, organizations, and the HRM function in particular, need to identify that *combination* of individual change and organizational change interventions which will be most effective to deal with the problems which exist. The HRM function needs to be aware of the legal implications for an organization of work-related employee stress and to ensure that they take all reasonable care for employees' mental and physical health

References

1. T Cox (1978), *Stress.* London: Macmillan Press.

2. H Selye (1956/1976), *The Stress of Life.* New York: McGraw Hill; H Selye (1974), *Stress without Distress.* Philadelphia: Lippinicott.

3. J W Mason (1971), A re-evaluation of the concept of 'non-specificity' in stress theory. *Journal of Psychiatric Research,* 8, 323.

4. R S Lazarus (1966), *Psychological Stress and the Coping Process.* New York: McGraw Hill; R S Lazarus and S Folkman (1984), *Stress, Appraisal and Coping.* New York: Springer.

5. A Ostell (1988), The development of a diagnostic framework of problem solving and stress. *Counselling Psychology Quarterly,* 1, 189–209; A Ostell (1991), Coping, problem solving and stress: a framework for intervention strategies. *British Journal of Medical Psychology,* 64, 11–24.

6. S Fisher and J Reason (Eds) (1988), *Handbook of Life Stress, Cognition and Health.* London: J Wiley & Sons Ltd. This volume contains a number of papers on the links between psychological states and health and illness.

7. C L Cooper and S Cartwright (1994), Healthy mind; Healthy organization – A proactive approach to occupational stress. *Human Relations,* 47, 455–471.

8. C L Cooper and J Marshall (1978), *Understanding Executive Stress.* London: Macmillan; C L Cooper, R D Cooper and L Eaker (1988), *Living with Stress.* London: Penguin Health.

9. C Maslach (1982), Burnout: *The Cost of Caring.* Englewood Cliffs N J: Prentice Hall.

10. A Ostell (1992), Absolutist thinking and emotional problems. *Counselling Psychology Quarterly,* 5,161–176; C Maslach (1982) op. cit.

11. K R Parkes (1994), Personality and coping as moderators of work stress processes: models, methods and measures. *Work and Stress,* 8, 110–129; R Payne (1988), Individual differences in the study of occupational stress. In C L Cooper and R Payne (Eds) *Causes, Coping and Consequences of Stress at Work.* London: J Wiley & Sons Ltd.

12. A Ostell (1993), Stress at work. *In* P Forrest (Ed) *Human Resources: Management and Strategy.* Kingston-upon-Thames, Surrey: Croner Publications.

13. C L Cooper and S Cartwright (1994), op cit; V J Sutherland (1993), The use of a stress audit. *Leadership and Organization Development Journal,* 14, 22–28.

14. R A Depue and S M Monroe (1986), Conceptualization and measurement of human disorder in life stress research: The problem of chronic disturbance. *Psychological Bulletin,* 99, 36–51; D Goldberg and P Huxley (1992), *Common Mental Disorders.* London: Routledge.

15. A Ostell (1986), Where stress screening falls short. *Personnel Management,* September. Institute of Personnel Management; A Ostell (1991), op cit.

16. C L Cooper and S Cartwright, (1994) op cit.

17. P Sterling and J Eyer (1988), Allostasis: A new paradigm to explain arousal pathology. *In* S Fisher and J Reason (Eds) (1988) *op cit.*

18. M Wallace, M Levens and G Singer (1988), Blue collar stress. *In* C L Cooper and R Payne (Eds) *op cit.*

19. P E Hodgkinson and M Stewart (1991), *Coping with Catastrophe: A Handbook of Disaster Management.* London: Routledge; D Spiegel (1988), Dissociation and hypnosis in post-traumatic stress disorders. *Journal of Traumatic Stress,* 1, 17–33.

20. J Earnshaw and C L Cooper (1991), Workers' compensation in stress-related claims: some thoughts for employers in the UK. *Work and Stress,* 5, 253–257 and (1994), Employee stress litigation: the UK experience. *Work and Stress,* 8, 287–295.

21. A Ostell (1988, 1991) op cit . Also see G R J Hockey and P Hamilton (1983), The cognitive patterning of stress states. *In* G R J Hockey (Ed) *Stress and Fatigue in Human Performance.* London: J Wiley & Sons Ltd (for a discussion of problems with the inverted 'U'curve and the pressure/performance relationship; see papers in S Fisher and J Reason (1988) *op cit* and J W Mason (1971) *op cit* for discussion of physiological differences between positive and negative emotion states).

Suggested Reading

C L Cooper, R Cooper and L H Eaker (1988), *Living With Stress.* London: Penguin Health. (A readable overview of much of the current research into stress at work).

T Cox (1978), *Stress.* London: Macmillan. (Somewhat dated now but provides a useful introduction to different models of stress and the physiological aspects to stress).

S Fisher and J Reason (Eds) (1988), *Handbook of Life Stress, Cognition and Health.* London: J Wiley & Sons Ltd. (More technical collection of papers worth reading for someone able to deal with the detail, particularly physiological/endocrine research).

M T Matteson and J M Ivancevich (1988), *Controlling Stress at Work.* San Francisco: Jossey-Bass. (Good review of strategies and interventions for dealing with workplace stress).

R Totman (1990), *Mind, Stress and Health.* London: Souvenir Press. (Interesting personal perspective on stress emphasising the importance of social support).

Questions

1. "Men are not disturbed by things but by the views which they take of them" (Epictetus). How does this observation throw light upon the phenomenon of psychological stress? What additional ideas would you use to help explain why and how people become psychologically distressed?

2. Describe the options available to an organization which wants to reduce stress problems among its employees. Evaluate the merits of the different options which could be used.

3. Discuss the ways in which stress levels within an organization can be determined and the problems of interpreting any data which are collected.

Case:

Is There Such a Thing as Positive Stress?

It is sometimes argued that there is positive stress which is beneficial for a person and negative stress which has a detrimental impact. The positive/negative stress distinction derives from Selye who called them *eustress* and *distress,* respectively (a response definition of stress). Unfortunately Selye did not explain precisely what the psychological and physiological differences were between these two states or how one might be converted into the other. Thus is there such a state as positive stress and how does it relate to negative stress?

Authors who attempt to explain these two forms of stress usually do so by adapting Selye's views and invoking some version of the so-called Yerkes-Dodson law. They argue that, in an occupational context, job pressures are curvilinearly related to performance through an arousal process, producing the inverted U curve (see figure 11.2). Accordingly, at low levels of pressure or demand arousal is low, performance is poor and people experience job dissatisfaction or boredom. As demands increase to some optimal level (which is different for different people) so does arousal and performance. Should demands exceed this optimal level further arousal leads to a deterioration in performance and to other disturbances in functioning. Thus it appears that negative stress is associated with either high pressure/arousal or low pressure/arousal while positive stress is associated with an optimal pressure/arousal state.

However, the model leaves many questions unanswered. For example, why under low pressure and low arousal can a person experience either distress or pleasure? It is argued that low pressure and low arousal at work leads to the distress of boredom, but low load and arousal when sitting at home or on a beach can lead to pleasure. People can also become very aroused and distressed when there are no work pressures upon them (e.g. people becoming furious because they believe that rewards have been distributed inequitably within their department, or anxious

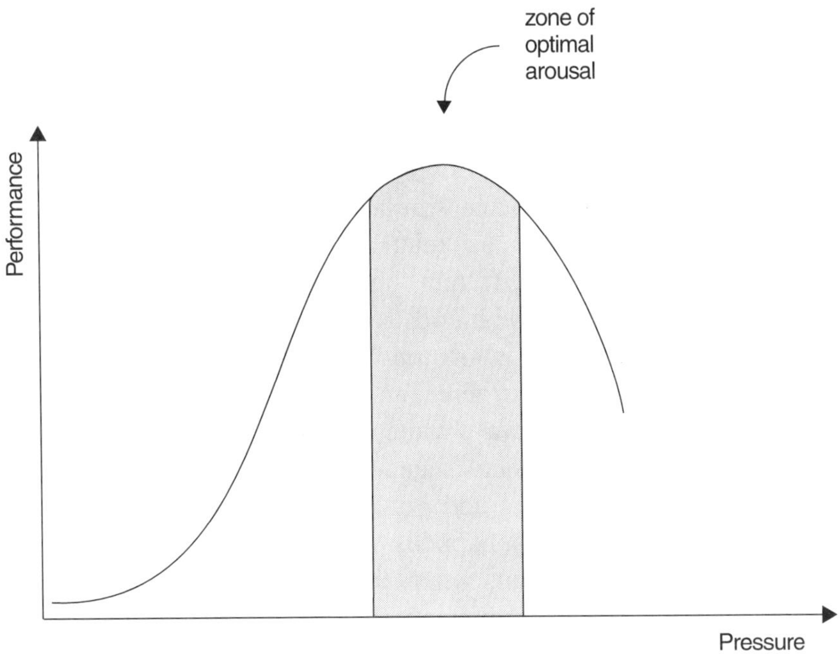

Figure 11.2. Hypothesised relationship between pressure and performance mediated by arousal.

about the failure to achieve promotion). Further, people can be distressed without being aroused (e.g. depressed about their poor performance). It is not clear whether the performance of people deteriorates above optimal arousal because their capacity is exceeded, or because their arousal is too high, or because of both? Thus, although it might be possible to demonstrate the inverted U relationship between pressure and performance in a specific situation, it certainly will not be true for the majority of stress situations. Of itself, the model also does not explain, in a convincing way, the underlying psychological processes which mediate the hypothesised relationship.

So how is it possible to account for the apparently positive and negative experiences associated with arousal. What is known currently is that when people are challenged or excited by a problem they sometimes *experience* a relatively pleasant state of arousal or heightened activation due to the increased output of certain hormones (e.g. adrenalin) into the blood stream, which they find enabling. However, when people doubt their ability to cope with a problem, or protest mentally about their circumstances, and so on, they also often notice similar physical changes, but these tend to be experienced as relatively unpleasant and have a detrimental impact. Different hormone combinations and concentrations occur in the bloodstream in this latter case. It is not that the latter people have too much, positive stress, or too high arousal, but that they perceive and react to the problem in a dysfunctional (stressful) way, while the former take a constructive view. The different physical states reflect the operation of quite different mental processes and not necessarily different levels of arousal. What commonly happens is that people view problems initially as challenges but, when the problems persist or prove difficult to handle, they then appraise their circumstances in a dysfunctional way with consequent negative changes in their experience and physical state.[21]

Within the framework adopted in this paper the term positive stress is meaningless and the Yerkes-Dodson law is a crude and misleading model to account for stress. Stress is a negative condition which refers to dysfunctional ways of perceiving and reacting to circumstances and events, which results in distress states, and is not specifically related to low or high arousal.

Part Three

Organization Development

Chapter 12

Working with the Law

Jonathan Winterton

Objectives

- To understand the institutions and origins of employment law in Britain;
- To analyse recent attempts at reform of labour relations through the law;
- To explore the scope of individual employment rights;
- To consider European law and the social dimension.

By the end of the Chapter, the reader should understand the pressures shaping the development of the legal framework of employment and recognize the key issues for the effective management of human resources.

Introduction

Employment law exists to protect individuals, regulate the employment relationship, and, increasingly, to provide remedies for practices of both employers and employees which are damaging to the interests of the other party. The trend towards 'juridification' of the employment relationship, whereby the law exerts an increasing influence on HRM and industrial relations, began in the 1970s and accelerated in the 1980s. Although much of the legislative innovation of the past 15 years has been directed at constraining trade union action, no manager can afford to ignore the employer's obligations with respect to employment security and discrimination. Moreover, it is important to be aware of the limitations of using the law to remedy perceived defects in industrial relations.

The extension of the law in the employment field has been profoundly political in character. The 1970 Conservative Government attempted to reduce trade union influence, while the Labour Governments of the period 1974–79 restored the union's legal immunities and extended employment rights as part of a Social Contract with the TUC. Conservative Governments since 1979 have focused on restricting trade union activities and reducing the scope of protective legislation. At the same time, European legislation, notwithstanding the UK Government's resistance to the Social Dimension, has extended social protection and will have an increasing influence in the second half of the 1990s.

This chapter seeks firstly to develop an understanding of the legal context by introducing the institutions of employment law and tracing the development of the legal framework of employee relations. The legal innovations since 1980 designed to reform industrial relations are considered in some detail in the second section. The changes over the past 15 years have been as profound as, and more numerous than, those of the previous 150 years. Also, the experience of collective labour law in the 1980s, though different from the experiment of 1971–74, equally demonstrates the tensions between the law and industrial relations. The third section is concerned with the individual labour law, specifically in relation to employment rights. Although individual rights have been eroded in some areas, basic protections concerning employment security and equality remain in place and are likely to be extended with the further adoption of the European Social Dimension, explored in the final section.

The institutions and origins of employment law

Legal technicalities will be kept to a minimum in this chapter, but it is useful to draw the distinctions between Common Law (made by the judiciary through ruling on cases) and Statute (laws passed by Parliament), and between criminal law (where prosecution is effected by the state) and civil law (where an action is taken by one party against another on the grounds that their interests are being unreasonably harmed). All four types of law are relevant in the employment field.

It is also appropriate to introduce the various institutions which are involved specifically in employment law, over and above those which have a broader legal remit, such as the County Court, the Court of Appeal and the House of Lords:

- Advisory, Conciliation and Arbitration Service (ACAS): an independent but state-financed body, established in 1974 and given statutory powers in 1975 to promote and extend collective bargaining and to improve industrial relations;
- Central Arbitration Committee (CAC): established in 1975 and arbitrates via a committee, with a chairperson and equal numbers from each side of industry, when asked to do so by both sides to a dispute, and in cases of disputes over disclosure of information to trade unions;
- Certification Officer: established in 1975 to maintain records of the financial and membership returns of trade unions and to

certify the independence of representative organizations from employer control or domination;

- Commissioner for the Rights of Trade Union Members: established in 1988 to provide legal advice and support to trade union members initiating legal action against their union;
- Equal Opportunities Commission (EOC) and Commission for Racial Equality (CRE): established in 1975 and 1976 to promote equality of opportunity and combat discrimination;
- Industrial Tribunals: established in 1964 and since 1972 concerned with unfair dismissal claims, they comprise a legally qualified chairperson and two lay members drawn from panels of employers and trade union nominees;
- Employment Appeal Tribunal (EAT): established in 1975 with a tripartite constitution similar to the Industrial Tribunals and chaired by a High Court judge, it rules on legal points raised at Tribunals, and cases may ultimately proceed to the Court of Appeal and House of Lords;
- European Court of Justice (ECJ): interprets European Law made by the European Council and Commission, which all member states are obliged to apply;
- International Labour Organization (ILO): a tripartite body with the objective of promoting fair working conditions on a global scale, once a Convention is ratified by a member state, the government is obliged to comply with its provisions, but there is no mechanism for enforcement.

Having identified the principal institutions of labour law, it is important to recognise that, historically, the law largely abstained from employee relations in Britain, a situation described as *voluntarism,* because:

- the parties preferred to establish terms and conditions of employment through collective bargaining;
- all parties wished to keep disputes out of the courts;
- management and unions sought to protect their autonomy.

The traditional view stressed the ineffectiveness of penal sanctions for the enforcement of industrial peace, and it was the absence of *restrictive* labour law, rather than regulatory and auxiliary laws, which characterized voluntarism. Since trade unions and industrial action are inherently unlawful under British Common Law, Parliament used the mechanism of negatively-expressed immunities to protect trade unions from judicial decisions.[1]

After the Combination Acts prohibiting trade unionism were repealed in the 1820s, the Courts used the doctrine of restraint of trade to curtail the unions, and Parliament gave unions relief from this in the *Trade Union Act 1871,* which formed the cornerstone for collective employment law for a century. The *Conspiracy and Protection of Property Act 1875* provided immunity from certain liabilities where the action was in contemplation or furtherance of a trade dispute, and introduced some restrictions on permissible actions to support a dispute. As a result of successful legal action by the Taff Vale Railway Company against the Amalgamated Society of Railway Servants in 1901, the *Trade Disputes Act 1906* was passed to grant unions and individual members further immunity from liabilities for inducing breach of contract. Similarly, after the Osborne case in which a union member had taken his union to court for using funds to promote political ends, the *Trade Union Act 1913* permitted political funds, provided the union concerned was acting within its own rules. As late as 1965, following the *Rookes* v. *Barnard* case, the unions were granted immunity by the *Trade Disputes Act 1965* from action over 'civil intimidation' arising out of a threat of breach of contract.

In the late 1960s, the voluntarist framework created by the structure of immunities was subject to considerable scrutiny by the Donovan Commission (see Chapter 13), which attributed Britain's industrial relations problems to the inadequacy of agreements, procedures and institutions, and advocated a voluntary reform of collective bargaining with the retention of legal abstention.[2] Nevertheless, the Labour Government proposed criminal sanctions in industrial relations,[3] and the Conservatives in opposition promised future legislation based on campaigning materials of the Party[4] and supporters in the legal establishment.[5] Labour's *Industrial Relations Bill* was withdrawn under TUC pressure, but the incoming Conservative Government was committed to a programme of legal reform.[6]

The *Industrial Relations Act 1971* (IRA) altered a century of voluntarism at a stroke, requiring all unions to register and publish rules specifying authorization of industrial action, in order to retain the immunities and tax status all unions had formerly enjoyed. The right to belong to a registered union was equated with a right not to belong to a union, registered or unregistered, although agency shop agreements differed little from closed shop agreements in practice. Collective agreements were held to be legally enforceable unless they contained a disclaimer clause to the contrary. Unfair industrial practices were defined and a new National Industrial Relations Court was established to hear complaints, including those relating to individual rights.

According to Clegg,[7] the Act failed because its success depended upon three assumptions:

- that unions would register and remain registered;
- that employers would use the law;
- that the NIRC's decisions could be enforced

Events demonstrated these assumptions to be false. The unions collectively de-registered to frustrate the Act and employers continued to accept closed shops and put the disclaimer 'TINA LEA' (this is not a legally enforceable agreement) to the vast majority of agreements signed.[8] When the Transport and General Workers' Union came up against the law, the Government secured the release of five jailed dockers on a legal technicality, and the sequestration of the Engineering Union's funds for contempt of court caused an anonymous party to pay the fine, averting an engineering stoppage of indefinite length.

Voluntarism was restored with the return of a Labour Government in 1974, which repealed the IRA and introduced the *Trade Union and Labour Relations Act 1974* (TULRA) as part of the Social Contract. The 1974 Act restored the traditional strike immunities and modified the unfair dismissal law by removing employers' liability for unfairly dismissing non-unionists under a Union Membership Agreement. Coupled with the *Employment Protection Act 1975* (EPA), the 1974 Act granted new statutory rights concerning trade union membership and organization: for example, a right not to be unfairly dismissed or victimized for membership of, or participation in, a trade union, and a right to take time off work to engage in trade union duties and activities. Independent trade unions had the right to initiate procedures to gain recognition, and to obtain fair wages, provisions which were subsequently repealed in the 1980s.

Employment law and industrial relations reform

When the Conservatives won the 1979 election, the Government was committed to a programme of legal regulation of industrial relations far more damaging for the trade union movement than the 1971 Act.[9] The programme, which continues at the time of writing, differs in three important respects from the earlier attack on voluntarism:

- the legislation has been introduced in a piecemeal fashion, each phase involving selected changes;
- its effectiveness does not depend upon the cooperation of the trade unions;
- employers have discretion to use the law according to specific conditions.

Soon after the 1979 election the first phase was introduced through the *Employment Act 1980*. The 1980 Act provided for payment towards the expenses incurred in holding *such ballots as may be prescribed;* ostensibly to encourage secret ballots, but it was used to promote *postal* ballots. Unions were forbidden from 'unreasonably excluding' persons (such as political extremists) from membership, and exemptions over non-membership of a union under a closed shop agreement were widened from 'religious belief' to 'grounds of conscience or deeply- held personal conviction'. Moreover, employers were able to deflect the compensation in such cases onto the union by demonstrating that the dismissal was made following pressure from the union. The immunity of individuals from civil action arising out of peaceful picketing, was restricted to picketing at a person's *own place of work*, thereby limiting the scope of the 1875 Act. The immunity of individuals from action arising out of a trade dispute was also removed from cases defined as *secondary action.*

The second phase of legislation arose out of the Green Paper *Trade Union Immunities*, which discussed ways of restricting union activities.[10] The *Employment Act 1982* built upon the restrictions imposed by the 1980 Act and made *unions* the subject of legal actions. The closed shop was further weakened, making it unfair to dismiss non-members under a union membership agreement except where the closed shop was introduced through a ballot held not earlier than 5 years before the dismissal took place. Such ballots were required to have a poll of 80% and to show 85% (of the poll) in favour. For persons unfairly dismissed on grounds of non-membership, the compensation introduced was substantial in comparison with normal unfair dismissal compensation. Employers were allowed to re-engage strikers *selectively*, three months after collective dismissal due to a strike. Union membership and recognition requirements in contracts for the supply of goods or services were prohibited, and the immunity from action was removed from any act done to bring pressure to impose such requirements. The Act repealed the immunity for trade unions and employers' associations from *certain actions in tort* (notably in connection with secondary action), and re-defined a trade dispute to exclude all disputes other than those 'between workers and their employer'.

The Green Paper *Democracy in Trade Unions* introduced the slogan of the third phase of legislation: 'giving the unions back to the members'.[11] The *Trade Union Act 1984* required unions to hold secret ballots for the election of every voting member of the principal executive committee, at least once every 5 years. The Act also specifies periodic secret ballots to enable unions to maintain a political fund or pursue political objects, effectively a return to the Osborne judgement. In all cases unions succeeded in securing exceptionally high majorities in favour of maintaining political funds. The Act required secret ballots to be held before industrial action could be authorized by a trade union, and removed all immunity from tortious liability where action was authorized without a ballot, effectively a return to the Taff Vale case. Remedies for apparent breaches of the procedures relating to industrial action under the 1984 Act were available to employers, customers and suppliers affected, and some employers used the new civil law against unions over picketing, secondary action and ballots.

The use of the law during the miners' 1984/85 strike marked a watershed.[12] The NCB drew back from using the law directly for fear of uniting the NUM and even the TUC (although hauliers and others were less reticent). While unused by the NCB, the civil law helped legitimize the extensive use of criminal law and police powers. Most significantly, the use of the law by individual members served to highlight the divisions within the Union, as well as ultimately contributing to the Union's defeat. Employers used the law more extensively after the miners' strike, mainly through securing interim injunctions. Employers still rarely took legal action against their employees or unions, but the threat of action was implicit and increasingly explicit.

Published after the 1987 General Election, the Green Paper *Trade Unions and their Members* promised further legislation to reduce trade union power.[13] Piecemeal and consolidating aspects of the *Employment Act 1988* concerned a complete ban on the post-entry closed shop; a requirement of postal ballots on political fund questions, and an extension of the statutory election requirements to non-voting members of union executive committees and union chief officers. The revolutionary aspects of the 1988 Act drew extensively on the experience of the miners' strike, and gave the right to trade union members not to be unjustifiably disciplined by their union, for failing to participate in industrial action, or for making allegations that union officials were acting contrary to rule, for example. In order to facilitate action taken by ordinary trade union members, the 1988 Act established a Commissioner for the Rights of Trade Union Members, to provide assistance and advice where members wish to take action against a union.

In the two White Papers *Building Businesses Not Barriers* (1986) and *Employment for the 1990s* (1988), and in the Consultative Document *Wages Councils* (1988), much of the protective legislation from the 1970s was held to operate as a disincentive to employment and entrepreneurial activity.[14] The *Employment Act 1989* was designed to reduce such labour market regulation by restricting the application of protective legislation, and imposing strict limitations on the rights of trade union lay officials to paid time off for trade union activities and training. The Green Paper *Removing Barriers to Employment* developed similar themes, but in relation to the closed shop and secondary industrial action.[15] Later that year, a second Green Paper was published on *Unofficial Action and the Law*.[16] These papers were reflected in the *Employment Act 1990,* which outlawed the pre-entry closed shop, removed immunity from all forms of secondary industrial action, made unions responsible for the actions of anyone able to authorize industrial action, specified further requirements in relation to ballots, empowered employers to dismiss leaders of unofficial action, and extended the role of the Commissioner of Trade Union Rights to include alleged breaches of the rule book. The *Trade Union and Labour Relations (Consolidation) Act 1992* (TULRCA) was designed to tidy up the existing legislation, rather than add anything substantive.

The Green Paper *Industrial Relations in the 1990s* looked forward to legislation requiring seven days notice of a planned strike, tougher regulation of strike ballots, legally binding collective agreements, annual agreement to maintain check-off facilities and the reform of the TUC Bridlington Rules.[17] These issues were addressed in a major new statute, the *Trade Union Rights and Employment Relations Act 1993* (TURERA), which received the

Royal Assent in July 1993. Among the more significant provisions are further requirements in connection with union elections and ballots; the financial affairs of unions; and union membership, including new requirements to authorize employers' deduction of subscriptions on behalf of the union. The Act also introduces new requirements in relation to industrial action, including postal balloting (although members may notify a workplace as their postal address), and seven-days notice to employers of impending action.

Individual employment rights

During the 1960s and 1970s a number of statutes provided a floor of individual employment rights, in relation to employment security and equal opportunity. In an effort to simplify the complex statutory framework in this area, provisions relating to the rights of employees were incorporated into the *Employment Protection (Consolidation) Act 1978.* Some of the protective framework was subsequently eroded by the Conservative legislation of the 1980s, while in other areas recent developments increased protection.

Provisions relating to employment security extended from the *Redundancy Payments Act 1965* (RPA), the IRA 1971 and the *Contracts of Employment Act 1972* (CEA) to the package of legislation under the Social Contract. The RPA provided compensation for workers facing redundancy, thereby securing cooperation in the labour shakeout through industrial restructuring. Employees with 2 years continuous employment are entitled to a compensatory redundancy payment, the amount of redundancy pay depending upon the length of service and level of pay.[18] The EPA gave workers facing notice of redundancy a right to paid time off during normal working hours to seek new employment, and required employers proposing redundancies to consult representatives of their recognized, independent trade union, the period of notice depending upon the numbers involved.

Under Common Law, an employee could pursue a claim for damages as a result of wrongful dismissal, for example if dismissed without due notice. The CEA introduced statutory requirements of notice of dismissal based on the length of continuous employment, although this did not affect the right of either party to treat the contract as terminable without notice by reason of conduct of the other party. Common Law provides no ultimate protection because the law will not induce an employer who has wrongfully ended a contract to re-engage the injured employee. These limitations, as well as recommendations of the ILO and the Donovan Commission, led to a new law relating to unfair dismissal in the IRA, part of which was re-enacted by TULRA. Every employee who had completed 26 weeks continuous employment had the right not to be unfairly dismissed by their employer. The qualifying period was extended to 52 weeks in 1979, and to 104 weeks in 1985. The qualifying period for part-time workers was 5 years, but is now the same as for full-timers.

An employee may make a complaint of unfair dismissal against an employer to an industrial tribunal, which must decide whether the dismissal was fair in the circumstances.[19] The onus is on the employee to show that they have been dismissed, and on the employer to demonstrate that the dismissal was due to a reason which was potentially fair, such as the conduct or capability of the employee. The tribunal must judge whether or not the decision to dismiss was reasonable. Remedies for unfair dismissal include an order for reinstatement or re-engagement, or a compensation payment comprising a basic award and a compensatory award. The basic award is calculated on the basis of the reasons for dismissal, the length of continuous employment and the employee's former earnings. The amount of the compensatory award is that which the 'tribunal considers just and equitable in all the circumstances having regard to the loss sustained by the complainant in consequence of the dismissal'. A dismissal can be held to be unfair even though the employee's conduct is accepted as grounds for dismissal, simply by virtue of the way in which that person has been dismissed (without due regard for agreed procedure, for example). In recognition of this, the law provides for the award to be reduced by virtue of the employee's conduct, and in cases where the employee had unreasonably refused an offer of reinstatement. The legal framework protecting employment security in Britain was least effective where it was most necessary – in respect of part-time and temporary workers. EC directives and ECJ rulings led to a decision of the House of Lords that part-time workers should be covered by the same provisions as full-timers with respect to redundancy and unfair dismissal.

The *Equal Pay Act 1970,* provides for men and women in certain circumstances to receive the same terms and conditions in their contracts, collective agreements and pay structures. The right to equal pay occurs in three situations: where a woman is employed on *like work* with a man in the same employment; where the work is rated *as equivalent* with that of a man in the same employment; and where a discriminatory *pay structure* or *collective agreement* exists. Where an individual complains to a tribunal that a term of her contract is less favourable than that of a man in the same employment, she must therefore show that the work is the same or of a broadly similar nature, or rated as equivalent, and that the differences are not of practical importance. The employer must then demonstrate *either* that the complainant is not doing similar work, *or* that the variation is due to a 'genuine material difference' between the cases compared.

The issue of equal pay for work of equal value became increasingly important in recent years in the UK, largely through the impact of European legislation.[20] Plumer analysed recent tribunal cases and found that there was significant variation in terms of the *choice of factors* to be taken into account when comparing jobs, the *scoring system* used, the *weighting* given to scores on each factor to produce an overall measure of two jobs, and the *interpretation of 'equality'*.[21] In some cases, jobs rated from between 79% and 98% of the value of a comparator job were defined as not equal, while in other cases jobs scoring 79% of the comparator were defined as equal.

The Social Contract included legislation designed to promote equal opportunity and reduce discrimination at work on the basis of gender or race, through the *Sex Discrimination Act 1975* (SDA), and the *Race Relations Act 1976* (RRA). The SDA renders unlawful certain discrimination on the grounds of gender or, in the employment field, marital status. The Act is worded in terms of discrimination against women but applies equally to men and introduced the important concepts of direct and indirect discrimination.[22] *Direct discrimination* occurs where a man discriminates against a woman on the grounds of her sex or treats her less favourably than he treats a man. *Indirect discrimination* arises where a person formally applies the same requirements to women and men, but the proportion of women who can comply with the requirement is considerably smaller than the proportion of men, it cannot be justified irrespective of the sex of the person to whom it is applied, and it is to the person's disadvantage that they cannot comply with it.

The SDA makes it unlawful for an employer to discriminate against a woman in recruitment, in access or opportunities for promotion, transfer or training, or by dismissing her. Similarly, it is unlawful for a trade union to discriminate against a woman in the terms on which she is admitted to membership, or by refusing her application. Exceptions to the unlawfulness of sex discrimination exist where 'being a man is a genuine occupational qualification for a job', for example by reasons of physiology (excluding strength), authenticity, or decency. The Equal Opportunities Commission was established to work towards eliminating sex discrimination and to promote equal opportunities between men and women, as well as to review the working of the SDA and the Equal Pay Act. The SDA is enforced through industrial tribunals and the burden of proof rests on the claimant, although the EAT has ruled that where a difference of treatment is established by comparison between a male and a female, a prima facie case of discrimination is raised.

The RRA made it unlawful to discriminate on racial grounds in similar circumstances to those in which sex discrimination is unlawful.[23] 'Racial' grounds under the Act refers to colour, race, nationality, or ethnic or national origins, but not religion. Like the SDA, the RRA covers both direct discrimination, where a person is treated less favourably on racial grounds, and indirect discrimination, where treatment is formally equal but has a discriminatory effect. The RRA makes discrimination by employers unlawful in recruitment, with respect to the terms offered or promotion. It is similarly unlawful for trade unions to discriminate against a person on racial grounds. Exceptions to racial discrimination again exist where 'being of a particular racial group is a genuine occupational qualification for a job', such an exception being authenticity in the entertainment field. The RRA established the Commission for Racial Equality to work towards eliminating racial discrimination, to promote equality of opportunity and good relations between persons of different racial groups, and to review the working of the Act. Complainants must bring their case, within three months of the act complained of, to the attention of an industrial tribunal, which is empowered to award compensation which may include elements for trouble, inconvenience and hurt feelings.

Recognizing the 'formidable obstacle to enforcement' which the burden of proof represents, the TUC recommended negotiating equal opportunity clauses in collective agreements, committing the parties to developing 'positive policies to promote equal opportunity in employment regardless of workers, sex, marital status, creed, colour, race or ethnic origins'.[24] Some agreements have broadened the concept of equality of opportunity to include religion and sexual orientation.

Important new rights were extended to women workers by the EPA. An employee absent from work wholly or partly due to pregnancy or confinement, in certain circumstances was granted the right to maternity pay and to return to work. A woman was required to notify her employer 21 days before absence began, that her absence was on grounds of maternity and, if she wished to return to work, that this was her intention. More stringent notice requirements were introduced by EA 1980. An employee was entitled to the usual protection against unfair dismissal on the grounds of pregnancy, unless her dismissal was because of inability to carry out her normal work (radiographers, for example) *and* the employer could not provide suitable alternative employment. The right to return to original employment was modified by EA 1980 to work of a kind 'suitable and appropriate', where it is not reasonably practicable to permit her to return to her original job. Maternity rights were only accorded to women who worked more than 16 hours per week and had been continuously employed by their employer for 2 years, but the right not to be unfairly dismissed on the grounds of pregnancy, was given to all employees with 26 weeks continuous employment. As with unfair dismissal in general, this entitlement was restricted in 1985 to persons with 104 weeks continuous employment, but as a result of European law, TURERA made the right not to be dismissed on grounds of pregnancy unconditional of length of service, and all women are now entitled to 14 weeks maternity pay irrespective of length of service.

European law and the social dimension

Law and policies are made within the European Union (EU) by a variety of institutional mechanisms, each having powers defined under the Treaty of Rome.

- The European Commission (EC) is headed by 14 Commissioners, each responsible for a different area of EC policy, whose Directorate Generals propose to the Council of Ministers new legal instruments for harmonizing the laws of members states. The EC also ensures that states implement EC law and is empowered to initiate proceedings against members states at the Court of Justice for non-compliance with EU law.
- The Council of Ministers, on which all member states' governments are represented, exists to ensure that all the objectives of the Treaty of Rome are attained. It makes decisions on legislation proposed by the EC and seeks the

opinions of the European Parliament and the Economic and Social Committee on draft legislation.
- The European Parliament is the democratic representative body which serves to legitimize EU activities and exercise advisory and supervisory powers over the EC. Its power, authority and constitutional basis is unlike that of national parliaments and its formal legislative role is confined to pressurising the EC to implement policies it considers to be important and suggesting amendments to the Council of Ministers.
- The European Court of Justice exists to clarify and interpret EC law and to ensure that members states apply the requirements of the Treaty. Cases brought by national governments, the EC or individuals, are ruled on by 12 judges appointed by national governments and 5 Advocates-General who give impartial advice.

Legal developments at the European level have had a profound effect on UK labour law, even with the UK having opted out of significant areas for the time being, as a result of Directives which have sought to guarantee fundamental social rights for workers and the decisions of the European Court of Justice, which is the European supreme court above the House of Lords. For example, TURERA 1993 enacted seven EU directives:

- a right not to be dismissed on grounds of pregnancy;
- statutory maternity entitlement of 14 weeks irrespective of length of service, on a rate no less than statutory sick pay introduced in October 1994;
- a right to a written statement of terms and conditions of employment for workers employed for more than 8 hours per week and having 2 months service;
- a right to refuse to work in unsafe conditions (believed to be in serious and imminent danger);
- improved contractual rights of employees in connection with a transfer of undertakings;
- strengthened consultation procedures in cases of redundancy.

As a result of EC directives and ECJ rulings, the Lords also ruled that part-time workers should be covered by the same legal provisions as those working full-time in relation to redundancy and unfair dismissal.

Legally-binding Directives on labour market issues were greeted with alarm by UK governments, who sought to oppose the social agenda on the grounds that it would undermine the competitiveness of industry. Nevertheless, as Leon Brittan noted:
Social protection alone does not make a country uncompetitive. A worker who receives high wages, long holidays, generous maternity leave and a good pension may still be comparatively productive if he or she is highly skilled, well educated and works in a country with high capital investment, good infrastructure and a strong emphasis on industrial research.

The 1992 Programme of the European Community to complete the single European market and establish economic and monetary union generated pressure to develop the 'Social Dimension'.[25] The benefits of European integration were largely seen to accrue to employers, and there were fears that the removal of barriers would create competition in labour markets which would reduce employment standards to the lowest common denominator. Such pressure, from the Christian and Social Democrats, labour and socialist parties, and the trade union movement led to the decision at the Maastricht EC summit in December 1991 to include in the Treaty on European Union a social policy protocol. The Maastricht protocol was concerned to establish social protection through increased EC intervention.

The UK Conservative Government, with an attachment to the pursuit of a free market and to a programme which has reduced state intervention and regulation substantially in 15 years, opted out of the Maastricht provisions, having refused to sign the 1989 EC Social Charter. The diverse views of governments of member states are no more significant than the differences apparent within states between employers and trade unions. There were three main arguments behind the social dimension:

- the single market would, in the absence of some regulation of the social dimension, facilitate 'social dumping' where transnational enterprises would be attracted to countries with the lowest labour rates and weakest employment protection legislation, generating in turn downward pressure on wage rates throughout the EU;

- the single market would intensify the international division of labour and exacerbate the inequalities between member states, especially to the disadvantage of the 'peripheral states';
- the social dimension was held to offer an alternative vision of promoting a European production norm based on highly-skilled labour, high quality, modern technology and high productivity, underpinned by the notion of 'social partnership'.

The social dimension has been important in making the single market more acceptable to the European labour movements, and thereby gaining their cooperation and support in the economic restructuring which accompanies 1992. The European employers' association, UNICE, like the UK Government, has opposed the social dimension on the grounds that it will reduce competitiveness, impose unnecessary burdens on business, act as a deterrent to entrepreneurial activity and therefore destroy jobs. As a result, the development of the social dimension has been slower than its proponents would have wished, and many contradictions remain. The original Social Charter, developed by the European Social Committee with support from the European Trades Union Congress and the Confédération Française Démocratique du Travail, began as a general political statement, but became more robust in intention when its adoption by the EC in 1989 included a commitment to the preparation of an action programme and associated legislative proposals.

Discussions within the Council of Ministers brought an emphasis on subsidiarity: member states (not only the UK but also peripheral states) were concerned to limit the constitutional influence of the EC and to protect national practice. Many amendments weakened the individual provisions of the Charter and no legislative commitment was made in two areas which had embodied important principles:

- right of fair remuneration;
- right to freedom of association.

Nevertheless, the action programme did include:

- establishment of minimum standards in respect of a range of working conditions: these included directives regulating the conditions of 'atypical' workers and workers sent to other EU countries, working time, maternity rights, contractual information, improvements in health and safety standards, and various initiatives to expand vocational training;
- information and consultation rights: these included new provisions on collective redundancy, and new (but at that time undefined) rights in respect of European-level companies.

The EC brought forward proposals in 1990 and 1991 for directives on contractual information, European Works Councils and collective redundancies, and by the end of 1993, the bulk of the proposals in the action programme had been adopted. The provisions in four areas, however, were substantially weakened:

- contractual information
- collective redundancies
- maternity rights
- working time

It was necessary for the EC to seek treaty revisions to establish EC 'competence' (jurisdiction) to legislate on a range of employment and industrial relations issues, and to extend qualified majority voting. The EC also proposed increased involvement of the social partners in consultation over EC proposals. The social partners' agreement on proposed treaty revisions of 31 October 1991 recommended that the treaty should provide for the conclusion and extension of EU-level agreements, and this was incorporated in the social chapter proposed at Maastricht. The UK government refused to accept the social chapter, even in a revised form, and the French government would not accept a treaty which did not include the extension of qualified majority voting on social policy issues. The social policy protocol to the treaty was therefore the compromise outcome, allowing the other 11 member states, without the UK, to adopt directives in the social policy field on the basis of what was proposed in the social chapter of the Maastricht treaty. While these provisions will not, for the time being, apply to the UK, the existing social policy provisions of the Treaty of Rome will continue to apply to the UK.

The extension of EC competence in the social policy field allows the Council to adopt directives by qualified majority voting without the involvement of the UK, which will apply to the 11 states, in such areas as:

- health and safety
- working conditions
- information and consultation
- equal opportunities

Unanimous voting is required for certain other areas, including:

- social security
- termination of employment
- collective representation of workers and employers
- codetermination

The extension of qualified majority voting and the involvement of social partners in the legislative process have profound implications for the extension of the social dimension in the EU, although in practice this is weakened by the exclusion of the UK. While the UK stays outside the scope of directives under the protocol, this may deter the extensive use of the new procedure, at least in areas where measures would add significantly to labour costs. Without a change in government, the UK is unlikely to agree to come under the provisions of the Maastricht social chapter, but increasingly UK companies are having to confront the EC legal requirements in order to operate across the EU.

Conclusion

- Traditionally, the law played a minor role in the employment relationship, but in the past 25 years juridification of employee relations has increased.
- The attempt to reform industrial relations through the law failed in the 1970s, and was followed by statutory support for collective bargaining and an extension of individual employment rights.
- From 1980, through piecemeal legislative innovation, the most hostile environment for trade unions this century has been created, and the scope of individual employment rights has been reduced.
- European law has acted as a countervailing influence to the deregulation pursued by UK governments and will increasingly bring into effect the provisions of the Social Dimension.

References

1. See K.W. Wedderburn, *The Worker and the Law,* Harmondsworth: Penguin, 1985; and B. A. Hepple and S. Friedman, *Labour Law and Industrial Relations in Britain,* London: Kluwer, 1986, pp. 39–67 and 260–6, for an explanation of the immunities and an analysis of the development of labour law.

2. Lord Donovan (ch) Royal Commission on Trade Unions and Employers' Associations 1965–68, *Report,* Cmnd. 3623, London: HMSO.

3. White Paper, *In Place of Strife,* Cmnd. 3888, London: HMSO, 1969.

4. Conservative Party, *Fair Deal at Work,* London: Conservative Political Centre, 1968.

5. Committee of Members of the Inns of Court Conservative and Unionist Society, *A Giant's Strength,* London: ICCUS, 1958.

6. P. Jenkins, *The Battle of Downing Street,* London: Charles Knight, 1970.

7. H.A. Clegg, *The Changing System of Industrial Relations in Great Britain*, Oxford: Blackwell, 1979.

8. B. Weekes, M. Mellish, L. Dickens and J. Lloyd, *Industrial Relations and the Limits of Law, Oxford:* Blackwell, 1975.

9. J. McIlroy, *The Permanent Revolution? Conservative Law and the Trade Unions,* Nottingham: Spokesman, 1991.

10. Green Paper, *Trade Union Immunities,* Cmnd. 8128, London: HMSO, 1981.

11. Green Paper, *Democracy in Trade Unions,* Cmnd. 8778, London: HMSO, 1983.

12. J. Winterton and R. Winterton, *Coal, Crisis and Conflict: The 1984–85 Miners' Strike in Yorkshire,* Manchester University Press, 1989, Chapter 5.

13. Green Paper, *Trade Unions and their Members,* Cm. 95, London: HMSO, 1987.

14. White Paper *Building Businesses Not Barriers,* London: HMSO, 1986; White Paper *Employment for the 1990s*, London: HMSO, 1988; *Wages Councils: Consultative Document,* (published with the1988 White Paper).

15. Green Paper, *Removing Barriers to Employment,* Cm. 655, London: HMSO, 1989.

16. Green Paper, *Unofficial Action and the Law,* Cm. 821, London: HMSO, 1989.

17. Green Paper, *Industrial Relations in the 1990s: proposals for further reform of industrial relations and trade union law,* Cm. 1602, London: HMSO, 1991.

18. C. Grunfeld, *The Law of Redundancy,* London: Sweet and Maxwell, 1980, 2nd ed; Institute of Personnel Management, *The IPM Redundancy Code,* London: IPM, 1983.

19. L. Dickens, M. Jones, B. Weekes and M. Hart, *Dismissed: A Study of Unfair Dismissal and the Industrial Tribunal System,* Oxford: Blackwell, 1985, Chapter 8; M.J. Goodman, *Industrial Tribunals: Practice and Procedure,* London: Sweet and Maxwell, 1987, 4th ed.

20. L. Dickens, 'Equal opportunities – a more encouraging approach?' *Employee Relations,* Vol.8, no.4, 1986, pp 27–32.

21. A.M. Plumer, *Equal Value Judgements: Objective Assessment or Lottery?* Warwick Paper in Industrial Relations No.40, University of Warwick, Industrial Relations Research Unit, 1992.

22. R. Townshend-Smith, *Sex Discrimination in Employment: Law, Practice and Policy,* London: Sweet and Maxwell, 1989.

23. B. Chiplin and P. Sloane, *Tackling Discrimination at the Workplace,* Cambridge University Press, 1982, Chapters 2, 4.

24. J. McMullen, *Rights at Work*, London: Pluto, 1983, 2nd ed.

25. J.T. Addison and W.S. Siebert, 'The Social Charter: whatever next?', *British Journal of Industrial Relations,* Vol.30, no.4, 1992, pp.495–513.

Guide to further reading

G. Pitt, *Employment Law,* London: Sweet and Maxwell, 1995, is a comprehensive text for the non-specialist.

J. McIlroy, *The Permanent Revolution? Conservative Law and the Trade Unions*, Nottingham: Spokesman, 1991, provides an excellent account of the legal changes of the 1980s from the perspective of the trade union movement.

Typical examination questions

1. Why was the UK characterised as 'voluntarist' and how has this situation altered?

2. What are the limitations to using the law to alter the behaviour of managers and workers?

3. Given the conflict between the European model of protecting workers' rights and the UK policy of removing burdens from employers, what would you expect to happen to employment protection?

Case Study

The electro-plating company employed 150 workers, about half of whom (mostly skilled workers) were members of the engineering union. The shop stewards enjoyed good relations with management, but there was no formal bargaining, nor agreed procedures. Skilled workers were paid above the industry average, but the semi-skilled rate was unattractive and there was consequently a high turnover of these employees. It was the tradition of this family business for the managing director to take ultimate responsibility for hiring and firing, guided by the management team.

In the past month, one of the semi-skilled workers, who had been employed for almost 3 years, had arrived late to work on four occasions and had been absent without explanation on two Mondays. The lateness and absence had caused production delays as the individual's job involved de-greasing components in preparation for electro-plating. When the managing director was apprised of the situation, he stormed into the degreasing shop, shouted at the worker concerned and dismissed the individual without notice. He had always taken a firm line on attendance because of the adverse effect which unscheduled absences had upon business performance and was surprised that the problem had not been brought to his attention sooner.

The managing director was also surprised when he learnt that the dismissed employee had made an application to an industrial tribunal on grounds of unfair dismissal. He believed in taking responsibility for his own decisions, so agreed to represent the company at the hearing. The tribunal chairman and, to his amazement, the lay member from the employers' panel, were highly critical of the company. His defence was that this employee had been treated no differently from others who had been persistently late or absent. The tribunal decision went in favour of the employee because the company appeared to have no proper procedure for disciplinary issues; no-one had explained to the worker concerned what would be the consequences of absence or lateness, and there was no progression through verbal and written warnings.

In the course of the tribunal hearing, it transpired that it was not uncommon for semi-skilled workers to be dismissed for poor time-keeping, whereas the skilled workers were invariably given an informal verbal warning by the foreman. The company acknowledged that the claimant's work had always been satisfactory and their time-keeping had been exemplary until the month in which they were dismissed. The claimant produced medical evidence that their daughter had recently developed asthma and had been taken ill at a time when her other parent was temporarily working away from home. There had been no opportunity to explain these circumstances to the company.

1. Why was the tribunal concerned about the absence of disciplinary procedures?
2. Why did the company treat the semi-skilled workers differently from the skilled workers?
3. The claimant, like most of the semi-skilled workers, was a woman. Does this raise any other legal issues?

Chapter 13

Managing Employee Relations

Jonathan Winterton

Objectives

- To explore the elements of employee relations in Britain;
- To identify the major attempts at reform of labour relations;
- To analyse the challenges to established industrial relations institutions;
- To consider options for developing employee relations in the 1990s.

By the end of the Chapter, the reader should understand how the system of industrial relations has evolved over the past three decades and recognise alternative approaches to employee relations and their contribution to the effective management of human resources.

Introduction

Employee relations encompasses some of the most complex and, on occasions, intractable, issues in the management of human resources. The traditional approach to managing employee relations has been pragmatic and reactive, rather than strategic and proactive. In the past 15 years, the influence of the trade unions has decreased and it has become fashionable to individualize employee relations. Therefore, while HRM has led to a more strategic approach to managing employee relations, the strategies have largely neglected the collective dimensions of industrial relations. If managers consider industrial relations to be irrelevant to the modern enterprise, they are not only mistaken, but also neglecting an important opportunity.

It would be a mistake to regard industrial relations issues as of largely historic interest, yet the recent history has largely created the contemporary industrial relations context. The future pattern of labour relations will not represent a return to the conditions of the 1960s, 1970s or 1980s, but already the 1990s are manifesting aspects of all three previous decades. While the general level of strike activity has been much lower in the 1990s, there have been small, short stoppages in manufacturing plants reminiscent of the 1960s, a few public sector pay confrontations like those of the 1970s and a continuation of the restructuring struggles of the 1980s. By analysing the attempts to reform industrial relations in recent decades, the present and future patterns of industrial relations can more easily be understood.

By ignoring labour relations issues because the balance of power is in their favour, managers run the risk of missing an opportunity to reconstruct employee relations to create the conditions for lasting competitive advantage. Any significant economic recovery will lead to new challenges from organized workers, but by using the current situation to develop and empower employees, management who have the courage to manage by consent may establish a high-trust relationship capable of transcending the 'zero-sum game' of traditional adversarial industrial relations.

This chapter is organized into six sections. First, the elements of industrial relations are examined to clarify the areas of interest. The special character of workplace industrial relations in Britain is highlighted by considering the problems of the 1960s, and attempts at reform. The next sections deal with the challenges of reconstructing industrial relations in the 1970s, and with the difficulties created by the collision of incomes policies with public sector workers' aspirations for wages comparable with the private sector. The nature of developments in the 1980s is explored by considering both the continuities and changes of the decade. The final section offers a brief prognosis of the prospects for a new era of industrial relations in the second half of the 1990s, drawing upon the lessons from, and strengths of, the previous three decades.

Elements of employee relations

Of the various approaches to the study of industrial relations,[1] one of the most influential has been the systems approach, which defines the actors and their institutional relationships within certain contexts. Obviously the key actors are managers and employees, but it is the interaction of their representative *institutions* which is the focus of industrial relations, rather than the relationship between individual workers and managers, which is more the province of HRM and inter-personal relations. In the UK, the character of trade unions, and other employee representative organizations such as staff associations, has had a determining influence on patterns of industrial relations. Employers' associations have generally reacted to trade union organization, and often companies are not affiliated to employers' federations, preferring to conduct negotiations independently.

The systems perspective, which has influenced the major schools of industrial relations in Britain and North America, views the essence of industrial relations as a *rule-making processes* whereby managers and workers, through their respective institutions, negotiate agreements to regulate their relationship, a process which we term *collective bargaining*. The rules produced by collective bargaining serve to regulate terms and conditions of employment (*substantive rules*), and to govern both the administration of substantive rules and the relations between the parties (*procedural rules*). The system therefore contains a degree of self regulation, indicated by the feedback in Figure 13:1. The rules need not be formal or written (codified) and in addition to voluntary agreements between management and unions, can include unilateral decisions by management, work group custom and practice, and government laws. The bargaining process itself includes the operation of sanctions (strikes and lockouts, for example) so that the 'settlement' arising out of bargaining need not

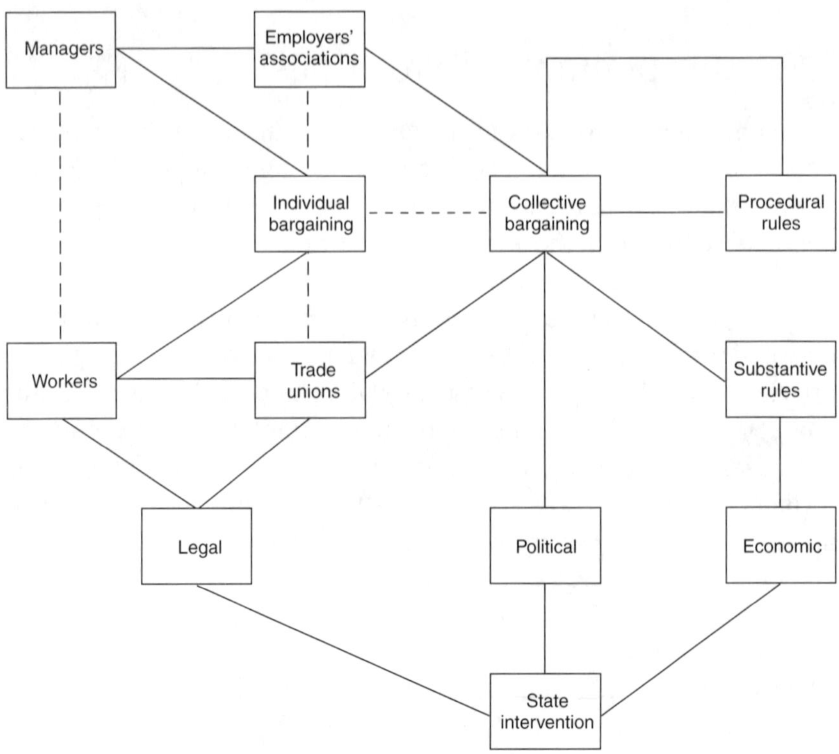

Figure 13.1. The System of industrial relations.

be agreement, let alone compromise. It is important to acknowledge that the system does not inevitably lead to the maintenance of order, but has considerable potential also for contributing to entropy.

The state intervenes in this relationship in a number of ways, and an analytical distinction can be made between legal, economic and political forms of third-party intervention. Each form of intervention affects the system at a different point, as Figure 13:1 shows. The role of *legislation* in industrial relations is evident at both the individual and collective levels. Collective employment law in Britain has traditionally been minimal, particularly when compared with the United States or Australia, although in the past 15 years there has been more statutory intervention than in the previous 150 years (see Chapter 12). Direct *economic* intervention in industrial relations, as opposed to general economic policies which impinge on the employment relationship, seeks to limit substantive agreements, either by imposing a ceiling to pay settlements through incomes policies, or by establishing minimum rates of pay in industries where collective bargaining was under-developed, as the Wages Councils once did. The *political* intervention distinguished in Figure 13:1 concerns the involvement in the bargaining process of state-sponsored institutions, such as the independent Advisory, Conciliation and Arbitration Service (ACAS), which assist the parties to resolve disputes and reach agreement.

Clearly the systems approach represents an over-simplification, and is of limited use as a theoretical framework.[2] The social psychologist may argue that such an institutional approach obscures the agency of individuals and neglects human relationships, while the political economist might object that attention is diverted from the locus and distribution of power in society. Both criticisms are valid, but taken as an abstraction from the real world, rather than a portrayal of reality, the model can be viewed as an heuristic device to define the boundary of the subject area and to identify its elements. The model can be used in this way to offer a systematic description, and a tentative analysis, of the key developments in British industrial relations over the past few decades.

Attempts at reforming the system in the 1960s

The 1960s represented a period when the established institutions of industrial relations came under significant strain as a result of tight labour market conditions, which were especially reflected in local shortages of skilled workers in manufacturing industries. The bargaining opportunities which this situation presented for key groups of workers resulted in a high and growing number of unofficial strikes in manufacturing, and was widely assumed to have contributed to Britain's perceived lack of competitiveness and low labour productivity. Under pressure to introduce legal restrictions on trade union action, the Labour Government established a Royal Commission on Trade Unions and Employers' Associations, which sat from 1965 to 1968, chaired by Lord Donovan.[3] The Donovan Commission produced the most extensive analysis of labour relations this century, and is a useful starting point because it highlighted many of the unique features of the British system.

According to the Donovan analysis, there were two systems of industrial relations in Britain: the *formal* system embodied in the official institutions and national agreements, and the *informal* system reflecting the actual behaviour of shop stewards and managers. In manufacturing industries, the formal, or external, institutions of collective bargaining were mostly sector level arrangements, typically known as joint national negotiating committees. In engineering, for example, an industry-wide agreement was negotiated between the Engineering Employers' Federation (EEF) and the Confederation of Shipbuilding and Engineering Unions (CSEU). In some industries, such as brewing and furniture, there was also collective bargaining at regional level, involving local employers' associations and the regional full-time officials of the relevant trade unions. The informal, or internal, system typically centred on work groups, represented by a shop steward, who negotiated with first line managers, foremen and supervisors. These two extremes of sector and work group bargaining, shown in Figure 13:2, were in conflict, and the extension of the informal system undermined the regulatory effect of the formal system, creating disorder in the form of unofficial stoppages, restrictive labour practices and wages drift.

The Donovan analysis emphasized the informality and autonomy of the informal system, where unwritten rules predominated and workplace customs were as enforceable as written national agreements. Where formal procedures for resolving disputes

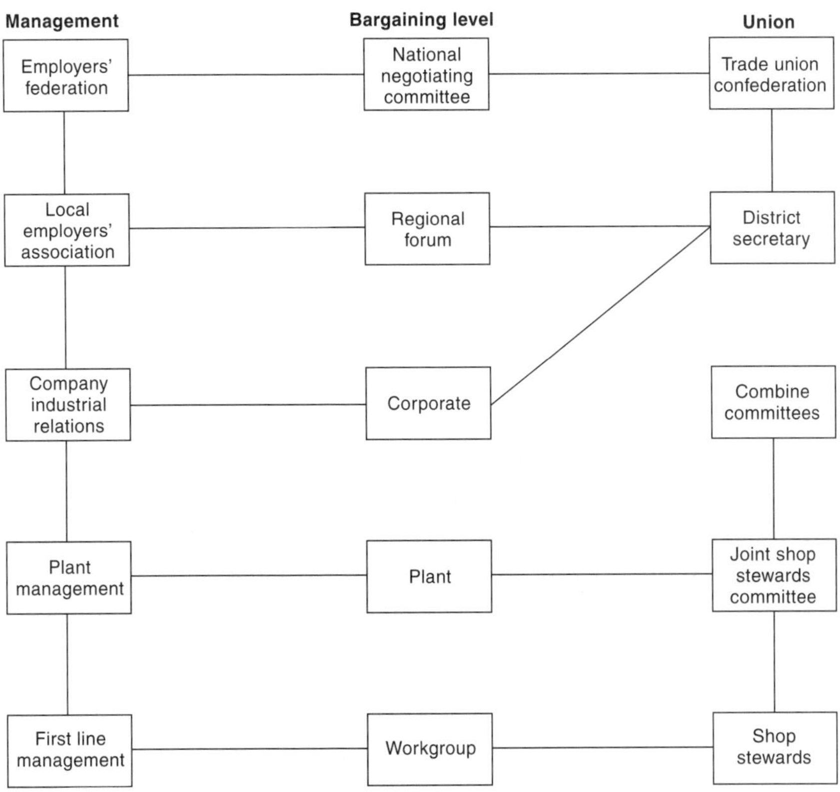

Figure 13.2. Collective bargaining structures.

existed they were often short-circuited; unofficial strikes (not sanctioned by the relevant authority of the union) were often also unconstitutional (in breach of the agreed procedure). The complexities of union structure resulted in a fragmented system of pay bargaining, which was beyond the control of union full-time officials and which generated disorderly pay structures at company level.[4]

In many respects, the story of employee relations in the 1960s was one of the resurgence of shop steward influence, a phenomenon which first became significant in the engineering factories devoted to munitions production during the First World War. The shop steward remained an informal, lay official and even in the 1960s, the majority of union rule books made no mention of them although most unions had some form of lay representatives at the workplace. Their origins, and power, lay in the social organization of work groups rather than the official bureaucracy of the trade union movement. From the Donovan era, shop stewards have been systematically examined by surveys and plant-level studies. On the basis of the workplace survey undertaken on their behalf, the Donovan Commission described the average shop steward as 'more of a lubricant than an irritant'. The majority of managers and trade union members did not regard shop stewards as the initiators of industrial action, although shop stewards did view themselves as being more militant than their constituents.[5] Shop stewards were often reported to be a restraining influence on members, discouraging 'wildcat' strikes,[6] and in the conflict-prone car plants of the 1960s, researchers identified 'unofficial-unofficial' strikes, stoppages which were not only unconstitutional and unofficial, but were also against the advice of local shop stewards.[7] While loyalty to their members may require stewards to support spontaneous action, they must also play according to the rules of the game if stable bargaining relationships are to be maintained with management.

The Donovan prescription rejected legal sanctions as ineffective and instead recommended introducing 'greater order into factory and workshop relations'. The reforms centred on the *formalization* of the informal system through the codification of local agreements and the adoption of agreed procedures at local level. Productivity bargaining had already begun to formalise workplace negotiations before the Donovan inquiry and had shifted the focus from the work group to plant bargaining. The Donovan prescription was also already under way in larger manufacturing enterprises, and was largely complete by the early 1970s. The formalization of plant bargaining enhanced the status of shop stewards and undermined further the authority of front-line supervision (who had acquiesced in granting informal concessions that effectively reduced the control of senior management). It also encouraged the development of joint shop stewards' committees (JSSC) to promote cooperation between the different unions represented at plant level. While the JSSCs reduced inter-union conflict, they also institutionalized the divisions between shop stewards and full-time union officials; shop stewards on a JSSC could find themselves committed to JSSC majority decisions that conflicted with the official policies of their union.

In a survey of industrial relations in federated (EEF) engineering establishments, undertaken towards the end of the 1960s, shop stewards were found to be present in all establishments, full-time convenors or senior stewards were found at 10% of establishments, while at a further 25% the leading stewards spent at least 10 hours per week on union duties.[8] The growth of workplace bargaining during the 1960s both reflected and enhanced the power of work groups (and hence of shop stewards) under tight labour market conditions. Where workplace trade unionism was highly developed, as in manufacturing and, especially, in the engineering and motor vehicles industries, shop stewards were able to exploit local labour shortages, employing unofficial, unconstitutional stoppages and contributing to the wages drift associated with the problems of the British economy from 1965. The survey of engineering plants found that stewards had a degree of unilateral control over such issues as labour mobility, manning levels and job demarcation in over one third of establishments.

Reconstruction in the 1970s

The reform of collective bargaining along the lines advocated by the Donovan Commission was largely complete by the early 1970s. Britain's strike proneness (number of stoppages per thousand employees) peaked in 1970 and thereafter the impact of institutionalization and formalization became apparent. At local level, management industrial relations strategies during the 1970s focused upon reforms designed to neutralize the impact of union activity and restore some of the managerial prerogative which had been eroded during the tight labour market conditions of the 1960s. Whereas the Donovan reforms had concentrated on negotiating procedures to *institutionalize* industrial conflict, during the 1970s, the emphasis shifted to *restricting the scope of collective bargaining,* especially at the point of production. Plant bargaining remained more important than industry-wide bargaining in most of manufacturing, but large companies also developed *corporate* industrial relations strategies and many initiated company-level bargaining on certain issues, or for certain groups.

In response to corporate industrial relations strategies, senior stewards in multi-plant companies attempted to overcome divisions and share information between different sites by establishing inter-plant Combine Committees. While the Combine Committees were the logical institutions for corporate bargaining, companies deliberately avoided negotiating with them, for fear of legitimizing a new tier of union organization, just as the JSSCs had enjoyed increased power with the formalization of plant bargaining. Instead, employers preferred to restore the influence of full-time union officials outside the enterprise, integrating the *external* representatives with the *internal* system. As Figure 13:2 shows, there was no automatic communication between regional full-time officials of a particular union and the lay officials serving on multi-union committees, so the dislocation between the internal and external system remained on the union side.

The comprehensive Warwick workplace survey at the end of the

1970s found shop stewards at 73% of all manufacturing plants and at 97% of large plants with at least 1,000 workers.[9] Where there were several stewards, there was usually a hierarchy; the likelihood of a senior steward or convenor is directly related to the size of the workforce and the number of shop stewards.[10] About 12% of establishments with stewards representing manual workers reported full-time convenors, but they were most common where wages are fixed by single- rather than multi-employer bargaining. Moreover, convenors usually came into being through managerial initiative and were clearly associated with larger *enterprises* (as well as establishments) and the existence of specialist industrial relations management. The Warwick Survey found that 29% of multi-union establishments reported cross-representation, whereby the steward of one union represents, in addition, members of another. In those where shop stewards' meetings were held, 52% reported meeting regularly, and a further 15% occasionally, typically as a JSSC. Beyond plant level, Combine Committees, were reported by 34% of establishments in the case of manual workers, and 44% in the case of white-collar workers.

Surveys have provided valuable information on the coverage of workplace union organization, whereas plant-level studies have illustrated the different ways in which shop stewards mobilize, and respond to, rank-and-file opinion. While there is a contrast between shop-floor representatives, who generally place a greater emphasis on leadership and the pursuit of union principles through industrial conflict, and staff representatives, both groups contain a range of interpretations of the shop steward role. Batstone and colleagues distinguished four types of shop steward according to the extent to which they demonstrated commitment to union principles and whether they saw themselves as representatives or delegates.[11] Stewards identified as *leaders* saw themselves as representatives in pursuit of union principles, while *nascent leaders* shared the pursuit of union principles but acted as delegates. *Populist* stewards were identified as carrying out the members' wishes, rather than following union principles, and differed from *cowboy* stewards only in so far as they were delegates rather than representatives.

In the studies of shop stewards, management were found to seek a strong bargaining relationship with the shop steward organization where convenors and senior stewards were able and willing to adopt a leadership role, and to avoid such a relationship with populist lay officials. In this way, shop steward leadership is reaffirmed by managerial action, often because management objectives can only be achieved with the cooperation of workplace union leaders. Purcell and Sisson considered how managers in the 1970s dealt with the challenge of trade unions and how they attempted to reconstruct workplace industrial relations in the light of this challenge.[12] The growth of giant corporations with interests spanning several industries, encouraged the development of senior management specialising in industrial relations. These managers have been involved in reforms intended to legitimize managerial authority and neutralize the impact of union activity by restricting the scope of collective bargaining, especially at the point of production, and negotiating procedures to institutionalize industrial conflict.

The formalization of plant bargaining increased the importance of shop stewards and convenors, but critics argued that it also incorporated them into management control structures through formal systems and written procedures.[13] Moreover, the emergence of shop steward hierarchies served to integrate senior stewards into the union bureaucracy and distance them from the rank and file membership. Others have argued that it was the managers who were incorporated into the shop steward system, recognising workplace union structures, and granting facilities which enhanced the lay officials' status.[14] Both perspectives are equally valid, and not contradictory. To the extent that 'incorporation' of each party occurred, it served to increase their mutual dependence and produce the stable bargaining relationships which were the foundations of pluralist institutionalization in the Donovan prescription.

Sources of instability in the 1970s

Historically, manual workers were highly unionized in most public enterprises before nationalization, and collective bargaining arrangements encouraged the growth of white-collar unionization. In 1948 all the nationalized industries together had a union density of 60%, compared with an average for all industries of 45%. By 1979 public enterprise union density was typically above 90%, compared with an average for all industries of 53%.

With a few notable exceptions, high union density was combined with a public sector norm of peaceful industrial relations, explicable in terms of the 'model employer' concept, the existence of career structures and 'lifetime employment'. Equally important were effective procedures to deal with discipline and grievances, highly-developed centralized collective bargaining and consultation arrangements, which served to institutionalize industrial conflict, and attractive redundancy arrangements when employment was run down in the public sector. Above all, there is the political contingency argument: governments wanted to keep the trains running and the lights on, as they would be blamed for stoppages.

However, the post-war public-sector consensus came under increasing strain during the 1970s as a result of incomes policies and the breakdown of comparability as the main principle of pay determination. Government is better able to control pay settlements in the public sector, so public-sector workers were affected more by incomes policies than were workers in, for example, private sector manufacturing. The pay of railway workers fell behind average earnings when the industry contracted during the 1950s, as did that of miners between 1957 and 1972. As a consequence, incomes policies, especially the 'n-1' policy of the Heath Government, which related only to the public sector, brought successive groups of public sector workers into direct conflict with governments in an effort to obtain settlements comparable with those obtaining in the private sector. The result was a wave of strikes involving postal workers, local authority workers, fire-fighters, railway workers, civil servants, health service workers, teachers and miners.[15]

In some areas of the public sector, a degree of decentralization of collective bargaining was introduced to provide flexibility and meet pressures to match wages in the private sector. For example, in local authorities and the health service, where workplace union organization has traditionally been underdeveloped, the National Union of Public Employees (now part of UNISON) established a shop steward system to deal with local bargaining. These changes in the structure of collective bargaining had a major impact on the power structure of unions.[16]

The centralized bargaining structures which existed in most of the public sector were less amenable to gaining wage concessions of the sort which manufacturing workers had won during the 1960s and into the 1970s. The traditions of local bargaining survived nationalization in steel, coal and the docks, where employee representation was particularly powerful both at national *and local* level. Pay rates tended to be determined nationally, while actual earnings were affected by local negotiation over overtime and bonuses (especially on the docks). Fluctuating earnings and strong union organization translated local bargaining opportunities into a relatively high level of conflict in these industries, which contrasted markedly with the generally peaceful industrial relations which has characterised the public utilities and other public enterprises.

In the case of coal mining, where collective bargaining had formerly been decentralised to the pit and the coal face, bargaining was elevated to industry level in the period 1966–71 by the National Power Loading Agreement (NPLA), which introduced standard shift rates for each coalfield in place of the rates established by district negotiation. The NPLA covered face-workers (including craftsmen and rippers) on power-loaded faces during a production shift and brought the most militant workers under the scope of national agreements. Coal mining had been overwhelmingly responsible for the number of strikes in British industry, even after the increase in manufacturing strike proneness during the 1960s, and the NPLA is widely accredited with bringing about the decline of coal mining strike proneness in the period 1966–1971. The proportion of strikes over allowances fell, there was a corresponding increase in the proportion of strikes over working arrangements, and the NPLA encouraged the use of the pit conciliation machinery because money could no longer be conceded in face negotiation.[17]

At the very time when decentralized bargaining was enabling workers in manufacturing to negotiate workplace additions, the miners were constrained by industry-wide rates and their relative earnings declined significantly. Declining earnings were accompanied by job losses; half a million jobs were lost from the late 1950s to the early 1970s, through falling coal demand and technological innovation. These trends, coupled with the new unity between areas created by industry-wide bargaining, led the National Union of Mineworkers to adopt a policy of pursuing aggressive wage demands and opposing further colliery closures. The 1972 miners' strike defeated the Government's pay policy, while the 1974 strike was perhaps the most dramatic example of public sector discontent, in that it contributed to the fall of the Heath Government. To avoid a continuation of the conflicts of the 1970s, the National Coal Board introduced Area Incentive Schemes in 1978, which fragmented bargaining once more, thereby making a national strike in support of a pay claim unlikely, and re-establishing divisions which were to prove critical in the 1984–85 strike against pit closures.

Restructuring and deconstruction in the 1980s

There is much debate over the experience of industrial relations during the 1980s, and the absence of consensus reflects the complex and contradictory nature of the decade's developments. Without doubt, the 1980s marked a fundamental departure from many of the traditions of British industrial relations. In particular, successive governments promoted a laissez-faire economic context in which the unions were seen as hindering the operation of free market forces (and restricting the freedom of individuals). Free market economic policies were supported by legislation designed to weaken the trade unions by providing remedies for employers and restricting the powers of union officials (see Chapter 12).

In this new context of industrial relations, some observers pointed to the development of more aggressive 'macho' management strategies, where unions were resisted and employees 'weaned off' trade unionism through HRM techniques designed to individualize employee relations.[18] It was predicted that employers would increasingly adopt "flexible firm" strategies, employing a core of permanent staff thoroughly integrated into the company, and a larger peripheral labour force comprising part-time and temporary workers with few employment rights.[19] Certainly, significant changes in management strategies in industrial relations are discernible, particularly in the public sector where there are several examples of the post-war structures of industrial relations being systematically dismantled, often after a bitter conflict.[20] In the private sector, however, most authorities believed that 'workplace organization and collective bargaining have remained largely intact as employers on the whole have not embarked on an anti-union rampage'.[21] Edwards similarly suggested that in large firms at least, managements 'have not been engaged in any systematic attack on unions'.[22] Pollert described the 'flexible firm' as a policy in search of practice, more evident as managerial fantasy than practical strategy.[23]

It is, perhaps, surprising that so many features of British labour relations survived the legal assault on the unions and the generally unfavourable economic climate which they faced throughout the 1980s. Perhaps this is further evidence of the pragmatism of British management and the absence of a strategic approach to human resources. In seeking to emphasise this continuity in British industrial relations, however, several authors have presented a *plus ça change* analysis which understates the extent of change. For example, after the defeat of the miners' year-long strike,

Richardson and Wood found 'no signs of a sustained frontal assault on the formal institutions of union representation and collective bargaining at the workplace level' in the coal mining industry.[24] Yet from the 1984–85 strike to privatization, the management of British Coal did not negotiate a single pay increase with the NUM, branch officials and union activists were disciplined and pit managers circumvented the local union.[25] Moreover, the coal industry provides an example of management pursuing various forms of flexibility as part of a coherent production strategy.[26]

For the trade unions, the 1980s presented their greatest challenges since the Second World War. The 1984 Workplace Survey found that fewer establishments with recognised manual trade unions had shop stewards present in 1984 than in 1980, the proportion having fallen from 70% to 65%.[27] This was a result of the changing size distribution of workplaces with recognized unions for manual employees. Only workplaces with small manual workforces showed a marginal decline in the presence of stewards. In other words, shop steward organisation held up in the bigger plants, but these plants declined as a proportion of the total. In contrast, more establishments with recognized non-manual unions had workplace representatives in 1984 than in 1980, the proportion having increased from 63% to 67% as a result of the general strengthening of white-collar trade unionism.

A postal survey of personnel managers in large manufacturing plants found that there had been a decline in the number of shop stewards in that sector between 1978 and 1983.[28] This was reinforced by the 1984 Workplace Survey which found a substantial decline in the number of manual shop stewards from 95,000 in 1980 to 72,000 in 1984 in private manufacturing. Nevertheless, if non-manual representatives are included, there was an increase from 317,000 to 335,000 over that period. The decline in shop steward numbers in manufacturing of 27% was offset by an increase of 18% in private services and a substantial rise of 31% in the public sector, which was concentrated in the white-collar grades.

Kelly noted that the loss of union membership between 1979 and 1982 was considerably less than in previous comparable recessions,[29] but there was a substantial decline in membership between 1980 and 1984. The number of representatives declined less than proportionately with membership, so that the average constituency of manual shop stewards fell from 26 full-time workers in 1980 to 23, including both full-time and part-time workers, in 1984. Between 1980 and 1984, most of the lay trade union representatives working full-time on union business at their place of work represented manual workers, but the proportion of manual convenors fell from 80% in 1980 to 66% in 1984.

Notwithstanding these developments, by the mid 1980s for the most part it was 'business as usual' so far as shop-floor trade unionism was concerned, particularly in major manufacturing plants.[30] The weak spots of trade unionism (small establishments, service industries) remained, but the strongholds of trade unionism had proved remarkably resistant to the assault. Even where the institutions remained in place, it was suggested that unions were abandoning militancy and adopting integrative bargaining methods in which shared interests with employers were emphasised.[31] This collaborative, accommodative approach, dubbed 'new realism', was presented as a modernizing tendency within the TUC, and contrasted with the 'dinosaurs' of the trade union movement, who continued to stress irreconcilable class antagonisms. The leaders of the electricians' union were the most notable 'new realists', and the union was expelled from the TUC for contravening rules on inter-union relations. The leaders of the engineering union, which subsequently merged with the electricians to form the Amalgamated Electrical and Engineering Union, were equally reformist but avoided breaching TUC rules. The General, Municipal and Boilermakers' Union leadership was more circumspect, but also adopted a more cooperative stance and took advantage of managements' willingness to promote moderate institutions and secure single-union and no-strike agreements.[32] While the new realists represented a minority of the TUC General Council, their policies affected the leaders of other unions, such as the Transport and General Workers' Union, who also signed single union deals.

Workplace industrial relations surveys during the 1980s demonstrated considerable continuity in collective bargaining. MacInnes argued that the emphasis on decentralized bargaining as a labour market strategy during the Thatcher era was not reflected in changes in bargaining levels: 'there was a slight shift toward company rather than plant bargaining in private manufacturing'.[33] Between 1980 and 1983, few employers reduced bargaining activity; in half of the plants surveyed by Batstone, respondents stated that there had been no change in the range or amount of bargaining, while in 25% bargaining was reported to have increased and in 20% to have diminished.[34] In almost three-quarters of establishments, shop stewards were reported to be negotiating over redundancy and discipline issues in 1983. The proportion of establishments reporting *negotiation* with shop stewards over labour mobility and manning levels in 1983 conforms closely with the responses from engineering plants in relation to *unilateral shop steward control* in the late 1960s. While the degree of shop steward influence had declined, the same issues were on the workplace agenda.

Moreover, signs of a steady erosion of collective bargaining increased through the 1980s. In 1980 JSSCs for manual workers were found in 41% of multi-union establishments and for white-collar workers in 24%. By 1984, the corresponding proportions had declined to 32% for manual workers and 20% for non-manuals. In 1980 JSSCs were much more common in workplaces where all the manual (or non-manual) unions negotiated with management as a single group than in those where they negotiated separately or in several groups. In 1984 the reverse was the case for manual JSSCs, and non-manual JSSCs were as common in workplaces with either type of negotiating arrangement.

The reassertion of managerial prerogative in the 1980s was facilitated by labour market changes and reflected a departure from the pluralist structures and bargaining norms associated with the Donovan era. Brown used data from the Workplace Industrial Relations Survey to demonstrate a significant contraction in the coverage of collective agreements, a narrowing in the scope of bargaining and a decline in the depth of union involvement.[35] The coverage of collective agreements throughout the economy (private and public sector) appears to have fallen from 72% of all employees in 1973 to 64% in 1984 and 47% in 1990 (although the bases of these estimates are not strictly comparable). The structure of bargaining has also altered. Brown characterizes the 1970s as a two-tier pay fixing system with multi-employer agreements (industry-wide) being explicitly supplemented by single-employer (company and plant) additions. Surveys showed that of those whose terms and conditions were established by collective bargaining, about 75% of workers in manufacturing were covered by single-employer agreements and 25% depended *only* upon multi-employer agreements. Since then, two-tier bargaining has declined: in 1984, of those private sector employees covered by collective bargaining arrangements (about 60% of the total), 67% were under single-employer agreements, while multi-employer agreements covered 33%. By 1990 of all multi-establishment firms engaging in single-employer bargaining, corporate bargaining accounted for 66% of manual and 80% of non manual cases in manufacturing and 90% of all in private services. Bargaining has become less fragmented and there has been a shift towards national single-employer (corporate) bargaining, rather than national multi-employer (industry-wide) bargaining.

Throughout the 1980s, the major conflicts in British industrial relations were in the public sector, where a dramatic reduction in employment was accompanied in some cases by a deconstruction of the institutions of collective bargaining.[36] The extent to which novel industrial relations strategies were pursued varied considerably between different public and recently-privatized enterprises. In those enterprises remaining in public ownership, there was less evidence that management actions were guided by a radically new industrial relations strategy. In the recently-privatized utilities water and electricity, there were major structural reforms of collective bargaining institutions, but for much of the decade management's approach to industrial relations was broadly unchanged. Privatization *per se* was relatively insignificant in accounting for the changes experienced by public enterprises, compared with the effects of organizational restructuring.

Some public enterprises changed almost beyond recognition in terms of their size and patterns of union representation, others experienced changes in bargaining structures, and in some there was been considerable institutional continuity but at the same time major changes to working practices during the decade. Some parts of the public sector underwent major changes to their structures, their technology and their working practices without conflict, but in others, conflict was the primary means of securing such changes. Whereas the public sector confrontations of the 1970s were concerned primarily with wages, most of the conflicts of the 1980s were caused by public sector borrowing limits, operational restructuring and preparations for privatization. Although the 1980 steel strike was ostensibly about wages, it formed the prelude to massive restructuring. Similarly, the water workers' pay strike involved wider issues related to privatization. The 1984–85 miners' strike was, of course, the most dramatic example of a conflict over restructuring, after which the institutions of collective bargaining established when the industry was nationalized in 1947, were thoroughly dismantled before the industry was privatized.[37]

Options for labour relations in the 1990s

Successive attempts to reform British industrial relations, in the 1960s, 1970s and 1980s, were not without effect, and for most of the economy, irrespective of whether the institutions of collective bargaining are unaffected, traditional industrial relations, involving zero-sum bargaining and frequent conflict, has been replaced and is unlikely to reappear. At this turning point, managers are able to make strategic choices about what is to replace the old industrial relations, and three broad alternatives can be contrasted:

- macho management: in most cases a reassertion of managerial prerogative with managers regaining control at the point of production and with a reduced scope of bargaining and reduced union influence, but in the extreme involving systematic union busting. This approach is expensive, and not necessarily effective; in the long run it may prove untenable. Employers who have adopted such an approach have often been underwritten by the state (e.g. coal, steel, docks) or by an employers' association (e.g. newspapers).

- modern paternalism: involving the workforce within clearly prescribed limits, enabling the employee to participate on management's terms, often through quality circles or TQM initiatives. This approach entails an assumption of an absolute identity of interest between the employee and the enterprise; sometimes termed 'empowerment', but does not involve any power sharing.
- employee-centred approach: in which the workforce is seen as a resource to be developed, not a cost to be minimized. The approach involves a variant of HRM, in so far as it is concerned with cost-effectiveness and integrating HR issues with corporate strategy. The key elements of such an approach are enskilling and empowerment: designing jobs to promote skill and autonomy, and developing a high-trust relationship with the workforce through whatever representative institutions exist.[38]

Since the growth of HRM has been accompanied by a resurgence of unitary values, some observers have concluded that HRM is incompatible with pluralist industrial relations, and have suggested that 'management is not practising effective HRM … [where] the door is left open for the unions to play a role'.[39] The adherence to unitary values explains why HRM has been prevalent in greenfield sites and enterprises having 'union-free' or anti-union traditions. The fact that in many cases HRM conforms with the unitary, anti-union managerial stereotype may be attributed to the current economic and political context because other anti-union activities can be cited which are unrelated to any adoption of HRM techniques (in public enterprises especially).

If HRM is inevitably and fundamentally unitary and individualist, however, then managements which adopt HRM practices run the risk of creating a pattern of workplace relations which is inherently conflictual. A paternalist pattern can be maintained only until workers become organized and oppose management, as a result of the differences which inevitably arise in the employment relationship. Managers adhering to unitary values deny the existence of such everyday disputes, and remain ill-prepared for the challenge of organised workers. Pluralist values were in the ascendant for most of the 1970s, and were displaced in some quarters by unitary values in the 1980s as unemployment rose and union power waned. Changes in government reinforced the process but were more symptom than cause; pluralism thrived under Heath's 1974–9 Conservative Government, which failed in its attempt to introduce much more modest legal regulation of industrial relations than was introduced in the Thatcher era.

The third way of an employee-centred approach entails welding together the most effective elements of the pluralist, collectivist traditions of industrial relations with those elements of HRM which entail developing and empowering individuals. Unitary values are symptomatic of trade unions weakened by an economy in recession, and to the extent that recovery restores union influence, there should also be a return to pluralist values. Since HRM does not inevitably entail unitary values, a sophisticated HRM strategy will establish a high-trust relationship with employees while the balance of power is in management's favour, by building upon the institutions of collective bargaining rather than seeking to circumvent them.

Conclusion

- The emergence of HRM, while integrating human resource issues more effectively with wider corporate strategy, has led to a neglect of collective aspects of employee relations.
- An understanding of the institutions of industrial relations is necessary for effective HRM where employees belong to representative organisations.

- Informal decentralized bargaining during the 1960s prompted reform of the industrial relations system.
- Formalization continued into the 1970s, alongside corporate strategies to restrict the scope of bargaining.
- Public sector discontent, mostly over pay in the 1970s and restructuring in the 1980s, has been a major source of instability in industrial relations.
- Trade union membership and influence declined during the 1980s, but much of the infrastructure of workplace industrial relations survived.
- Management have the opportunity now to develop an employee-centred approach to HRM, through enskilling and empowerment, to develop a high-trust relationship with the workforce and their workplace representatives.

References

1. See T. Keenoy, *Invitation to Industrial Relations,* Oxford: Blackwell, 1985; and P. Blyton and P. Turnbull, *The Dynamics of Industrial Relations,* London: Macmillan, 1994, chapter 2, for an introduction to industrial relations theory.

2. R. Hyman, *The Political Economy of Industrial Relations: Theory and Practice in a Cold Climate,* London: Macmillan, 1992.

3. Lord Donovan (ch) Royal Commission on Trade Unions and Employers' Associations 1965–68, *Report,* Cmnd.3623, London: HMSO.

4. H.A. Clegg, *The Changing System of Industrial Relations in Great Britain,* Oxford: Blackwell, 1979.

5. S. Parker, *Workplace Industrial Relations,* Report SS402, Government Social Survey, London: HMSO, 1968; W.E.J. McCarthy and S. Parker *Shop Stewards and Workplace Relations,* Donovan Research Paper 10, London: HMSO, 1968.

6. W.E.J. McCarthy, *The Role of Shop Stewards in British Industrial Relations,* Donovan Research Paper 1, London: HMSO, 1966.

7. H.A. Turner, G. Clack, and G. Roberts, *Labour Relations in the Motor Industry,* London: Allen & Unwin, 1967.

8. A.I. Marsh, E.O. Evans and P. Garcia, *Workplace Industrial Relations in Engineering,* London: Engineering Employers' Federation, 1971.

9. W. Brown (ed) (1981) *The Changing Contours of British Industrial Relations,* Oxford: Blackwell, 1981.

10. W. Brown, R. Ebsworth and M. Terry, 'Factors shaping shop steward organisation in Britain', *British Journal of Industrial Relations,* Vol.16, no.2, 1978, 139–59.

11. E. Batstone, I. Boraston and S. Frenkel, *Shop Stewards in Action,* Oxford: Blackwell, 1977.

12. J. Purcell and K. Sisson, 'Strategies and Practice in the Management of Industrial Relations', in G. Bain (ed) *Industrial Relations in Britain,* Oxford: Blackwell, 1983, 95–120.

13. R. Hyman, 'The politics of workplace trade unionism', *Capital and Class,* No.8, 1979.

14. S. Dunn, 'From Donovan to … Wherever', *British Journal of Industrial Relations,* Vol.31, no.2, 1993, 169–87.

15. D. Winchester, 'Industrial Relations in the Public Sector', in G. Bain (ed), *Industrial Relations in Britain*, Oxford: Blackwell, 1983, 155–78.

16. I. Boraston, H.A. Clegg and A. Rimmer, *Workplace and Union,* London: Heinemann, 1975.

17. J. Winterton, 'The trend of strikes in British coal mining 1949–1979', *Industrial Relations Journal,* Vol.12, no.6, 1981, 10–19.

18. L. MacKay, 'The macho manager: it's no myth', *Personnel Management,* January 1986.

19. J. Atkinson, 'Manpower strategies for flexible organisation', *Personnel Management,* August 1984.

20. J. Winterton and R. Winterton, *Coal, Crisis and Conflict: The 1984–85 Miners' Strike in Yorkshire,* Manchester: Manchester University Press, 1989.

21. J. Kelly, 'Trade unions through the recession 1980–1984', *British Journal of Industrial Relations,* Vol.25, no.2, 1986.

22. P. Edwards, 'Managing labour relations through the recession', University of Warwick, Industrial Relations Research Unit. 1985 [mimeo].

23. A. Pollert, 'The "flexible firm": fixation or fact?', *Work, Employment and Society,* Vol.2, no.3, 1988, 281–316.

24. R. Richardson and S. Wood, 'Productivity change in the coal industry and the new industrial relations', *British Journal of Industrial Relations,* Vol.27, no.1, 1989, 33–55.

25. J. Winterton and R. Winterton, 'Coal', in A. Pendleton and J. Winterton (eds) *Public Enterprise in Transition: Industrial Relations in State and Privatized Corporations,* London: Routledge, 1993, 69–99.

26. J. Winterton, 'Flexibility, new technology and British Coal', in P. Blyton and J. Morris (eds) *A Flexible Future?*, Berlin: de Gruyter, 1991, 275–94.

27. N. Millward and M. Stevens, *British Workplace Industrial Relations 1980–84,* Aldershot: Gower, 1986.

28. E. Batstone, *Working Order: Workplace Industrial Relations over two decades,* Oxford: Blackwell, 1984.

29. Kelly, *op cit.*

30. Millward and Stevens, *op cit.*

31. J. McIlroy, *Trade Unions in Britain Today,* Manchester: Manchester University Press,1988.

32. P. Bassett, *Strike Free: New Industrial Relations in Britain,* London: Macmillan, 1987.

33. J. MacInnes, *Thatcherism at Work: Industrial Relations and Economic Change,* Open University, 1987.

34. Batstone, *op cit.*

35. W. Brown, 'The contraction of collective bargaining in Britain', *British Journal of Industrial Relations,* Vol.31, no.2, 1993, 189–200.

36. A. Pendleton and J. Winterton (eds), *Public Enterprise in Transition: Industrial Relations in State and Privatized Corporations,* London: Routledge, 1993.

37. J. Winterton and R. Winterton, 1993, *op cit.*

38. C. Molander and J. Winterton, *Managing Human Resources,* London: Routledge, 1994.

39. D.E. Guest, 'Human resource management: its implications for Industrial Relations and Trade Unions', in J.Storey (ed) *New Perspectives on Human Resource Management,* London: Routledge, 1989, 41–55.

Guide to further reading

The most up-to-date analysis available is P. Edwards's *Industrial Relations*, Oxford: Blackwell, 1995, which is a successor to the collection edited by Bain and referred to in this chapter. In addition, the following texts offer a comprehensive introduction to the area:

M.P. Jackson, *An Introduction to Industrial Relations,* London: Routledge, 1991.

P. Blyton and P. Turnbull, *The Dynamics of Employee Relations,* London: Macmillan, 1994.

Typical examination questions

1. What lessons can be drawn for the 1990s from the attempts to reform industrial relations in the 1960s and 1970s?

2. How have recent trends of labour relations in the public sector differed from those of private manufacturing industries?

3. Given that workplace trade union organization survived the 1980s in a weakened form, what effect would sustained economic recovery have upon workplace employee relations?

Case Study

The food processing plant operated throughout the year with a skeleton workforce of about 50 'regulars'. For the 'campaign' during the summer months, when the majority of produce was available from farms in the area, a further 350 'casuals' were employed, for periods ranging from 12 weeks to a fortnight. The factory operated two 12-hour shifts over 5 days, with maintenance and cleaning work at the weekend. The regulars were union members and received additional pay during the campaign for supervising the casual workers. There was considerable resentment among the casuals that the rate of pay for very arduous work in unpleasant conditions was considerably less than that of the regulars.

The retorts, where the canned produce is pasteurized, had become a bottleneck of production because they had not been expanded in proportion with the increases in the speed of the filling lines feeding them. Casual workers were carefully selected for working in the retort area and the operatives required more training than for any other job. When the pace of work had reached its peak for the season, casual workers on the night shift who were operating the retorts threatened strike action on behalf of all the casuals for parity of pay with the regulars. They were not union members and the union condemned their action. The company threatened dismissal unless they agreed to work normally, and the other casual workers, who had earlier voiced support during the break in the canteen, continued to work normally. The would-be strikers reluctantly agreed to work normally without having their demands considered.

As the season came to a close, the retort 'militants' anticipated being the first to be laid off, but several were kept on to the end of the season as it would have been costly to train others for the few weeks that were left. Nevertheless, those involved in the threatened action were never re-employed by the company in subsequent years, and the management believed the problem had been resolved.

Over the remainder of that season and in the following years, the incidence of spoiled produce increased. A proportion of the cans which were rejected from the line as being under-weight were found to contain foreign matter, such as a newspaper or a pepper pot from the canteen. The perpetrators were usually identified, and summarily dismissed, but the problems continued to reappear. More worrying was the number of cases involving sabotage in the retort ring, where produce was found to be spoiled from 'over-cooking'.

1. Were the collective discontents of the casuals ever adequately resolved, or was their expression simply suppressed?
2. Why did the existing trade union representation fail to represent the interests of the casuals and how might appropriate institutions and arrangements for consultation and negotiation have been established?
3. Would it have been more or less damaging for the company to have had conflict expressed overtly at the collective level, or covertly at the individual level?

Chapter 14

Designing Organizations

Andrew Pendleton

Objectives

- to identify the reasons for organization re-design
- to identify the main dimensions of organization structure
- to consider the problems ('dysfunctions') that the main dimension of organization structure often give rise to
- to outline the main forms of company organization
- to provide a check-list for those embarking on organization re-design

Introduction

The design of an organization is its configuration of tasks and the relationships between organization members and units performing them. Organization design has become a pressing issues for organizations throughout the industrialised world because of the need to improve efficiency, cut costs and improve product quality. In some cases total overhaul of organization structure has been undertaken. More commonly, the distribution of tasks and functions between parts of the organization has been modified whilst other parts of the organization have been left unchanged. Even so, organization re-design is now coming to be seen as a persistent feature of organizational life, and many fear that long-term careers within organizations will not longer be possible.

Much of the impetus for organization re-design has come from the perceived imperative to cut costs. In the private sector this is often attributed to the growth in global competition since the 1970s. Many newly industrialising countries are now able to under-cut producers in the developed world. In the public sector, pressures to contain the growth in public expenditure have meant that pressures for cost-cutting have been just as strong. In these circumstances, organization design is about rationalising structure, so that the current workload can be achieved with fewer employees. For those seeking to make these economies, a fortuitious development since the 1970s has been the rapid pace of change in information technology. Electronic data processing and communications have meant that much of the traditional information processing role conducted by middle managers and employees can be dispensed with, and it is now possible for top managers to monitor directly the performance of units at the bottom of the organization.

A further motive for organization design has been concern to improve the quality of decision-making by employees, and hence to improve organizational performance. This is reflected, for instance, in the long-standing trend for large multi-plant organizations to re-organise themselves into the divisional or M-form structure. Head office becomes responsible for strategic planning and capital allocation within the firm, whilst operating units concentrate on producing and selling particular products or services. The theory behind this development is akin to that of 'comparative advantage' in economics: by concentrating on the function for which they are most suited, each part of the organization will be able to improve the quality of decision-making. At a wider level, all types of organization have perceived a need for decentralisation of decision-making in recent years. It is argued that decentralisation takes organizations 'closer to the customer' and hence makes the organization more responsive to market forces or other consumer pressures. Furthermore, giving more scope for decision-making to those in the lower reaches of the organization seems likely to improve motivation and commitment (see Chapter 6).

In recent years a concern to improve product and service quality has added to the pressures for organizational re-design. Those subscribing to the fad of the late 1980s – Total Quality Management (TQM) – suggested that quality could be improved by setting up quasi-market relationships within the organization so that departments 'purchase' goods and services from each other. By introducing these producer-customer relationships, 'market power' can be exerted to force product improvements. This approach has dominated recent structural changes in the UK public sector, though not necessarily with any explicit references to TQM. Separation of service specification from actual provision has been at the core of reforms in the UK National Health Service. Health-care providers (e.g. hospitals) have been separated from those responsible for purchasing health care provision on behalf of the population (health authorities). A similar principle underlies the introduction of competitive tendering in local government and the creation of 'executive agencies' in the civil service. The most recent innovation, however, is that of Business Process Re-Engineering (BPR)1. This approach dicates that the traditional features of organization structure – vertical hierarchy and departmental specialisation – should be replaced by multi-function process teams comprising all those involved – finance managers, administrators, human resource managers, production managers, technicians etc. – in producing a particular product or part of a product. Aligning organization structure with product processes in this way, it is argued, will lead to higher quality products and better quality decision-making.

For the most part, attempts to re-design organizations are aimed at changing the behaviour of those who comprise the organization. Those initiating reorganizations generally make what can only be described as heroic assumptions about the impact of structural innovations on employee behaviour. Whilst it is undoubtedly true that structure and context have a profound influence on human behaviour, formal reporting relationships and allocation of job tasks (as exemplified by the organization chart) are only one influence on what employees actually do. Organizations are such complex entities that formal structure can only provide an imperfect guide to how things should be done: employees frequently have to 'work round' the correct procedures to get the job done. In addition, groups of employees develop group norms and patterns of interaction which are distinct and possibly even opposed to organization objectives and procedures.[2] Furthermore, employees bring to their work expectations and perspectives derived from outside the firm and these inevitably permeate their attitudes to their tasks and the organization.[3] Organization re-design, therefore, can only have a partial impact on employee behaviour. Indeed the prevailing 'social system' is likely to have a powerful impact on how the reorganization works in practice, possibly leading to outcomes unanticipated by organization designers. It is imperative, therefore, that those initiating organization re-design have an adequate understanding of the social system of the organization as well as long-standing principles of organization structure and design.

In this chapter we outline the main dimensions of organization design and highlight how the objectives of those creating organization structures can be subverted by the wider social system of the organization. We then provide a series of steps that those embarking on organization re-design should follow to increase the chance that the re-design will be successful.

The Dimensions of Organization Structure

Organizations are complex configurations of people and tasks organised in a way which seems conducive to the achievement of organizations goals. In essence, the tasks of the organization are broken down so that they can be performed by individuals and groups. The design of individual jobs is known as job design, and the principles that should govern job composition are discussed in Chapter 15. Once tasks have been broken down and allocated in this way it is then necessary to coordinate and control them and the job activities of each organizational member. In most cases the breakdown of tasks involves some measure of functional specialisation whilst the requirement for coordination and control is believed to require hierarchy and organizational rules.

Any consideration of organization structure inevitably needs to refer to the work of German sociologist Max Weber (1864–1920) who provided the first systematic analysis of the characteristics and foundations of modern organizations.[4] He suggested that the modern bureaucracy rested on the emergence of rational-legal authority. In modern societies action is justified by its intended consequences, rather than its intrinsic religious or moral worth. The main feature of this type of authority is that systematic laws and rule are created, based on the principle of rationality, to govern the behaviour of individuals and groups in a routinized manner. Thus it is unnecessary for an individual leader to exert authority on every occasion that action is required from a subordinate. Instead, the rules guide individual behaviour for most of the time. In fact it is difficult to imagine the the myriad tasks of an organization being carried out on any other basis.

Weber drew attention to a number of characteristics of modern organizations – encapsulated in the notion of an 'ideal type' of bureaucracy – which he believed differentiated them from earlier forms of organization. These included hierarchical distribution of authority, functional specialisation of task roles, coordination and control by rules, and appointment and promotion of organization members on the basis of merit rather than patronage. In practice, it is possible to identify elements of modern organizations where practice is other than that proposed by Weber, i.e. the recent tendency in the UK for senior appointments to QUANGOs to be made on the basis of political patronage rather than merit. In general, however, the modern organization more or less incorporates the principles identified by Weber, though they do not always lead to the efficiency advantages he claimed for them.

In terms of structure there are three key elements of Weber's model: the degree of centralisation, the extent of specialisation and the extent to which coordination is achieved by formal rules and standardized procedures. We now discuss each in turn

i) Centralization

Virtually all modern organizations, other than the very smallest, have some form of hierarchy composed of two or more levels of authority, with those in upper levels having authority over those in lower levels. A central issue for those designing organizations is how many levels there should be and the distribution of decision-making authority between them. In practice there tends to be a partial association between the two: where there are several levels there is a tendency for decision-making to be centralised. In these circumstances decentralised decision-making would probably leave a limited role for some higher levels of the hierarchy and pressures could develop for 'de-layering' in response. Where there are only a very small numbers of tiers in the hierarchy there will have to be some decentralisation of decision-making if the top levels are not to become overloaded.

Underlying these considerations is the notion of the 'span of control': the number of people that can be overseen by a superordinate. Classical management theory, developed by Fayol and Urwick, suggested that between three and six subordinates per supervisor was most effective.[5] However, search for an ideal ratio is now widely accepted as a misguided exercise. In practice, the most effective span of control will be strongly influenced by the distribution of decision-making between employee and supervisor.

Where decision-making is relatively decentralised, the span of control can probably be wider than where it is relatively centralised. Social relationships within the organization will also be an influence. Where employee-management relationships are conflictual and 'low trust' in character, there may need to be more supervisors than where relationships are consensual and 'high trust'.

As might be expected, however, the size of the organization has a very powerful influence on the number of tiers in the hierarchy (all other things being equal).[6] Larger organizations tend to have more hierarchy. However, in recent years many managers have criticised multi-layered hierarchies on the grounds that they tend to encourage centralised decision-making. This leaves little decision-making scope for managers at the 'sharp end' of production and service provision. This is thought to be demotivating, to 'insulate' these organizations from external (i.e. market) pressures, and to make decision-making a slow and protracted affair (because ground level managers will need to refer upwards for instructions). In short the capacity for organizations to innovate is stifled. Furthermore, it is argued that the function of middle-levels of these hierarchies is often little more than a 'mail-sorting' operations – they process information from the bottom of the organization for transmission to the top, and relay orders from the top to the bottom. Recent developments in information technology have now made much of this function redundant. For this reason 'de-layering' and decentralisation have been widespread developments in organization design in recent years.

However, reductions in hierarchy do not necessarily lead to greater decentralisation. This is because centralisation/decentralisation is neither a simple one-dimensional phenomenon, nor a once-and-for-all event. Whilst ground level managers may acquire greater authority to make decisions in a decentralisation initiative, at the same time they may become more accountable to higher level managers i.e. the monitoring procedures may be made more effective, and the sanctions for inappropriate decisions increased. It is also common, especially in single product/service organizations, for formal decentralisation to be followed by attempts by higher level managers to retain control (using their power over finances and promotions for example) to ensure that ground level managers do not take initiatives which have harmful repercussions for other parts of the organization or other products. Many ground level managers soon discover that decentralisation is more apparent than real. Attempts at organization re-design of this type, therefore, seem as likely to lead to new tensions between organization levels as much as a decisive shift in the balance of organizational power.

ii) Specialization

The horizontal dimension of structure is the extent to which tasks and functions are specialized. A key feature of industrialization has been a division of labour in which it is generally believed to be more efficient and effective for individuals to specialize in certain tasks or components of tasks, rather than making a product or service in its entirety. This principle is a central organising principle of most organizations. Chapter 15 deals with the principles that govern individual job design. Here we will be concerned with the tendency to group individuals doing similar or related tasks into larger groups or departments. In all but the smallest organizations, there are typically a number of departments carrying out the main functional tasks of the organization as perceived by organization designers. The strength of departmental boundaries varies quite widely between organizations. In some cases functional departments are almost like 'mini-organizations' in their own right: they possess their own hierarchy, with career progression occurring solely within the department, and members of the department are not subject to the authority of more senior members of the organization located within other departments. In others, departmental boundaries are much looser. At a given level functional specialists work most closely and report directly to the general manager for that level rather than the functional manager at the next level of the hierarchy. They may, however, be responsible to the higher functional manager on certain issues. In these circumstances it is common for there to be conflicts of loyalty. Functional managers may give more weight to decisions emanating from their functional superior than their formal boss.

There are both advantages and disadvantages associated with strong functional specialization. On the positive side, it facilitates the development of strong specialist expertise, by allowing employees to devote all or most of their working time to the specialism, and by providing a career structure based on accumulation of specialist knowledge, expertise and experience. This can be deeply motivating for the staff involved. On the negative side, specialist functional departments tend to pursue their own specialist interests rather than those of the organization as a whole, as was found by Selznick in his study of the Tenessee Valley River Authority in the USA in the 1940s.[7] A similar development occurs when an especially indispensable functional department manages to imprint its own goals on the wider organization. Organizations with a strong technical infrastructure, such as railways and telecommunications, tend to be dominated by technical departments to the extent that commercial objectives are coloured by technical considerations. These organizations are often said to be 'engineering led'.[8]

A further problem with strong departmental specialisation is that lateral communication and cooperation between deparments tends to be inhibited. Coordination of departmental activities has to take place at the top of the organization. There is therefore an association between centralization of decision -making and departmental specialization. In recent years many organizations have attempted to weaken the power of functional groupings. In the UK health service, for instance, the management cadre that has emerged during the recent health service reforms has attempted to weaken the power of specialist professional groups such as doctors, and to encourage patterns of resource allocation which are dictated by a broad range of organizational priorities, rather than immediate perceived medical need. Human resource managers have also been victims of this trend as organizations have attempted to pass some aspects of human resource management to line managers at the 'sharp end' away from 'ivory tower' professionals.

iii) Control and Coordination

A persistent issue for those designing and running organizations is how the work of employees and organization sub-units are controlled and coordinated so that organizational goals are achieved. In part this is a technical problem of synchronisation, since large organizations are complex entities. But there is also a deeper problem that employees' interests may not be congruent with those of the organization, and they may therefore wish to behave in different ways to those prescribed by organizational leaders. Furthermore, as the previous section illustrated, some features of the organization itself – such as departmental specialization – can generate and reinforce a divergence of interests. Finally, those analysing modern organizations from a Marxian perspective, argue that there is a fundamental divergence of interests at the societal level, between those who comprise the foot-soldiers of organizations and those who own them or run them on the owners' behalf. They have suggested that the fundamental objective of employers in capitalist society is to gain control of the workforce. In the academic literature there have been a number of attempts to identify management strategies to secure control of workforces, such as Braverman's work on de-skilling, Edwards classification of 'simple', 'technical' and 'bureaucratic' control, and Friedman's distinction between 'direct control' and 'responsible autonomy'.[9] Valuable though these discussions have been, it has been argued that they are limited by their implicit focus on production workers, and by their assumption that there are over-riding management strategies with these aims. Many of the techniques of organizational control are more mundane and ad hoc in character, though taken together they can be grouped into a number of basic approaches.

We believe that in contemporary organizations four approaches to control and coordination can be discerned, and each is outlined here in turn.

a) personal instruction

In this approach, senior members of an organization take a personal, directive role, issuing instructions to their subordinates as circumstances demand (cf. Edwards' notion of 'direct control'). This approach is found in virtually all organizations since there are limits to the extent that action can be guided by formal rules and procedures. On occasion, difficult choices have to be made between the application of two or more procedures. However, personal instruction tends to be the main form of coordination and control in small organizations in an early stage of development. Typically, the owner-manager takes a 'hands-on' approach to all aspects of running the organization. However, once organizations of this sort grow in size, this individual tends to become 'overloaded' with supervisory tasks, often at great frustration to themselves, and at the expense of effective communication with other members of the organization. Bad decisions can be made, and employee resentment at autocratic management may develop. At this stage of development, a new approach to coordination and control should be adopted – that of formalisation and standardisation of work procedures – since the job has come to be too big for one person. Unfortunately many owner-managers resist this logic because such a bureaucratisation of 'their' organization seems to run counter to the entrepreneurial creativity they experienced when the firm was born.

b) rules and procedures

This approach to control and coordination is characterized by specification, standardization and formaliszation, and is a key feature of modern organizations identified by Weber. Employee behaviour is to be governed by formal (usually written) rules, standardized to cover all similar situations. These rules can cover all aspects of the organization's activities (e.g. 'all visitors must report to reception', 'staff must not leave their work-station without their supervisor's permission', 'all cash deposits must be recorded individually' etc.) and are sometimes brought together in a company rule-book. More typically, they are recorded in a variety of different formats: the contract of employment, procedure manuals, memos, collective agreements between management and employee representatives etc. Using a phrase borrowed from industrial relations research, organizations can be viewed as a 'web of rules', and it is extremely difficult to envisage how modern complex organizations could function without formal rules and procedures.

However, research into organizations, as well as more popular critiques of bureaucracy and 'red-tape', has found that rules also have a number of negative effects ('dysfunctions'). In an early investigation, American sociologist Robert Merton identified what he called the 'bureaucratic personality' – emphasis on rules resulted in organization members paying more attention to following the rules than achieving organization goals.[10] In a similar vein, fellow sociologist Peter Blau identified the phenomenon of 'goal displacement': adherence to the rules leads employees to pursue intra-organizational objectives (ie. maintaining the rules) rather than the main objective of the organization.[11] A good recent example of this in the UK concerns the ill-fated Child Support Agency established in the 1990s to ensure that divorced and separated husbands made adequate maintenance payments to their former wives. Although the agency was apparently set-up to pursue those who made no contribution to their former families, the rule that Agency staff maximize maintenance settlements led staff to concentrate their efforts on those already making maintenance payments, because they were easier to identify and track-down. Many of these had previously made settlements which were viewed as fair and appropriate by both former wives and the courts. Meanwhile those making no such payments were frequently ignored by the Agency.

Other analysts have noted how rules can be turned against those formulating them. Chris Argyris has shown how rules stifle individual initiative and prevent individuals reaching true maturity (ie. defined as accepting full responsibility for their actions). By building immaturity into the system, organizations encourage immature behaviour by employees, shown at its most extreme by individuals taking pleasure in subverting the rules and goals of the organization.[12] In a similar vein, Alvin Gouldner and Michael Crozier have both pointed out that rules can illustrate to subordinates what is unnecessary as well as what needs to be done. They therefore function as a useful guide to what employees can get away with. Employees use these 'gaps' in the rules to pursue their own interests, such as minimizing work effort or advancing the power position of their particular group. A typical response by managers in these circumstances is to tighten-up the application of these rules or to generate additional rules, thereby intensifying the low-trust dynamic already in place.[13]

c) consent and commitment

These negative consequences of relying on rules to achieve control and coordination has led some commentators to argue that it is preferable to generate commitment to the organization instead. If employees are committed to organization goals and values, rules will be less necessary to control employee behaviour. In other words they will do what is required of them without being told. If anything, their work performance is likely to be better than in the traditional bureaucratic organization because freedom from rule-bound constraints is likely to lead to greater motivation and creativity. This approach is particularly associated with American consultants Peters and Waterman, and first popularized in their book *In Search of Excellence* in the early 1980s.[14] More recently Peters has taken the message much further, arguing for a state of anarchy within organizations. The free-rein given to individual creativity, it is suggested, will, overall, lead to improvements in collective performance, despite the difficulties of formal coordination and the tendency for mistakes to be made.[15]

Most would argue that this is taking things too far and that there is not much hard evidence to back up these ideas. However, there is plenty of evidence of good performance among organizations where employee consent is valued. In the USA there is a wealth of evidence that firms who seek to win employees consent by facilitating employee participation perform better financially than firms who do not.[16] In the UK there is some evidence, as yet unpublished, that university departments characterized by consent and collegiality produce better quality research output than those with more autocratic modes of decision-making. However, there is also a great deal of evidence to show that attempts to generate employee consent can conflict with more traditional forms of coordination and control. There is always the danger that employee ideas about new ways of doing things will be discarded by their superiors because they transgress existing rules and conventional forms of coordination and authority. In these circumstances employees quickly learn that consent and involvement is more apparent than real, and lose interest. This fate befalls many an employee involvement initiative, and accounts for the short-lived existence of many quality circles and similar innovations.

d) internal contract

This approach to control and coordination, which has become fashionable, especially in the UK public sector, attempts to push the discipline of the markets and contracts into the inner reaches of the organization. Instead of using rules to govern and coordinate inter-departmental relationships, contracts are struck between departments for the supply of goods and services. Real or notional payments can be made on receipt of these, whilst failure to deliver contracted services can result in withholding of payments or purchasing power being taken elsewhere. The rationale for this innovation is that traditional forms of control and coordination – based on rules and procedures – lead to sub-optimum outcomes at the organizational level because there are few incentives for individual employees or departments to maximize performance. Furthermore, an enormous amount of organizational time, which could be devoted to more productive activities, is spent on generating rules to overcome problems of coordination and control.

A good example of the use of internal contracts is found in the British Broadcasting Corporation which reorganized itself into a number of 'Directorates' in the early 1980s, with relationships between Directorates put on a contractual basis. For instance, a programme-maker now contracts with staff from the production directorate for the supply of technical services. The programme maker can minimize costs by threatening to use external firms instead if the in-house service is too expensive. It is argued that this system has cut costs within the BBC, has made the cost basis of programme making and delivery more transparent, and facilitated more effective and efficient allocation of resources. However, the new system also has its critics, who allege that an inordinate amount of organizational time is now spent on contract negotiations, and on devising rules to govern such negotiations. In effect, one bureaucratic system has been replaced with another. A particular casualty of the new approach, it is argued, is that creative staff are diverted from their proper function into administration. Overall, critics allege that the internal transaction costs outweigh any benefits of the new system of management. A similar claim is made in relation to the health service, where the introduction of an internal market has been associated with a steep rise in the number of managers and administrators at the expense of those more directly involved in patient care, such as doctors and nurses.

A further problem with internal markets is that they reinforce one of the traditional problems with departmental specialization: pursuit of departmental objectives rather than those of the organization as a whole. Indeed the very concept of an internal market sets departments against others in a competitive fashion. This can be damaging in those organizations which are dependent on cross-functional teamwork, and where information sharing across the organization is important for organizational success. At the extreme, a particular department could function in a way that seriously damages other departments, and hence the organization as a whole. To prevent this happening most organizations with an internal market have a regulatory system to keep competitive behaviour within certain parameters. However, it is arguable that this adds to the bureaucratization of relationships between departments whilst limiting the potential benefits of an internally competitive system. It also encourages centralization of decision-making, because the regulatory system will have to operate above the competing units, typically at the top of the organization.

Structural Types

The preceding analysis has explored the key structural dimensions of centralization and specialization, and outlined the main forms of coordination and control. A multitude of different configurations of these dimensions are possible. In each case organization structure will be determined by the interplay of environmental context, the organization's objectives and managers' perceptions of appropriate structural forms. In practice most organizations fall into a small number of categories. Burns and Stalker suggested that organizations tend to be either mechanistic (ie. with fairly procedures) or 'organismic' (ie. more flexible).[17] In most cases, however, structure is not the outcome of a single, high-level strategic decision. Instead, structure evolves in response to a multitude of more operationally-focused decisions concerning the division of work tasks between small numbers of employees. Furthermore, the actual working of the structure – how individuals work with each other – may differ in practice from formal definitions of structure contained within the organization chart.

Organization design is complex in most organizations. It becomes more complex still when an organization operates in a number of different markets or environments, and has to develop new structures to both coordinate the operation of the organization as a whole, whilst leaving sufficient flexibility for sub-units of the organization to tailor their operations to their specific context. The growth of giant multi-product firms and the development of transnational companies in the second half of the twentieth century has encouraged the emergence of a number of different types of company structure. Each form provides a different solution to the relationship between head office and constituent business units , and the distribution of decisions between them.

Three main types of structure can be discerned.

Functional (U-Form)

The functional or U-Form type of structure embodies the principles of centralisation and specialisation in a relatively simple way. Organizations of this type are structured on a hierarchical and departmental basis. The organization is divided into a number of key functional departments (production, marketing, human resources etc.) with reporting relationships being concentrated within departments.

The functioning of these departments is coordinated at the top of the organization. As a result decision-making tends to be centralised since, if lateral communication between departments is discouraged, initiatives likely to have implications for other departments will need to be referred upwards for resolution. In practice there is often some degree of lateral communication – indeed some contact is likely to be necessary for the organization to function at all on a day to day basis – but major decisions involving several departments will almost certainly always have to be taken in the higher reaches of the organization. It is often said therefore that these organizations tend to be inflexible and that initiative tends to be stifled. In other words the functional form of organization can be said to exhibit the characteristics of the 'mechanistic' organization mentioned earlier.

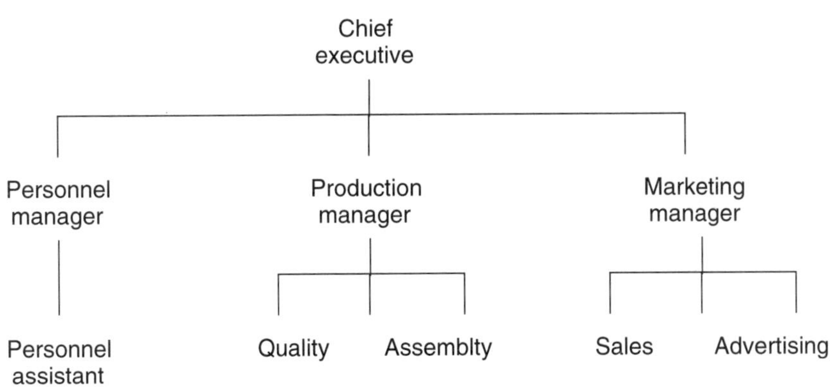

Figure 14.1. Functional structure.

This organizational form can be appropriate for single site operations but becomes problematic in multi-site operations, because the difficulties of co-ordinating departments are multiplied by the requirement of coordinating the geographical units. This problem does not appear to be insurmountable, however, in organizations where there is a single product or service, delivered by a single, dominant department. A stable environment is also helpful, since pressures for important strategic decisions at local level will be relatively weak. The functional form is now relatively rare in large multi-site manufacturing firms in the UK and the USA, but is widespread in manufacturing firms in Japan and Germany. It is more common in UK service organizations, where a common service is provided at all branches, and is also the main form of organization in government departments.

Multi-divisional (M-Form)

Most large British and American manufacturing companies are now organized along multi-divisional lines. In this model the operating units of the company are organized into separate divisions, overseen by a divisional general manager or chief executive, based on distinct products or localities. Overall coordination of the firm takes place at head office. In theory, head office is responsible for devising strategic direction – deciding which markets to operate in – and for allocating investment funds between the divisions. The divisions themselves are primarily production or service delivery units, whose pattern of operations can be tailored to particular markets or environments. The rationale for this structure is that it allows successful adaption to diversity – it enables firms to move into (or exit) markets with minimum disruption to other parts of the firm. It also facilitates strategic decision-making whilst enabling decentralized operating management. A recent development is for sub-units of divisions to be established in a way which mirrors the relationship between division and head office. Divisional general management determines overall strategy within certain markets, whilst the sub-units – often called profit-centres or strategic business units (SBUs) – focus on production and service delivery

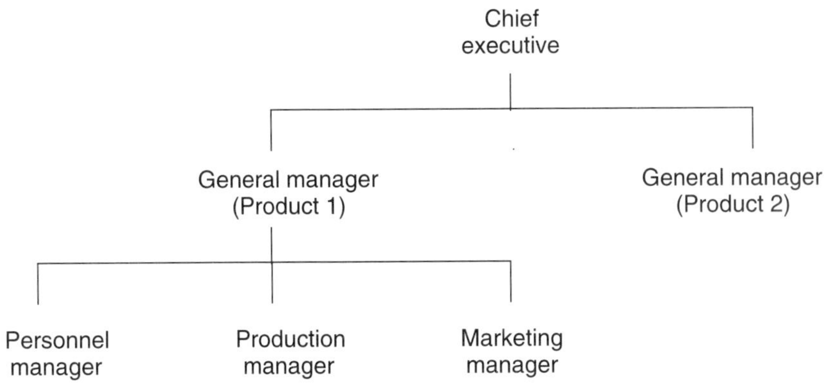

Figure 14.2. Divisional structure.

This pattern of organization was pioneered in the USA in the 1920s when hitherto U-Form firms moved into new geographical markets. It became a common organizational form somewhat later in the UK.[18] Many UK firms took a holding company or H-Form instead as they expanded. Many UK firms have expanded by acquisitions and mergers rather than organically, and, typically, when firms have been purchased by others their organizational structure and strategy has been left more or less intact. They continue to function as virtually independent companies, with the main difference being that the profits pass to the holding company. In the H-Form structure, then, the head office takes an inactive role in strategic direction, and decision-making of all types is comparatively decentralized. From the 1960s onwards, however, many of these firms have rationalized these structures into something more akin to the multi-divisional form.

However, the clarity of roles and decision-making in the M-Form model is not always found in practice, and it is arguable that this model should be viewed as an 'ideal type' against which to measure reality. Research has shown that the notion of a strategic decision is not fixed- managers tend to define what is most important at the time as strategic. Thus, what might be classed in the model as operating decisions – industrial relations for instance

– may be the subject of head office decision-making on occasions.[19] In practice there are differing models of the head office role in multi-divisional firms in the UK, ranging from a 'hands-off' approach to divisional management, to a highly interventionist approach where the head office controls much of the constituent divisions' activities. Research suggests that no form is necessarily more appropriate than another. There are cases of good performing firms in both categories.[20] However, there is some evidence that a high degree of decentralization to divisions and below can be harmful in some sectors – such as electronics- since it can inhibit the research and development upon which the future of the firm depends. Individual units tend to focus on short-term financial performance and are often unable to sustain the level of research activity necessary for long-term competitive success.

Matrix form

The third form of organization structure is somewhat rarer than the previous two, though elements of matrix-style reporting relationships are found in a very large number of organizations. In a such an organization employees typically report to two or more managers or departments, on the grounds that this will encourage these employees to take full account of the priorities of all management functions concerned. It is thought to be particularly appropriate for project teams where team, members need to take account of both technical and commercial considerations. The advantages it may confer are that it breaks down departmental boundaries and allows decentralized coordination.[21] The matrix form was pioneered in the American aerospace industry in the 1960s, but it has not been widely adopted because of the problems experienced by many organizations experimenting with this form. It has re-emerged in a new guise in the new fashion for Business Process Re-engineering.[22] In this model, functional departments are replaced by multi-function process teams who oversee all aspects of the production or delivery of a particular product or service.

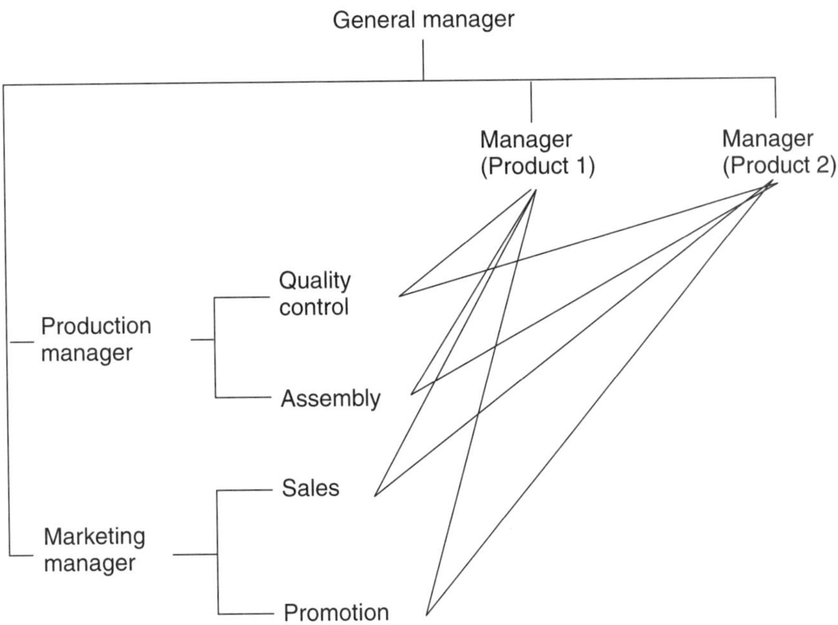

Figure 14.3. Matrix structure.

Matrix forms of management are usually introduced to encourage creativity and break down departmental boundaries. However, a change to structure of this sort will not necessarily lead to changes in employee behaviour. Where employees have a strong sense of departmental or functional identification they may continue to give priority to decisions emanating from superiors from within their own traditional function. Alternatively, lack of clarity in reporting relationships can be destructive. Employees may be uncertain what to do when conflicting instructions are received from superiors, and contrary to the intention of the initiators of the matrix structure, this could lead to caution and inertia. In these circumstances there is the danger that senior members of the organization create new rules to regulate those areas of potential conflict, and this further stifles creativity. In general, matrix organization may be appropriate for organizations or parts of organizations in the innovatory stage of the product cycle. Attempts to invigorate mature organizations with the matrix form can be fraught with danger, as existing problems may be intensified rather than solved.

Approaches to organization re-design

The foregoing discussion has indicated that organization design and re-design can take many forms. It can involve a small-scale change involving relatively few employees, or can involve a transformation of the structure of the whole organization. In all cases, however, those responsible for re-design should take heed of the social processes and relationships within the organization as well as the formal structure, since these will have a substantial impact on the operation of new structures. Given these considerations, how they go about their task? The following discussion attempts to highlight the main steps.

1. The company's basic goals and objectives need to be formulated, taking account of any long-held organization philosophies.

2. The organization's external environment and its response to it needs to be analysed using SWOT analysis (Strengths, Weaknesses, Opportunities and Threats) or portfolio analysis (to assess the opportunities for growth in profitability and market share).

In these two initial stage, the organizational designer is attempting to determine what the organization is trying to do, whether its objectives are realistically attainable, and whether there is a pronounced gap between desired and actual performance. If the environment is such that the organization cannot realistically improve its performance, then market withdrawal and an accompanying re-design may be necessary. Alternatively, re-design may be necessary to prepare the organization for new market or environmental opportunities. If, for instance, a hitherto mass market has evolved into a set of 'niche'markets, change from a functional to a multi-divisional structure could well be beneficial.

3. To discern the internal blockages to desired performance, designers will need to collect information on individual and collective behaviour and performance. Relevant data may be obtained using job analysis, by a programme of interviews, or by using information gathered during the staff appraisal

(making sure that any confidentialities are not breached). It may be that use of external consultants is the most appropriate way to gather information on behaviour, since the designers themselves may not be viewed as impartial. Employees may be reluctant to provide truthful information to senior managers from within the firm for fear that they could prejudice their own future career opportunities within the organization.

4. The data gathered will need to be rigourously analysed to determine whether the existing structure is presenting genuine obstacles to desired performance. Those undertaking the analysis should be able to distinguish the behavioural effects of structure from behaviour which has different antecedents.

5. Once the data has been analysed, any proposals for change can be formulated.

6. The proposed changes and their rationale should be communicated to all organization members. Ideally, the nature of the plans should be discussed directly with all those likely to be affected by them. This can be a particularly difficult part of the process since re-organizations are often synonymous with contraction and redundancy, and they can therefore be deeply threatening to employees. It is difficult to judge at what point employees should be informed and consulted. In general early notification is desirable – indeed there are minimum statutory periods where redundancies will result – but equally it can be argued that too long a period of uncertainty can be damaging to morale and performance. However, it is possible that employee's representatives will want to consider and amend proposals for re-design, so adequate time should be allowed for the consultation process. Insufficient time can mean that re-organization is delayed.

7. The implementation stage will involve re-assignment of job holders to new posts, reformulation of job duties and modifications to reporting relationships. However, actual relationships and division of tasks between organization members cannot be read-off in their entirety from organization charts, so it is essential that time is allowed for those affected

by re-organization to work-through how their tasks relate to those performed by colleagues in other parts of the organization.

8. Finally, the impact of the change should be monitored and assessed, paying particular attention to the impact of structural change on individual and collective behaviour

If conducted properly, organizational re-design may secure benefits for both the individual employee and the organization. In practice, however, restructuring often has the opposite effect. Both the Kings Cross fire on London Underground and the Clapham Junction crash on British Rail in the late 1980s occurred shortly after major re-organizations, and official inquiries into both incidents identified organization re-structuring as important contributory factors.[23]

A fundamental problem is that those responsible for re-designing organizations have generally received little training in the analysis of organizations and social systems, and there is the danger that their approach may be more influenced by current management fads than serious analysis. Those most likely to have these analytical skills – human resources professionals- are rarely at the forefront of organization re-design. Their involvement is often limited to the implementation process, e.g. handling job transfers and redundancies.[24] The danger, then, is that organization re-designers misinterpret the causes of performance problems, viewing them as the outcome of structural problems, when in fact they may arise for different reasons. Furthermore, they may fail to realise that 'softer' innovations in organization development, e.g. training in communication skills, might be necessary to supplement substitute for 'harder' structural change. This is not to argue that those generally initiating structural change are unaware or disinterested in behavioural issues. Instead, the problem is often that they assume a simplistic relationship between structural form and behavioural outcomes

Conclusion

The main argument of this chapter has been that there is more to organization design than formal structure. Formal structure is designed to influence employee behaviour, but the relationship between them is far more complex than is often assumed by those embarking on organization re-design. A given configuration of hierarchy, specialization and coordination can have both positive and negative effects on employee performance. Furthermore, employee behaviour will also be influenced by factors outside the firm. Finally, the operation of a re-designed structure can be as much determined by prevailing patterns of employee behaviour as by the behavioural impact of structural innovations.

In this area of organization re-design there are three possible options for the human resource manager. The first is to accept a subordinate position, and deal primarily with the 'nuts and bolts' issues of implementation, such as issuing new job descriptions and administering job transfers. The second, more pro-active, option is to attempt to influence those redesignng organizations, with the objective of raising their awareness of the complex relationships between structure and behaviour. The third is to get to the core of strategic decision-making. Here, human resources managers themselves are involved in organizational re-design. To achieve this position of power is not easy, given the traditional role of personnel management. It will be necessary to reconceptualize personnel management to strategic human resources management, and to assert the close links between organizational success and sophisticated human resource management.

References

1. See M. Hammer and J. Champy, *Reengineering the Corporation: a Manifesto for Business Revolution* (London: Nicholas Brealey, 1993).

2. As occurred during the Hawthorne Studies in the USA in the 1930s. See M. Rose, *Industrial Behaviour* 2nd edition (London: Penguin, 1988), chapters 11–12. for a good discussion of Elton Mayo, Human Relations and the Hawthorne Studies.

3. This was a key finding of the Affluent Worker project in the 1960s. See J.Goldthorpe, D. Lockwood, F. Bechofer and J. Platt, *The Affluent Worker: Industrial Attitudes and Behaviour* (Cambridge: Cambridge University Press, 1968)

4. See S. Andresik, *Max Weber on Capitalism , Bureaucracy and Religion: a Selection of Texts* (London: Allen and Unwin, 1983) and H. Gerth and C.W. Mills *From Max Weber: Essays in Sociology* (London: Routledge, 1991).

5. See J. Child *Organization: A Guide to Problems and Practice* 2nd edition (London: Harper and Row, 1984), p.45.

6. This was a key finding of the Aston studies into organization structure in the 1960s. See D. Pugh and D. Hickson *Organizational Structure in its Context: the Aston Programme volume 1* (Farnborough: Saxon House, 1976).

7. P. Selznick *TVA and the Grass Roots: A Study in the Sociology of Formal Organization* (New York: Harper and Row, 1966).

8. E. Batstone, A. Ferner and M. Terry *Consent and Efficiency: Management Strategy and Labour Relations in the State Enterprise* (Oxford: Blackwell, 1984), A. Pendleton 'Structural re-organization and labour management in public

enterprise: a study of British Rail' *Journal of Management Studies,* Vol. 31, No. 1, pp. 33–54.

9. See H. Braverman Labor and Monopoly Capitalism (New York: Monthly Review Press, 1974), R. Edwards *Contested Terrain: The Transformation of the Workplace in the Twentieth Century* (London: Heinneman, 1979), and A. Friedmann *Industy and Labour: Class Struggle at Work and Monopoly Capitalism* (London: Macmillan, 1977).

10. R. Merton 'Bureaucratic structure and personality; *Social Forces,* vol 18, pp. 560–568.

11. P. Blau *The Dynamics of Bureaucracy* (Chicago, Chicago University Press, 1955).

12. C. Argyris *Personality and Organization: The Conflict Between Systems and the Individual* (New York: Harper and Row, 1975).

13. A. Gouldner *Patterns of Industrial Bureaucracy* (New York: Free Press, 1954). M.Crozier *The Bureaucratic Phenomenon* (Chicago: Chicago University Press, 1964).

14. T. Peters and R. Waterman *In Search of Excellence* (London: Harper and Row, 1982).

15. T. Peters *Thriving on Chaos: Handbook for a Management Revolution* (London: Pan, 1989)

16. See M. Conte and J. Svejnar 'The performance effects of employee ownership plans' in A.Blinder (ed.) *Paying for Productivity* (Washington DC: Brookings Institution 1990).

17. T. Burns and G. Stalker *The Management of Innovation* (London: Tavistock, 1961).

18. See A. Chandler *Strategy and Structure: Chapters in the History of the Industrial Enterprise* (London: MIT Press,

1962), A. Chandler and H. Daems (eds.) *Managerial Hierarchies: Comparative Perspectives on the Rise of the Modern Industrial Enterprise* (London: Harvard University Press, 1980) , L. Hannah (ed.) *Management Strategy and Business Development: an Historical and Comparative Study* (London: Macmillan, 1976), D. Channon *The Strategy and Structure of British Enterprise* (London: Macmillan, 1973)

19. D. Hickson, R. Butler, D. Cray, G. Mallory and D. Wilson *Top Decisions: Strategic Decision-Making in Organizations* (Oxford: Blackwell, 1986).

20. M. Gould and A. Campbell *Strategies and Styles* (Oxford: Blackwell, 1987)

21. K. Knight *Matrix Management* (Aldershot: Gower, 1977).

22. M. Hammer and J. Champy , *Reengineering the Corporation: a Manifesto for Business Revolution* (London: Nicholas Brealey, 1993).

23. D. Fennel QC *Investigation into the King's Cross Underground Fire* (London: Department of Transport, 1988, Cm. 499). A. Hidden QC *Investigation into the Clapham Junction Railway Accident* (London: Department of Transport, 1989 Cm820).

24. A. Evans and A. Cowling 'Personnel's part in organization restructuring' *Personnel Management,* October 1985.

Further Reading

J. Child *Organization.: A Guide to Problems and Practice* 2nd edition (London:Harper and Row, 1984)

R. Butler *Designing Organizations* (London: Routledge, 1991)

Human Resource Management Journal, Vol. 5, No. 2 1994–95 special issue on innovations in organization structure

Exam questions

1. What are the main dimensions of organization structure, and what are the problems that often result from structural characteristics?

2. What are the key differences between functional, divisional and matrix organizations

3. Why does organization re-design often fail to live up to expectations?

CASE STUDY

Bradford Design Company

Background

Bradford Design Company (BDC) is a packaging company which offers a design capability for product packaging as well as manufacturing cartons and boxes for a range of clients. Initially, the firm (set up by a former marketing consultant Archie Smith in 1963) concentrated on package design, with the clients making their own arrangements for manufacture of the packages. Early on, however, it became clear that BDC could also profitably offer a manufacturing service, since its clients preferred to deal with just one organization for this part of their production process. BDC sub-contracted package manufacture to a range of other local firms. This approach, though welcomed by BDC's clients, was not entirely successful for BDC itself, since after initial success profit margins declined. Indeed, in some years this part of the operation was not profitable. Although the firm considered pulling-out of this part of the business on a number of occasions, caution always prevailed since it was believed that BDC would lose a substantial part of its design activity to other firms as a result. BDC therefore pursued an alternative strategy – that of bringing a manufacturing capability in-house. When the owner of local packaging firm, Bradford Packaging Company (BPC), decided to sell her company BDC jumped at the opportunity to buy this firm. BDC, employing around 500 in the expanded business, thrived for a while but in recent years it has been beset with internal problems.

The design arm and the manufacturing arm of the company function in effect as two separate operations, and there is frequently conflict between the two. The mainly blue collar workers in the manufacturing facility view the employees of the design function as 'ivory tower types' who have little understanding of making packaging materials. Too often the designers come up with impractical designs which require costly alternations to machine settings. It is rare for the designers to consult with their manufacturing colleagues in the formative stages of package design. For their part the designers believe that those employed in the manufacturing part of BDC (including the production director) are unimaginative, and that it is pointless to involve them earlier in the design stage since they will find a host of reasons why a particular design approach should not be used. On occasions a particular design will be 'sabotaged' by the manufacturing function, leading to delays in delivery, excessive costs and friction with clients.

Overall BDC is organized on a functional basis: both design and manufacture are organized as separate departments, alongside a small finance function (created mainly from that acquired from BPC). The sales function is a branch of the design department. Design has a flatter structure than manufacturing: three levels in the hierarchy against six in manufacturing. Supervisors and managers in the latter are often critical of their limited decision-making powers. The main grievance among employees in design, however, is that promotional opportunities are limited. At the top of the company, Archie Smith is an active Managing Director and likes to be involved in all of the major decisions taken by the design and manufacturing departments. He acts as an arbitrator in the frequent conflicts between the two departments, though he is perceived by many to be more sympathetic to the manufacturing department.

Task

Archie Smith has recently become exasperated by the internal strife in BDC and has appointed you – an expert in organizational analysis – to 'sort the company out'. He is expecting a set of recommendations to change the way the company is organized.

What are your recommendations?

Chapter 15

Managing Change

David T H Weir

Objectives

- To take the perspective of a manager involved in a change programme and review
- The reasons for change
- The types of change which affect organizations
- The process of change
- Its effect on individuals
- The role of external helpers
- The methods by which change can be managed
- Why change goes wrong

Introduction

In the first edition of this book Sir John Harvey-Jones, at the time of writing, Chancellor of Bradford University wrote, "All this ferment of change is impacting on business organization and is going to force major re-appraisals of the ways in which we relate to, manage, motivate and reward people. To look at things anew and adapt to the future one requires a profound understanding of one's craft and its practice."

It is important for the manager to recognize that this topic is not an arcane wisdom reserved only for a few senior corporate leaders, or the specialist preserve of a small group of talented and highly trained experts. It is the lot of every manager. Understanding how change occurs and how to ride the waves of change is an essential part of the manager's tool kit and of the craft of management.

In this chapter we take the perspective of the manager who may be involved in, or take major responsibility for, managing a change programme. But change is a process which takes place over time, so we deal with the way change starts and the reasons for it, the types of change which affect organizations, the process of change, and its impact on individuals, the role of external consultants or change agents and the methods by which change can be managed.

If it is an exaggeration to say that "All management is the management of change", nonetheless the study of the management of change leads inexorably into a consideration of the problems of management in general. The idea of change is very topical. But several thousand years ago the Latin playwright Terence advised "there is change in all things" Perhaps he was echoing the well known maxim of Heraclitus that "a man never puts his foot into the same river twice".

Some American writers proclaim that, 'we are living in the era of the most rapid change known to man,' and have made great fortunes out of the gullible by such concepts as "future shock" and "the management of chaos". There is some, but not much, evidence to justify this apocalyptic excitement. It is by no means certain that managers in our generation have to cope with more change than ever before. Though some indices of the transmission of information and the speed of computation show a substantial improvement over the powers available to earlier generations; in other ways the statement is clearly overdrawn. Today's generation of managers, in the United Kingdom at least, will typically not have had to fight in a world war or to emigrate to find work and shelter; they are less likely to have seen their children and contemporaries die of unpreventable and unremediable disease and they will have lived most of their lives under stable regimes of government. Few of these advantages of stability were available to our parents' and grandparents' generations. Perhaps it is more judicious to say that our generation is one of the first to learn that it is possible to *manage* change.

But most professional managers *will* have to deal with change at some time during their working careers. They will be better prepared if they live in expectation of this, and develop skills and habits of mind in advance, which help to prepare for the inevitability of change.

Organizations which are led by those who are better trained to adapt to changing circumstances may be more likely to survive than those which are not.

What is Chance?

Change can be defined as some kind of major intervention by managers to overcome what they perceive as inertia in respect of major organizational goals. The politics and culture of organizations are important frameworks in the analysis of change.

Not all change works out the way it was planned. But once change processes are started it is difficult to stop them.

The *momentum* of change is important. Revolutionary change can lead to a process of evolution in which the change is consolidated and absorbed. Incremental change can be punctuated by discontinuous changes of a more revolutionary kind. Some of the incremental changes can be described as "fine tuning", in which change processes become adjusted to the expectations of organizational actors and the emerging and unpredictable realities of the environment. But some changes are "mould breaking". They involve major technological innovations or changes in the pace of operations or severe breaks in product life cycles. The ensuing organizational and personnel discontinuities affect the whole structure of work. In such cases, organizations may need to go "back to basics."

Grinyer and McKiernan show that some organizations – which they characterise as "sharp bending" – can be on an apparently downwards trajectory. The experience of a change programme may, with hindsight, represent a significant watershed in behaviours and perceived outcomes for the organization and the individuals who participate in it.[1] But it is not always possible to predict, in advance, when the 'sharp bend' is going to occur. It is like being told that the way to an Irish destination is to turn right one mile before you get to Murphy's Bar.

> *For the purpose of this chapter we define the "management of change" as that aspect of management that is concerned with restructuring, which may be evolutionary but involves a fundamental re-positioning of an organization in relation to its product or supplier market. This usually implies a re-orientation of the 'soft' as well as 'hard' elements of organization structure. It is concerned with new ways of making sense of the same reality as well as with continuing ways of making sense of a changing reality.*

Major changes of this kind include:

1. Changes of leadership.
2. The introduction and implementation of novel product market strategies: entering a new market, expanding geographically, and new products introduction.
3. A decision to build a major new production facility or to introduce a significantly different production technology.
4. Major change in a distribution network.

5. The modification of organizational structures and the proposed re-distribution of authority.
6. Reaction to changes in the external environment caused by any or all of the above, the activity of competitors, changes in consumer tastes, and the effect of the business cycle.
7. Merger or acquisition with another organization.
8. The introduction of new methods of control and distribution of information.
9. The growing expectation amongst organizational participants that change involving some (or a combination) of the above, is about to happen.

When managers in different industries talk, for example, of "markets" they may be using the term in quite distinct ways for the judgements they make are rooted in different "recipes" – or different ways of organizing the reality they face. In some industries "change" is part of the recipe, in others it is not. An essential part of the understanding of change is the understanding that there are differing social constructions of change itself.

Organizations sometimes act as if they hoped to avoid change, or at least its uncomfortable aspects. They operate by attempting to impose their own view of the world on their environment. This makes it easier for them to plan, but may drive them further away from the changing market and the requirements of their clients. When the need for change is finally recognized it may be already too late.

So organizations tend to create structures which they hope will outlive the vagaries of the immediate changes in their operating environment. That may be sound common sense for the enterprise, but is a dangerous wisdom for individuals. If organizational participants believe their own organizational myths of stability and coherence they may not see the point of developing those skills which will enable them to cope with change.

To talk of "planned change" may be misleading, because it reinforces a top-down view of the organization. *Change* in fact is feared by many and is not necessarily welcomed even by those who understand its inevitability on an intellectual level. These managers (and nearly all operatives) know from experience that all change is not necessarily for the better, at least for them.

Some contemporary writers celebrate "chaos" or "liberation management", but middle managers know that we do not normally have to celebrate chaos in order to understand change.

The dominant paradigm in many organizations is that the management of change is a specialist activity best managed by specialists. These may be identified as "Change Manager", "Facilitator", "Organizational Development Specialist" and the like. It is a paradigm which believes that the management of change involves the use of specialist skills which only a professionally qualified or hierarchically superior elite has the responsibility to manage. But it is a dangerous illusion that the management of change demands superhuman attributes from managers which nothing in their previous experience has trained them to possess.

> *The management of change is something that quite ordinary managers do, and do successfully. It is not an Olympic event for heroes.*

Organizational change can be facilitated by having some spare resource to undertake specific tasks. So external consultants and third parties may play a useful role. However, many organizations which manage change successfully do so by harnessing the already existing internal reservoirs of skill, experience and the hard-won knowledge of product and market which have created its existing structures and special competitive advantages.

It is unlikely that change will be successfully managed if it does violence to the essential nature of the organization itself and the events and histories which have given it competitive advantage. So change must be consistent with the models of the organization and its business carried in the heads of organizational participants and those who do business with it.

The beginning of wisdom in managing change is to understand what business your organization is in, and how it got where it is.

The Processes of Change

Change may be planned or unplanned, continuous or discontinuous. Some changes may be described as degradational and others as evolutionary. Programmes of change with a limited life capability may be started with a flourish but go downhill. Like summer love affairs there is a natural period to their existence. Change processes initiated by managers who have come to remote outstations with the message "We have come from Head Office to help you" are likely to fall into this category. They may only last as long as their utility to their authors' career progression. Other middle managers learn to recognize the signs and take avoiding action.

All of these considerations lend force to Wilson's judgement that "The notion of planned change, on the surface a seemingly rational and eminently appropriate task for managers, is not so unproblematic as it may seem."[2]

The specific problem of some change programmes is how to change the inertia, which is characteristic of organizations which have achieved an apparently settled pattern of organization, into the momentum which will be supported by the shared visions of an adequate number of organizational participants.

Change involves a fundamental repositioning of an organization in relation to its product markets and its internal ways of working. It entails a re-orientation of the soft, as well as the hard, elements of organizational structure, thus creating new ways of making sense of what has been taken hitherto to be objective reality. Sometimes it starts by offering a new picture of an apparently well understood organizational world. Successful change recognizes an organization's heritage but also introduces new ways of playing the organizational game. It may generate more specific design criteria for creating structural flexibility and identify tools of design and methodologies for measuring progress and techniques of performance analysis to determine the success of the desired transition.

Wilson provides a more sophisticated typology of change, identifying four types of change, according to the degree of change, from preservation of the status quo to revolutionary transformation. He introduces the distinction between operational and strategic dimensions. Thus, in the revolutionary strategic change type is characterized by the redefining of the existing parameters of the organization as a whole.

Wilson also distinguishes two paradigms of change, of systemic conflict and strategic choice. In the first, the implicit tensions or contradictions within the system provide the impetus for change, the second emphasis as the manager as doer and as the entrepreneur of the change process.

Wilson argues that human resource management has to produce managers who are more autonomous, more generalist in corporate perspective, more entrepreneurial and who view themselves as arbiters of strategic choice.

This is an encouraging, and to some extent flattering, portrait of the manager and one that will appeal to many readers of this chapter. But defining oneself as an entrepreneur or an agent of change does not necessarily conjure up the resources to implement such a role successfully, and to publicly identify oneself in this way may create expectations which are not capable of being satisfied. The result may be disillusion or a loss of impetus for the change programme.

Different types of change require different modalities of change and different skills in those who are charged with managing the change process. McWhinney, distinguishes four basic modes,

1. *Analytic* in which change is achieved by imposing policies that have been developed by testing an idea against empirical data. Thus, change is conceived of as a rational process and is driven by an authority which embodies, perhaps unilaterally, the highest manifestations of that process.

2. *Participative* change is achieved by developing a value consensus in the relevant group, action follows from shared involvement, the source of power is democratic, guided by a rational relation to data in which individuals feel they have made some choices.

3. *Imperative* change is achieved by leadership of a charismatic or agent of authority.

4. Emergent change is achieved through creating and accepting a new idea that may have emerged from the groups which are involved in the process.[3]

While these distinctions have some merit in forcing us to examine aspects of the change process, it is not clear that they represent real organizational situations, for many real life change programmes involve a mixture of all of these four aspects. Change is always more complex and surprising in reality than it appears to be on paper.

The manager, in considering the sources of his or her authority, has to understand the concept of "myth". An appropriate mythology or collective history has to be created and sustained throughout the change process, so that individuals can relate their own actions to a pattern of values which defines what is right for them in their organization. Thus, change has to come to be embodied into some conceptualization of, "The way we do things around here" and the rightness of change has to be tested against the core values of the organization.

When these conditions are met, the change will be owned by those whose careers and prospects in the organization are affected by the change. When they are not present these managers may create and indeed deserve "resistance to change".

The Pressures for Change

A successful programme of change management must be closely allied to the strategy of the business.

This has become a key consideration for many large organizations operating in a transnational or global environment. Technological change may provide a boost to an organization by improving a production method, or introducing a more satisfactory material for a particular product, or by increasing access to a market through more efficient distribution. The increasing sophistication of markets, the growth of knowledge intensive products, the increased emphasis on product design and the introduction of flexible manufacturing may provide a shot in the arm, in the short term, for an organization which is confident in its ability to manage. But in the medium term none of these factors are without impact on the process of management itself, and most issues of this kind tend to resolve sooner or later into “people” issues.

The pressures of privatisation, increased consumer awareness, trans-national bodies, such as those of the European Union, or the creation of wider trading areas, as in both North America and Europe, mean that managers have to conceptualize their approach to management in such a way that they are able to deal with the demands of other markets and cultures than those which they have experienced hitherto, and in which their learning has taken place.

Large organizations typically operate in dynamic and turbulent environments, where the relation between strategy and structure is not clear cut. In the 1970s and 80s organization theorists and personnel managers emphasized the importance of creating the “best fit” between an organization’s internal processes and the demands of its strategic path through the environment, but now the emphasis is on structural flexibility and the management processes which can create and sustain this flexibility.

While organizations need to become more alert, responsive and pro-active in relation to their environment, not every organizational participant can in practice do everything. Not every organization can respond to every changing requirement of the market. Pettigrew argues that there are few studies of change that allow the change process to reveal itself in a temporal or contextual manner. Moreover, many accounts of change are anecdotal, episodic, or unrelated to the real historical environment in which these change processes actually occurred. So the learning which a manager in one organization can expect to get from understanding how a nother organization has successfully managed a change process is inevitably limited and might lead to deeply misleading conclusions.[4]

There is not likely to be *one* correct model of change or *one* recipe which, if followed, will guarantee a successful outcome. Indeed it may be that not all organizations are in shape to consider change. There may be situations in which it is better to simply wipe the slate clean and start again. We can also learn from the histories of, once moribund, companies which have successfully managed a programme of change by stopping in their tracks and starting again in the green field situation. But for most managers this is not an option. They have to deal with what they know. They have to make different dishes from original ingredients, to create nouvelle cuisine out of what currently conjures up only cold porridge.

Change inevitably takes time. Twenty years ago I was told by a manager in Babcock Power the parable of the elephant. Change, my informant told me, is like making love to an elephant. "It will take a long time and no results will occur for at least two years because this is the period of gestation for the elephant. You need some technology, not too much, but at least a ladder. You will need the support of your friends to hold the ladder and to get you quickly out of the way in case the elephant does not like what you are doing to it. But in that case be quick, because the elephant will make a terrible noise, roll rapidly over on to its side and crush you under its weight. So be very sure that you have all of those pre-requisites before you put your own best foot forward." This is still good advice for the line manager invited to become involved as a "change agent" or "change manager". Nonetheless the rewards of success may be very attractive and, win or lose, the process will be an exciting one.

The first few months of a change programme will be decisive. I once asked Don Revie, the successful Leeds United Team Manager of the 1960s and 1970s, if he would talk me through his first "hundred days" as manager of the greatest club side in the world at that time. "I can describe to you what I did in the first hundred minutes", he answered.

Eccles warns, however, that the deliberate manipulation of crisis situations in order to provoke a desired chain reaction may blow up in its initiator's face. He says, "Many organizations have thought that a smart way to galvanize people would be to generate a drama, only to find that they had opened a Pandora's box and created a full blown fiasco." In such circumstances it is not wise to personally light the blue touch paper, even if the manager proposes to retire to a safe distance. The ensuing retirement may be more terminal.[5]

Change may be endogenous or exogenous, driven from within or by external forces. In practical terms, for the manager caught in the middle, the difference between these two is that the second is likely to be more sudden, swift, brutal and to lack consideration of alternatives. New owners may come in with their ideas of the proper way to do things: the choice for the manager is to stay and do it or leave and offer his skills to a (possibly uninterested) market. This philosophy was summed up for me by a chief executive who advised that he used the FIFO method of motivating senior managers in a situation of rapid change. I had met FIFO as a method of stock valuation and inquired how it related to senior management decision making. "Fit in or f--- off", replied my informant.

Eccles introduces the useful concept of organizational viscosity, defined as a perceived resistance to change based on some conflict or unmanageable complexity in the value systems of the organization. Many change programmes fail because they do not create a preferred value system which will retrospectively justify the change. The viscosity is too great. The new ideas do not flow through. New situations do not take root.

Eccles summarizes the preferred pre-requisites for change to work successfully.

1. There must be *pressure for change* from somewhere. This may come from inside or out. Sometimes it may be present or latent in the organization but liberated by some action or announced intention.
2. The change must embody, or at least announce, the intention to agree on a *clear, shared vision* of where the organization will be after the transition. This must appear to be a right action or at least a defensible one as far as the organizational participants are concerned.
3 There must be some *effective liaison* or trust and a process through which this can come about.
4. There must be *will and power to act.*
5. For this to take place the *change must be owned* by some individual or element within the organization which is, or feels itself to be, empowered to act.
6. There have to be, within the organization, *capable people and sufficient resources* to effect the change.
7. As well as the specific skills of leadership and direction, we may need third parties, consultants, or outside supporters. But for these to be effective there has to be a skill basis within the organization to support these capabilities. This will certainly involve *training.*
8. There has to be an *appropriate structure of rewards* related to a parallel system of accountabilities. The question, “what’s in it for me?” has to have a reasonably clear – but not necessarily simple answer.
9. Change must start with *actionable first steps* and there must be a *feedback* loop, in the organization, which enables it to learn and adapt from the mistakes it will inevitably make.

Leadership for Change

Leadership is a key element. Change will not come about unless individuals have the capability to offer appropriate leadership to the organization and are prepared to take the risks intrinsic in acting on those capabilities. *Unless the chief executive owns the change process, and is seen to be identified with it, change will not occur.* The leadership style, the tone of the campaign, the urgency with which the message is transmitted and the energy with which the actions are taken must be manifest in the leaders style and own method of handling situations. This is true at all levels, but it is more true the higher up the organization. Eccles puts this bluntly in an echo of Urwick and Fayol, "The more senior you are, the more responsibility you must take." He calls this the rule of proportionate responsibility. Not all leaders survive the change process they have initiated.

A popular buzz word at the moment is "empowerment". It is a concept which engages the enthusiasm of many organizations. Empowerment is both likely to be a cause and an effect of a successful programme of change. It is through an active philosophy of this kind that successful change programmes take their shape, define their processes and create their structures.

Empowerment, as a concept, suffers from a conceptual confusion. To empower someone implies that the active part is taken by the doer, and the passive part is taken by the one who is gaining the benefit. But this is the opposite of reality in complex organizations. Those who are to be empowered have power of their own already; but it is normally the power to deny, to restrain, and to avoid. It is negative power. "Empowerment" is about transmuting these restraining influences into a dynamic element which will support the positive direction of change. So in order to be in a position to empower, the chief executive has to recognize the limitations on his or her own freedom of action. Then his or her task must be to liberate the positive potential among colleagues and subordinates.

Empowerment on its own is not likely to be the whole answer, though organizations which do not know how to handle power or are uncertain in their trust in those who are empowered will typically find the process of change difficult and, perhaps, disabling.

But when an organization feels it is ready for change, top management may delay the institution of a change programme at its peril.

By the time senior management has successfully negotiated its own conceptual and practical hurdles, has had its workshops, its away days, its guru briefings and its team building exercises and is preparing to break the crucial news to its juniors that "the times they are a – changing", they generally find that their colleagues are there already and know in their water that "A change is gonna come". They may also have already worked through some of the options. These may be more radical in fact than those which senior management have restricted themselves to.

The successful change programme in the Tannoy Company emphasizes this point. A downturn of the product market imposed a perceived need among senior managers for speedy cutting of costs, which would inevitably mean redundancies. However, their diffident efforts to sell this bad news to the representative body of the workforce was met with a specific list of those individuals who might be most easily spared. When this list was acted on, there was no objection even from the victims.[6]

It is not easy to determine who, in this kind of situation, could confidently claim to be empowering whom. The management of change, in today's organization, involves moving from the Win Lose philosophies and habits of mind of the traditional organization, to the Win Win expectations of the empowered organization.

Teams

The chief executive has a very specific role in managing strategic and organizational change. The chief executive and board must lead from the front to create a positive culture involving ongoing honest appraisal and commitment to quality throughout the enterprise. Communication and the taking of appropriate responsibility must be emphasized, for "team building" on its own is unlikely to represent the whole answer. There is a price to team working and it may be paid in delay, confusion, and sometimes unnecessary conflict played out on unsought and irrelevant battlefields. Team decision making, is not necessarily intrinsically superior to individual decision making providing that the trust to empower in an upward direction is balanced by the experience that decisions, when they are made, are normally ones which can be supported.

Team building is, nonetheless, a common part of the change process and provides a focus for generating organizational commitment. Teams typically go through the phase of "forming", "norming", "storming", and "performing". In the first phase the team gets together, in the second and third, values and beliefs are exposed and the team may go through a period of unrelated and even conflicting behaviours. It is only in the fourth phase that the team will start to perform according to the expectations of its members.[7]

If the team and membership of it is not a priority to those who are part of it, other elements of organizational performance may take precedence. This will devalue the team and create problems for those members for whom the team is a more central part of their commitment to the organization. So the vision and strategy of the change programme have to be generated before the teams are set up.

Certain roles have to be manifest in the team for it to perform effectively. This presents particular challenges for the leadership team. The leader has to determine what kind of leadership role may be appropriate in the circumstances of the specific culture and structure of the organization. Once these questions have been answered, the leader can offer clear directions and create a climate which can stimulate high performance

The team itself has to be managed. Results do not come naturally or simply, by nature of the fact that the team is operating on a particular problem. The performance of team members has to be defined and monitored, and appropriate rewards and punishments instituted. Managing change is not about being especially nice to people. In extreme situations, selective execution is a legitimate tool of management and may do wonders for the encouragement of waverers. The leader must therefore be sensitive to his or her effect on the team's overall ability and on the team's internal dynamics, as well as conscious of the management of the external environment and its expectations.

Members of the team must have a clear expectation of what they are intending to do and what goals may be legitimately targeted. Being a member of a team bringing about a process of change will clearly not, for most managers, be the sum total of their continuing commitment to the organization: most will also "have a day job"; the day job is likely to be something they are more familiar with and will have more short term and precise expectations attached to it. So there is a considerable danger that the existing commitments may seem to embody more realistic and manageable performance targets than does membership of a team or a temporary structure, which may be nebulous or changing and which is directed towards perhaps more intangible and contentious longer term goals.

Communication

All of those involved in programmes of change need to pay particular attention to communicating what they are doing to other members of the organization. They need a perception of *how* change will come about, *what* the organization needs to do, *where* the programme will start and *when* certain specific activities will occur. These particular "how", "what", "where" and "when" questions will probably be more meaningful to many managers than will the "why" question. In most organizations the "why" is pretty well understood by organizational participants, even before top management announces that there is a crisis and something must be done. Most employees have far more trust in their senior's ability to read the obvious signs than may appear justified to outsiders.

From 1976 to 1989 I was involved in a major change programme in the Babcock Power Group. The company had realised that its dependence on the power station building programme of the CEGB and the declining predictions of UK power requirements meant that they had no forward orders for the following year. I became involved in an "employee communication" exercise to transmit the message to the workforce that things would have to change. The senior management of Babcock expected there to be hostility, resentment and conflict. But instead, the overwhelming sensation was one of relief that management had belatedly woken up to the realities which the workforce had already well understood.

It is sometimes argued that rank and file employees are concerned above all things with the security of their own jobs. But the Babcock experience also showed that in many situations the workers, particularly in an organization with a long history and in a settled community environment, may be more concerned with job prospects for their children and may realise that, in order to safeguard these hopes, change is inevitable. But they still expect to be communicated with and their fears and anxieties appropriately recognized in the change programme.

The communication process needs to be both top down and bottom up. Sometimes well intentioned senior management abdicates the responsibility to give clear messages, in the hope that "a democratic process" will fill the gap and the answers will well up through natural pressure from the workforce as a whole. This usually does not happen. The communication process itself has to be managed. If there are too many layers of management, the complexity and difficulty of the communication process tends to increase.

In managing expectations, many techniques are available. It is almost a truism to say that there can never be too much communication. At Babcock, a video presented by a well-known TV figure was the catalytic communications medium. But it was backed up by briefing groups led by line management. These managers themselves had to be briefed. All who saw the video were given the opportunity to make both immediate and longer-term comments on how the process would affect them. In so doing, they also improved the access of the senior management to the nitty-gritty of underlying points of conflict and pressure within the organization. The processes of feedback and communication became formalized. The collective undertaking of the nature of the change was incurred by the process of participation.

Most organizations now understand the value of communications and that responsibility for the communication strategy of the organization is that of senior management. Responsibility for the communications involved in a Change Programme is, a fortiori, the responsibility of senior and middle management combined. So weekly meetings, monthly review meetings, the incorporation of overall objectives into appraisal meetings, management conferences on an organization-wide level, newsletters, posters, news clipping boards, and quality circles or the like, must all be part of a formal communication strategy.

Communication itself is part of a cultural change in which telling people what is going on is seen as a desirable organizational objective as well as a useful management technique. So senior managers must model in their behaviours the roles and processes they wish to encourage. It is here that "management by walking about" comes close to the best practice of organizations which can handle change. It is a crucial part of the change management skills of the Japanese and other national management cultures in which the hierarchical structures still often found in British organizations are not so noticeable.

The essence of communication is *listening.* Listening skills are central to many organizations' training programmes. But they need to be reinforced and to become embedded in the way management at all levels does its business. Sometimes this can become frustrating when the senior manager has to cope with the same message, perhaps put in the same way, from a large number of organizational participants. But it is nonetheless vital that frustration does not lead the senior manager to devalue the experience of receiving negative messages. It is not easy for organizational juniors to tell their bosses that they are doing something wrong. When they do it, it is likely to be significant, not least for the bosses themselves.

Training in "listening skills" may seem a humdrum way to underpin a programme of change dealing with markets, governments, clients, and technology. But it is almost certainly an effective part of every successful change programme, and a very good way to start the change process going.

Asda formalized the process of listening in their "Tell Archie" memos. Archie Norman was a new chief executive who came in from a City background without the experience in retailing which many middle managers felt to be essential in this industry. But by signalling that he *knew* that he didn't know and that he was prepared to remedy the deficiency, he set new cultural bounds to the relationship between senior management and the organization. Employers must believe that these seniors want to be told the truth, even if it's bad news.

Suggestion schemes, open forums and walking the job are essential skills for the manager who wants to learn how to listen. Formal training has an important role to play too. Managers can also listen through networking and through being available in a range of informal situations.

But listening, which is the core of communication and, communication which is the core of the management of change, can themselves be overdone if they lead to a weakening of the executive's resolve to manage change effectively. Top Management will inevitably receive many messages and some of these will be opposed to the change programme itself. These oppositions may be based on legitimate and honourable motives, but sometimes they will be defensive positions erected around selfish interests. So the manager involved in a change programme learns to test reactions and solicit the views of other interested parties. In order to do this, open communication is essential. Appearing to be open to alternatives will tend to reinforce the change manager's position if it then leads to action, but not if it leads to inaction, indecision or delay.

Sometimes the role of the change manager is expressed as that of "coping with ambiguity." However this is only part of the story. Sometimes it is the manager's job to create ambiguity or to demonstrate that ambiguity already exists in the organization's present ways of doing things. Essentially, however, the change leader has to be perceived to have the competencies and goodwill to harness and control the ambiguities which exist, without creating chaos and unnecessary distress. Change managers are doers, so change management cannot normally be solely undertaken from within a specialist personnel or human relations function unless that function is closely allied to the interests and structures of line management.

To be able to care for an organization and its tasks normally means having some ability to do essential tasks oneself and to be knowledgeable enough to understand what the organization is about. *This means that change management can be most successfully undertaken from within the organization by those who have the experience to give them credibility amongst those who need to change.* Outside agents and consultants can be a part of the process but the change programme itself has to be driven by those who will still be there after the deluge.

At the highest level of the organization, the change programme has to be integrated into the organization's evolving strategy. This has to be decomposed into a series of action steps which can be taken by managers and staff in the organization as a whole. In order for this to work, the needs of the users of new systems have to be taken into account. This will inevitably bring technical experts, systems people and information specialists into close proximity with physical processes and those who manage the detail of them. This is usually a more complex activity and takes longer than senior management expects when it initiates the programme.

Insiders and Outsiders

It is helpful to distinguish the inside and outside aspects of change. Senior management may need to spend a good deal more time than usual in explaining, justifying and obtaining resources for the change programme from sources outside the organization, including shareholders and other stakeholders. A good top management structure is often found in the military Chief-of-Staff-pattern of organization, in which the General and his team cope with grand strategy and the Chief-of-Staff with the detail. Where this works, as with Montgomery in the Western Desert before El Alamein, it frees the General for doing the essential job of networking and restating the mission, the purposes and the likely outcome of change to participants. Montgomery did this by spending every afternoon prior to the battle touring all the units in the army and giving a ten-minute pep talk followed by ten minutes of questions which were, he comments, "normally to the point and to do with latrines." But the message itself cannot be delegated and has to be owned by the leading figure in the organization if it is to be transmitted and thus owned by the common field soldiers. Montgomery understood that it was the "poor bloody infantry" whose jobs, and in this case lives, were on the line.

Leadership of a change programme involves developing an influence strategy to get support for change. This inevitably means working with main boards and with customers. The change must be sanctioned by those who are expected to benefit from improved performance. The surest way to ensure that a programme of change becomes bogged down and does not lead to improved performance is to create a structure and behave in such a way that people come to the conclusion that the change is nothing to do with them. This is demoralizing. Ownership of the change process must be located amongst those who will be most affected by it.

Factors in Successful Change Programmes

Taylor identifies a number of key factors common to the British companies who have successfully transformed their business in the past ten years. While each business has its own specific problems and each chief executive has his personal leadership style the common themes are:

1. *Stretch goals:* a set of objectives which are sufficiently ahead of the organization's current performance to draw out vastly enhanced performance. Each company has a leader who has communicated a credible vision of the company's future and a sense of direction for attaining that vision. Each has also introduced a leaner organization structure often involving major surgery of unnecessary bureaucracy.
2. *New culture:* in most of these companies the executive team has made a deliberate attempt to change the management style and the employee's attitudes.
3. Many of the companies who have successfully managed change have done so by endeavouring to attain to *world standards,* by benchmarking against the acknowledged world leaders in their type of business.
4. Each of the successful organizations has undertaken a *review of their performance* in terms of specific targets. This identified targets for individuals and work teams and transferred ownership into these areas so that individuals and teams can take responsibility for their own performance.
5. The management of performance has also identified *specific training* needs.

6. Individuals are given *regular feedback* on their own performance. When excellent performance occurs it is recognized and rewarded.
7. Many companies have gone beyond total quality into *total innovation.* As Taylor says, "It is not enough to do the same things better. The challenge is to harness the creativity of the workforce to do new things and to do things differently". This means tolerating a certain amount of chaos and disorder, relaxing controls and letting the employees take charge.
8. Finally this relaxation of hierarchy has led to management through partnerships and networks in which *trust and co-operation* rather than control and hierarchy are the chief sources of management authority.[8]

This process can create casualties as managers trained in older methods find it difficult to keep up and to accept the increased pressure of enhanced responsibilities. The managers who survived develop new styles in which long term strategic imperatives are supplemented with short term financial controls. This has led to new structures and the elimination of unnecessary layers of management – the process of "delayering".

The centre should be an early casualty of delayering. Head Offices become smaller because the central strategic players in the organization are in the field, preaching the gospel of sharing, openness and learning. They are building the special skills and knowledge into the operating management at large, not hoarding it in Head Office. Head Office itself should become more visible and more accountable.

The concept of promotion also changes, as careers no longer merely lead to a higher position in the corporate hierarchy. With reduced hierarchy, de-layering and a smaller central core of permanent staff, the typical promotion route for the senior manager may be through a succession of projects as much as through progressing upwards to positions of increasing general responsibility. The horizontal move once derided as "sideways promotion" may become the norm.

This implies new attitudes towards information. In the de-layered organization, information of corporate significance will no longer be the prerogative of those at the very top. BP distinguish between three types of information. Primary business information is the responsibility of, and specific to, a relevant business network. Secondary information is based on primary but tailored to specific needs, and Core information is commonly defined and freely available across all corporate levels.

Communication and openness and sharing of information are the fundamental element, in the management of change. Where information is shared, openness and trust are created and wide consultation becomes the preferred mode of decision making. In this structure dissent is seen not as treasonable betrayal of senior management's instructions but as a creative and synergetic process.

The Transition of Change

In change programmes it is often easier to get started than to continue. Many organizations go through a phase of initial euphoria only to become to disillusioned at the perceived lack of progress. In this "reality shock" the organization realises that a large gap exists between its high expectations of performance and the reality of the situation which it inhabits. This may be succeeded by a phase of denial. Managers use such phrases as "the market has got it wrong". The organization may revert to undertaking only the activities which it understands and with which it feels comfortable. This usually creates a cosy pattern of behaviours, which may even be justified by strategic alibis such as "cutting back to core business", or "removing unnecessary diversity", or "de-complexifying our future". This may be a disastrous mistake. In the next phase the continuing bad news from the market place may provoke the increasing realisation that change is really necessary, coupled with the depressing insight that the organization does not possess the skills to bring the change about. This creates a perception of incompetence, leading to feelings of frustration and low self esteem. Once the inevitable is accepted it is possible to "let go" and give up trying to cling on to the habits and beliefs of former times. This has parallels with the situation in a marriage approaching divorce. The organization starts to look for new clothes and experiments with a new hairstyle. It gets out and about and starts to meet new people.

The revised acceptance of reality leads to a period of testing in which new behaviours and approaches are tried out, some are rejected but others seem to make sense, and to fit the new realities. But not all are a success and there will be periods of conflict, anger and frustration. New people are brought in, and not all stay for very long. There may be angry recriminations that the chief executive has "introduced unnecessary complexity" while the CEO may retort that the organization is at last emerging from the 'dark ages' and is coming to terms with the coruscating realities of a more diverse and faster moving environment. This may not be a happy time and some may wish that the instigators of the change had left well alone, but most will recognise that, this is an opportunity to try things out. Budgets may get out of control, and unproductive investment may be made. This can also be a dangerous period, but it is a necessary one.

When the dust has settled and the organization obtains a clearer view of what has happened to it, there will be a search for understanding and a period of introspection, of "emotion recollected in tranquillity" though the tranquillity may be only relative to the seething torments of the newly experienced frustration.

Finally, if the medicine works, the organization emerges into the sun-drenched uplands of prosperity and will have a new position in a strong market, bolstered by a new perception of itself as a success story, and with new meanings and myths incorporated into new behaviour.

The transition from 'Before' to 'After' is not undimensional. Kilmann identifies the "five tracks" of: culture, trust and commitment; managerial skills; team building; structure and strategy; and reward systems.[9] Kilmann's view is that it is useful to start in most cases with the first track. He therefore proposes that all organizations should start to question their culture and open up restraints on required actions and start projects. Simultaneously, action should be taken to improve management skills to build teams and to review strategy, structure and rewards. But the first actions should be taken at the cultural level, asking questions about the existing culture, and what values are implicit in it and what behaviours are sanctioned by it. Perhaps most important of all, it is necessary to ask what have been the impediments to asking these questions in the first place? This process of questioning and reviewing whether the existing culture does, in fact, support agreed organizational goals, will lead to consideration of whether the culture is in line with new philosophies and will start to put on the agenda the crucial question of legitimacy. If something does not appear to be right, or there appears to be a disjunction between what is stated in one aspect of the culture and what is apparently done in the behaviours which the current culture sanctions, this will provide the impetus to start the change process.

But Kilmann is quite open-ended about the techniques which will put the culture question on the agenda. He recommends that change programmes should be proactive and opportunistic and, above all, should have a review process built in. In looking for some of the culture gaps which may provoke the required sort of reaction, Kilmann asks us to question the standing of groups against individuals, whether there is a predisposition in favour of the status quo and against the kind of questioning which will lead to innovation in tasks. Are individuals and their goals preferred over teams and their goals? How do individuals stand in relation to the organization? Are individuals perhaps comfortably supported in their view that the organization which provides their main income is merely one of their many clients?

Another way of looking at Kilmann's five distinctions is that they are points of leverage within the organization. Bearing this in mind, it may be that, in practice, it is not essential to start with the culture dimension. For one thing, an overt attack on a culture and a way of life in which organizational participants have been nurtured and which has supported them over many years is not necessarily the best way of getting them on side. In some cases working at the reward system, supported by team building and skills development, would create the climate in which the existing culture may appear, in principle, to be questionable.

Kanter offers a different set of criteria for change projects. They should be trialable, reversible, divisible, concrete, familiar, congruent and, above all, *sexy.*[10] This is down to earth talk, and it may well appeal to the practical manager. The last is by no means an insignificant dimension. If people are not intrigued enough to want to do something different, they will tend to go on doing what they know. For this reason, even programmes which apparently fail or do not succeed in all of their objectives may have an important role to play.

Organizations which successfully manage change need to be open-minded in one sense and closed-minded in another. They are directed towards the achievement of certain goals and should not be deflected from these. But they will be open as to means and to the likely opportunities for learning on the way.

Organizations which survive change must create conditions in which the behaviours which reinforce change are rewarded. They celebrate success and they enjoy successful outcomes. They will consist not merely of hierarchical elements and horizontal components (as in the classic matrix organization) but they will inhabit their matrices with teams who are flexible, small and have freedom of action to pursue their own goals. Organizations which manage change do not all conform to Senge's paradigm of the "learning organization" but they do have mechanisms for learning.[11] They relate to their environment, customers, employees, consultants, and owners in an interactive way. Barings failed to survive a predictable crisis because the centre had not learnt from the operational part what kind of controls were really needed in an unfamiliar situation. Unexpected success may be as misleading as unexpected failure, and, when the reasons for it are not understood, it may be twice as damaging.

As organizations are moving from the known to the unknown, their reward structures will also need to change in unpredictable ways. Those new modalities may well seem "unfair" to those conditioned to the old ways of working. Where product champions are expected to take responsibility they will feel they are entitled to at least some share in rewards. Where organizations have parts which have survived the challenge of change they will feel unjustly denied if they do not profit, perhaps at the expense of those who have preferred the easier route of sticking to their original knitting. Each side will see the outcome as unfair. *Organizations which manage and survive a process of change will not necessarily do so in the way they thought they would when they started the change process.* But in order to survive the inevitable unpredictabilities they will have had to gear up to a higher level of activity than they had thought they were previously capable of.

How to Start

McCalman and Paton identify seven methods of initiating change in organizations.[12] Surveys are useful: they provide essential data and involve those who are most likely to be affected by a change. To ignore them is not merely bad manners but will lead to unnecessary resistance. But it is unnecessary to undertake a full attitude survey in every case. What is often required is something reasonably quick and dirty which can have credibility amongst those involved in the problem or in the proposals for changing it.

It is usually impossible to predict in advance what new processes will work precisely, but it is important to at least attempt a *timetable* based on a reasonably clear vision of what things will look like after the events in the programme. Consultants who offer a proprietary survey sometimes insist that only their methodology is likely to produce results. Managers are often frightened of asking simple and obvious questions about these methods. They should not be. It is their jobs that are at risk. The consultants will walk away from any ensuing debate. If managers don't understand the consultant's approach, their subordinates will not either.

Insight can often be gained from *team building* exercises. Examination of the composition of a team in terms of behavioural types such as the Myers Briggs typology may provide the dynamic required to get a programme started.

Nominal group analysis, in which the pressures of the immediate situation are taken off and respondents asked to distance themselves, is useful. Other pencil and paper techniques include mental mapping, brainstorming, and focus groups. O'Connor's Handbook for Organizational Change provides a useful summary of some of these techniques. Clarkson's book offers a stimulating analysis of the change process based on the insight of psychotherapy and the core competencies of clinical psychology.

Often a training session off premises led by an *external facilitator* can get the ball rolling. The important thing is to find a basis to start by talking about what is really happening. McCalman and Paton quote Pugh's basic rules for managing a change process:

1. establish that there is a need
2. think it through thoroughly
3. discuss it informally with those likely to be affected
4. encourage the expression of all objections
5. make sure you are willing to undertake change yourself
6. monitor the changes and reinforce them at all points

If managers can do these six things in their normal operations they will normally expect to manage a change programme successfully. *However, it is worth remembering that if they really could do all these things all the time there probably wouldn't be a need for the change programme.*

There is, however, a need for change managers to understand the processes, techniques, tools and approaches which can support the change process. Change managers should be able to describe the current situation, possibly by using a SWOT analysis or a simple presentation in chart form of pressures on the business and some attempt to quantify them. Once an agreed format, for example forcefield analysis or mental maps, is decided on it can be adopted across the organization.

Another useful approach is to chart the sphere of influence of the change team. If time and budget permits, attitude surveys into organization culture, or organization culture inventories, can be useful. But the forces opposing change can seize upon the inevitably mixed findings of such surveys and the complexity they reveal to create new focuses of resistance to the change programme. Similar points can be made about mission statements. Because a mission statement is logically a prior level of activity, it does not mean that it is psychologically appropriate or even feasible to start by getting consensus across the whole organization on a mission statement.

In principle, techniques which look outward and beyond the individual and groups existing limitations will create the most dynamic. Training activity in areas such as listening skills, negotiation skills and indeed any interpersonal facilitation activity, will inevitably support the change programme. It will also very probably throw up new bases for conflict or provide the arena for the working out of, in an overt form, of conflicts which may have, up until then, been latent. This does not mean that a valuable function is not being served, however.

There are no absolutes in this field. Organizations may, for no apparent reason, turn against a particular technique or approach and even against the hapless change managers who come to be associated with it. In these cases, do not be over-proud and over-committed to a particular intellectualisation of the technique. If it works it's good, if it doesn't move on. Try something else. Better still, try something that the people whose views you are trying to change think they thought of first.

The Role of Consultants

A major decision which managers have to make is whether to bring in outsiders such as consultants at all. Outsiders can be helpful in starting the process. Sometimes their knowledge of other organizations can be directly helpful. In other cases it can provide assurance that others have gone through the same or similar trauma. Once questions have been asked an intervention has been started and the change process has been initiated. External consultants or change agents are crucial in many change programmes. Some consulting companies claim special expertise in the management of change. Some indeed have proprietary methods, involving specific questionnaires, interviewing techniques, or even rigid pro formas and timetables.

Reliance on a formulation which may have worked in another organization is not, by itself, enough to guarantee success in quite different situation. But the real reason for failure, in, these cases, is almost certainly not due to the consultants themselves or the irrelevance of their methods. It lies in the prior derogation of responsibility by senior organizational managers, and in their belief that they can pass on the responsibility for managing the change process to others who will bear the burden of the battle and the responsibility if things go wrong.

But the consultant will not be there for the long haul and will not have to live through the wreckage of an inadequately specified change programme based on unclear priorities and carried by misunderstood communications. The consultant will simply pack his tents and take his instant panacea and simplistic initiative to the next potential client. *The change process, to be successful, must be owned by the organization and must be consistent with its own managing styles.*

W Warner Burke's comprehensive overview of organizational development contains a useful and sensible review of the strengths and weaknesses of external consultants.[13] He identifies ten primary abilities as essential to the effectiveness of an OD consultant. They are also equally relevant to the qualities required of the change manager internally. The effective consultant should have the abilities to tolerate ambiguity, to influence, and he or she must, in a sense, be able to enjoy the power and complexities of persuading other people.

The change consultant must be able to confront difficult issues that members of the organization are sometimes reluctant to face themselves. But this must be balanced by the ability to support and nurture and sustain others, even in times of adversity when conflict and stress are widespread. Few change programmes can avoid stress and conflict.

The consultant must remain interested in what respondents are saying. Perhaps he or she is hearing their moans for the nth time but it is the first time as far as *they* are concerned. This means empathizing with the goals of others without necessarily taking their view of the situation as the correct and only one. Consultants must be able to recognize their own feelings and distinguish these from the objective facts of the situation.

They must be able to conceptualize in a variety of different levels and linguistic styles. They will have to deal with a wide and disparate range of people inside and outside the organization. Sometimes customers offer the clearer analysis of an organization's failures. (It is students and employers who may see where universities need to change). They must be energetic and be able to discover and mobilize the energy of others. They should be able to teach and create learning opportunities. The training environment is a key focus for change managers. First, last and all the time they must have a sense of humour. The only true law of change management (as it is of management in general) is that Murphy's law will operate and if things can go wrong, they will.

There are several legitimate reasons for using outside help. In the first place, managers may not know what is wrong, or may have incorrectly diagnosed what is wrong and attempted to act on that basis. Moreover, they may not know what kind of skills are available elsewhere or what kind of knowledge is available in other organizations. Several times I have used the device of bringing in managers from organizations which have successfully managed part of a change programme or have problems which are both like and unlike those which one is trying to work on in the client organization. It is very rare indeed that no learning comes from these situations. But, in any event, the external consultant cannot carry the whole burden. It is the kiss of death to say "Oh, we have had McKinseys in (or Andersens or Coopers or anybody) and *they* are handling the change management." The process must be a *joint* one between the inside and outside teams.

However the change comes about and whoever claims credit for its operation, by the end of the process the change must be owned by the client organization and not by the consultant. The consultant or change agent has to help the organization define the problem, and to offer help in resolving it, and like a good physician to be able to walk away once the healing process is underway.

It is clear that not all of these skills will be found amongst the very young or those who lack experience or indeed those who only have experience in a limited range of contexts. Consultants must be acceptable, or be prepared to work to become so. They must have excellent interpersonal skills. They must have the support of the CEO, coupled with the objectivity to report unwelcome truths. They should base their recommendations on a sincere empathy for the industry and its technology. Above all they require endless stamina.

Why Change Programmes Fail

With so much agreement as to how successful change programmes work it is surprising that any fail. However, in many organizations, change programmes do not take root and do not succeed even when the conditions initially appeared propitious. Failures are usually due to a disjunction between the verbal acceptance of the need to change and the actual behaviours which are implied by the verbal assent. Top managements, in particular, are good at saying one thing and doing another. They tend to talk of satisfying customers needs, building relationships, encouraging teamwork, investing in people and asking for long term commitment on the basis of delegation and empowerment. However, they simultaneously ask middle managers to exercise restraint in their own resource requirements, and then introduce short term performance goals which re-organize and destroy relationships, they manage by divide and rule tactics, reduce training budgets, keep all significant decisions themselves, and overreact to short term pressure. Sometimes their own salaries and reward packages are improved while they call for restraint in other people's rewards, or even create redundancies. It does not impress middle managers to find that, when the whole organization is thrown into a state of chaos, the top team has found a mechanism for increasing their own rewards, based perhaps on some obscure or irrelevant performance parameter. This lack of consistency can ruin the whole change programme.

Some senior managers focus only on short term performance improvement, give only verbal assent to openness and create a situation in which teamwork is unlikely to occur. Still others focus only on changes which need to be made *below* them and see the higher management structures and their visible failings as above analysis. Failures can also occur because, while the vision and overall objectives are clearly specified, the mechanisms for the attainment of them are not articulated and thus cannot develop. But the single most prominent feature of failure in the management of change is a *lack of commitment from the top.* This is often coupled with a lack of feel for organizational processes and a lack of orientation to the real needs of the clients and customers. The top in many organizations may be more out of touch than the rank and file.

It is tempting to summarize all of these failures as due to an inadequate leadership and inappropriate corporate strategy except that these behaviours can occur in enterprises which have demonstrated success over a period of years by demonstrating these very same behaviours. Some change programmes fail because initial expectations are set too high or expectations once set are adhered to rigidly. Another reason for failure lies in internal organizational politics. It is naive to assume that all changes will be equally valued by all organizational participants. Where departmentalism is strong, and hierarchical structures still predominate, sub goal optimisation may take place and groupings within the enterprise come to see their own objectives as of more salience than those of the organization as a whole. The chief reason for the failure of change projects is a lack of commitment and support from top management. Without driving from the top or at the very least consistent, quiet and flexible support no change programme will gain the credibility it requires to win over the uncommitted.

Other change programmes fail because the objectives for change are not clearly identified or are seen to be incompatible with other organizational objectives. Still others fail because line and functional managers are not sufficiently involved. In some change programmes they are deliberately and explicitly kept out because senior managers distrust their commitment. This can produce the very result which the change programme is designed to amend.

Other reasons for failure are of a more conventional managerial kind. Responsibilities for tasks need to be clearly defined and allocated to individuals. If change managers ignore problems until they are too late or monitor progress in a haphazard way, then corrective actions may be delayed or ignored. If the project group does not work as a team or the leaders of change projects lack the right mix of skills, the change will be impeded.

Clausewitz' classic dictum 'Time spent in reconnaissance is seldom wasted" is always relevant and it is important to invest adequate time and effort in planning.

Problems can occur when key people are left out of discussions or when departmental or sectional interests are seen as greater than organizational ones.

What Happens when Change Programmes go Wrong?

What does it mean for change programmes to go wrong? Change programmes may be partially successful but may end up in an inadequate fulfilment of the original goals. Some change projects end at the point where greater effort has been called on but objectives have not been clarified. This is likely to devalue the experience and organizational participants will not give the process of change the legitimacy it requires.

In other projects, spending more money, perhaps on bringing in expensive outside consultants is seen as an end in its own right.

Sometimes senior management becomes sold on a particular approach or a particular guru or other outside source of wisdom. The search for an all embracing panacea carried by a special language can force a superficial unanimity in the organization. The problems of cultural diversity will not therefore be tackled. This will normally last until the CEO meets another Messiah. The organization will breathe a sigh of relief and collapse into its old ways.

The translation of problems from one context to another, without being solved, but merely relocated on to some other manager's patch, will also discredit the change programme. In other projects the means of change apparently take precedence over the goals and cost cutting, for example, comes to be seen as an end state rather than a change modality.

The authors of the change programme may lose their nerve half way through and start to question their programme and processes. The opposite failing is to plough on regardless of the feedback that things need to change even within the programme of change itself. Some senior managers become disheartened by the inevitable opposition and others become infuriated by what they see as the base motives of those who do not see things the same way that they do. So they simply give up. Perhaps a decent equanimity and a still place at the heart of the ceaseless energy is also required. Change managers may gain comfort from the Arab proverb that "The dogs bark but the caravan moves on."

Conclusion

Managing change is a fundamental skill of general management. It involves the clarity of insight, the 'helicopter' ability to perceive where the organization is, and the strength of vision to perceive where it can and should be going to.

It is based on strong interpersonal skills, listening, team building, effective handling of meetings, whether as chair or facilitator, and on open communication.

Good networking, customer awareness and learning from good practice elsewhere needs to be balanced by a continuing appreciation of what the organization is like in its heart of hearts, a concern for its texture, its myths, and the expectations of those who inhabit it.

The change manager will need the help of others, some of whom will bring useful or challenging skills, specialist techniques and a fresh perspective. But the responsibility, the costs and the rewards of change are initially located in the organization, and the change manager will undoubtedly be the culprit if things go wrong. The change manager must therefore possess many of the attributes of the good consultant, especially the stamina.

The most useful and general advice to the change manager is undoubtedly that offered by Robert Townsend, author of "Up The Organization" and CEO of Avis. "If all else fails," Townsend advised "… try honesty. It really works."

References

1. P.H. Grinyer, D.G. Mayer and P. McKiernan: *Sharpbenders:* Basil Blackwell: 1988

2. D.C. Wilson: *A Strategy Of Change:* Routledge: 1992

3. W. McWhinney: *Paths Of Change:* Sage: 1992

4. A. Pettigrew, E. Fergie and L. McKie: *Shaping Strategic Change:* Sage: 1992
5. T. Eccles: *Succeeding With Change:* McGraw-Hill: 1995

6. M. Weir and J. Hughes: *Participate, Damn You:* MCB: 1989

7. P. Clarkson: *Change In Organizations:* Whurr: 1995

8. B. Taylor: *Successful Change Strategies:* I.O.D.: 1994

9. R.H Kilmann: *Managing Beyond The Quick Fix:* Jossey-Bass: 1989

10. R.M. Kanter: *The Change Masters:* Simon and Schuster: 1983

11. P. Senge: *The Fifth Discipline:* Doubleday: 1990

12. J. McCalman and R.A. Paton: *Change Management – A Guide To Effective Implementation:* Paul Chapman: 1992

13. W.W. Burke: *Organization Development:* Addison Wesley: 1993

Suggested Reading

1. J.A. Belasco and R.C. Stayer: *Flight Of The Buffalo:* Warner: 1993
2. D. Boddy and D.A. Buchanan: *Managing New Technology:* Basil Blackwell: 1986
3. P. Dawson: *Organizational Change:* Paul Chapman: 1994
4. T. Eccles: *Succeeding With Change:* McGraw-Hill: 1995
5. N. Foy: *Empowering People At Work:* Gower: 1994
6. P.H. Grinyer, D.G. Mayer and P. McKiernan: *Sharpbenders:* Basil Blackwell: 1988
7. R.H. Kilmann: *Managing Beyond the Quick Fix:* Jossey Bass: 1989
8. J. McCalman and R.A. Paton: *Change Management – A Guide To Effective Implementation:* Paul Chapman: 1992
9. C. O'Connor: *The Handbook For Organizational Change:* McGrawhill: 1993
10. P. Sadler: *Strategic Change:* Pergamon: 1995
11. B. Taylor: *Successful Change Strategies:* Institute Of Directors: 1994

Questions

1. What did Don Revie do in his first 100 minutes as Manager of Leeds United?

2. When should senior management bring in outside consultants in your organization? How would you brief them?

3. Have you been involved in a change programme that did not succeed? What lessons would you derive from that experience?

4. What changes would you, as an individual manager, like to introduce in your lifestyle and work habits to fit your organization's needs more appropriately?

Case Study:– Babcock Power

Management of Change Chapter

In the late 1970s Babcock was in decline. Its key market for heavy tubes, drum, pressure vessels and pipework was the United Kingdom power generation industry. Diminished projections of demand for electricity led to the cancellation of key power station orders on which Babcock had relied. Babcock Power was the major employer in Renfrew, to the west of Glasgow in Scotland. The future looked bleak with no forward orders, obsolete technology, confrontational industrial relations and no experience in competitive international markets.

The change programme followed three phases:

1. The first priority was to create work for the immediate future. The only way of doing this was to persuade the Government to change its mind on the cancellation of a specific power station project. The then Labour Government made it clear that it would require the combined agreement of both sides, management and the workforce, represented by the official trade union movement before they would listen to a case. *"Exercise impact"*, in which a fundamental re-analysis of the economic and technical aspect of a cabinet decision involved both unions and management and the creation of a secretariat to generate the appropriate data, provided the first opportunity for unions and management to work together in a concerted way on a common problem.

2. Once mere survival had been obtained management and unions looked to the medium term future. On approaching their main board for a critical investment programme to revitalize the machine shop they were told that the main board would require a positive expression of commitment from both management and the workers on two dimensions which have previously been regarded as beyond negotiation. They were skills flexibility and a substantial de-manning.

A massive communication exercise involving management at all levels and the entire workforce then ensued. Outside consultants were brought in.

A video was made to high professional standards. The key themes of the video were the need to restructure to meet the competitive challenge of overseas manufacturers, especially those in the Far East, the need to fundamentally review working practices and to undertake all this with a smaller workforce. This video was shown on one day to the entire plant in the apposite work groups.

Management indicated its commitment to the process of communication by offering the workforce the facility to make their own video. This took the form of the filming of an open session in which management sat on a platform to answer specific and tough questions. This event turned out to be, not so much confrontational, as an opportunity to restate an agreed level of mutual commitment from both sides.

There was fundamental rethinking at the top of the organization. Task forces and teams were set up across the many areas of the organization's business. A newsletter was introduced. The manager who had been responsible for the communication programme and communication impact became a full time change manager. Management laid the basis for open discussion on manning levels by offering an unconditional guarantee of no involuntary redundancy provided natural wastage occurred.

3. In the next phase it was agreed that the competitive threat should be examined firsthand and mixed teams of management and employees went to Japan to analyse the competition's secrets. The learning from this phase can be summed up in a quote attributed to a trade union member of one of the teams who reported back, that in his opinion *"these Japs were nae sae f...ing clever"*. The workforce started to grow in confidence. The rebuilding of the machine shop then took place. It provide a model for future physical restructuring.

After a phase of latency, in which these changes were absorbed into new ways of working, a new change programme was initiated through the *"Greenfield Project"* in which outside consultants worked with *"Deep Slice"* teams of managers and employees on precise change programmes for their individual factories. Against a norm of best practice and what would now be called benchmarking the teams were able to report after twelve weeks of regular meetings that, in principal, it was possible with minimal capital investment to replicate the best practices of competitor organizations. This whole process took approximately six years.

Questions

1. Why did the Babcock Programme apparently take so long?

2. Would the communication techniques adopted by Babcock work in your own organization?

3. If senior management is asking for a commitment from the workforce, what kind of commitment should it be prepared to give on its own part?

Chapter 16

Empowerment, Culture Change and Human Resource Management: Drawing the Threads Together

Christopher Molander

Objectives

- To define the meaning of the term empowerment
- To offer reasons why the concept is currently in favour
- To describe the various types of empowerment
- To link empowerment with culture change
- To describe empowerment as good human resource management

Introduction

Organizations operate in a turbulent environment – facing uncertainty and change. It was ever thus. The following only hint at the kind of pressures facing them: increased demand for quality and value for money; intensifying international competition; increasingly complex and fast changing technology; higher workforce expectations from work and the need to maintain competitive advantage by reduced labour costs.

These are some of the major reasons for reawakened interest in empowerment. Nowhere is this interest more pronounced than when it goes hand in hand with globalization; for the impact of the one on the other is of great practical importance. Decentralized globalized organization structures will be unworkable unless managers have been empowered to operate with very much less control than has hitherto been the norm.

The Background to Empowerment

It is therefore more than ever important that employers find successful ways of releasing employee creativity, intelligence and initiative at every level and that efforts are integrated in the achievement of a common purpose.

All this amounts to a change in organization culture, producing internal and external behaviour which is more rational and appropriate in the current climate.

Organizations need to become more exciting and rewarding. We must find ways of reducing bureaucracy and 'macho' leadership. Leadership must become more empowering and less controlling. Peters[1] and Belasco[2] have both made much of this point.

HR managers will once again fail to deliver if they see the essence of organizational survival as one mainly of providing more training courses managed by the human resource department. Important though this is, it pales into insignificance against the key task of changing the organizational climate. The track record of professional HR managers in terms of delivery at the strategic level has been traditionally poor. Can they do better now?

HR people have a crucial role to play. They should be leaders of organizational change and not just advisers and specialists. They should have the contacts and the knowledge to analyse and diagnose organizational needs, and to design and implement change programmes along with line managers.

Organizations will need to become obsessed with customer satisfaction. They will survive the threat of increased global competition only if they bring to market faster the higher 'value added' products which the customer wants to buy. As one Chairman of a large international company recently said: 'We have the potential and the infrastructure. What we lack are the vision, will and skills to pull it off'.

The change in corporate culture is one of increasing innovative risk taking and team playing. For this to occur, there will have to be structural change in most organizations. The structural characteristics of 'winning organizations' will be flat, decentralised, lean, Matrix-based and customer-oriented. In a word 'empowered' rather than 'bureaucratic'. Bureaucracies, like the dinosaurs of Jurassic Park have had their day.

Chief executives must be commited to the culture change and not just pay it lip service. HR managers must think wider than administration and reactive 'establishment control' and record-keeping. The change in title of many personnel departments is a recognition of this change. Hopefully the change signifies a greater strategic concern.

So when we talk of empowerment, it is not something picked out of the air. It is more than a technique, it is a survival strategy in a globalized market place. It liberates the creative and innovative potential of employees. It constitutes the culture change necessary for survival.

Empowerment – Working Definitions

In itself the term is not new. American in origin, it has been in use for more than a hundred years in political circles. Originally it described the process of gaining power, especially in minority groups. More recently, business groups have adopted and overexploited it. In practice there is often much less to empowerment than meets the ear.

There are at least three levels at which the term is used:

Personal Involvement – another term for consultation. This is the approach adopted by McDonalds, for example, and is well established. Many firms using quality circles fall into this category. (Marchington)[3] Information is given to the team usually by the first line manager and information is collected from the team for upward transmission. Team briefing, as enthusiastically recommended by the British Industrial Society, is similar in effect.[4] Suggestion schemes are an example of an older, more primitive but essentially similar notion. The power-based structure and managerial style remain unaffected.

Job Involvement – Job re-design, allowing employees to use a variety of skills, often in teams, is more radical than the personal involvement referred to above. In this form managers assume a more supportive role, allowing staff to achieve their goal with minimum interference. Employees at all levels, are expected to pursue goals and objectives without the constant intervention of supervisors. Decisions, once the prerogative of management, are vested in the employee. For example, customer service clerks might decide on customer compensation; employees approve their own expense accounts or stop the production line if they think quality is deficient.

Job involvement does not, however, involve strategic decisions about organization structure, power and rewards. These are still seen as senior management's responsibility.

The introduction of quality circles can be seen as an example of this approach to empowerment. Typically they consist of four to twelve people from the same work area who meet on a regular basis to identify, analyse and solve their own work related problems. The circles present solutions to management and are often involved in implementing and monitoring those which management accept. There is increasing evidence of employee resistance and failure. The main reason appears to be the dissonance between the philosophy of employee involvement and managerial control needs. (Russell and Dale)[5]

System Involvement – Employees are not only involved in decision making related to their jobs or how effectively their team performs, but in the performance of the whole organization. Every aspect of the empowered organization is different to the control oriented one. Information is shared and spread horizontally and vertically in a delayered structure. Profit sharing and employee ownership are standard elements. Human resource planning is geared to strategic objectives.

An apposite example of empowerment at this level is British Petroleum's 'Project 1990' which heralded the start of a fundamental cultural change throughout the entire company and which is still ongoing: (Simon)[6]

It is clear form the above that this third type of empowerment is quite different from the other two. It is based on a coherent philosophy from which it is possible to derive an integrated set of plans to change managerial behaviour.

As Block[7] observed, 'Empowerment is not changing the rules but changing the rule makers'.

Gandz[8] asks 'Who gains in the empowered organization'? and answers: 'Anyone interested in the bottom line' – shareholders,

BP's Culture Change

The Old		*The New*
	Structure	
Hierarchies		Teams
Boundaries		Connections
Internal Focus		External Focus
	Relationships	
Smothering		Empowering
Distrusting		Trusting
Controlling		Supporting
	Behaviour	
Analysis		Action
Risk Avoidance		Risk Taking

Figure 16.1. BP's Culture Change.

employees and so on. Who loses? Only those managers who believe that it is their function to organize, direct and control. In other words, the losers are the followers of traditional management theory; the bureaucracy of Max Weber[9] and the organisational philosophy of Henri Fayol[10] – still reported in textbooks as the basis on which good management is practised.

It is dangerous to argue that 'systems involvement' is always appropriate. Much depends on the special circumstances of the organization and the cultural environment in which it operates. It is possible that for cultural reasons some employee nationalities do not take easily to changes in traditional working relationships. The relative balance between direction, support and autonomy should vary according to circumstances. In every case there will be limits. The HRM department has an important role to play in the recognition and setting of them.

HRM Implications of Empowerment

If empowerment is to succeed and not be seen as simply a modish talking point, in the way that MBO and sometimes even TQM are treated, minimal prerequisites must be in place. They all involve the HRM function and serve admirably as a summary of the areas of concern of the HRM department in the modern organization.

Culture Management The dominant concern of management in the 80s was control, and organizations were encouraged to become finance-led. Greater control was exercised at every level from the centre. Finance led organizations were keen to adopt mechanisms such as performance related pay. Where assessment is linked to individual achievement of objectives, absurdities and waste of time tend to result. (Molander,[11] Deming)[12]

Without a reduction in the degree of central control, it is impossible to introduce a form of empowerment other than the most basic – in which there is no perceptible change in the balance of power.

Managers must have faith in the employees. There is no return without risk. The organization itself must support its risk-taking managers. In the 80s organizations were run by auditors and controllers. Unless more managers ask: 'What is the problem?' rather than 'Who is to blame?' there will be no risk taking.

The risks of empowerment can be minimized by training; but there will be crises, so management must expect that mistakes will be made and expect to take the responsibility for the actions of others even if they do not directly control them.

Managers must reinforce faith with the capacity to become coaches rather than supervisors and directors, giving employees the opportunity to develop the necessary skills to minimize risk when exercising increased responsibility.

HRM professionals at the highest level must press for an integrated approach to change, in which empowerment is a reflection of a sympathetic culture.

Change Management HRM professionals should have knowledge of the factors which affect individual commitment to change and be able to work with top management in the development of methods of introducing change. This process will involve developing and introducing systems relating to communication, participation and performance. It will also involve the development of mechanisms whereby identification with the company's mission can be developed along with the necessary attitudes and behaviour to support the culture change.

Employee Resourcing Employees will need skills to perform not only in their present role but have the capacity to develop further. Analytical and decision-making skills will be required. It is clear that the HR director must constantly monitor the recruitment process, to ensure that the organization looks for only those who have a place in the developing enterprise.

There is much room for the design and development of improved selection methods. Despite decades of evidence that the interview lacks reliability and validity as a selection technique, many firms have done little to reinforce it with other more effective methods.

Employee Development As long ago as 1959, Herzberg[13] noted that it is not possible to empower employees to do things if they cannot do them. It is common to find that organizations which seek to empower employees have inadequate training and development budgets.

Technical training is obviously required but so is development of decision making and team building skills. Enhancing the capacity of employees will help ensure that the teams become more than the sum of their parts and that improvement in performance and motivation will actually follow the introduction of team working – in the context of autonomous work groups, for example.

With regard to team building skills, it is salutary to consider the changing role of the first line manager, whose job is now much more concerned with networking, liaison and representation than it is with supervision. (Mallory and Molander)[14]

Traditional methods of succession planning will prove too inflexible and require replacement with more individually tailored responses, closely linked to line management-led appraisal. It will be necessary to identify those who need easing out (exiting), as observed by Hunt.[15]

It is through the education and training process and involving people in quality improvement programmes that total quality management can become a reality. It is an important aspect of the HRM professional's role to encourage top line management to invest in training and development at every level of the organization. Training effort must be related to both organizational need and the needs of individuals to improve their knowledge base. So long as training is seen as an unpleasant and peripheral activity and of an occasional nature, empowerment will remain a theoretical goal. The learning organization and empowerment go hand in hand.

Organization Design The structure of the organization must be relevant to empowerment – delayered, decentralized and matrix in form. Macey[16] found that the most common stages relating to product improvement programmes were structural and involved a move towards 'flat, lean structures and multi-skilled activities in the team context'.

HRM specialists ought to have the behavioural science knowledge to understand the significance of structure for individual behaviour. An important element in structural change will be the quest for flexibility, with the consequent need for a more competent workforce if the best use is to be made of it. It is important then that HRM people are both aware of the alternative organization structures and sensitive to their situational relevance. They must delight in being involved in the redesign of jobs to cater for projected changes in product, technology and organization design. It is organizations which empower people by providing them with more or less opportunity to take responsibility at the point at which it matters – the contact point with client or customer.

Reward and Performance Management When employees reduce costs, raise quality and eliminate low value-added work. the benefits must be shared between those who have achieved. Flexible reward systems, broad band payment systems and individual contracts are necessary to facilitate targetting of rewards. Incremental pay scales and collective bargaining should be phased out.

Traditional job evaluation methods of linking pay to predetermined levels of mental and physical effort will be abandoned. New forms of evaluating the managerial role are needed now in particular. The highest rewards will go to those who maintain and develop empowered staff. Bonuses, company shares and other special payments will become more common than position based compensation systems.

The boundary-less organization will be one in which status distinctions are abandoned in favour of harmonized conditions of service – for example communal canteens, the abandonment of status related classes of travel, and the provision of uniform pension systems. Non performance related distinctions hinder the empowerment process.

Now is a good time for the HRM professional to consider cafeteria systems of reward, so that people can have more power over such basic issues as the form in which they are recompensed – money, time, personal development opportunities and so on.

Fundamental to performance management is, of course, performance review. This is the means whereby performance expectations are defined and which form the basis of rewarding people on the basis of their contribution.

In practice, difficulties abound in identifying managerial contribution on an individual basis as we have seen in an earlier chapter. Systems of group-related performance review reduce the demotivating effects of these schemes. It is by no means out of place with regard to empowerment, with its potential for autonomous group working and job enrichment.

Performance review provides an opportunity to clarify objectives and to measure performance against these objectives. The performance review process is the main vehicle for agreeing improvement and development plans and is at the heart of performance management.

Performance management with its emphasis on joint target setting and task assessment (not personality assessment) is itself an essential element in the empowerment process. It encourages employee ownership of task definition and evaluation of results.

Employee Relations It is difficult to talk of empowerment without assuming the existence of direct communication with employees. The implications for the traditional adversarial shop floor relationships between management and union is that they are likely to be replaced with a more cooperative climate; a new realism on the part of both management and unions with an individual rather than a collective basis.

This does not deny the need for some collective representation however. Despite the more strident American versions of HRM, it appears analytically naive to consider the workplace as anything other than made up of legitimately competing interest groups; the views of which can perhaps best and most efficiently be represented though union recognition. One or two examples of gross top management pay settlements in a climate of wage restraint might suggest to the reader the appropriateness of methods for expressing collective disquiet!

It is likely in any case that if the unions did not exist management would have to invent them in order to communicate in the most effective manner. (Monks)[17]

Arguably, unless employees are empowered by the employment contract to express views which are from time to time inconvenient to management, the term empowerment might be misconstrued as a politically acceptable means of re-establishing a managerial philosophy better suited to an earlier economic and social period.

In this chapter we have argued that there is nothing new about the idea of empowerment – it has a long history in philosophical and political thought. Its potential during the last decade of the twentieth century lies not in theory but as the practical means by which the idea of the multinational corporation becomes plausible. It is clear that the process of international spread and empowerment are closely related – the one leading to the other. HRM professionals have an important role to play in turning managerial theory into practice. In order for them to be seen as a credible force for change, they must themselves take a critical look at their own power base.

Traditionally seen, with good reason, as limited in their vision and administrative in their orientation, they must abandon the old personnel management ground. They must return to line managers their responsibility for managing the people who work for them and instead assume a more strategic and analytical approach to organization development. Success will be theirs only if they gain membership of the most senior management groups and carry these senior colleagues with them.

By arguing that empowerment is human resource management, we have demystified the term and hopefully rescued it from the oblivion which has awaited managerial panaceas in the past.

If people are selected competently, trained, motivated and rewarded all within an appropriate organization structure, employees will have been empowered. If it is viewed as a set of techniques rather than a culture change, nothing much will come of it.

Happily the pursuit of this view has led us to recapitulate the major preoccupations of human resource management, a fitting point at which to conclude this collection of essays.

Conclusion

The most recent World Competitiveness Report ranked Britain 40th of 48 nations for its motivation to retrain. Armstrong, Director General of the UK Institute of Personnel and Development has argued that 'it is time the UK began to adjust more effectively to the realisation that it can no longer assume it has a big share of world trade. It is painful to discover that many of our standards of efficiency, quality and design are not globally competitive. We have to transform through education, training, technology and investment in all these areas. It is the only way to move up the value chain. Competitive strength will not be achieved by having the lowest labour costs – that route would be folly'.[18]

Whilst empowerment is obviously relevant to the process of organization renewal, it is in danger of becoming misused and so ill-defined as to be something to which no one could take exception – rather like 'motherhood and apple pie'. There are however different types of management style each producing in practice different types and levels of empowerment.

Empowerment reflects a type of organization culture and is the result of the strategic introduction of human resource management principles. If the HRM practices which follow from these principles are in place then the workforce will be empowered. We have seen, however, that organizations often find mechanisms to apparently introduce HRM principles and, in fact, leave the distribution of power as it was.

Increasing the non managerial content of an employee's job does not constitute empowerment. It involves an increase in risk-taking by managers. The notion that they are still responsible for outcomes, although not in control of day to day behaviours, requires a change in managerial style and the development of different and more appropriate 'hands off' structures and relationships.

Empowerment is about support rather than control. It is not about managerial abdication. Readers might care to consider the recent merchant bank collapse in the light of this last comment.

Still less is it about techniques. If it continues largely to be seen as something which can be introduced as a process, rather than as a strategic reflection of culture change, it will sink into oblivion.

References

1. Peters, T., (1989) *Thriving on Chaos,* London, Collins

2. Belasco, J., (1990) *Teaching the Elephant to Dance; Empowering Change in Your Organization,* New York, Century Business

3. Marchington, M., Goodman, J., Wilkinson, A. and Ackers, P. (1992) *New Developments in Employee Involvement,* Manchester School of Management, Employee Department Research Series, No. 2

4. Industrial Society (1974) *Practical Policies for for Participation,* London, Industrial Society

5. Russell, S., and Dale, R., (1989), *Quality Circles – A Broader Perspecetive,* WRU Occasional Paper No.43

6. Simon, D., (1990), *'Managing Cultural Change at BP', Management Development Review,* Vol. 4 No.3

7. Block, P., (1987), *The Empowered Manager,* San Fransisco, Jossey Bass

8. Gandz, J., (1990), 'The Employment Empowerment Era', *Business Quarterly,* Autumn

9. Weber, M., (1946), *From Max Weber: Essays in Sociology, Oxford,* Oxford University Press

10. Fayol, H., (1949), *General and Industrial Administration,* London, Pitman

11. Molander, C.F., (1970), 'Management by Objectives in Perspective', *Journal of Management Studies,* Vol. 9, No. 1

12. Deming, W.E., (1988), *Out of the Crisis: Quality, Productivity and Competitive Position,* Cambridge, Cambridge University Press

13. Herzberg, F., et al., (1959), *The Motivation to Work,* New York, Wiley

14. Molander, C.F., and Mallory, G.R., (1989), 'Managing in the Front Line: The Changing Role of Supervisors', *Journal of General Management,* Vol. 14, No. 3, Spring

15. Hunt, J.W., (1984) 'The Shifting Focus of the Personnel Function', *Personnel Management,* February

16. Macey, B.A., (1986), 'An Assessment of US Work Improvement and Productivity Efforts, 1970 – 1985', *National Academy of Management,* Annual Meeting, August

17. Monks, J., (1994), 'The Union Response to HRM: Fraud or Opportunity?, *Personnel Management,* September

18. Armstrong, G. (1995), in Wade, G., 'Missing that Personnel Touch', London, *The Guardian,* 21 October

Further Reading

Storey J., and Sisson, K., 'Vision, Mission and Culture Management: Customer orientation and Quality in the New Management of Labour' Ch. 8 in *Managing Human Resources and Industrial Relations,* Open University Press, Buckingham, England, 1993

Wickens, P., *The Road to Nissan: Flexibility, Quality and Teamwork,* Basingstoke, Macmillan, 1987

Marchington, M., Goodman, J., Wilkinson, A., and Ackers, P., *New Developments in Employee Involvement,* Manchester School of Management, Employee Department Research Series No. 2, 1992

Questions

1. Examine the view that empowerment cannot be introduced other than as an element in a culture change programme.

2. What examples of empowerment in action have you come across personally? Into which of the three categories defined in this chapter do they fit, and why?

3. With regard to empowerment, what practical consequences follow from the difference between managerial *control* and managerial *support?*

CASE STUDY

A Problem in the R&D Department

The Delta Slag Company was a large British concern. The plant involved in this case was one of the largest in the company and had been established to fill the needs of a growing market. The primary product of the plant sold well, as its quality was high, and the capacity of the plant, though large, was continually oversold. In the manufacturing process a by-product was produced and was drawn 'off the stream' in such quantities that it was thought of as a co-product rather than a by-product; it also required a high degree of purification.

A large technical department was headed by a technical director who had several assistants, each of whom was in charge of a given phase of the department's activities. One of these assistants, Mr. Roberts, was in charge of a group of chemists and chemical engineers whose primary duties related to the important by-product. The men in this group reported directly to Mr Roberts. He, in turn, reported to the technical director. Research problems, product development, quality and the like were handled by the personnel in this group, reviewed by Mr Roberts and passed along to the technical director. Since the purification operations and quality control associated with the by-product were so technical in nature, the group members also served as supervisors for the operating crews of the by-product plant.

Joe Green, a chemical engineer, was a member of the technical group under Mr Roberts' supervision. He became completely absorbed in the research work in that area and set out to' learn everything there was to know about it'. At the start of the project, he was pleased with the potential it held and would half jokingly say: 'I'm going to make myself an expert in this field'.

Elaborate research was conducted for about a year and Joe thought the results he achieved were well worth the effort. However, after about six months, Joe sensed that his work was being taken for granted and that his superiors had not given the project the importance that it deserved. Joe did not let this lack of recognition affect his work however; and the quality and value of his work and research findings remained high. He expressed his feelings to some of his associates, but since they were not as close to the problem as he, their replies were more humorous than serious. This reaction did not help Joe's feelings one bit, but he increased his efforts and did an excellent research job.

He reported the results completely and thoroughly in a well written and well documented report. As was the practice in the group, all copies of the report were delivered to Mr Roberts, who was to review the report, present it to the technical director and arrange for necessary meetings to discuss practical applications of the findings.

Joe waited about a month for action on his work; but none came. He was given some other minor assignments and he helped on routine work. He found it difficult to approach Mr Roberts concerning the report and was put off time after time.

Mr Roberts was called away on a business trip and Joe was assigned the duty of standing in for him whilst he was away. One day the technical director gave Joe the key to Mr Roberts' desk and asked him to get a file which he knew was there. When Joe opened the desk, he saw all the copies of his report lying there apparently unread. This discovery caused Joe considerable trauma, since he was confident that by this time some of the copies had been delivered to the technical director and other company officials.

Joe's feeling of worth was reduced to nothing and with it went his feeling of pride in his work. He was so shaken by this experience that he began to look for employment elsewhere.

He was soon hired by a competitive concern where his success has been outstanding.

Questions for discussion

What were the main motivational needs of Joe Green? Which one apparently motivated him most?

What does this case explain about the motivation of scientific, technical and professional personnel? How does this tend to differ from the motivation of rank-and-file employees? What does this indicate for management in the future?

Index

References in italic indicate figures or tables.
HRM = human resource management.

Human Resource Management in Practice

Mulvie, A. & McDougal, M

Real-life practices and problems in Human Resource Management are tackled by these carefully selected case studies set in a variety of industrial/commercial and public sector organisations. Based on real situations, they meet the needs of both tutors and learners, as well as experienced managers wishing to broaden their perspectives.

ISBN 0-86238-279-3, 200 pages, 1990 pbk, £7.95 + £2.35 p & p

The Structure of Competence – Models for Management

Hall J

33 chapters by experts like Argyris, Lewis, Likert, Hall, Blake, Mouton and Janis on motivation, power, leadership, group dynamics, agreement, conflict, trust and other concerns, providing a complete reference and source of inspiration for anyone, trainer, manager or student, who is interested in the role of the behavioural sciences in the work setting.

ISBN 0-86238-394-3, 520 pages, 1996, pbk, £25 + £2.35 p & p

Starting to Manage: the essential skills

Blair G

Many people become managers simply because they are good at the job they are doing - not because they know how to manage. Yet few people are then given the appropriate training. For these, and others who aspire to a management role, this book provides a key to achievement. It is a know-how-to guide for people with responsibility for small teams and projects.

ISBN 0-86238-336-6, 175 pages, 1993, pbk, £10 + £2.35 p & p

Qualitative Methods in Management Research

Gummesson E

This book is an analysis of the roles and methods used by academic researchers and management consultants when working with change process in companies and other organisations. It deals with case studies as a research method and advocates more involvement by the researcher and consultant through increased application of participant observation as used in anthropology, and through action research/action science (which is a method to combine the roles of researcher and the consultant), and other qualitative methods. In particular, the book stresses the problems of access, pre-understanding, and awareness of one's own paradigm.

ISBN 0-86238-197-5, 202 pages, 1988, pbk, £13.95 + £2.35 p & p